PREHISTORIC FIGURINES

'Outstanding – a daring and authoritative treatment, wonderfully wide-ranging . . . a fascinating treatment that ranges from early farmers to Barbie Dolls – a superb comparative work in visual culture. The way archaeology needs to go.'

Michael Shanks, Stanford University

'The book is ambitious, wide-ranging and coherent. It is clearly going to be the authoritative account on the subject . . . Bailey writes accessibly and shows a clarity of thought lacking in most authors who tackle this kind of material. In short his account is scholarly, judicious and balanced, but also interesting . . . This book ought to be mainstream reading in archaeology, anthropology and studies of visual culture, at advanced undergraduate and postgraduate levels.'

Richard Bradley, University of Reading

'Challenging and provocative, successfully engaging European prehistoric evidence with wider studies of visual culture . . .'

Alasdair Whittle, Cardiff University

Prehistoric Figurines presents a radical new approach to one of the most exciting but poorly understood artefacts from our prehistoric past, and transforms the study and interpretation of prehistoric figurines from Neolithic southeast Europe. The book explores the ways in which people use representations of human bodies to make subtle political points and to understand their own identities and to negotiate their relationships with friends and enemies. Moving beyond the traditional mechanisms of interpretation, the argument is an original and coherent interpretation of prehistoric figurines from southeastern Europe.

The author isolates and examines four critical conditions: figurines as miniatures; figurines as three-dimensional representations; figurines as anthropomorphs; and figurines as representations. From these discussions he propels the debate past the limitations of the out-dated interpretations of figurines as Mother-Goddess and investigates individual prehistoric figurines in their original archaeological contexts and in terms of modern exploitations of the human form. He examines not what figurines were, but how and why they fulfilled the variety of roles that they might have played, asking what it is about a figurine's physical and visual condition that makes it successful as a votive, portrait or other manifestation of material and visual culture. The book benefits from the author's close understanding of the material culture and the prehistory of the Balkans and from recent developments in the fields of visual culture studies and social and cultural anthropology.

Douglass Bailey is Head of Archaeology at Cardiff University and a world authority on the prehistory of eastern Europe. He has conducted fieldwork in Romania and Bulgaria and written on a wide range of topics including art, architecture and the politics of archaeology. His *Balkan Prehistory* (Routledge 2000) is the standard text on the southeast European Neolithic.

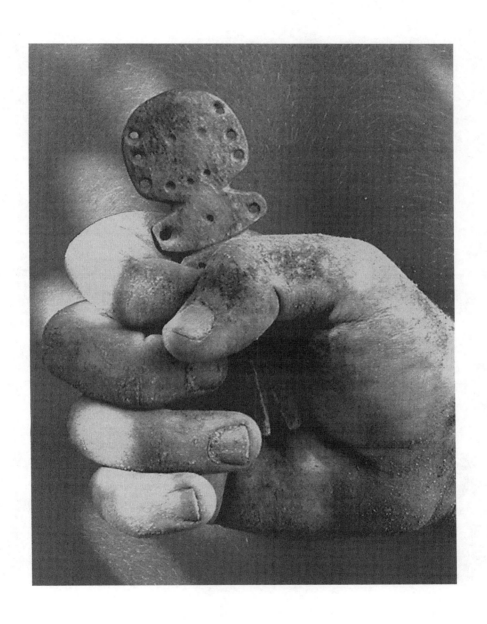

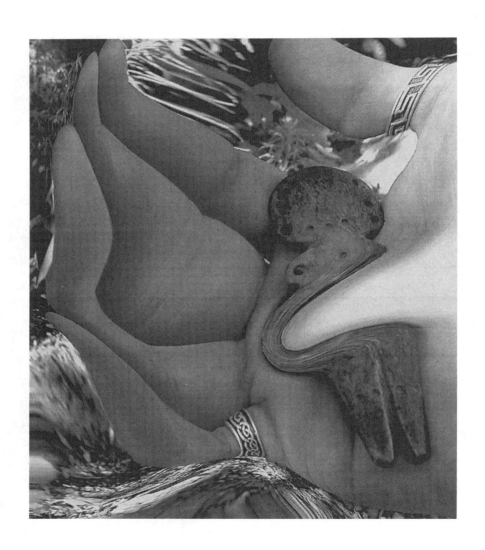

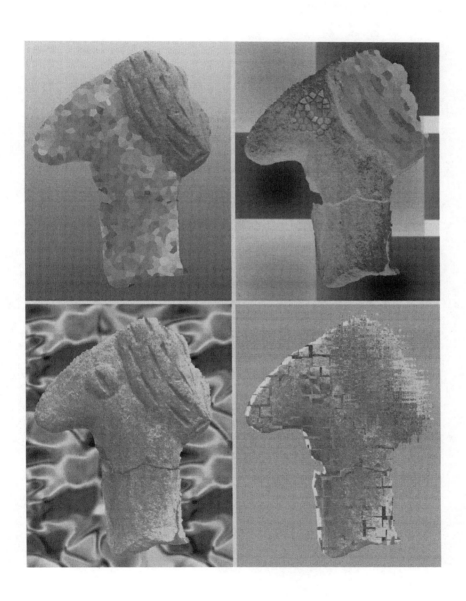

PREHISTORIC FIGURINES

Representation and Corporeality
in the Neolithic

Douglass W. Bailey

LONDON AND NEW YORK

First published 2005
by Routledge
2 Park Square, Milton Park, Abingdon, Oxon OX14 4RN

Simultaneously published in the USA and Canada
by Routledge
270 Madison Ave, New York, NY 10016

Routledge is an imprint of the Taylor & Francis Group

Transferred to Digital Printing 2010

© 2005 Douglass W. Bailey

Typeset in Garamond by
Keystroke, Jacaranda Lodge, Wolverhampton

All rights reserved. No part of this book may be reprinted or reproduced
or utilized in any form or by any electronic, mechanical, or other
means, now known or hereafter invented, including photocopying
and recording, or in any information storage or retrieval system, without
permission in writing from the publishers.

British Library Cataloguing in Publication Data
A catalogue record for this book is available from the British Library

Library of Congress Cataloging in Publication Data
A catalog record for this book has been requested

ISBN 0–415–33151–X (hbk)
ISBN 0–415–33152–8 (pbk)

FOR ILKA ANGELOVA

CONTENTS

List of figures		xv
Preface and acknowledgements		xvii
1	Introduction	1
2	Miniaturism and dimensionality	26
3	Hamangia	45
4	Anthropomorphism: dolls, portraits and body parts	66
5	Cucuteni/Tripolye	88
6	Visual rhetoric, truth and the body	122
7	Thessaly	147
8	Subverting and manipulating reality	181
9	Corporeal politics of being in the Neolithic	197
	Notes	205
	Bibliography	217
	Index	236

FIGURES

1.1	Figurine discovered by the Southern Romania Archaeological Project, Teleorman Valley	2
1.2	Method proposed by Ivan Vajsov for analysing Hamangia figurines	13
1.3	An example of Peter Biehl's study of motif disposition on Bulgarian figurines	14
1.4	Comparison of Palaeolithic figurine and the body of a pregnant woman	17
1.5	Joyce Marcus' reconstruction of figurines in an Oaxaca house	21
2.1	Miniature objects from Ovcharovo	26
2.2	Miniature book from the collections of Stanford University's Green Library	30
2.3	Bonsai tree	31
2.4	Penjing tray landscape	31
2.5	Michael Ashkin's *No. 43* (1996)	34
2.6	Alton Delong's experimental rooms	37
3.1	*The Thinker* and *The Seated Woman* from Cernavoda	45
3.2	Hamangia figurine from Cernavoda	47
3.3	Hamangia figurine from Cernavoda	48
3.4	Hamangia figurine	49
3.5	Traditional typology of Hamangia figurines	50
3.6	Main sites of the Hamangia Culture mentioned in the text	52
3.7	Plan of Hamangia site at Ceamurlia de Jos	54
3.8	Hamangia phase graves from Durankulak	61
3.9	Hamangia figurines from Baia-Goloviţa	64
3.10	Hamangia figurines from Baia-Goloviţa	65
4.1	Figurines from Selevac	66
4.2	Gertrude Käsebier's *Blessed Art Thou Among Women* (1898)	69
4.3	Anatomical doll use in court	71
4.4	Eli, Matilda and Eli's Barbie Doll	74
4.5	Hans Bellmer's *Les Yeux de la Poupée* (1935)	76
4.6	Two images from Alfred Stieglitz's serial portrait of Georgia O'Keeffe (1919 and 1918)	79
5.1	Cucuteni figurines from Dumeşti	89
5.2	Hora-pot stand from Frumuşica	90
5.3	Four Cucuteni figurines as they were found at Ghelăieşti	91

FIGURES

5.4	PreCucuteni figurine from Traian-Dealul Viei	92
5.5	PreCucuteni figurine from Tîrpeşti	93
5.6	Cucuteni A figurine from Poduri	94
5.7	Cucuteni A figurine from Drăguşeni	95
5.8	Cucuteni A3 figurine heads from Truşeşti	97
5.9	Tripolye C figurine from Kočeržincy	98
5.10	Cucuteni B figurines from Costeşti-Baia and Ghelăieşti	99
5.11	Figurines from Vîhvatinti and Ghelăieşti	100
5.12	Main sites of the Cucuteni/Tripolye cultures mentioned in the text	104
5.13	Plan of the PreCucuteni and Cucuteni phases at Tîrpeşti	107
6.1	Figurine from Sitagroi	123
6.2	Jacques-Louis David's *Bonaparte, Premier Consul, Fraichissant le Grand Saint-Bernard, 20 mai 1800*	124
6.3	Alexander Gardner's *Hanging at Washington Arsenal; Hooded Bodies of the Four Conspirators; Crowd Departing, Washington, D.C.* (1865)	128
6.4	Alexander Gardner's *Lewis Payne, a Conspirator, in Sweater, Seated and Manacled* (1865)	128
6.5	Dorothea Lange's *Destitute Pea-Pickers in California; a 32-Year-Old Mother of Seven Children* (1936)	136
6.6	Example of a negative that has been 'killed' by Roy Stryker of the Farm Security Administration	139
7.1	Figurine from Achilleion	148
7.2	Figurines from Roidies and Bei	149
7.3	Figurines from Orenia and Bezil	151
7.4	Acrolithic figurine from Rachmani	156
7.5	Figurine from Achilleion	157
7.6	Figurine from Panagou	158
7.7	Figurine from Achilleion	160
7.8	Figurine from Orenia	161
7.9	Figurine from Kyriaki	162
7.10	Seated figurine from Larisa	163
7.11	Seated figurine from Koutsouro	164
7.12	Main sites of the Thessalian Neolithic mentioned in the text	167
7.13	House model with figurines from Plateia Magoula Zarkou	170
8.1	Figurine from Achilleion	181
8.2	J.M.W. Turner's *Snow Storm: Hannibal and his Army Crossing the Alps* (1812)	182
8.3	Walker Evans' *Squeakie Burroughs* (1936)	184
8.4	Hannah Höch's *Das schöne Mädchen* (1920)	188
8.5	Andalusian carnival participants	192

PREFACE AND ACKNOWLEDGEMENTS

This book has two origins. As a Master's student, I attended a lecture on the east European Neolithic which included a series of slides of anthropomorphic figurines. They were striking objects and though the lecturer (it was either Colin Renfrew or Ian Hodder, I do not remember which) convinced us that these objects were not representations of goddesses he did not offer any better explanation. I was intrigued. I spent the next several years putting together a PhD about the figurines from the Bulgarian late Neolithic site of Ovcharovo (Bailey 1991) in which I attacked the goddess argument and tried, not very successfully, to build something to take its place. From that research, I spun out a couple of articles but never felt that I had done justice to the material.

A second origin came a number of years after I had completed my doctorate and when the majority of my research energies were directed towards studying the Neolithic landscapes of southern Romania. I received a letter from Chris Scarre, editor of the *Cambridge Archaeological Journal*, asking if I would contribute to a 'Viewpoints' discussion entitled 'Can we interpret figurines?' which Naomi Hamilton was organizing for the journal. I was cautious. I was not so sure that I had anything new to offer. Chris suggested that I cut loose and write whatever I felt needed to be said, that the journal wanted to push the debate in new directions. At about the time that Chris's letter arrived, I had been reading some essays on the history of photography, including Susan Sontag's *On Photography* (Sontag 1973). The more I read of that and other books, the more uneasy I became with the explanations that continued to be offered for prehistoric figurines. Worse, I became increasingly convinced that my own published contributions had done little better. So, I accepted Chris's invitation; in the piece that eventually appeared in the *Cambridge Archaeological Journal* (Bailey 1996), I started to explore avenues that I had not considered before. This book is the product of that original invitation to cut loose.

In addition to thanking Chris Scarre for that invitation, I am in debt to a large number of people who have contributed to the project: to Colin Renfrew and Ian Hodder who started me on the topic; to Andrew Sherratt who, quite rightly, questioned my original conclusions; and to a long series of particularly dynamic seminar discussions that followed the presentation of my more recent thinking, notably those that took place at the Archaeological Institute of the Romanian Academy of Sciences, the University of Bucureşti, the University of California at Berkeley, UCLA, Columbia University, Cornell University, New York University, the University of Pennsylvania and Sheffield University. Thanks as well to Robin Skeates for inviting me to participate in his session on Visual Culture at the European Archaeological Association meetings in Thessaloniki and to Marian Neagu in Călăraşi (Romania) for inviting me to participate in his museum's symposium programme.

PREFACE AND ACKNOWLEDGEMENTS

I am in debt to specialists from many different museums and institutes who contributed their time, expertise and criticism: Radian Andreescu, Cătălin Bem, Peter Biehl, Fiona Campbell, John Chapman, Meg Conkey, Whitney Davis, Marcia-Anne Dobres, Aleku Dragoman, Dragoş Gheorghiu, Costel Haită, Jonna Hansen-Ulin, Kostas Kotsakis, Catalin Lazar, Richard Lesure, Katina Lillios, Christina Marangou, Silvia Marinscu-Bîlcu, Cristi Mirea, Dan Monah, Marian Neagu, Dragomir Popovici, Nerissa Russell, Evangelia Skafida, Stella Souvatzi, Laurens Thissen, Henrietta Todorova, Ruth Tringham and Ivan Vajsov. I am especially grateful to Michael Ashkin, Alton Delong, Roy King and the Little Artists (a.k.a. John Cake and Darren Neave) who took the time to talk about their work and about the potential overlap in our interests.

In the final stages of research and writing this book, I was privileged to spend a year as a Visiting Associate Professor at Stanford University's superb Archaeology Center. Cardiff University and the Arts and Humanities Research Board supported that visit with a Study Leave Grant. Many thanks to all who made that year a success, particularly the staff and students at the center, the Department of Cultural and Social Anthropology, and the Arts and Green Libraries: Ashish Chadha, Ellen Christensen, Fernando Fumero, Joel Leivick, John Mustain and Chris Witmore. Special thanks are due to Ian Morris, Ian Hodder and John Rick who made my time at Stanford possible (and positive). Extra-special thanks to Bill Rathje who offered a sane perspective when chaos threatened. Much of the critical secondary research would have been impossible without the help of the staff at the Sackler Library at the Ashmolean Museum in Oxford.

At Cardiff, I am especially lucky to have the support of colleagues, students and staff, especially the students of HS 2401 (The Archaeology of Art and Visual Culture) and HS 2367 (Balkan Prehistory); the Master's students on the Europe in the Neolithic degree and PhD students (Andy Cochrane, Ollie Harris, Dani Hofmann, Jo Seely). Steve Mills has long offered his help without proper acknowledgement. Howard Mason was invaluable (as always) in producing the line-art and in discussing the particularities of many of the figurines; Ian Dennis was instrumental in helping with producing final images. John Morgan made the photographic side of the project proceed so smoothly, and Aled Cooke provided critical support when systems collapsed. Don Shewan worked his usual magic turning poorly reproduced, often inaccurate and conflicting originals into superb maps.

In particular, I thank the following who provided original photographs: Amelia Hennighausen at *Discover Magazine* who went (way) out of her way to find a picture of the Alton Delong experiments; David Gilmore who was very generous in making his original slides available from his research into the Andalusian carnivals; Deborah Koreshoff for offering her *bonsai* images for reproduction; Joyce Marcus who made available images from her published projects; Kostas Gallis who made available his art-work of material from Plateia Magoula Zarkou; Sheriff Marcia Morgan who allowed me to reproduce an image from her work on police interviewing techniques; Radian Andreescu who made available the material from his excavations at Vitănești as well as the material from the Romanian National Museum of History in Bucureşti; and Leroy McDermott who supplied photographs from his seminal research on Palaeolithic figurines. Richard Stoneman, Celia Tedd and Julie Tschinkel (Routledge), Maggie Lindsey-Jones (Keystroke), Richard Willis (Swales & Willis), and Jane Olorenshaw steered the project from prospectus through to the book you see in front of you.

I am particularly in debt to Alasdair Whittle who commented with precision on much of the text and to Laurens Thissen, Kostas Kotsakis, Richard Bradley and Julian Thomas

PREFACE AND ACKNOWLEDGEMENTS

who commented on particular chapters. Many conversations with Mike Pearson have helped me to think in new and exciting directions. In the critical phases, especially when ideas were just emerging, Michael Shanks offered vital support and advice: the book would not have survived without his calm but incisive suggestions. Many thanks to Emma, Alexander and Hannah as well as to my parents for their continued support.

Finally, working on material kept in local east European museums and excavation archives has never been easy, before or after the changes of 1989. None of my work on Neolithic figurines would have been possible if not for the original openness and generosity of Ilka Angelova of the Turgovishte Regional Historical Museum in Bulgaria, who welcomed a very young and very inexperienced PhD student into her office, opened a drawer, took out a battered cardboard box and started teaching me about the figurines from northeastern Bulgaria. As a much delayed, but never diminished thank you, I dedicate this book to her.

Stanton and Palo Alto
Summer 2004

One of my male patients recollects that in the masturbation fantasies of his youth there was a little, imaginary, female figure which he always carried in his pocket and from time to time took out and played with. . . . You will already have guessed that this man's sexual potency was very inconsiderable.

(Ferenczi 1955)

1

INTRODUCTION

Looking up from my fieldbook, I saw one of the students running, full tilt. She was coming from the other side of the valley, from the flat lands, across the river. Was it Jo, one of the Third-Years? She was struggling, arms flailing awkwardly as she tried to keep her balance, fists clenched; unsuitable boots made her progress a challenge. Every couple of steps her foot would catch a rabbit hole hidden in the grasses or she would half-trip on an old plough furrow. She stopped across the stream bed from us. Red-cheeked, face streaked with dirt, frizzy red hair matted to her forehead, bent over, hands on knees, head up, wheezing in sharp, shallow gasps, she forced out an explanation. '. . . found . . . grid 145 . . . eroded surface. . . . Steve says get you . . . bring camera, more bags . . .'

Leaving the mapping team to log in the rest of the river course, I drove the Land-Rover, through the ford, up the bank opposite and threw the door open for Jo to haul herself up and in. Bumping our way back across the grassland, we could see the Grab Team up ahead, clustered around Steve, some on their hands and knees, others bent down pushing back the grass looking at the ground. Still wheezing (why do asthmatic students smoke?), Jo filled me in.

She had been working with Steve's team recording one of the 7,000-year-old Neolithic settlements that we had found in the valley bottom the week before. On the surface of the ground, the site was nothing more than pottery sherds, flints and clumps of burnt clay-and-straw building material. Today's collection of all the finds from the area and the mapping of the densities of finds would reveal how large this new site was and it would give us some idea about where to drop test-trenches if we decided to have a better look later in the summer or perhaps during the next season.

Earlier in the day, in the cool, quiet, early light just after dawn, I had left Steve and his team laying out the collection grid, marking grid numbers on the grass with spray-paint, assigning teams of grabbers to the squares, labelling and handing out finds bags and starting notebook entries. Jo said that after about two hours, work had stopped when one of the First-Years had let out a yell. Either the student had cut the hell out of her hand, had disturbed a snake or a rat, or she had found something extraordinary. Jo finished her report as we slowed to a stop by Steve's team: the survey team had turned up a small, badly preserved, fragment of a clay female figurine (fig. 1.1).

INTRODUCTION

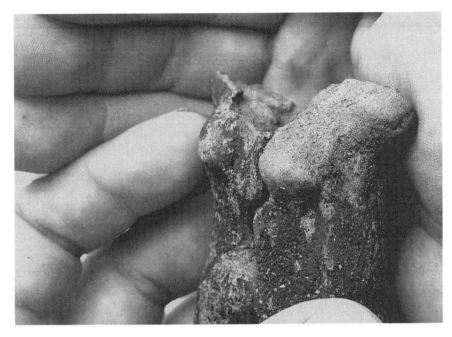

Figure 1.1 Figurine discovered by the Southern Romania Archaeological Project, Teleorman Valley.

Introduction

Why do prehistoric figurines evoke such strong emotions? Why, in this example from our work in Romania's Teleorman Valley, did the discovery of one, broken, out-of-context, surface-find create such a stir among the students? Most of them knew that the significant finds would be tallies of numbers, the densities of the more mundane sherds and flint scrapers? Why do specialist studies of figurines account for a disproportionately large number of pages and illustrations in excavation reports? Why are objects such as figurines deemed appropriate, desirable enough, to be included in Sotheby's or Christie's auctions, to take pride of place in museum cabinets and displays? Why are you reading this book? Why, indeed, am I drawn to write it?

The answers to these questions come from an investigation not so much about figurines themselves, in the sense of stylistic typologies or imaginative reconstructions, but about figurines as dynamic visual events. Because of this, the book before you is about many apparently disconnected subjects, discontinuous periods, separate regions and places. There will be no exhaustive compilation of figurines, their find-spots, and no discourse on culture-historical similarities among figurines from neighbouring or distant sites. Valuable though such descriptive studies are for making typological, cultural and chronological comparisons, I am looking for a different kind of answer, a different type of meaning.

The goal is to understand how and why objects such as figurines evoke the strong responses that they inevitably stimulate in you, in me and undoubtedly in their

INTRODUCTION

prehistoric makers and users. In understanding the how and why of figurines as visual culture, we will find a better understanding of Neolithic figurines. In a better understanding of Neolithic figurines from southeastern Europe, we will refine our understanding of the people who made, looked at, used, held, thought about and threw away these objects.

Starting in the middle of the seventh millennium BC, people in southeastern Europe made clay, bone and stone anthropomorphic figurines. Though figurines were produced in other periods of Europe's prehistoric past (e.g., the Upper Palaeolithic and its so-called Venuses), the Balkan Neolithic provides the largest body of material: hundreds of thousands of figurines were made. In the Balkans,[1] the phenomenon is tightly restricted to the Neolithic (6500–3500 BC); figurines appear with the first settled, pottery-making farmers and they disappear abruptly with the abandonment of the Neolithic way of life that marks the start of the early Bronze Age in the middle of the fourth millennium BC.[2] What was it about the Balkan Neolithic? What are the social, economic, material and political contexts in which Neolithic figurines were made? How did the people of the Neolithic Balkans live?

The Neolithic of Southeastern Europe

At a general level, the Balkan Neolithic is a collection of communities that lived their lives in similar ways.[3] Diversity along regional and chronological dimensions distinguishes different groups. Important variations lie in the ways people shaped and decorated pots, in the size, shape and permanence of their habitations, in the manner in which they handled death and displayed status, and in the intensity of exploitation of food resources. The traditional approach to this diversity identifies formal variation in material culture, mainly ceramic vessels, and assumes that these variations distinguish different cultural groups of people. Archaeologists thus generate schematic correlations that arrange cultures in time and separate them across the space. At the pan-regional level, there is more similarity than difference. Viewed at a finer resolution, of course, there was tremendous variation along these dimensions: between different parts of a region, within single river valleys or plateaux, between two adjacent settlements, between individual houses, huts, and even between individuals within a household. At the regional level, however, the similarities force us to think of a broadly common way of life.

Though the different Neolithic communities of the Balkans share many characteristics, they are distinct from those that occupied the region in the millennia before 6500 BC. These distinctions are important; they suggest that the people living in the region after the middle of the seventh millennium BC thought about the world in radically new and different ways, indeed that they possessed a new philosophy of life. On the ground, there was no absolute transition of a way of life; there was no revolution as we understand that concept. The changes were radical, with fundamental, if unintended consequences, but they occurred over a long period time, in various spurts and retardations, emerging in some areas sooner than in others and co-existing with other, particularly pre- and non-Neolithic, ways of life. Figurines were one of several key components in this new way of living.

3

INTRODUCTION

The built environment

One of the most important components of the new philosophy was the relationships that linked people to particular parts of the landscape: the explicit marking of repeated engagement and alteration of the terrain. The non-Neolithic Balkans was defined by temporary occupations and mobile existences that made short-term uses of caves and open-air sites; the Neolithic was about huts, camps and villages. It was about settling down.[4] Neolithic people physically built their own social environments; architecture offered shelter but, more importantly, provided the mechanisms for people to engage and create place. Some Neolithic built environments were little different from the places that mobile Upper Palaeolithic groups had used: small huts with simple, single-roomed floor plans, lined pits dug into the soil, covered with a roof, surrounded by walls made of saplings.[5] Distinct and novel for the Neolithic, however, were more substantial structures of one or two rooms, built at ground level, containing simple interior features such as a hearth or an oven. Both pit- and surface-level structures formed loose aggregations without formal spatial arrangement; most accurate analogies are drawn to short-term camps, places lived in, abandoned, reused and then abandoned again perhaps on a seasonal basis.

At the same time in other parts of the Balkans, people created more substantial built environments with larger buildings (up to 10 m on a side) made of thick wooden posts, sunk into foundation trenches, interspersed with smaller wooden poles around which were entwined branches and twigs which, in turn, were covered with a mixture of mud, clay and grasses. In some buildings, sun-dried mud bricks or stone foundations made walls more stable and structures more permanent. Many buildings contained four, five or more rooms in which particular areas were dedicated to specific activities such as parching, grinding and storing of plant foodstuffs. Larger, more permanent structures were grouped together in highly organized ways, forming villages, often tightly packed with little extra open space. In other cases, building arrangement left significant areas of open space, areas in which people shared activities and resources, ate and talked.

Significantly the larger, more orderly arrangements of buildings had long lives. Older structures were repaired; replacements were constructed directly on top of buildings that had collapsed or, frequently near the end of the Neolithic, had been burned down intentionally. In many places, when buildings were replaced, great effort was made to rebuild in precisely the same location with earlier floor plans carefully replicated. With many regenerations of buildings, villages grew into substantial tells rising from the landscape, becoming highly visible statements of monumental settlement. Tell villages represent communities' commitments to particular places for settlement; attention to location and forms of rebuilding established links between living and past generations of village residents.

Though commitments to settlement and architecture are common across the Balkan Neolithic there is variation in the degree and in the timing of their appearances. In northern Greece, for example, substantial, long-lived villages made with durable stone and mud brick occurred early, from the second half of the seventh millennium BC. To the north, along the lower Danube, such substantial construction materials never appeared and monumental tells did not emerge until the middle of the fifth millennium BC, 1,500 years after pit features and surface structures first appeared in the area. Neither to the north nor south did tells dominate; Neolithic Balkan landscapes were mixtures of

4

INTRODUCTION

different degrees of settlement permanences. To the west in Serbia, for example, tells appeared at the same time (and in the same landscapes) as did less permanent habitations, though tells were less frequent than flat settlements that spread horizontally through successive phases of building. In southern Bulgaria another pattern reveals only tells.[6] Perhaps the most accurate reconstruction of Balkan Neolithic settlement patterns includes different manifestations of the built environment depending on variation in activities, seasons or political reasons.

The social and political significance of Neolithic Balkan architecture cannot be over-emphasized. Houses and villages created tangible, physical, and relatively permanent boundaries around groups and their activities. The physical presence of houses established and reinforced cohesion of small co-resident groups. Houses pulled together group members at the same time as separating them from other groups. Membership in households was maintained over time by repeated rebuildings that secured physical links with earlier generations of houses (i.e., the long-term occupation of tells), or by repeating the form and size of a structure nearby (i.e., a thin, horizontal spread of occupation). Houses incorporated individuals into groups at the same time as they excluded other individuals. Similarly, aggregations of buildings incorporated individual houses (and their households) into the larger social institution of the village.

The social and political consequences of the Neolithic developments in Balkan architecture were fundamental. Benefits of incorporation were shared resources and labour, reduced risk for an individual or household, and other co-operative spin-offs of communal living. More dramatic were negative consequences: tensions and conflicts inherent in shared living, competition for limited resources, the ill-ease that exclusion generates. To realize the benefits, to reduce the tensions, and to overcome the threats to community coherence, Neolithic village living required not only new materials but also less tangible, political mechanisms. Resolution of conflict and tension was a major part of Neolithic life and was played out with new objects and raw materials, developments in attitudes to the dead, and changes in the scales of economic activities.

A new materiality

As significant as the adoption of architecture was a dramatic increase in the number and range of objects that people made and used. The most important element of this change was the adaptation of a ceramic pyrotechnology (Vitelli 1989, 1993, 1995). Balkan Neolithic potting developed through two stages: an early experimental encounter of the technology followed by a longer phase during which the elaboration of forms, techniques and uses expanded. The experimental phase consisted of casual attempts at potting; a few people making one or two vessels of simple design, irregular construction and uneven firing. Most likely, the first potters were people with experience in locating, gathering and processing other, special, raw materials; they knew where to find plants for food and, particularly, for medicines and for making mood-altering substances. Esoteric knowledges needed for collecting and transforming a raw resource such as a plant into a consumable, medicinal potion could easily have been adapted into the knowledges required for locating, collecting and processing a new raw material, such as clay. The abilities to find, extract and work clay and then transform it, by firing, from a natural, malleable, perishable medium into a permanent one were special skills. As Karen Vitelli has argued, early potter-gatherers may have played special roles in Balkan Neolithic communities.

5

INTRODUCTION

Equally important, the transformative process of pot-firing and the special identities of pot-makers most probably invested early ceramic objects with equally special meanings.

It is relevant, therefore, that early ceramic vessels were not used for cooking or storage, uses that only developed as ceramic technology stabilized and became a more commonly held knowledge. With time, vessel shapes became extraordinarily diverse; potters became technical specialists producing many pots of regular shape and decoration. In this the more developed phase of Balkan Neolithic potting, vessels were used for cooking, for storage, for transportation, for display; ceramic was now the medium of preference for container technologies. Ceramic vessels facilitated the accumulation and exclusive storage of plant or animal products, and pots were also social objects, playing important roles in feasting and exchange and in expressions of group and individual identities.

Appreciation of the transformative character of ceramic technology is an important consequence of the adoption of pottery-making. Creating a permanent medium from an impermanent one and making the perishable durable are significant material and spiritual transitions. In the experimental potting stages, pottery-making and pottery use must have evoked the magical and the other-worldly; ceramic practitioners would have been magicians, shamans and respected or feared possessors of special knowledges. In the more developed phases of potting, the significance of the transformation can be recognized in the roles that pottery vessels and other ceramic objects played as they carried messages of status and imagery.

The introduction and development of pottery-making was only one part of a wider new materiality that characterizes the Balkan Neolithic. Stone, both ground and flaked, was made into axes, scrapers, blades and other tools such as grinding-querns and grinders. Animal bone was made into spoons, awls and scrapers: animal horn into digging-sticks, shaft-hole axes and adzes, hammers and pounders. Though not preserved, other objects of perishable materials were widely used: containers of woven plants and gourds; wooden pots;[7] leather straps and coverings; net bags; textile clothing, rugs and wall-coverings. Though not all of these objects were new to the Neolithic, the variety of form, the scales of their production, use and consumption, and most especially the impact of a new, malleable but permanent medium such as clay would have been fundamental: the Balkan Neolithic was a time of material objects. The increase in made objects documents a new way of living, of people and possessions, of increased scales of production and consumption, of technological evolution, of collection and hoarding, but also of giving, receiving and sharing. The adoption of a ceramic technology was significant and novel, although in reality the gross increase in frequencies of objects may only be a consequence of the more radical change of people marking out space with structures, buildings, camps and villages repeatedly occupied over time.[8]

Expressive material culture

An important component of the new materiality that defines the Neolithic Balkans was the production, use and strategic deposition of intentionally expressive objects, particularly those made of fired clay. Anthropomorphic figurines are one example of the new, permanent, and specifically expressive, objects. Animal as well as human forms appear in the shapes of pots as well as in the two-dimensional images depicted on vessel surfaces. Representations of buildings, their façades as well as their interiors, also appear in miniature as house models.

INTRODUCTION

More striking were new materials that appeared through the fifth millennium BC, materials with particular, visually provocative, physical characteristics. The use of copper, first for cold-hammered trinkets and pendants and then for extravagantly large tools, is matched by the use of gold for body ornaments. These are sensually stimulating materials used to make objects displayed and consumed close to the body. Similarly, white shell of the marine mollusc *Spondylus gaederopus* was made into bracelets, rings, beads and pendants; graphite and gold solutions were used to decorate pot surfaces. Copper tools, gold and *Spondylus* jewellery, and brilliantly reflective pottery surfaces provided tremendous new potentials for the expression of individual and group identities. Significantly, many of these new, visually expressive, objects were deposited in burials.

The emergence of permanent, intentionally expressive material culture and the more general increase in the number and varieties of things that people made and used had consequences for the ways in which people acted out who they were and what they intended as their relationships with others. The use of pottery decoration as a means (even unconscious) of expressing and recognizing affinities to groups complements the senses of incorporation and exclusion evident in the growth and development of houses and villages as social institutions. Expressions of membership in a household or village must have taken advantage of the potential presented first by the almost infinitely malleable (and decoratable) medium of clay and second by the more general potential presented by the arrangement (hiding, hoarding, sharing, displaying) of all objects intentionally expressive or not. Importantly, the new materiality of the Balkan Neolithic provided, if not the recipe, then at least the ingredients needed for making expressions of individual, household and village identities.

Treatment of the dead

The built environments and the new materialities of the post-6500 BC Balkans provided potent mechanisms with which people and their communities negotiated and contested their lives and their relationships. Contemporary developments in mortuary ceremony supplemented these mechanisms. In the southeast European Neolithic, the deposition of the deceased was closely tied to the occupations and meanings of building space and village space. Neolithic ideas about landscape, of people making places by the establishment of camps and villages, included the deposition of the dead into the new, anchored, social environments. Buried individuals included young and old, male and female, although the predominance of children's burials is striking. For all ages and both sexes, the ranges and numbers of grave-goods were limited: individual pots, a few bone or shell beads. In some regions, interment included animal bone, teeth and antler. In terms of the number of people living in houses and villages, inhumation was an infrequent event and it is difficult to read any significance into patterns of age, sex or differentials in grave-good distribution. The occasional inclusion of disarticulated human body parts into the burial of a separate individual, the dismemberment of skeletons, and the recovery of unassociated fragments of human bone across sites suggest that whatever rules applied to deposition of the dead they were not applied equally to all people. The majority of bodies must have been disposed of in ways that have left no traces; perhaps they were exposed or left for scavengers in places unconnected to settlement or other activity areas.

INTRODUCTION

In the fifth millennium BC, however, important developments in mortuary ritual are evident. Most striking are the inhumations of the deceased in extra-mural cemeteries, often with disproportionate distributions of grave-goods. Large concentrations of burials (up to 600 graves) are dramatic though it is difficult to determine whether the number of bodies reflects a long period of use for one cemetery or whether it signals the deposition of a high proportion of a single community over shorter phases. It is clear, however, that death and its celebration now played a significant role in strategies to maintain, manipulate or contest claims for social status and social positioning within and between village communities. Men, women and children were buried in cemeteries, but there are clear disparities in the numbers and types of associated grave-goods: adults were buried with a larger number and more exotic grave-goods than were children; adult women were buried with fewer, less exotic grave-goods than were men; men were buried with special objects such as large copper chisels and axes, golden jewellery and body appliqués. While these patterns are not absolute (some women were interred with concentrations of exotic objects) in terms of effort invested, the mortuary realm now received greater attention than it had in the previous millennia and more of that investment was directed to adults than to children and more to men than to women.[9]

The extra-mural dislocation of death from the village and the space of the living is significant and suggests that by the fifth millennium BC, many Neolithic communities listened to both cemetery-centred, publicly expressed, ceremonial statements of status and power-relations as well as more house- and village-focused, more private, quieter, versions of reality (Bailey 1994a). The publicly broadcast version involved the consumption of the new especially expressive materials (gold, copper, *Spondylus*) which were deposited during the death ceremonies of particular individuals. Along with the elevation of the public mortuary ritual as a main stage for social positioning, it is not surprising that mock burials took place at times when the need for reaffirmation of status was greatest (i.e., the often misunderstood, so-called, cenotaphs).

Plants and animals

In the light of developments in architecture, material culture and burial, the changes in exploitation of plants and animals in the Balkan Neolithic were not as dramatic as traditionally assumed.[10] True, new technologies for exploiting plants and animals and the introduction of new species are important distinctions of life in the Balkans after 6500 BC. Domestication of local animals such as pig, dog and cattle, the introduction of animals of foreign origin, such as sheep and goat, were matched by the introduction of novel cultivation technologies and plant species: wheats, barleys and legumes. New species and new technologies required new knowledges and skills. Individuals able to manage plant-growing and animal-rearing occupied new positions within communities. If the traditional economic division of food-gatherers from food-producers still holds any value for defining the revolutionary difference of the Neolithic, then that value rests in the social and political consequences of growing plants and grazing animals.

In important ways, new animal species represented no change; eating the meat of herbivores was nothing novel. The way in which the meat was packaged, however, was different; the role of cattle and its large body-size had important social repercussions for animal slaughter and meat distribution. To consume one bovid required the aggregation of a large group; meat distribution of a large animal thus provided opportunities to be

8

INTRODUCTION

grasped and problems to be avoided. Again, there is continuity with previous millennia, specifically with the distribution and consumption of large-bodied animals such as red deer. The significant difference is that the domesticated animals of the Neolithic were investments of labour, care and fodder; events of meat distribution followed new rules and entitlements, values and consequences.

In the Neolithic, the character of the relationship between people and animals had changed. Connection of human to domestic animal was established well before the events surrounding the kill; in the more mobile communities more common before the Neolithic, the human–animal relationship and, critically, the rules and responsibilities of meat distribution, were established only with the event of the kill or the hunt. In the pre-Neolithic, hunting and the distribution of meat from a large-bodied animal were important mechanisms of group aggregation and for individuals to express status, identity and power. In mobile communities of fluctuating memberships and sizes, meat distribution was a critically important social and political mechanism. In the Neolithic, the distribution of meat from large animals was also important but its significance was complicated by the competing and, perhaps, more forceful mechanisms of social organization provided by the built environment, mortuary ritual and the new materiality.

It is significant that the new animal species (i.e., sheep and goat) introduced intermediate-sized packages of meat, much smaller than cattle but larger than pigs and dogs. The social repercussions of slaughtering and consuming animals of sheep and goat proportions are important: the size of the group fed fits most closely with the size of the groups that focused their lives and activities in Neolithic houses. Compared with earlier millennia, the social and political potency available to individuals distributing meat would have been much reduced. With time, the role of large-bodied domestics, especially cattle, took on new significances, perhaps played out at a village level, of a more public order and more closely matched with the ceremonies taking place in the extra-mural cemeteries than they were with more private, household events. Indeed, by the end of the Neolithic cattle had attained a special importance within Neolithic communities with zoomorphic figurines and, in a few instances, gold appliqués created in their image.

The adaptations of new plant species and technologies are also important for the social and political consequences of their implementation, consequences that varied with the scales of cultivation and the scheduling of activities in the agricultural cycle. As with potting, the exploitation of new technologies and plant varieties in the Balkan Neolithic proceeded through early, experimental, phases before accelerating into more intense and standardized systems of planting, tending, harvesting, processing, storing and consuming. Small-scale garden horticulture tended by individuals required little investment of time, labour or long-term residence. More complex commitments of swiddening required greater investment in preparing the land (perhaps clearing areas of forest and scrub) and longer sequences of residence. Neither system is incompatible with a semi-mobile existence in which small communities spent only parts of seasons in places of cultivation. Nor is either system excluded from a more permanent system where people stayed in one place for several years before moving on, perhaps to return after a year or two. Such patterns of small-scale planting characterized much of the Balkan Neolithic, though more intense regimes appeared early in some regions, particularly to the south.

Dramatic changes in the scale of cultivation occurred at the same time as did the shift to extra-mural cemeteries, the emergence of new expressive material culture and the

INTRODUCTION

appearance of tell villages in the northern Balkans, namely from the late sixth millennium BC. From this time, significant efforts were made to alter the land before planting and to employ cattle for traction in ploughing. Cows and goats were now exploited for dairy and textile materials as well as for their meat. Indeed part of the increasing status of cattle over time may have been due to the animal's new value derived from its secondary uses; investments of labour, care and foddering made cattle a true (live)stock. Growing wheats and barley in large fields was not unusual and tell villages contained large grain silos full of carbonized grain. Grinding-stones are frequent finds in houses and very large storage vessels are common.

Food production had intensified and with the scale of intensification came important social and political consequences. First among these were the requirements of labour, time and knowledge needed, especially the ability to manage the labour required and to retain, distribute and store the plant-goods produced. Management of labour for large-scale cultivation was complex.[11] Some stages in the agricultural cycle, such as planting or harvesting, were disproportionately labour- and time-consuming; large numbers of people were needed to work intensively over a short period of time. Other stages, including the majority of a crop's growing time, required very few people doing very little. The bringing together and, critically, the sending away of people were potential management problems. Abilities to co-ordinate and coerce human resources were socio-political skills. Special technical skills and knowledges were also required; critical to success were knowledges of when to plant and when to harvest. Miscalculations of either would have been disastrous. Equally important were skills and experience in processing harvested grain: threshing, winnowing and, especially, parching were crucial and not necessarily equally available across a community.

The potential problems inherent in organized, especially large-scale, cultivation required socio-political solutions. Tell villages, as political institutions, may have provided one solution: a focus for residence, for labour, for storage. Other phenomena of the Neolithic undoubtedly contributed. The loud, public expression of status and identities in mortuary ceremony, the accumulation of people and goods in houses and in villages probably advertised the power of a village at the same time as identifying the individuals who were in control of decisions and resources. The role of visually expressive objects and their display contributed to such socio-political solutions. At the same time, it is important to see the darker side of these consequences and solutions. Expressions of status differentiation and management of labour investment were just as easily used as tools of exploitation and coercion as they were mechanisms of co-operation and collaboration. The Neolithic means of incorporating and excluding were ideally suited to creating and maintaining divisions within communities and to establishing disproportionate distributions of resources and materials.

Socio-politics

In the Balkans after 6500 BC people started living their lives in new ways. This included very substantial changes in people's relationships to each other, both within and between groups and especially in the ways individuals thought it appropriate to identify themselves and their own places of residence and activity. Changes included new conceptions of landscape and appropriate ways of inhabiting and exploiting the land and its resources. Significant changes occurred in the particular components of the natural world that

INTRODUCTION

people chose to exploit, in the ways they exploited them, and in the ways they consumed the resources exploited and the things made. An important part of these changes was a daily life increasingly full of a widening variety of new objects.

The house, the household, the village and, eventually, the cemetery, were the key social institutions of the Balkan Neolithic. Houses and villages created tangible, physical and relatively permanent boundaries around groups, their activities and their possessions. Memberships within households and villages were as much products of incorporation as of exclusion; the physical boundaries manifest in house and settlement were matched by a new perspective of death which viewed the disposal of the corpse as the appropriate focus for ceremonies that expressed differentiation (and similarity) among individuals within and between communities.

If, therefore, the Balkan Neolithic is defined in terms of incorporation and exclusion, then attention must focus on the means of expressing identities, of rights and entitlement to residence and to participation in village life (and death). Burial and settlement practice played major roles in identity expression. Similar roles were occupied at a more mundane, though no less important level, by the material culture of life, not only by the exotic and visually stimulating, but also by the more quotidian objects of living and the ways in which they were used, shared or hoarded, hidden or displayed, preserved or discarded.

From all of these patterns emerges a socio-politics of the Balkan Neolithic in which life was run through with series of tensions and conflicts, contestations and usurpations. Clearly some of this took place on the big stage of mortuary rituals (either in the burial of children in house floors or in extra-mural cemeteries) and of ceremonies of house construction and rebuilding. Other currents of tension ran deep below the surface and can only be sensed in the delicate and incomplete traces of political intention and coercion.

Figurines and their links to the key phenomena

Based only on this general understanding of their Balkan Neolithic context, what can we say about anthropomorphic figurines? Does a better understanding of the key economic and social phenomena of the period begin to move us toward a better understanding of figurines? As ceramic objects, figurines were part of the new Neolithic materiality. As such they were one of many categories of things through which people expressed, maintained, negotiated and contested identities and realities. That they were made of a new durable, transformative and perhaps transgressive material must be significant. That they were one of a number of different, particularly expressive, materials is equally important. Also telling is the fact that, with one major exception, figurines were used and consumed in houses or at the very least within the boundaries of village space; their absence from burials is conspicuous.

Perhaps most importantly, however, figurines are objects that appeared within a period during which critically important questions were continually being asked about who people were, about where people belonged, and about what relationships existed between individuals and among groups. All of these issues must be addressed in moving towards a fuller understanding of Neolithic figurines. That is the purpose of this book.

11

INTRODUCTION

Previous approaches to figurines

A detailed assessment of previous research on figurines from the Balkan Neolithic requires a book of its own. Even a descriptive review of the appearance of figurines in local, Balkan, and international publications exceeds both the scope and purposes of this chapter: to highlight the challenges that face figurine research and to suggest how work can move forward.

The present trend in figurine research is historiographic: to research not the figurines themselves but to examine the studies of figurines, the schools of interpretation and proposed interpretations. Important texts on figurine historiography include Richard Lesure's recent article (Lesure 2002), two papers by Meg Conkey and Ruth Tringham (Conkey and Tringham 1995; Tringham and Conkey 1998) and a collection of shorter comments in the *Cambridge Archaeological Journal*'s 1996 Viewpoint section entitled 'Can we interpret figurines?' (Bailey 1996; Haaland and Haaland 1996; N. Hamilton 1996; J. Marcus 1996; Ucko 1996). Many analyses concentrate on Goddess interpretations given life by Marija Gimbutas.[12] Some investigate the gendering of figurine studies, highlighting the damage that, paradoxically, Mother Goddessism has done to a feminist archaeology.[13]

Historiographies aside, figurine scholarship consists of excavation reports and interpretive essays. Of these, many propose specific meanings or functions for figurines. In addition to the Mother Goddess interpretations, the common references are to ritual, religion and spiritual life. Most propose anecdotal functions: figurines as dolls, toys, magical items, afterlife accessories, sexual aids, fertility figures, effigies, talismans, ritual figures, concubines, slaves, puberty models, training mechanisms, votive and healing objects, items used in initiation ceremonies, contracts, territory and identity markers (Meskell 1998).

Few attributions of function offer substantive argument to support their interpretations. Many avoid explicit discussion of the assumptions upon which preferred interpretations rest. As explanations, the results are pleasing. Why else the success and continuity of Mother Goddessism? But they are also simplistic, offering anecdote in the place of explanation, avoiding the transparency of approach that a rigorous, reflective method requires or the theoretical reasoning that underpins modern archaeology. Worse still, unreflective approaches are exclusive. Authors provide complete and seamless interpretations; readers are not given the opportunity to trace the ways that the data are joined with particular interpretations. As such, anecdotal interpretations eliminate the potential either for criticism or for the development of alternative meanings for particular figurines. Everything is simple and clear. There is neither debate nor even reason to stimulate debate. The worst news is that the majority of primary publications of figurines follow this anecdotal approach. Why is this the case? What are the alternatives?

A special rhetoric

A critical reader of excavation reports and journal articles on the Balkan Neolithic quickly realizes that figurines possess strange attractive powers that seduce and overwhelm archaeologists and editors. It is as if figurines, on their own, out of context, in publications or museum displays, function with an intangible, inherent and perhaps unquantifiable rhetoric. It is a rhetoric that convinces journal peer-reviewers and publishing house

12

INTRODUCTION

referees that it is appropriate to devote disproportionately large proportions of their volumes to the presentation of Neolithic figurines. It is a rhetoric of essentialism; figurines just *are* important. The figurine rhetoric convinces us of the primacy of their study and, more worryingly, makes us believe that there is no need either for explicit justifications of their scholarly importance or for proof of figurines' value to reconstructions of prehistoric life. The implicit assumption is that figurines are essential components of life (both Neolithic and modern archaeo-academic). Figurine essentialism is damaging; it has restricted the intellectual breadth of research and conditioned many scholars to accept figurines as an easy and simple category of material culture.

Empirical solutions

Within figurine essentialism, some analysts have reacted against undefended acceptance of unsupported, anecdotal interpretations. Turning away from implicit reasoning and unverifiable conclusion, they place a premium on scientific examination, description and measurement (e.g., Podborský 1983, 1985). Increasingly common in final excavation reports, these analyses contain abundant data: lists of measurements, descriptions of colours (Munsell codes are mandatory), fabric identification, bibliographic references, photographs and often redundant line-drawings. A good example is Milojković's chapter analysing the figurines from the late Neolithic, Vinča culture site of Opovo (Milojković 1990); every figurine is described with full descriptive and excavation information. Another example is Vajsov's work on Hamangia figurines from northern Bulgaria and southern Romania (Vajsov 1992b) (fig. 1.2); multiple measurements of body parts are proposed as a key, though it is not clear what door such a key will unlock. Milojković and Vajsov's intentions are honest and well-intentioned: the inclusive presentation of information that openly provides the scholarly community with as much data as

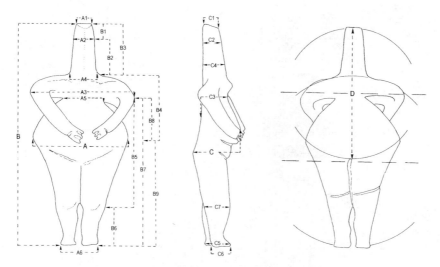

Figure 1.2 Method proposed by Ivan Vajsov for analysing Hamangia figurines (after Vajsov 1992b)

INTRODUCTION

is possible. Such inclusivity allows a fullness of further research that the anecdotal interpreters, unfortunately, do not provide.

Where the unsupported anecdotal interpretations are frustrating for their absence of argument, explicit assumptions of method and the data-rich treatments are exasperating for their blind empiricism.[14] Important questions are left unasked. Is all of the information so carefully gathered and presented for use? Is each measurement necessary? If so, for what? If so, why is so little done with this information? One exception is Peter Biehl's detailed recording and analysis of Gradeshnitsa-Krivodol culture figurines from northwestern Bulgaria (Biehl 1996, 2003). Biehl attempts to combine a typological analysis of attributes with information about form, content and context in order to elaborate the rule-generated systems by which figurine-makers worked. He identifies and documents individual decorative motifs and assesses the statistical significance of the placement of different motifs on different areas of the figurine's body (fig. 1.3). With this information, Biehl tries to link motif patterns and frequencies to codes of production. Though the argument is not entirely convincing, the study is a refreshing application of empirical rigour to an anthropological question.

In many other works, however, a fetishism of measurement is at work and it is far from obvious that it is of any value for the interpretation of material culture like figurines. It is unclear even if it is of use for traditional culture-history typologies and chronologies; do the variables that are recorded in such detail provide insight into geographic or diachronic variation? There are other problems particular to the rules of empirical documentation. For example, when measuring the sizes of figurine heads from different types of figurines (Hamangia figurines are one case; Thessalian ones another), it is unclear how one can determine precisely where the head ends and the neck begins? There is also the

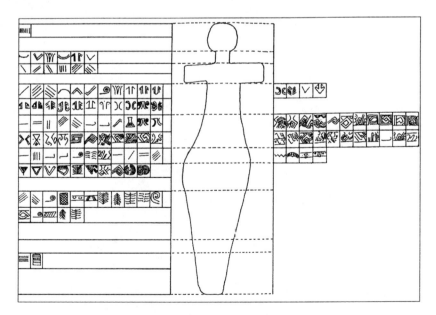

Figure 1.3 An example of Peter Biehl's study of motif disposition on Bulgarian figurines (after Biehl 1996)

INTRODUCTION

huge challenge presented by the overwhelming fragmentation of the material (see Chapman 2000a: 68–79). Most figurines survive as bits and pieces long since broken: arms, heads, thighs, torsos. How does one measure what has not survived? Often the answer is to create types from complete figurines and assume that standardization of size and form is the norm; then an individual disarticulated body-part can be measured and complete figurine measurements deduced. In most Balkan Neolithic figurines attempts to reconstruct a whole from a part is challenging at best. More worrying is the failure to ask if the differences in the variables recorded are important. If, for example, there are strong patterns of size differentiation, then why do these patterns exist? What might they tell us about how Neolithic people thought about the figurines? If the proportion of the size of a particular body-part, such as the head, to the body varies in a significant fashion, what might be the interpretive consequences of recognizing such a pattern? In what ways can such minutely detailed description move our understanding forward?

Critical questions

Significantly, neither the anecdotal nor the empirical approach asks the fundamental questions. What makes an object a figurine? When is something simply an oddly shaped stone, bone or lump of clay and when is it a representation? When is that representation anthropomorphic? Indeed, what is a representation and what are the cognitive or political significances and consequences of making representations? What of viewing representations? Of handling them? When is an anthropomorph a representation of a man and when of a woman? When of a child? When of an animal? Are these categories exclusive?[15] Are they significant? Are there not important problems inherent in the identification and rigid definition of boundaries that are necessary for empirical description? So often, in their reaction against the anecdotal and imaginative interpretation, the empirical alternatives offer no interpretation at all. They let the numbers, tables and illustrations stand for themselves. They trust that their fear of offering interpretation will be dispersed by overzealous measurement and increasingly detailed columns of description.

These comments touch on only a few of the most common ways that figurines have been treated in publication and how they are processed in museums, on excavations and in people's perceptions of them. A very good, recent, and more inclusive, overview is that of Richard Lesure and the interested reader is directed there for a fuller discussion of other trends in figurine analysis from both the Eurasian and American contexts (Lesure 2002).[16] Each trend and school of thought is, of course, legitimate in itself, within its own conception of scientific or social reality (i.e., Indo-European studies; Eco-Feminism; Naïve Empiricism); indeed how else could the many examples of each have to come to print in reputable journals and in volumes from established academic publishing houses?[17]

Moving forward

Many existing approaches are unsatisfying because they ask the wrong questions: questions about typology and chronology (what is the difference between figurines of Hamangia Type A and Hamangia Type B?); questions about the gender balance of societies and the search for matriarchies and patriarchies (was the Vinča culture dominated by men or women?); and questions about the rosters of pantheons (was the Bird-Goddess or the Bull Consort present?). Most importantly, they ask questions and employ methods

INTRODUCTION

that betray a radical misconception or ignorance of the complexities and dynamics of material culture and, more critically, of visual culture.[18] There are, however, several important exceptions, studies which take different angles of approach and which push the discussion in new, more exciting directions. It is worth considering these exceptions in more detail.

Representing females

In a major contribution to the study of figurines, Leroy McDermott and Catherine McCoid transformed our understanding of Upper Palaeolithic Venus figurines (McDermott 1996; McCoid and McDermott 1996). Their work is important because it approaches the material from the point of view of the person who made the objects. McDermott and McCoid see parallels between the particular and standardized proportions of female Venus figurines and the view that a pregnant woman would have of her own body (fig. 1.4). Their approach has radical implications for the way we think about Upper Palaeolithic figurines but also for looking at Neolithic anthropomorphs. The status of the image shifts from a sexualized representation viewed by an Other to self-conceptions viewed by one person, who is both the subject and the object. The consequences for understanding the emergence and manipulation of the self, identity and personality are large. How did people in the Upper Palaeolithic or the Neolithic conceptualize themselves? As objects? As beings? How did representations of the human form reshape prehistoric ideas of what it was to be human? What are the consequences of taking account of who is looking and why? What are the consequences of thinking about who is being looked at and why? How could we redefine figurines if we think more deeply in terms of the visual and the roles that the spectator plays and if we examine the power relationships that develop around acts (and mechanisms) of being looked at? What are the politics of looking and being seen? Of wanting to be seen? To be seen in a particular way? To possess particular characteristics of form and of material essence?

In another important paper, Gunnar and Randi Haaland (Haaland and Haaland 1995) wrestle with one of the fundamental, but little investigated, premises of most figurine research: that a figurine is a direct reflection of actual beings, whether they are human or divine. Starting with a critique of Gimbutas and the Mother Goddess movement, the Haalands attack two assumptions: that a predominance of images of women in a society reflects a society in which women hold dominant positions; and that the predominance of female imagery is a characteristic of matriarchic societies. The Haalands examine ethnographic studies of communities that have an abundance of female imagery, and they use their own fieldwork among the Fur of western Sudan.[19] They focus on the relationship between the roles that women play in communities and the presence and uses of female imagery. For example, a richly developed female imagery exists among Fur communities. Its use and meaning is linked to the concept *Bora Fatta* (i.e., white or mother's milk) as well as to particular rituals, colours, substances and intra-group relationships. For the study of figurines, the importance of Fur female imagery is that its meaning emerges in crises of the life cycle and in interpersonal relations, events that usually involve ritual solutions: healing, warfare, circumcision, rainfall. Significantly, these crises and relationships are dominated by men. Fur female imagery is a part of attempts to establish trust and support within a community consisting of poorly developed corporate groups and within which social solidarity is fragile. With the Fur, then, abundances of female

16

INTRODUCTION

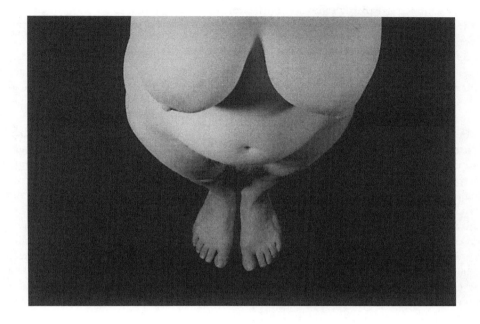

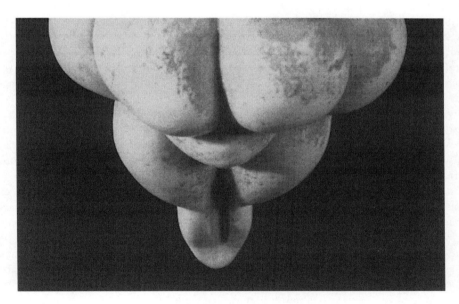

Figure 1.4 Comparison of Palaeolithic figurine and the body of a pregnant woman (after McDermott 1996). Courtesy of Leroy McDermott.

INTRODUCTION

imagery cannot be read as a reflection of the dominance of women in society. Imagery is involved in deep, complicated systems of meaning and negotiation within communities where men dominate in public.

Clearly, it would be possible to find ethnographic case studies that document a match between abundances of female imagery and female political dominance.[20] The important point is not the dominance-status of the relationship (i.e., do women or men hold positions of social power in communities with abundant female imagery?), nor is it even that many ethnographic case-studies, the Haaland's examples included, suggest that an abundance of female imagery correlates with a subordinated role of women.[21] Rather, the interesting issues are, first, that a relationship between sexed imagery and community power structures exists at all and, second, that it is more frequently expressed and manipulated through images of women and not of men.[22] We are forced to ask why does female imagery work in this way? Why do female symbols possess the potential to evoke particular kinds of associations? What may figurines say about human relationships? Why does an imagery modelled on attributes of the female body convincingly express ways of engaging these relationships? Critically, the Haalands distinguish between asking what a figurine is an *image of* and asking what a figurine is an *image for*. To ask the latter question demands that we accept that figurines are active material representations and that there is an inherent potential within such material to affect people and their perceptions of reality.

In her study of Early Iron Age Greek bronze figurines, Susan Langdon adds further dynamism to the relationship between the gender of representations and social reality (Langdon 1999). Langdon suggests that asymmetries in male and female figurines reveal new strategic uses of gender to validate imbalances in male and female roles in the development and participation in Iron Age cult. The majority of figurines (81 per cent) are male. Male figurines are depicted engaged in a greater range of activities than are the female figurines. Furthermore, male figurines depict more dynamic activities than do female ones: males are shown, for example, herding animals to sacrifice, drawing back a bow, and working at metal-smithing; females' activities are more passive, for example, standing or holding a pot. Also, in their broader stylistic developments, male figurines are less static than are the female ones; newly introduced types are more often male than they are female. Finally, male figurines depict social identities that refer to life beyond the limits of cult; female ones are restricted to particular cult roles.

Langdon proposes that we understand these patterns in the context of contemporary changes in religion and cult and in attempts by men to dominate the new institutions that result. Between 1000 and 700 BC, religion assumed a greater symbolic value. New cults were founded and existing ones were reorganized. The number of bronze offerings at sanctuaries increased. Langdon argues that bronze anthropomorphic figurines played a role in revising and communicating gender definitions and norms for religious and cult activities. She argues that figurines were used aggressively to propose and reinforce a male domination of religious development. Through the display of bronze figurines, gender emerged as a significant factor within visual discourse. Langdon's work raises important questions about the potential that figurines have for socio-political struggle and for proposing alternatives and inverting the status quo. What is it about the character of figurines that make them potential agents in these contests? Why aren't other objects or other materials employed? What is the socio-political significance of differences in frequencies, activities and styles between male and female images?

INTRODUCTION

Linda Conroy's discussion of the emergence of gender in the Upper Palaeolithic asks similar questions about figurines and about potential meanings of gendered representations (Conroy 1993). Conroy argues that the interest in distinguishing between male and female imagery in figurines is a product of modern ways of thinking about gender. Provocatively, she suggests that males and females share the same body morphology and that variation is restricted to a common spectrum: variation of the human form. Because of this the important observation is to see how different communities choose to emphasize differences or similarities between humans. Conroy suggests that we think about the conventions used to differentiate between women and other, sex-neutral, beings. In this light, it is easier to understand the significant numbers of figurines that are neither male nor female.[23] Upper Palaeolithic cultural constructs were created through material emphasis on female anatomical attributes. Female sexual morphology underpinned a gendered stereotype; figurines were a medium for projecting that stereotype. For Conroy images are potent mechanisms that influence shared beliefs and attitudes to the world. Gender is a social institution best encountered through practical activities such as looking, describing, categorizing, abstracting and inferring from parts to wholes. Conroy sees a link between Upper Palaeolithic figurines and the emergence of gender. In doing so she asks critical questions. How do conventions of human depiction arise? How are they maintained? How do stereotypes grow? Perhaps most importantly, Conroy forces the question, what is it about these images that makes them convincing, that powers them?

The work of Haaland and Haaland, McDermott and McCoid, Langdon and Conroy suggests that, at the very least, the presence of male or female imagery cannot be read as a simple reflection of social organization, structure or reality. At a more penetrating level, they deflate the Mother Goddess readings. As it is invoked for Neolithic southeastern Europe, the principal of Mother Goddessism is the equation of a dominance of the female imagery with the dominance of the status and power of women over men (Meskell 1998: 53). The rupture of the link between female imagery and female dominance has major, undoubtedly fatal, consequences for adherents to the Goddess anecdotes.[24] Mother Goddess-bashing aside, the Haalands' research and Meskell's arguments open important new debates in the study of prehistoric figurines and generate a series of critical questions. What is the status of the representational relationship contained in a figurine? Is it direct and easily read (like a reflection) or is it complex and potentially aggressive, combative and ideological? If representations are political then how do Neolithic figurines engage the contemporary socio-politics? If they are political, then what is it about miniature anthropomorphs that make them succeed as political objects? Why not other objects, materials, or forms of representation? These are the critical questions of a socio-politics of figurines-as-representations which the present book attempts to answer.

Other worlds

As important as the status of representation is the relationship of figurines and other worlds. Important stimulus comes from Christine Morris and Alan Peatfield's study of Bronze Age figurines from Crete (Morris and Peatfield 2002). Morris and Peatfield examine the physicality of gestures depicted in figurines from peak sanctuaries, particularly at the site of Atsipadhes Korakias, and suggest that gesture and body are fundamental to figurine function. The authors read figurines as records of ceremonies in

19

INTRODUCTION

which the participants alter their states of consciousness and transcend the mundane world of routine life. In these contexts, the human body behaves in rituals as a vehicle to facilitate communication with the transcendent. This recognition that figurines may play a role in altering the way that prehistoric people thought and felt, even to the extent of allowing a transcendent experience, is exciting. Also, Morris and Peatfield highlight the physical intimacy that develops among worshipper, ritual act and votive figurine. By emphasizing the physical interaction of figurine and ritual participant, the authors probe relationships that stimulate new understandings of peoples' sensual engagements with figurines as material culture. Equally refreshing is the suggestion that the human body plays an important role in attempts to communicate with the transcendent or in efforts to move into altered states of consciousness.

Morris and Peatfield provide exciting glimpses of the neuro-physiological basis to the body's response to embodied experiences (i.e., dramatic changes in brain-wave patterns and the production of bio-chemical compounds). The work on peak sanctuary figurines provokes important questions. Why did Bronze Age Cretans believe that anthropo-morphic figurines were appropriate objects with which to represent the ceremonial entry into altered states of mind? What is it about figurines that make them successful media for representing the other-worldly? If some of the anthropomorphic representations function as votives (as Morris and Peatfield suggest), then why and how do they succeed to that purpose? Is there something particular to miniature anthropomorphs that makes them work particularly well as votives? What are the physical, cognitive, psychological mechanisms involved? Although the core of their approach reduces figurines to passive representations (and thus prevents the authors from moving forward to ask questions about how the objects worked in these activities), the links between altered states of consciousness, ritual and figurines bring important issues to the surface. The questions that develop from the discussion of the peak sanctuary figurines focus our attention on the potential, active, roles that figurines may play in ceremonies where they are more than simple depictions of participants.

Like Morris and Peatfield, Joyce Marcus suggests links with other worlds in her study of Early and Middle Formative (1800–500 BC) figurines from Mesoamerica (J. Marcus 1998). Marcus argues that women made and arranged figurines in ritual scenes in houses and that these scenes provided venues through which the spirits of recent ancestors could return (fig. 1.5).[25] Just as Haaland and Haaland suggested for the use of female imagery and the *Bora Fatta* among the Fur, Marcus contends that the Formative figurines from the site of Oaxaca succeeded in expressing and maintaining social obligations among individuals, descent groups and ancestors.[26] Women modelled and decorated figurines with various body positions, hairstyles, costumes and ornamentation in order to depict age, marital status, social rank and gender of specific ancestors. While these details provided links to particular ancestors, the figurines were not exact, realistic depictions; figurine faces, for example, show little variation and fit into widespread types. In their houses, women arranged figurines into scenes that formed the focus for socially integrative rituals in which descendants and ancestors could participate together. To animate figurines, women addressed them by name, dressed, consulted, fed, scolded, petitioned and reminded their ancestors of their responsibilities. After the rites had been completed, the women broke or defaced the figurines and discarded them so that people outside of the household could not use them. The Oaxaca Formative figurines are predominantly female, though male figurines were made; the intention was to invoke recent female ancestors.[27]

20

INTRODUCTION

Figure 1.5 Joyce Marcus' reconstruction of figurines in an Oaxaca house (after Marcus 1998).

Marcus argues that the female figurines used in household rituals relate to ancestors of minor significance who were not of importance to the entire community or region. In this, the female figurines were distinct from contemporary men's ancestor rituals that took place in the men's building. Women may have been central to the domestic ancestor ritual but they were peripheral to the rites conducted in the men's ancestral hall. Although, over time, some deceased males attained positions of publicly honoured ancestors, the group of ancestors honoured in private domestic rituals became increasingly female. Indeed, Marcus argues that with the rise of the Zapotec state (from 300 BC), the non-influential ancestors of the household rituals become much less significant than the ancestors of royal or noble families. Thus figurines disappeared from the archaeological record and ancestor rituals continued with a different set of objects: sculptures of nobles and drinking vessels. The multiplicity of types and significances of ancestors and the correlative division of the community along gender lines are important, suggesting not only that there can be more than one set of ancestors being depicted and ritualized, but also that figurine imagery can be made and used by women and can refer to women even when women are a subordinate component of a community. This is another warning of the dangers of the assumption that figurines can be read as direct representations of rulers or divinities.

Marcus' detailed work is invigorating. It marries a high level of contextual information with contemporary socio-political contexts. The proposal that figurines were parts of the rituals that engaged both the living and the spiritual worlds is exciting. That suggestion that figurines acted as venues though which ancestors could return to participate in rituals

INTRODUCTION

and thus remain part of the maintenance of social reality is important. Equally stimulating is the process of animating the figurines by speaking to them and by handling them. By physically engaging the figurines, women entered another world, the one in which the ancestors dwelt, or at least one which both ancestors and living humans could occupy together. Taking this work forward are questions about the ways in which Oaxaca figurines functioned to provide a believable inter-world venue. Why were figurines deemed the acceptable medium for the movement of the ancestors (and of human participants) in the rituals? Why not other categories of material culture? Why were the ancestor depictions represented in three dimensions and not two? What does three-dimensional representation offer that two-dimensional imagery does not? Why did the ancestors need to be represented in a material medium at all? What is so special about the tangible and what actions and thoughts does it facilitate that intangible representation does not? Why could oral presentations and invocations not have functioned just as well? Is there something particularly powerful when several miniature anthropomorphs are grouped together and used as they were in the ritual scenes?

Thinking new thoughts

In his short paper on the aesthetics of Vinča culture figurines, Miodrag Pavlović (Pavlović 1990) offers a glimpse at similar dimensions of figurines that are usually overlooked. Pavlović urges us to think of figurines as attempts to create something that pleases the senses, as something intended to stimulate the imagination. He describes figurines as early models of the human form that are linked to new orders or new conceptions of beings; figurines thus raise critical issues about the ontological dimensions of being human and representing the human. These ideas are exhilarating and provocative. It would be exciting to see these ideas played out through a body of material. It would be particularly stimulating to consider the consequences of such a perspective for our understanding of Neolithic socio-politics. Pavlović raises the point, perhaps obvious, but never directly addressed in detail, that as representations, Neolithic figurines are merely abstractions and do not provide complete or exact portraits; what does it say about Neolithic people that figurines are only abstractions? In his brief note, Pavlović shifts the discussion in important directions.

In a detailed attempt to recover figurine meaning, Peter Biehl studied almost 400 figurines from 33 sites of the Gradeshnitsa-Krivodol culture (Biehl 1996, 2003). The analysis combined a compilation of the motifs that appear on the bodies of Gradeshnitsa-Krivodol figurines and a rigorous statistical testing of the location of different motifs on different parts of the body. Biehl's work is important as it focuses on the figurines themselves as material culture and because it sets aside assumptions of anecdotal meaning and interpretation. Meanings are not assigned but patterns of important symbols are documented. Importantly, Biehl recognizes that the whole concept of anthropomorphic representation was as abstraction of the human body. Indeed, as Pavlović had noted, Neolithic figurines are not complete representations. What is the significance of these observations? What does it mean that the humans depicted are not realistically portrayed? Biehl suggests that the symbols on the figurines sent abstract messages to the people who saw and used them. What is the significance of the abstractness of the symbols and of the human form? Do these conditions help us to better understand the ways in which people thought about them?

INTRODUCTION

Also provocative is Ruth Tringham and Meg Conkey's critique of Palaeolithic and Neolithic figurine studies (Tringham and Conkey 1998). Tringham and Conkey suggest that we should devote more effort to reconstructing and understanding the use-lives of anthropomorphs: how were figurines modified, used, broken, reused, repaired, decorated, disposed of? Tringham provides a case-study of the figurines from her excavations at Opovo in Serbia (ibid.: 29–35). She grounds her analysis firmly in a contextual study of the locations in which figurines were found at the site. She argues that people intentionally deposited them outside of houses, and she suggests a strong link between the use or meaning of pits (where most figurines were found) and the use or meaning of the figurines themselves. The analysis is rigorous, based on detailed excavation recovery techniques and opens up new and destabilizing questions: why was it that, at Opovo, figurines were the objects that were intentionally deposited in these places and in these ways?

Tringham and Conkey argue that figurine analysts need to probe the broader implications of the meanings and roles played by representational material culture. They urge us to ask new questions. Why would Upper Palaeolithic or Neolithic people have found images of females meaningful? What is the significance of making a miniature of the human form? If some of the Neolithic figurines appear to wear masks, then what is the significance of covering the face and, in particular, why do so few of the masked figurines have mouths depicted? They suggest that we should speak about anthropomorphic objects and not of 'figurines'. They urge us to ask how objects such as figurines work within the construction, enactment and transformation of ideologies and the negotiations of power relations.

More questions

Even though in these examples archaeologists acknowledge the complexity and ambiguity of life and of visual culture, they resist moving beyond a preliminary level of understanding. I have neither the intention nor the expert knowledge to deny that particular anthropomorphic figurines may have worked within politically motivated misrepresentations of power structures, or that others played a role in the emerging dominance of new elites. Indeed many figurines may have functioned as images of divinities or ancestors who were worshipped. These suggestions for figurine function are not assessable. No mechanisms exist for evaluating the accuracy of anecdotal suggestions. It is not simply a matter of developing a more complex set of hypotheses or applying a more rigorous statistical analysis, or even of acquiring better contextual information during excavation, of wet-sieving and of 100 per cent sampling. In the end, our inability to assess these propositions is not important; even if you and I could prove (or even agree) that a particular figurine represents a goddess or an ancestor, both the proof and the equation are irrelevant.

Proof and equation are irrelevant because it is not of primary importance for us to know what is represented by a figurine. Is it of interest? Yes. But, is it fundamental to a fuller understanding of prehistoric figurines? No. It is more important to understand the ways in which miniature anthropomorphic representations succeeded in being the political tools, goddess images, votive offerings or ancestor portraits that different figurine analysts have suggested. How and why could figurines play the roles that they did in domestic negotiations of identity, in the manifestation of the other-worldly, in the presencing of

23

INTRODUCTION

the deceased? Why weren't these roles filled by other types of material culture? Why not by oral culture? Why not by other media of representation or other objects? Why not by objects made by different raw materials? What are the powers and consequences of representation in general and of representation of the human body in particular? What is the significance of human representations made in miniature? What of anthropomorphs modelled in three dimensions?

These are the questions that this book asks. In doing so it moves the debate forward in important ways; it bypasses the arguments about Mother Goddessism; isn't it important enough, on its own, to accept that modern men and women think that these figurines are images of an Earth Mother? It bypasses the debates over the proportion of male to female representations in figurine corpuses; isn't it better to focus on the consequences of representing the human form? It even ignores the calls for fully contextual analysis; will total recovery of figurines from a site or the millimetre-specific recording of the location of all finds around a figurine really help us understand how the object was perceived in Neolithic minds?

A new approach

It would be easy to choose any of the examples presented in the preceding section of this chapter and simply play it out against the figurine material and archaeological context of the Balkan Neolithic. Indeed the interpretation that Marcus develops for Formative figurines at Oaxaca fits the Balkans with seductive ease: the recovery of figurines from household contexts; the predominance of female figurines; the fragmentary nature of the material; the contemporary social and economic conditions; the similar disappearance of figurines at the end of both the Formative and the Neolithic; their replacement by similar phenomena (drinking vessels and the rise of more individualized ancestor respect or rituals). To apply any of Marcus' interpretations to the Balkan Neolithic would be a mistake, regardless of the strength of the analogy; such an application would get us no closer to understanding how and why figurines work. In this book I have preferred to follow the questions provoked by the studies outlined above. This book is about asking a different set of questions about prehistoric figurines. It asks why figurines work in the ways suggested by the research reviewed above. It is a teasing apart of figurines as material and visual culture, as representation and as socio-politics.

The book suggests that figurines are unsettling, that they work within a vortex of contradictions and paradoxes. Because figurines are unsettling and paradoxic, people react to them in irrational ways. The best example of such irrational reactions is the enormous body of figurine literature that follows both the anecdotal and the overly empirical approaches. Part of the project of this book is to ask what causes this reaction, both for modern western archaeologists, curators, publishers and antiquities' auctions as well as for Neolithic inhabitants of southeastern Europe. Why do figurines have the effect that they have on people as they observe or handle them?

Based on these questions, three main types of inquiry will follow. First this book investigates the phenomena of miniaturism and three-dimensionality (Chapter 2). What is the significance of a figurine's miniaturism? What happens when an object is reduced in scale? What effects does miniaturizing have on a person looking at and handing objects like figurines? Is it significant that figurines are three-dimensional? What is specific to three-dimensional objects that set them apart from two-dimensional things? Next, this

24

INTRODUCTION

book considers the phenomenon of anthropomorphism and the socio-politics of representation (Chapters 4, 6 and 8). Does the human form have particular evocative powers that are not present in other representation? What is the political potential of figurines when they are defined as visual culture? How do representational objects work to support and, more provocatively, to block and invert, existing power structures? Indeed what is representation and what are the consequences of the material representation of the human form?

These investigations proceed with reference to studies and analyses of many different disciplines, regions and periods. Throughout, I assume that despite vast differences in the material, environmental and economic matters, the cognitive abilities of Neolithic and modern people are the same.[28] Thus, the discussion that follows includes many topics and examples not normally associated with the Balkan Neolithic, let alone prehistoric archaeology. Examples from the history of photography, research into the human perception of scale and perspective, the development of anatomical dolls for interviewing child victims of sexual abuse, André Kertész's surrealist photography, Walker Evans' and James Agee's project on tenant farmers of the US Depression, the Barbie Doll, Renaissance architectural tools, nineteenth-century *cartes-de-visite*, the provocations of the Young British Artists of the late 1990s, and the collaborative work of Alfred Stieglitz and Georgia O'Keefe. There are many other touchstones with the modern world.

While this book is firmly set in discussions of these modern examples, it also wrestles with the particularities of the data: Neolithic figurines. The photographs that started this book provide the first engagement with the material of the period and they hint at the direction in which it is heading. There are chapters on figurines from three regional varieties of Balkan Neolithic figurines: Hamangia (Chapter 3), Cucuteni/Tripolye (Chapter 5) and Thessaly (Chapter 7). These chapters are not exhaustive reviews of work on these regional variations, nor are they complete typologies and chronologies of the material, though reference to the key works and sequences is provided. Rather, the intention is to let the material work through some of the ideas that are argued for in the more theoretical chapters: i.e., on miniaturism, anthropomorphism and the socio-politics of representation.

25

2
MINIATURISM AND DIMENSIONALITY

In the late 1970s Henrietta Todorova directed the excavation of the fifth millennium BC village at Ovcharovo in northeastern Bulgaria (Todorova *et al*. 1983). In the debris of a building in one of the later phases of the village's long life the team uncovered a collection of 26 miniature objects (fig. 2.1). Included are the following objects.

Four anthropomorphic figurines, each of which is of similar size and shape, each decorated with red-painted design, and each *c*. 8.0 cm tall. Arms reach out from the shoulders or curve gently upwards. Heads, without facial features (though one has a pinched face that models a nose), taper upwards from the neck. Painted decoration is restricted to chest-shoulders and waist-hips-thighs; both areas are densely covered with rectilinear and, in one case, curvilinear designs.

Three standing, footed, two-sided, rectilinear clay plaquettes, each measuring no more than 6.0 cm wide and 5.0 cm high. Surfaces are decorated with painted sets of lines that run to the plaquettes' edges: concentric circles or perpendicular, crossing lines and sets of angles fill surface centres.

Eight chairs and three tables. The tables are square, four-legged and squat; one has small raised dots at each corner of the surface. Chairs are also squat and four-legged; each has an arched back. Neither tables nor chairs are decorated.

Three bowls and two pans. Bowls are small (2.0 cm in dia.), generic, open, rounded forms. Each has a separate lid. Bowls are undecorated; the top surfaces of the lids have

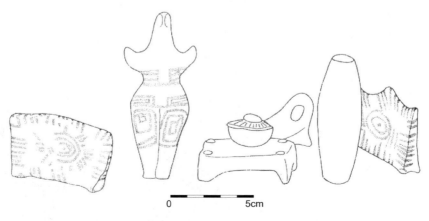

Figure 2.1 Miniature objects from Ovcharovo (after Todorova and Vajsov 1993).

MINIATURISM AND DIMENSIONALITY

short, straight incisions that run from their centres to their edges. Two lids have knob-handles at the centre of their tops. Proportionately, the two pans are larger than the bowls (e.g., the pans are too wide to fit on the tables). One pan is undecorated; the other has painted lines on its interior of similar design to those found on the footed plaquetttes. Three tapered cylinders are interpreted as drums. The largest is 5.0 cm tall; the others are slightly smaller.

Though it is difficult to account for post-depositional or curatorial effects, the surface wear on all of the objects suggests that they were well used or at least had a long life: the cylinders are smooth and shiny; five of the chairs have broken backs. This collection of miniature objects was found along the southern wall of a square, one-roomed, building on the eastern edge of the village (Todorova *et al*. 1983: 38). Nearby were three large pots. Though there is little published detail, the excavator calls the pots pithoi, so we should assume that they are large and probably used for storage. Along the inside of the building's western wall ran a low bench upon which rested many other pots; in the middle of the eastern wall is the structure's only door. In the middle of the northern wall is a square hearth. In the corner, between the hearth and the platform are grinding-stones. Near the platform was found another miniature, a clay house replica. Thirty cm on each side, it is complete with oven, platform, door and walls all arranged as in the house itself.

Besides these miniature finds, there is nothing special about this building: its size (6 × 6 m) is typical, as is its orientation (NS–EW). Information about the range of activities that took place here is limited, though there were a number of large pots. Other buildings of the same phase of the village have rooms of similar dimensions and collections of artefacts and furniture, as do other buildings in earlier and later levels of the site. Other miniature objects come from other houses in this, earlier and later phases of the village; almost 100 other anthropomophic figurines, a smaller number of zoomorphic miniatures and many building replicas suggest that the collection of miniature finds from Building 7 is not unique. That the excavators found them together is unusual, though this may be as much a factor of deposition (were they stored in a pot when the building collapsed or was destroyed?) as it is a factor of recovery techniques (if modern screening techniques had been employed would other examples have been recovered?).

How are we to understand these miniature objects? The excavator interprets them as a cult scene: the plaquettes represent altars, the cylinders are drums (used in rituals) and the figurines represent attendants to the divinity bodies shaped in poses of adoration (Todorova 1974; Todorova *et al*. 1983). The house in which they were found is understood as a Neolithic shrine and the decoration on the altars documents the emergence of the cult of the sun, the moon and the natural elements (Todorova 1986: 197–8). Christina Marangou uses the Ovcharovo set as one of many examples of the way Neolithic people assembled miniature objects for initiation rites or rites of passage, for narrations before audiences, or for the interchange of ritual information (Marangou 1996a: 196). For Marija Gimbutas these objects are a ritual assemblage that attest 'to the Goddess's association with music' (Gimbutas 1989a: 71); the cylinders are drums, the figurines have wings, the plaquettes are altar screens, and the decoration of the plaquettes 'suggests that this miniature tableau might have replicated an actual ritual for the Bird Goddess in which drums were used' (Gimbutas 1989a: 71, 73).

A more productive approach is to think about the people who would have looked at and held these objects during the fifth millennium BC. How would they have reacted?

27

MINIATURISM AND DIMENSIONALITY

What are the particular physical and evocative conditions inherent in these objects? How might such conditions stimulate specific reactions and thoughts in the people who handled these small things? What was going on when someone placed one of the tiny lids onto one of the tiny bowls and then put them on the top of a tiny table and pulled up a tiny chair and stood one of the tiny people next to it?

Introduction

People perceived, and thus understood, the Ovcharovo objects in terms of at least two important conditions: their small size and their three-dimensionality. This chapter makes two propositions: first, that size reduction and three-dimensionality are processes that have important psychological effects on viewers and handlers; and second, that an understanding of these processes and their effects will refine, perhaps even transform, our understanding of Neolithic figurines. When we examine the mechanisms and consequences of size reduction, an important distinction emerges, separating factual models from miniatures. Furthermore, the processes of abstraction and compression play important roles in our perceptions of these objects; one consequence is the ability that miniaturism has to make accessible alternative worlds and alternative world-views. This chapter identifies several key conditions of miniaturism, conditions that both enable and prohibit understanding, and thus that affect our search for the meaning of Neolithic figurines. With the recognition of the conditions of miniaturism comes a realization that the use of three-dimensional media in making representations has important consequences as well. Emphasis will centre on the intimacy that is demanded (yet implicit) in objects that are both small and palpable. The chapter ends with the conclusion that the meanings of objects such as figurines are found within the collisions of a set of paradoxes, paradoxes of the miniature and the three-dimensional.

Size reduction

There are various ways to think about the processes of reducing the size of an object. One is to view a small thing as an object that has been reduced in proportion to an original. This is to think in terms of scale. Qualification (indeed quantification) by scale to the original is taken for granted in much that we do whether it is using a map, buying toy cars for our children (or ourselves), or digitally manipulating the size of images and text on computer screens. It is not surprising that, in general, we agree about the appropriateness of the different scales-to-originals that we employ. In many cases the job at hand determines the scale-to-original we use; balancing the advantages and disadvantages of different scales produces best practice. Toy cars work well at 1:16, 1:24, 1:32 or 1:40 scales. Ship models are most often made at 1:48, 1:64 or 1:96. Trains seem to work best at 1:89 (i.e., HO scale). Architects build models at 1:480 where 40 feet are reduced into one inch (King 1996: 12–14).[1] If any rules apply they are general ones. Too small a scale (i.e., one that produces a very small version in relation to the original) blurs details or makes it impossible for fine rendering. Too large a scale is redundant or, at its most extreme, physically impossible; can you imagine a road map drawn at the scale of 1:10 (one kilometre of motorway represented by 100 m of paper)?

A second way to think about size reduction is to take the human body as the ultimate, essential measure of scale. In this sense there is only one scale relationship (human body-to-object) and only three significant size categories: life-size, smaller than life-size, and larger than life-size. Thus, thinking about representations in the scale-to-human is a different exercise to thinking in terms of scale-to-original. Thinking of the relationship between the body and the thing-reduced forces us down into an anthropocentric world where the scale of the human dictates all spatial relationships.

Thinking about size reduction in the human scale has important consequences for understanding Neolithic figurines because, unlike cars, trains or architectural models, figurines are anthropomorphic representations. Depicting the human is a large and complex action and a full discussion follows in Chapters 4 and 6. Before we reach that discussion we need to further define small things, specifically by illuminating the critical distinction between a model and a miniature.

Models

Models are attempts at precision. They strive to reproduce an original in a factual manner. They seek exactitude and completion. The goal is to reproduce reality in reduced dimension with the maximum detail retained. Models are accurate and authentic (King 1996: 19, 227). The architect's presentation models are good examples of this principal. Since the early fifteenth century, architects have used models of buildings for a variety of purposes (Millon 1994). Building models serve a variety of purposes: as teaching aids, as guides and templates during construction, as prototypes subjected to tests (e.g., for wind shear), as entries in competitions and tenders for contracts, or as presentations to potential clients (for approval) and authorities (for permissions).

In all of these uses, the model buildings rely on the accuracy with which the modeller is able to reproduce the proportioned details of the original structure. In a similar way, if not necessarily for the same purposes, many other types of factual models pursue accuracy in their manifestations: ship models (in bottles, naval museums or elsewhere); model steam engines; metal and plastic pre-made or Airfix car kits; lead, tin or plastic soldiers, and creatures from history or science fiction. These factual models evoke strong, perhaps subconscious, reactions that are powered by the viewer's recognition of the skills required to work at small scale and of the knowledge of the original that is required to model authentically. Similar responses are generated by tiny books, paintings or other nano-art (fig. 2.2) (Rugoff 1997, 2000; Stewart 1997). We react to these objects with wonder, with respect for the abilities and dedication displayed by the creators, the artists, the modellers in their quest for reproducing accuracy at tiny scales.

Miniatures

Miniatures are different from models. Miniatures are small things that do not seek accuracy in representation, that are not precise or exact. Furthermore, miniatures result from human experimentation with the physical world (Lévi-Strauss 1972); they are cultural creations. In this sense there are no naturally occurring miniatures; each one is a person's utilization of eye and hand to manipulate the world (Stewart 1993: 55; 1997: 79). Good examples are the tiny trees and the tiny landscapes that make up *bonsai*, scholars' rocks and *penjing*.

Bonsai (or the Chinese *punsai* or *pensai* from the Chinese characters *Pen-tsui*) have been popular in the West since the Second World War. Though the histories of growing small

MINIATURISM AND DIMENSIONALITY

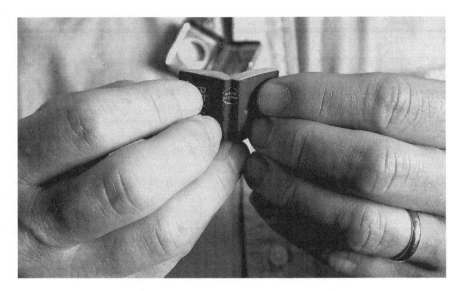

Figure 2.2 Miniature book from the collections of Stanford University's Green Library.

potted plants in Japan and China are very deep, any search for a single origin or meaning of processes of *bonsai* meets with failure.[2] *Bonsai* are natural trees made small. It is a replacement of the complexity of the life-size tree with the simplicity of convention. *Bonsai* compresses information and detail about the texture of bark, the subtleties of colour, and the structure of fine branches (fig. 2.3) (Fontanills 1997). Similar processes are at work in other oriental nature arts such as scholars' rocks and *penjing*.

Scholars' rocks are stones that have been sculpted into evocative, richly textured miniature landscapes (R. Rosenblum 1997, 2001; C. Brown 1997; Stuart 1997) (fig. 2.4). They provide a physical stimulus, a tangible yet imaginary vehicle for travel through an imagined landscape. The rock sitting on a scholar's desk both provides a concrete reality and suggests places that belong to the other worlds of established mythologies. Scholars' rocks work because they posses the capacity to suggest imaginary retreats; while some detail stimulates memory, the specific details, of cloud and water for example, are left to the viewer's imagination (C. Brown 1997: 57, 75). Similar phenomena are the *penjing*: tray-sized landscapes made up of artistically created miniature versions of natural scenes (C. Brown 1997: 57; Zhao 1997: 112). *Penjing* have a deep history in Chinese scholarly art, dating from the Qin and Han Dynasties (221 BC–AD 220) with origins resting in the class of *penjing* literati, a stratum of erudite men of high literary education and cultural sophistication, who shared an aesthetic based on four concepts: aloofness (*gugao*); sparseness (*jianjie*); refined elegance (*ya*); and plainness (*pingdan*) (Zhao 1997: 7).

Perhaps most significant to an understanding of miniaturism is the concept of sparseness (*jianjie*) and its reference to the viewer's perception of complex patterns in objects and phenomena which appear at first sight to be very simple (Zhao 1997: 51–3). In representing trees, rocks and landscapes, the artists creating *bonsai*, scholars' rocks and *penjing* manipulate scale to transform the real world into separate, intimate alternatives (R. Rosenblum 2001: 47; Stein 1990: xxii). They create images of reality that flip back

Figure 2.3 Bonsai tree (after Koreshoff 1984). Courtesy of Deborah Koreshoff.

Figure 2.4 Penjing tray landscape (after Koreshoff 1984). Courtesy of Deborah Koreshoff.

and forth between the natural and the cultural worlds (R. Rosenblum 2001: 21). In flipping from one to the other and then back again, these miniature creations transform viewers' ways of seeing and thinking.

Bonsai, scholars' rocks and *penjing* are very different from models of ships, cars or buildings. They are manipulations of the form and content of an original in order to create something that does not exist but which retains some reference to the real world. *Bonsai* are trees, they are alive, but they are not natural; they have been radically manipulated. *Bonsai*, *penjing* and scholars' rocks are not only different ways of seeing the world, they present alternative realities. They are miniature manipulations.

Abstraction and compression

Miniature manipulation of reality works from two processes: abstraction and compression. Miniaturism's reduction of size is more than mere diminution of physical dimensions: miniaturizing reduces detail. The resulting, intentional, understatement provides much of the power of a miniature because miniaturism demands selection. One result of abstraction is that the viewers of a miniature are cheated. They are not shown everything nor are they shown the full detailing of those elements that are selected for representation. The fact that some elements are not included in the miniature critically warps the relationship between the observer and the representation and, unavoidably, radically, alters the observer's understanding and comprehension of the object. The brevity that comes with abstract representation forces the viewer beyond the information that is provided. The abstraction of a miniature demands that the spectator draw inferences.[3] Thus, a person who contemplates a *bonsai* in a pot or a scholar's rock on a desk or who stares at a Neolithic figurine in its case in the museum or as it is uncovered in an excavation trench, is drawn, almost without realizing it, to think of what is not there, of what has been left out. Where are the other trees? Where are the little birds that should surround the *bonsai*? Where is the rest of the mountain evoked by the scholars' rock? Where is the detail of human expression on a faceless figurine?

Through abstraction, a miniature is an object made active; it forces the viewers to do something that otherwise they would not do. Making the viewer draw inferences about what is not represented in a Neolithic figurine or a *bonsai* tree has important consequences for the understanding that the viewer develops about the miniature object. Critically, the range of inferences that any one viewer can draw are almost limitless; constraints depend only on each viewer's beliefs, understandings, interests, backgrounds and desires. The potential for a miniature to stimulate different inferences means that the responses and understandings of a miniature object, such as a figurine, are many. In this sense then, miniatures are critically opposed to factual models which, though capable of evoking powerful reactions (of awe and respect), aspire to precision and accuracy. As miniature objects, figurines do not propose exactitude, complete knowability or comprehensive meaning. On the contrary, via forced inferences, they suggest that there are many different meanings and reactions, all of which, within reason, are equally valid.

Compression further contributes to the distancing of miniaturism from factual modelling. In addition to the power that it derives from abstraction, miniaturism gains force from its inherent condition of compression. In miniatures, values are enriched. Miniaturism concentrates and distils what is normal in peoples' routine day-to-day activities and thoughts and then produces a denser expression of a part of that reality. At the same time as miniaturism reduces elements and properties it multiplies the weight of the abstracted remainder.[4]

The effects of miniaturism on the viewer/handler

Understood in terms of abstraction and compression, miniatures have important effects on the person seeing or handling an object such as a figurine. First, miniaturism enlarges the spectator. Physically, it makes the viewer gigantic, omnipotent and omniscient. It insists on a transcendence by the viewer. Thus, miniaturism empowers the spectator. It allows physical control over a homologue of a thing; intellectually it facilitates a better understanding. With a miniature, knowledge of the whole precedes knowledge of the parts and this gratifies the intelligence (R. Rosenblum 2001: 21). By reducing the world-at-large's reality, a miniature provides a way of making sense of that world. Literally, it makes the world manageable (Betz 1998). Furthermore, miniaturism comforts the spectator. By providing the better understanding and physical control over a thing, miniaturism suggests security and thus brings pleasure. By creating a world in which the human scale matters most and dictates all spatial relationships, miniaturism reassures and liberates the viewer. In doing so and in making the viewer powerful and all-knowing, a miniature object makes the viewer free to indulge in flights of fantasy (Darling 1998). Finally, and perhaps paradoxically, miniaturism unsettles the spectator. It confronts and stimulates the viewer in a way that would not usually occur in such abstracted and compressed forms.

One of many good examples of how miniaturism liberates the viewer, freeing him to indulge in fantasy is the work of Michael Ashkin, an artist who creates table-top industrial and urban landscapes (fig. 2.5). In these works, one of Ashkin's intentions is to give the viewer a better sense of how people have degraded the earth's environment; Ashkin's miniature landscapes are full of industrial debris and abandonment, of asphalted and paved space. In his pieces, Ashkin reproduces the damaged landscapes of our cities in miniature; the work affords the viewer a better sense of the environment's degradation at the hands of men, as well as the haunting beauty of this decay (Model World 2002: 3).

Ashkin has worked at 1:89 scale, though he eventually settled on 1:160 scale (i.e., N-scale in the world of railroad modelling). The choice of the correct size to work in was a measured decision. For Ashkin, there always has to be enough detail so that the viewer can feel what it would be like to actually stand on the surface of his miniature landscapes. When this is possible, the viewer looks at the piece and the viewer's self changes size to accommodate the change in scale. Ashkin's decision about the correctness of the scale to use takes us back to the essentialness of the human scale. Basically, at some point the scale gets too small and the viewers can no longer project themselves bodily into the piece. In Ashkin's words, 'it is as if a smaller version of myself/not myself is in the tiny landscape and, for this new version of myself, different possibilities become newly available' (Ashkin pers. comm. 2002). While creating his miniatures, Ashkin feels himself stepping into the scaled-down space so that he can experience the results of his work; when he needs to add a new piece to the work and has to walk over to the table-saw to cut the piece, Ashkin feels himself stepping out of the miniature world. When making his miniature landscapes, he is drawn into their worlds in a narcotic way.[5] It was as if, for the duration of the creative process, Ashkin exists within the separate space of the

Figure 2.5 Michael Ashkin's *No. 43* (1996). Wood, masonite, dirt, cement dust, N-Scale models, Enviro Tex (39 × 36 × 19.5 inches). Courtesy of Andrea Rosen Gallery, New York. © Michael Ashkin.

miniature. When he is at work, transported into the miniature spaces of his scaled-down landscapes, he feels that the perspectives that he creates extend out from him indefinitely.

Spectators of the miniature experience a sense of being drawn into another world; Michael Ashkin's experiences are not dissimilar to more common engagements with more mundane miniature landscapes. Modern miniaturized landscapes often provide the contexts for play. Miniature golf, storybook villages, Legoland's reconstructions of Big Ben, and children's zoos are fantastic creations invoked on a miniature scale, visited by adults and children alike. These worlds of the fantastic are brought to life through miniature, three-dimensional representation (Stewart 1993: 59).

Alternative worlds

The effects that miniaturism has on the viewer combine to give miniatures their most important power: the ability to create and allow access to alternative worlds and realities (Stewart 1993: 54; King 1996: 47). It is the world into which Michael Ashkin steps when he works on his industrialized landscapes; it is the alternative realities of so many of the world's signature buildings and monuments that populate Legoland. The process of miniaturism creates a dimensional space that is distinct from the real world that surrounds it.[6] This miniature space is a separate physical place as well as an alternate psychic one. It is the place where imagination and fantasy have an advantage over practical and rational logic and activities. In these senses, miniaturism opens up a set of actions, of narratives, of histories that are outside the field of perception that exists in the reality of the everyday routine.

Disneyland

One of the best examples of a miniaturized alternate-dimensional place is Disneyland in California. Walt Disney and his Hollywood-trained engineers and artists used miniaturism as a tool to create a set of alternative worlds. The designers of Disneyland manipulated size and scale in order to enlarge the visitors, to make them feel bigger, to relax and comfort them.

One of the most striking uses of size to falsely enlarge and soothe the spectator is experienced by every Disney visitor. A critical feature of Disneyland is Main Street, a recreated slice of small town America. Main Street is a physically unavoidable part of everyone's visit to Disneyland. When they enter the theme park, all visitors are guided down Main Street; there is no other way into or out of the park. Though the buildings that line Main Street appear normal and life-size, they are not. Walt Disney built Main Street as a scale model, at 5/8ths real size (Jacobs 1996: 170–1; 1997: 79–80; Shackle 1985: 323–4).

The reduction in size is unnoticeable in an unconscious way. Measurement with a tape would show that everything is smaller than it should be. Indeed, the upper storeys of buildings became smaller and smaller as one moves up and away from street level. Disney employed forced perspective to trick the viewer, standing on the sidewalk, into believing that the buildings appeared much larger than they actually were (Jacobs 1997: 79–80). The scale of the architecture makes visitors to Disneyland feel larger than they are. The result is that people walking along the street and entering its shops are provided with a subtle, unperceivable boost to their sense of well-being; they are empowered, comforted, made secure. On Main Street, life suddenly seems pleasant, manageable and nice; things make sense in an intimate and neighbourly way (Jacobs 1997: 82; Doss 1977: 181).[7]

In light of these efforts to enlarge and empower the Disneyland visitors, it is not surprising that the origins of the park lay in Walt Disney's desire to create a refuge from the real world, to provide a nicer, safe, more comfortable and soothing place to be (Schickel 1985). Disneyland was intended as a place of amusement but also one of escape, of a utopian, better, America, a land more pleasant than the America that visitors suffered in their own homes, on their own main streets and which they had left, out beyond the boundaries of Disneyland (Jacobs 1995: 31).[8] Walt Disney's intention was to build a place where nothing could go wrong (Jacobs 1995: 35). He believed that art was a refuge from the problems of the world and Disneyland was a particular refuge from the trials of everyday life that thrived in the suburban strip-mall reality of 1950s America (Doss 1997: 181).[9] It is not surprising that the people who designed Disneyland were Hollywood art directors, people at ease with the conceits of illusion in order to evoke look, feel and smell in popular audiences (Jacobs 1996: 58). The genius of the Disney parks was Herb Ryman, a man who, even his critics said, could make images hang in the air like exotic perfume, pungent but elusive, palpably there, but hard to describe afterwards with any degree of precision (Jacobs 1997: 69). When asked about his desire to create Main Street as a scaled-down version of reality, Disney replied that although the street had been more expensive to make at 5/8ths scale, he had intended it as a toy for the very reason that imagination plays more freely with toys (Schickel 1993: 323).[10]

MINIATURISM AND DIMENSIONALITY

Temporal compression

Disneyland's uses of miniaturism to create alternative worlds are good examples of how the process of miniaturism can physically and emotionally take people into other places, places in which the visitors feel empowered, at ease, relaxed and in control. Miniaturism can also provide access to another type of other world, a separate mental place. In 1983, Alton Delong published a remarkable piece of research on the effects of miniaturism (Delong 1983). Delong, an architect with interests in how humans react to differently sized physical environments, designed an experiment to see what happened when people were asked to carry out the same task in two differently scaled surroundings. In the experiment, subjects played the computer game, *Pong*, on two different televisions: one had a 7-inch screen, the other a 23-inch screen (Delong 1983, 2000). Results suggested that subjects' performances and perceptions differed significantly depending on which sized screen they used.[11] When subjects played on the smaller screens, they performed better[12] and scored points more quickly than they did when they played on the large screen. Interpreting the records of EEG output recorded for subjects during play, Delong concluded that people were more alert when they played on the smaller screen. The shift in relative amount of brain power generated across different frequencies meant that, in a scaled-down environment, the human brain is more alert and capable of processing more information (Delong 2000: 8). Furthermore, when Delong asked subjects to estimate how long they had been playing, small-screen players thought that they had been playing for much longer than, in fact, they had been playing.

Delong concluded that when the size of peoples' environments is compressed, important things happen to how people behave, how well they perform and how they perceive time. A reduced-scale environment speeds up the central nervous system; the larger a person is relative to their surroundings the faster that individual's brain experiences time. Conversely, the smaller a person is relative to the environment, the slower one's brain processes time. The important consequence of this is that in different-sized environments, people experience time at rates that differ from the rate of the clock; in other words, brain-time differs from clock-time depending on the size of one's surroundings. In the *Pong* experiment (and in other research), Delong found that the compression of space and time are proportional.

Thus, while miniaturism can transport the viewer to another physical place or to another, more comforting place, as it does when you walk down Main Street, it can also take you to another mental place, a place where the most rational elements of our existence (such as a perception of time) may be stretched out of shape or compressed. These consequences and effects of miniaturism apply generally to any media of size reduction whether it is the flat-screen virtual tennis court of *Pong*, or *bonsai* trees, or *penjing* landscapes, or Michael Ashkin's work.

Three-dimensionality

Neolithic figurines are not only miniatures, they are three-dimensional miniatures. When the process of miniaturism is released through three-dimensional media, further dimensions of its power emerge. An object that has volume, that is to say is made in three dimensions, is distinct from an object created in two dimensions and the differences have consequences for understanding miniature objects such as figurines. If abstraction and compression are important conditions that cause miniatures to have the effects they have on the spectator, then such effects are multiplied when miniaturism emerges in three-dimensional form. Furthermore, three-dimensionality invokes a critical human sense, the tactile, and thus expands our experience in the worlds of the palpable and the intimate. If size reduction in two dimensions allows spectators and viewers to visit alternative worlds and radically alters their experience of basic conditions such time, what happens when scale reduction takes place in three dimensions?

In addition to the *Pong* experiment into performance and time perception, Alton Delong investigated the effects of three-dimensional size reduction (Delong 1981). If the *Pong* experiments had revealed important consequences of two-dimensional size reduction, then what happened if scale reduction took place in three dimensions? To find out, Delong designed an experiment to see what happened when people were asked to imagine themselves in differently scaled, three-dimensional, surroundings. In the experiment, subjects were shown one of three scaled-down model rooms: 1/6th, 1/12th or 1/24th real size (fig. 2.6). Delong asked the subjects to imagine that they were in one of the small rooms and that they were waiting for a friend to meet them there. Subjects were asked to manipulate a scaled-down human figure in the room, for example choosing a place for the figure to sit and wait. Subjects were not allowed access to clocks or watches and were asked to report when they thought that 30 minutes had expired.

Not surprisingly, the subjects' estimates of 30 minutes were inaccurate. What was shocking, however, was the degree of inaccuracy of the estimates and the correlation between a subject's estimate and the particular scaled-down room in which they had been imagining themselves. On average, subjects who were waiting in the largest room (i.e., 1/6th scale) thought that the half hour had expired in 5.43 minutes, those in the next smallest room estimated 2.66 minutes, and those in the smallest rooms (i.e., those made at 1/24th scale) suggested 1.49 minutes (Delong 1981, 2000). As with the *Pong* experiment, therefore, when people were asked to carry out a task in a reduced-scale environment, their perceptions of time were affected. Compression of space leads to compression of time as measured by subjects' brain-clocks.

Thus, strange things happen when reality is scaled down, when things are miniaturised both in two and in three dimensions. The process of miniaturism and its condition of

Figure 2.6 Alton Delong's experimental rooms (1/24 and 1/12 scale). Courtesy of Ascher Derman.

MINIATURISM AND DIMENSIONALITY

compression is magnified when reduction occurs in three dimensions. Delong notes how the magnitude of the reduction increases significantly when it occurs in three dimensions. A 1/12th scale model has linear dimensions that are 1/12th of the original: length is 1/12th of the original length; width 1/12th the original width; and height, 1/12th the original height. In this sense, a 1/12th scale replica is the same as a 1/12th reduction of a drawing or a photograph. However, in terms of the volumetric reduction that occurs in three-dimensional space, a 1/12th scale-model is actually a 1/1728th reduction (Delong 2000: 8). Thus, whatever processes are at work in miniaturism along two dimensions, they are multiplied when taken to the third dimension.

Intimacy

In addition to the increase in the scale of reduction that occurs when miniaturism occurs in three dimensions (and hence, undoubtedly, the increase in the evocative power that accompanies miniaturism), reduction in three dimensions alters the type of interaction that a viewer has with an object; miniaturism promotes the position of the spectator's body when one looks at or handles a small thing. The combination of three-dimensionality with miniaturism in a figurine creates an exceptionally intimate object. Intimacy introduces important limitations and potentials for viewers. A reduction in size demands close scrutiny in a truly physical sense; you have to be close to see the small thing properly. The resulting encounter of intimate proximity provides the viewer with a new way of seeing and thus with a new way of understanding the small thing being observed. This of course applies as easily to two-dimensional miniatures as it does to a Neolithic figurine. However, a three-dimensional object such as a figurine demands a physical engagement that two-dimensional media are not concerned with.

Penetrating the intimate space

The decision to understand or engage a miniature, three-dimensional thing demands that the spectators publicly and physically display their commitment to that engagement. At the very least they have to get close and peer into the miniature world. With a three-dimensional object, you must take that little world in your hand. The encounter with such a thing is a personal one. It is an encounter that takes place within reach of the body, in the personal space of the individual. Importantly, it is in this personal space that the core of an individual's reality resides. If one of the fundamental powers of a miniature is to transform reality and offer other, alternative worlds, than the significance of its presence within the core of a person's personal reality is powerfully transformative. Thus a miniature, three-dimensional object demands that if viewers want to understand the object then they must bring it within the physical world of their personal spaces. One of the most important characteristics of a figurine is that it must be within arm's reach to be engaged.

The difference between looking and touching is important. Looking at objects or other people primarily allows the viewer to establish relationships, at a distance, *among* the things or people being observed. For example, I can see that the man is standing next to my car or that an apple is in the bowl on the table. The visual space that I perceive allows me to establish the physical relationship between distant individual objects or people. It is a very different matter, a tactile matter, when I want to establish the relationship between myself and an object or person that I am looking at. The most precise way of establishing this relationship is through touch, through the tactile space that physically regulates relationships between viewers and what they see.

If people are forced to bring a miniature three-dimensional object, such as a figurine, within their reach in order to understand it, to read it, to see it, to handle it, then such an engagement has proxemic consequences. Forty years ago, Edward Hall's classic work (E. Hall 1966) on proxemics showed that not only does there exist a series of required distances for different types of encounters between people (intimate, personal, social, public) but also that the distance that people maintain between each other is a fundamental regulator of personal relationships and of social organization within communities.

The same principles that apply to the spatial relationships among individuals also apply to the relationships between people and things. Thus the things that are within a person's intimate reach possess a power, meaning and value quite different from objects that are beyond that reach. Indeed these objects are the materials most often used to proclaim identity and status (e.g., jewellery, clothes, what you carry in your hands, what you keep in your pockets).[13] Therefore, if this is the case for objects that are within one's reach then it means that objects that are brought into this intimate zone take on an elevated status or identity, an identity that is newly linked to that person.

The contention that understanding a figurine requires tactile engagement is significant. Miniature, three-dimensional objects force their ways into peoples' highly emotive, meaningful, signifying, personal spaces. Furthermore, because figurines force themselves into intimate spaces, they are potent vehicles for carrying meanings, symbols into these personal realms.

Perspective and the paradox of three-dimensionality

In addition to intimacy, there is another condition of three-dimensionality which contributes to the power of a figurine or a *bonsai*: three-dimensional objects are paradoxes of comprehension. With very few exceptions (Van Eyck's *The Ambassadors* is one, much of the surrealist project is another), two-dimensional representations dictate, authoritatively, the perspective that a viewer may take. The use of perspective in two-dimensional representation ensures that there is only ever one position from which, for example, to see a painting. Granted, spectators may move around and change their position, they may peer close-up or they may back away, but, as long as they stay in front of the image, the perspective they have of the painting, drawing or photograph remains the same. In two-dimensional representations, the artist/author dictates the correct perspective for the spectator to take. In this sense there is only one way to understand, visually, the two-dimensional representation: the way intended by the artist.

A three-dimensional object is fundamentally different. Although a three-dimensional object may have a front and a back (i.e., a sculpted torso may face one direction) the object is always available in the round. Provided space allows it, the viewer is free to move around the object (if the object is large) or move the object itself, in one's hand for example, if it is small. The view from the 'rear' is very different to the one from the 'front'. Also different is each view that is available from each of the, almost infinite, number of positions a spectator can occupy while moving around an object. In this sense then, three-dimensional representations allow complete comprehension. They give the spectator the

MINIATURISM AND DIMENSIONALITY

highest degree of authority to change their position of viewing and thus of understanding; every side can be seen, nothing is left to the imagination, nothing is hidden or left out.

On the other hand, and this is the paradox, in moving around the sculpture or turning over the figurine in one's hand, the spectator (or the handler) never holds the entire view at any one time. The spectator cannot be both in front and behind the sculpted torso at the same time, nor can she or he be at both sides simultaneously. In this sense, three-dimensional objects escape complete comprehension. They can never, simultaneously, be viewed in their entirety. So, at the same time, a three-dimensional object is both open and closed to complete understanding. This is the paradox of comprehension that lives within three-dimensional objects. The paradox of comprehension is yet another source of the inherent power of objects such as figurines to stimulate reaction among viewers (and handlers). The paradox of the three-dimensional distinguishes representations in the round from the two-dimensional representational world.

In light of the consequences of intimacy and of comprehension, there is little surprise in the number and range of attempts to manufacture the illusion of three-dimensional reality, especially in the world of public entertainment. Eighteenth- and nineteenth-century dioramas used translucent images to create three-dimensional scenes that appeared real but that were not. Viewers were compelled to study these scenes intensely and to make constant comparisons with the real thing; such manufactured illusions of three-dimensionality encouraged viewers to make a long series of imaginative leaps into and then back out of other worlds (Kamps 2000: 7). Even more popular than dioramas were stereoscopic images. Invented in the 1840s as one of the early manipulations of photography, stereoscopy used two almost identical photographs of the same image in order to create striking three-dimensional illusions (Jones 1976; Herbert 1997: 9). As Mirzoeff has argued, stereoscopy created the illusion of a depth of visual field that stepped away from the viewer in a foreground, a middleground and a background (Mirzoeff 1999: 94). Many other visual artifices have exploited the mechanisms and the implicit attraction of the constructed three-dimensional image: the 1950s fade for 3-D movies,[14] holograms, waxwork museums such as Madame Tussaud's in London,[15] and the 1970s toy craze in the US for View-masters (i.e., individual stereoscopic viewers into which could be slotted rings of images of popular television shows). All of these phenomena rest on the same differentials of power that distinguish the two- from the three-dimensional representation.

The priority that the three-dimensional holds over the two-dimensional is at the core of what the visual thinker John Tagg has called the ability to suture (Tagg 1988: 201). Comparing the different erotic successes of a pornographic photograph of a woman and an inflatable sex doll, Tagg has suggested that the two-dimensional photo fails to provide the 'orgasmic pleasure of illusionary wholeness' that the three-dimensional doll does. The contradiction between the flat actuality of the photographic paper and the fullness of the desired body is too large; the distance between reality and representation is closer with the rubber doll.[16] There is another reason why the inflatable doll succeeds erotically where the photograph fails: the size of the representation. Here again the relation to the essential measure of scale, the human body, is paramount. The sex-doll is life-size and as such it allows engagement at a one-to-one scale. The doll's amorous suitor cannot get inside the photograph of the naked women but, literally, he can enter the doll.

The power implicit in one-to-one engagement was also harnessed by the Disney engineers. A good example is the ride, *Snow White's Dangerous Adventure* (Jacobs 1995:

40

MINIATURISM AND DIMENSIONALITY

75). To transport you and your family into the world of Snow White, the illusionists of Disneyland make you and Snow White's world the same size. They do this by miniaturizing you, by reducing the size of your body, by sitting you in a carriage and then by taking you through a landscape that is an enlargement of a cartoon world, blown-up so that it comes to life at your living-size. It places you in the movie or in the storybook. The manipulation of size makes you into Snow White, and allows you, as Snow White, to encounter the Seven Dwarfs and the Evil Witch. By taking you on this ride, Walt Disney performed magic and transported you, a living rational human, into a completely fictional, but physically tangible place.

By manipulating the real sizes of your body and of Snow White's world, Disney fashioned a one-to-one encounter. The human visitors are made small and through the powers of miniaturism they are taken into another world. In making the individuals in the carriage small, Disney was debasing them, taking away the controlling omniscience that, as parents, or even as children, they normally possessed over Snow White and her world. Disney's Imagineers (as members of the Disney design team were termed) invoked the one-to-one engagement in other parts of the park. On *Tom Sawyer's Island*, the bears and Indians are full-sized and invite participation; as Schickel notes in his classic work on Disney, what boy did not want to be Tom Sawyer: boys could be Tom Sawyer on an island at Disneyland (Schickel 1993: 324). Perhaps the most successful of Disney's one-to-one transformations are the cartoon characters that wander the park posing with very excited children (and their parents) for photographs. For many visitors, the highlight of their trip to Disneyland is their encounter with Daffy, Goofy, Minnie, Snow White, and Mickey (you can visit his house and have breakfast with him – but only if you make a reservation far ahead of time).[17]

This, of course, was the original magic of Disneyland: to transform characters, scenes and narratives that originally existed in two-dimensional media into three-dimensional reality. Disney was the first to understand the massive marketing potential that has been realized ever since by toy companies that merchandize children's (and adult) cartoons, movies and comics and fill the shops with Snoopy dolls, Batman action figures, popstars and television characters in miniature statuette form.

Again, like miniaturism in general, or intimacy, the paradox of three-dimensional comprehension on its own is interesting but nothing more. The dynamism of figurines gathers speed from the combined conditions of miniaturism, abstraction and compression, and with the other conditions of three-dimensionality noted above, of the forced entry into the intimate and the personal, and the paradox of comprehension. There are a lot of things going on within each. No one of these conditions, on its own, is itself overly powerful. Taken together, however, they combine in a dynamic fashion. Other elements particular to anthropomorphic representation in general (Chapter 4) and to Neolithic figurines in particular (i.e., the social, political and material contexts within which they emerged and lived) will further explore this inherent dynamism.

Conclusions

In this chapter we have redefined figurines as miniature, three-dimensional objects and we have broken down these concepts. Having done so, we are faced with a series of contradictions. These contradictions collide in the visual event of seeing and handling a miniature object. The paradox of three-dimensional comprehension is one such collision.

41

MINIATURISM AND DIMENSIONALITY

There are other paradoxes, each of which further intensifies the impact that miniature objects have on our visual and tactile senses. Individually, each paradox makes a figurine a more powerful manifestation of representational material culture; taken together they make figurines perceptually explosive objects. It is in these paradoxes that the fundamentals of the meaning of figurines are to be found.

The paradox of size

Through compression and distillation, something that is physically smaller becomes more powerful than what is larger. The small stimulates very big thoughts about larger worlds. Even more importantly, the reduction of quantifiable dimensions increases levels of significance.

The paradox of multiple scales

There exists more than one scale of things in the world. I hold a miniature in my hand and my hand is not in proportion to its new world; my hand and, in fact my body, become the background to another equally valid scale. By playing with scale, especially scale as proportioned to the human body, miniature objects dislocate us from our normal field of reference and disrupt the belief that there is only one rational scale (Rugoff 1997: 68–9).

The paradox of multiple worlds

There are alternative worlds in addition to the one that we inhabit and these worlds can be accessed through manipulations of scaled objects. Perplexing is the realization that these other worlds are shaped by images and components with which we are familiar, such as the human body, or fictional cartoon characters but also chairs and tables, and lidded bowls.

The paradox of being/not being there

At one and the same time, we want to be both inside and outside of the other, minia-turized world. This is impossible; we cannot be both in this world and in the miniature world simultaneously. As Michael Ashkin suggests for his miniature landscapes, the spectator or handler continuously fluctuates between being in the miniature space and being outside of it. The result is an irresolvable tension that points to metaphysical issues inherent in all perceptions, indeed what Ashkin compares to the effects of a narcotic.

The paradox of the uncanny

While an object like a figurine is a familiar, knowable form (the human shape), it is at the same time very different, eerie, and uncanny (Carriker 1998: 13). The miniature engages the life-size object through formal reference to the known while making the representation appear strange (Stewart 1997: 88). This, perhaps, is the ultimate paradox: the thing represented in miniature is not what it purports to be. It depicts something recognizable but it does so by invoking incompatible associations. The familiar thus is also the distant (Krauss 1977).

MINIATURISM AND DIMENSIONALITY

Relevance and moving on

How does this discussion help us to understand the Ovcharovo miniatures with which this chapter began? None of the arguments and examples presented is intended to suggest that Neolithic figurines are some sort of Balkan *bonsai* or *penjing*, or that we should understand them as prehistoric characters in a Disneyesque facade. The Ovcharovo miniature tables and chairs were not pieces of furniture placed on a miniature, prehistoric, table-top landscape. The Ovcharovo figurines do not replicate children's storybook characters. However, each of the non-archaeological examples presented in this chapter suggests a way in which miniaturism, and three-dimensional miniaturism especially, contribute to the sensory effects that small representations have on people.

The relevance of the examples cited is that the meanings of Neolithic figurines are to be found by thinking in terms of particular visual and palpable conditions. Important are the consequences that these conditions have when a person looks at, picks up and thinks about a figurine. Critical is what happens when someone arranges eight little chairs around three little tables. Both Disney's illusionary use of scale, the forced perspective and the manipulation of the spectator's size, as well as Delong's experiments in temporal compression reveal the radical effects that changes in scale have on how humans perceive, think and act. The series of contradictions that emerge from, literally, thinking in miniature provoke an unbalancing of the mind of the spectator-handler and it is this imbalance that powers objects such as figurines to deliver and act and inspire.

This leaves several questions unanswered. First, if we accept that miniaturism creates powerful responses, if they stimulate people to think in other ways and worlds, then what are these responses and what are in these other worlds? What suggestions are being made? Answers to these questions follow the positioning of Neolithic figurines and other miniatures with their social, political and material contexts. Positioning starts in Chapter 3 and continues in the chapters that follow, culminating in Chapter 9 where larger reconstructions of Neolithic worlds are proposed. As we complete those culturally specific reconstructions, we must address two other questions: what is the significance of the human form as representation (and this is the topic of Chapter 4); and what are the potentials for visual representation to create and maintain or contest and subvert socio-political power relations (the theme of Chapters 6 and 8).

All of the discussion so far has taken place on a high, partially theoretical, level. The example presented at the start of the chapter, the Ovcharovo miniatures, was not integrated in the discussion. However, in terms of the issues raised so far, we can begin to see these objects in a new light. We feel more uneasy with the interpretation provided by the site's original excavator and her designation of them as a cult scene, an interpretation that now sounds hollow, perhaps even empty of any real meaning. In the contexts of this chapter, the Ovcharovo miniatures, the tables, chairs, pots, screens and people suggest many new meanings. Delong's research on what happens when people interact with scaled-down environments and when they imagine themselves in smaller worlds is particularly relevant. Certainly similar issues of alternative ways of thinking, of the compression of time, of an increased attention span and of mental ability revolve around the use of the Ovcharovo objects.

When we start to think about these artefacts in this way, it becomes less important to know whether or not they were used by children as toys or whether, indeed, they were part of some ritual activity that involved priestesses (represented by the figures), altars (represented by the tables), votive offerings of food (represented by the bowls), cosmic

43

imagery (the lightning-like representations on the screens) and ritual music (played on the drum-cylinders). In this sense, the Ovcharovo miniatures have no specific function. Indeed it is best to avoid assigning a function to them; it would be misleading to do so. We should not reconstruct narratives of a person fashioning miniature pots out of clay and making these objects with a particular purpose or a specific intention in his or her Neolithic mind. It is better to know that when a person, child, adult, shaman, priest or any other individual drew the little chairs up to the little tables, they had entered another world, a world with a different set of rules about time and, undoubtedly, about other thoughts and conceptions of other realities.[18]

3
HAMANGIA

Essences of Hamangia figurines

Hamangia figurines are sensually striking objects. Two particularly provocative pieces were discovered in the 1950s during rescue excavations at the Cernavoda cemetery (fig. 3.1) (Berciu et al. 1955; Berciu 1960).[1] The first of these, which the excavator named *The Thinker*, sits on a low, four-legged stool, with feet flat on the floor, knees raised, elbows on knees, hands on either side of the face; the figure's cheeks rest in the palms of the hands.[2] The second figurine, *The Seated Woman*, is similar in proportion and sits on the ground, with one leg sticking straight forward, the other bent at the knee upon which rest the figure's hands.

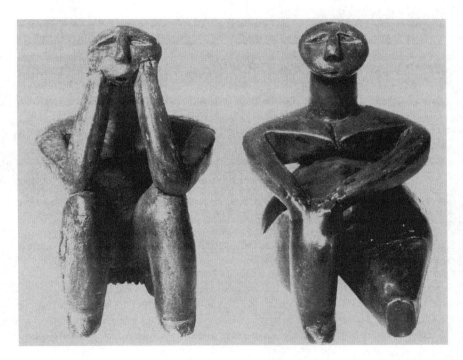

Figure 3.1 *The Thinker* and *The Seated Woman* from Cernavoda (courtesy of the Romanian National Museum of History).

HAMANGIA

Trapezoid or ovalish heads rest at the top of extraordinarily long necks. Faces tilt upwards, chins jut forward, eyes look ahead. Eyes are formed with horizontally impressed triangles; raised thin triangles of relief are noses. Eyes are widest in the middle of the face and diminish to a point near each side of the head. Eyes and the long, pointed noses are shaped with simple modelling; mouths are round. A fragment of a figurine similar to the seated one was found in another grave at Cernavoda. A figurine head, similar to those of both *Thinker* and *Seated Woman*, but broken from its neck, was found in another part of the Cernavoda cemetery.

The Thinker and *The Seated Woman* unsettle me. At first, they appear realistic, their faces and body positions are expressive. I feel that I know them; I sympathize with them. When I look into their faces, I connect. I recognize a mood or even convince myself that the three of us share an emotion. When I step closer, however, when I look more deeply, peer into their eyes and try to understand the expressions of their faces, of their mouths, I find myself unexpectedly lost. I understand and connect yet I feel excluded. On the one hand there is clear and particular detail. Eye-pupils, for example, are depicted, but only just. It is not especially clear if eyes are open or closed. Indeed, it is impossible to tell for certain. On the fragmented figurine head from Cernavoda, six, small, circular impressions run across the forehead, three over each eye. How do I understand these? What are they? Do they represent something specific? Why can't I tell what they depict? Is my ignorance purely a factor of the six and a half millennia that separate us or is it something more? Even in the fifth millennium BC, when these objects were made, even then, was there ever a single, correct, intended, understanding?

The mouths of the two seated Cernavoda figurines are small oval impressions made at the most forward corner of the face, shaped as if the lips are puckered or pursed, though lips are not shown. Are these mouths singing or are they blowing? Are they sucking in air through their teeth? Is it shock, disapproval, joy? Are they speaking, shouting, whispering? It is impossible to tell. The flat, oval heads perched on top of the long necks are tilted up, chins raised, foreheads thrown back. The expression with which I originally connected is not easily comprehended; I cannot imagine holding this position nor can I imagine seeing someone facing me, angling up their face in such a way, looking towards me along the line of the nose. The more I look the less I understand. My inability to understand troubles me. It makes me uneasy, but, in a strange twist, the unease grades into a seductive power with which each figurine holds me. I want to pick them up, hold them in my hands. I want to run the tip of my finger along the smooth, curving lines of their thighs. I want to slip them into my pocket and take them away with me, out of the museum.

While the two Cernavoda figurines are exceptional and extraordinary, my reactions to them are matched by my responses to other, more common, but less realistic Hamangia figurines. Unlike *The Thinker* and *The Seated Woman*, almost none of the Hamangia figurines has face or head depicted (fig. 3.2). If I have trouble understanding my reaction to the two Cernavoda figurines, then what hope do I have with the overwhelming majority of Hamangia figurines which are without faces or even heads? Almost every Hamangia figurine has an unnaturally long neck, most often triangular in section. The necks appear identical from one figurine to the next. Without markings or decoration, necks rise out of the shoulders, stretch upwards, straight or, in a very few examples, curved slightly forward. They stop abruptly in a flat triangular surface emphasizing the neck's triangular cross-section: a neck soaring upwards but halted as if sliced straight

46

HAMANGIA

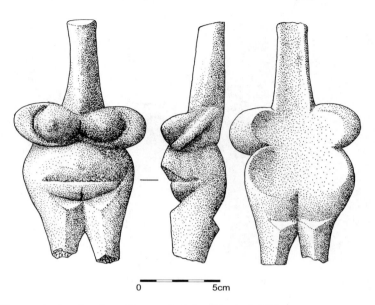

Figure 3.2 Hamangia figurine from Cernavoda (after Berciu 1966).

through with a knife. Is there something missing? Were separate heads slipped onto these necks? If so why have none been found? If they haven't survived because they were made of wood or grass or cloth or leather or some other perishable material, why weren't they made of clay? How do we understand these headless figures?

The shoulders, the torsos, the hips, indeed the entire bodies of Hamangia figurines are wide and full. Arms, where they are depicted, are often tightly tucked up across the chest or under conically pointed breasts. In some cases, these breasts are clearly female; in others it is less obvious. On some figurine chests, it is difficult to determine whether the modelled clay is intended to represent breasts (male or female) or whether it is an indistinct combination of forearms and hands. On other Hamangia figurines, arms are modelled more clearly, bent at the elbows with hands meeting over the abdomen. Most hands have no fingers; arms end in undefined mittenish abstractions. On a few, fingers are recognizable, though bizarrely some hands have only three fingers, others have four but lack thumbs. On many figurines, the arms are short and stubby, sticking straight out to the sides from the shoulders. These have no details of hands or fingers and one doubts that there was ever intended to be anything below the elbow. Perhaps the arms are folded back on themselves at the elbow? It is impossible to tell. On other figurines, it is equally difficult to determine whether the modelling around the shoulders represents arms, breasts or merely some undefined bulkiness.

The widest part of almost all Hamangia figurines is at the hips which form an angular or rounded junction for the torso to meet the legs. On some figurines, straight lines incise a simple pattern at the front of the lower abdomen (fig. 3.3). Occasionally, these lines form clear triangles. On other figurines the pattern is less straightforward and one can say nothing more than that there are two parallel lines, an upper one that cuts into the belly (like a belt or, perhaps, some sort of ligature) and a lower one that curves in its

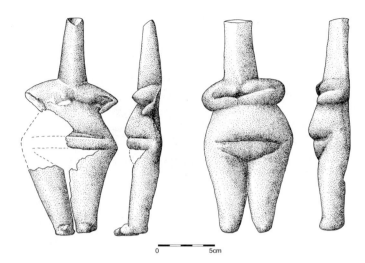

Figure 3.3 Hamangia figurine from Cernavoda (after Berciu 1966).

middle down towards the crotch. On a few, a short vertical incision has been placed in the middle of the bottom line. Is this to depict labia or could it be a penis? The lack of fine detail prevents answers.

While many Hamangia figurines have legs extended straight as if standing or lying down, others have legs tucked up under their bottoms, modelled to sit flat on the ground. Occasionally, dense parallel, incised lines decorate the thighs and legs (fig. 3.4). For most, however, hips, thighs and legs are smooth and undecorated, with only a shallow line to show where one leg meets the other. A very few have one leg pushed forward, separated from the other, bent at the knee, with foot placed flat on the ground to the front. For the extended figurines, some have legs modelled tightly together, delimited one from the other with an incised line running from crotch to feet. Others have legs slightly apart, decreasing in diameter as they reach the feet. Very little detail is given to the ankles or the feet; many legs just dwindle into undefined stubs. In some cases, a pinch of clay depicts a knee or a slight kink forward represents an ankle.

Overall, Hamangia figurines are particular in their lack of detail in body parts or facial features. Absences of faces or even heads for the majority are particularly striking. The formless muddle that occupies the chest and shoulders of many is complemented, compounded even, by the generic, low-level depiction employed in the representations of legs and feet. Abstraction is at work here: a deselection and exclusion of most detail within the human form. What is included is compressed into powerful little concentrations: the faces where they are present, the necks on all of them, the breadth of the hips. In addition to these reactions, one is struck by the serial repetition of a common style of anthropomorphic depiction for each figurine, a repeated form offering little variation in feature or shape. One senses stylistic rules and canons. Are these the symptoms of constraint imposed (or inherent) in the Hamangia way of modelling the human body in miniature or is there information on offer here about corporeal similarities and differences that worked within negotiations of human identities?

HAMANGIA

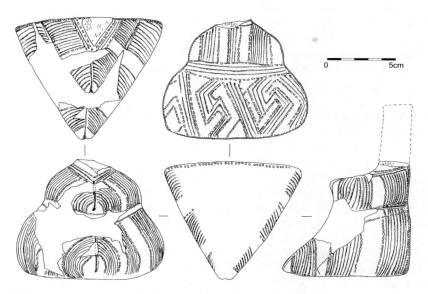

Figure 3.4 Hamangia figurine (after Todorova and Vajsov 1993).

The combination of these features is unnerving and exciting but at the same time not easily understood. Despite the absence of modelled features and the repetition of one very simple form, Hamangia figurines are provocative. They arrest and unbalance the spectator. The surfaces of almost all are highly burnished: smooth and soothing to the touch, shiny, reflective. In a few cases, painted or incised lines cover thighs and hips.

All of the Hamangia figurines are small objects, very few are taller than 20 cm. They sit especially well in my hand; they offer a satisfying and seductive cocktail of pleasurable weight and slippery surface. The most striking aspect of their character however, is an apparent contradiction: their little bulkiness. They are tiny yet they appear over-inflated, as if about to burst. Absence of most facial or anatomical detail adds to the visual power of their bulky, bloated, blodgy character. The absence of heads compounds and concentrates this stimulation. In my hand they feel like very intimate objects. I am intrigued and bewildered by these little Hamangia figurines. What are they and why do they appear and feel as they do? What brought people to make them as they are and to what purposes were they put? How do we understand these figurines? Traditional attempts have been accepted as satisfactory, but do they really help us?

Traditional studies of Hamangia figurines

The main account of Hamangia figurines is found in Dimitre Berciu's 1966 seminal volume *Cultura Hamangia*. The key text is the chapter 'Arta culturii Hamangia' (Berciu 1966: 86–108) in which Berciu provided the basic typology that Puiu Haşotti followed in his more recent accounts (Haşotti 1985, 1986a, 1997: 42–6) and which Ivan Vajsov refers to in his important Bulgarian articles (Vajsov 1987, 1992a, 1992b). Berciu's primary attention (repeated by Haşotti and Vajsov) focused on typologizing Hamangia figurines in terms of body morphology, material of manufacture and surface treatment. Thus, while the vast majority was made of fired clay, a handful was fashioned from marble, a couple of stone and a few of bone. More numerous than these latter ones, though less frequent than the clay examples, were figurines made from shell.[3] While incompletely fired, poorly preserved, exceptions have been found at Durankulak and Medgidia Cocoaşa, most ceramic Hamangia figurines were made of fine clay fabric, well fired and highly burnished.

Berciu devoted the majority of his analytical energies to defining three categories of Hamangia figurines based on body position: Types A, B and C (fig. 3.5). Type A figurines are most numerous and are distinguished by their standing position. Type B figurines are less numerous and are defined by their seated (or semi-seated) position and by a tendency to be more massive than Type As. Type Cs are very few in number and are defined by their 'maximum realism'; the Cernavoda *Thinker* and *Seated Woman* are Type Cs as are the disarticulated figurine heads found at Grădiştea-Coslogeni, Medgidia-Satu Nou, and Tîrguşor-Sitorman. Chronologically there is little to differentiate among the three types. Examples of both of the two most numerous types (A and B) come from separate parts of the Cernavoda cemetery and are deemed to be contemporary (Berciu 1966); furthermore, figurines of both types have been found in two different Hamangia phases at Baia-Goloviţa and at Tîrguşor Urs. Though the absence of absolute dating and the infrequency of multi-strata sites make chronological conclusions difficult, it appears that figurines of all types were made and used throughout the Hamangia phases.

In addition to typology, the interpretation of Hamangia figurines comes originally from Berciu, though Haşotti and Vajsov as well as Marinescu-Bîlcu (Marinescu-Bîlcu

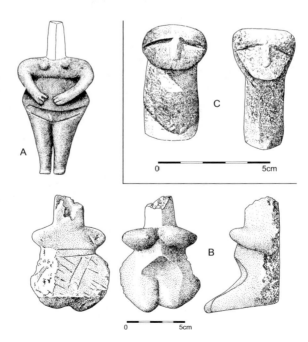

Figure 3.5 Traditional typology of Hamangia figurines.

HAMANGIA

1964, 1977a, 1977b, 1985, 1986) and Marija Gimbutas (Gimbutas 1989b: 183; 1991: 249) have made important contributions. In these treatments, figurines are presented as valuable sources of information about two things: cultural genealogy and cosmic spirituality. As in most Balkan prehistoric archaeology of the past half century, a major interpretive goal has been to place Hamangia figurines in their regional and extra-regional cultural contexts. To this end, similarities in figurine form have been used to draw analogies with material at Haçilar in central Anatolia (Haşotti 1997: 43). More general connections use figurine body-shape to suggest similarities across Anatolia and beyond (e.g., with Çatalhöyuk, Jarmo, Ras Shamea, Tell Mureybet and Abu Hureya) (ibid.: 45). Further links are traced to mainland Greece (e.g., with Nea Nikomedia, Dikilitash, Achilleion, Sesklo and Tsangli) (Marinescu-Bîlcu 1985). Additional parallels have been proposed for figurines from Bulgaria, Crete and Cyprus. In all, claims for resemblances between figurines range over a huge area, centring on the Near East but reaching from southeastern Europe to Iraq and Syria (Berciu 1966: 52–7; 1961: 514; 1960: 432). The general similarities of form used to establish these broad links are complemented by more specific comparisons of particular features. Thus similarities have been noted between the face of the Cernavoda *Thinker* and the faces of figurines in other regions and in other periods; these similarities have been used as arguments for contacts and cultural origins among different Balkan Neolithic communities: between Hamangia and the PreCucuteni communities to the northeast (Marinescu-Bîlcu 1964, 1977a), between Hamangia and the Dudeşti culture in southcentral Romania (Comşa 1959); and between Hamangia and the Vinča culture in Serbia.[4]

The second predominant understanding of Hamangia figurines reads them as inventories of information about Hamangia divinities and religious ideas (Haşotti 1997: 42). Attention is drawn to the width of figurine hips, the bulky abdomens and the depiction of pubic triangles; conclusions follow that these are objects belonging to cults of fertility and fecundity. Indeed, Gimbutas identified the Cernavoda *Thinker* as a god of vegetation (Gimbutas 1989b: 183; 1991: 249). These interpretations are as unsatisfying as are the ones that seek to create trans-regional cultural connections based on similarities of figurine form from distant regions. As I suggested in the introductory chapter, dissatisfaction rests with the types of questions that these anecdotal and culture-historical suggestions attempt to answer, questions that fail to move us towards a better understanding of our reactions to the Hamangia figurines that we see in publications, in museum cases or which we hold in our hands. If the traditional typologies and interpretations of Hamangia figurines are unsatisfying, how might archaeological evidence help? Can an examination of the archaeological and social contexts of Hamangia figurines provide the information and satisfaction we seek?

Hamangia contexts

Hamangia refers to a collection of Neolithic settlements and cemeteries in southeastern Romania and northeastern Bulgaria (fig. 3.6). Berciu's *Cultura Hamangia: Noi Contribuţii* (Berciu 1966) is the classic text. Subsequent work, especially by Puiu Haşotti, has refined Berciu's original theses and added material from more recent excavations, particularly in Romanian Dobrogea.[5] Equally important work has taken place in northeastern Bulgaria with Henrietta Todorova's excavation of the settlement and cemetery at Durankulak on the Black Sea coast (Todorova 1983, 2002a, 2002e; Dimov 1992a, 1992b).

51

HAMANGIA

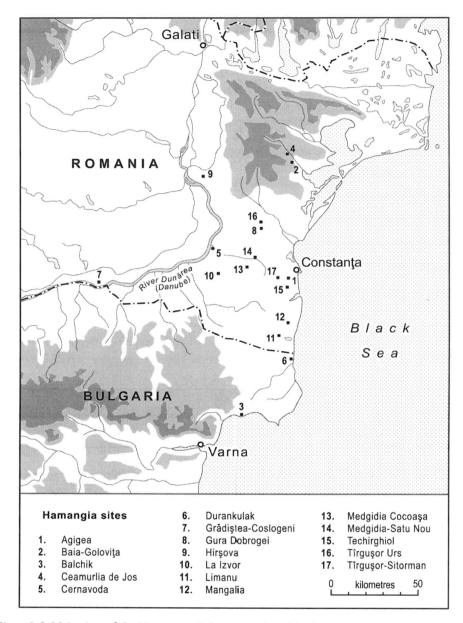

Figure 3.6 Main sites of the Hamangia Culture mentioned in the text.

Hamangia dates from the middle of the sixth millennium through the middle of the fifth millennium BC. More precise dating of features or even more generally of sites or cultural phases is difficult. Paucity of radiocarbon dates is a major problem; chronologies are cobbled together by integrating fortuitous discoveries of Hamangia material in non-Hamangia sites (e.g., in the Boian-Giuleşti culture-contexts at Bogata in Călăraşi county;

HAMANGIA

Haşotti 1997: 21) or by drawing parallels with better-dated sites from Romania (e.g., Hîrşova) and from farther afield.[6] Another problem is the absence of stratigraphic links between the Hamangia sub-phases, whether they are the ones originally proposed by Berciu (Hamangia I–V) or as adapted by Haşotti (Hamangia I–III). With very few exceptions, habitation sites have only one cultural level[7] and cemeteries only offer occasional, fortuitous, relationships where a later grave cuts an earlier one.[8] Attempts to sequence sites chronologically and to correlate Hamangia material with other culture-complexes rely heavily on comparisons of ceramic style and form. As with other north Balkan Neolithic communities of the sixth and fifth millennia BC, Hamangia people were small-scale cultivators and plant collectors, making pottery, herding and hunting animals, investing sufficient effort and time in constructing places for living, and following particular shared understandings of what was the necessary and appropriate manner of dealing with death.

Settlement

Hamangia settlements consisted of small buildings with rectilinear floor-plans and thin walls made from saplings and small tree-trunks, stuck in the ground and then joined together with horizontal interweavings of branches, covered with packed mud and clay mixed with grasses and other plants. Buildings contained the full range of materials, tools and facilities common to small-scale cultivator-herder-gatherer-hunter communities. Most structures contained ovens (or at least open hearths), collections of flint blades (almost 600 from one building at Tîrguşor Urs) and large quantities of pottery vessels (both coarse and fine wares, the latter made into small burnished bowls and cups with channelled decoration). In some instances, the ground was levelled and packed down before buildings were erected; at Tîrguşor Urs the surface may have been hardened first by burning. The permanent fixing of a grinding-stone into the floor of Building 2 in a late (Hamangia III) phase of Ceamurlia de Jos suggests that in some instances people made commitments to building-use over long periods of time and that perhaps such commitments increased towards the end of the Hamangia phases.

In addition to the rectilinear, surface-level buildings, Hamangia people built living-places with floors that were dug below ground level; these pit-structures were oval or irregular in plan, ranged greatly in size, and were covered with wood, clay, mud and straw roofs. Some pits were very small and it is difficult to imagine that many had any purpose other than storage or rubbish deposition. Others were larger, had internal walls dividing space into separate rooms, and contained ovens and larger concentrations of tools and domestic debris: caches of microlithic flint blades; granite axes, chisels, hammers, grinders and grinding-stones; bone and horn digging-sticks and smaller tools such as spatulas and spoons.[9] One of the most clearly documented pit-structures comes from Durankulak in northeastern Bulgaria (Dimov 1982; Todorova 1983; Skakun 1982). The building is large (8 × 5 m) and has three rooms, separated by clay walls. The central room contained a hearth, the northern room an exterior door, the southern room a bench. Similar Hamangia pit-structure sites have been excavated at Ceamurlia de Jos (Berciu 1966: 119–231), Baia-Goloviţa (ibid.: 232–79), Medgidia-Satu Nou (Haşotti 1980, 1987), and Techirghiol (Slobozeanu 1959; Comşa et al. 1962; Necrasov and Haimovici 1962).

Surface-level and pit-structures were arranged into villages, though perhaps it is more accurate to think in terms of camps, as there is little evidence for long-term permanence

53

of occupation (fig. 3.7). Unlike other parts of the Balkans at this time, there is no evidence for consecutive sequences of new structures built directly on top of older ones. It is possible that the horizontal spreads of Hamangia buildings represent contemporary, spatially distinct, occupations. More likely, these sites may represent episodic reoccupations of a settlement area: new buildings constructed in open and unused areas adjacent to older pit-structures which, over time, filled up with rubbish from the new phases of residence. Settlements concentrated on terraces overlooking river and stream valleys, on the slopes of hills and along lake shorelines. Caves at Gura Dobrogei and La Izvor also contain traces of Hamangia activities though it is unclear whether such cave-use qualifies as settlement (Hartuche 1976).[10] Some habitation sites covered large areas. Haşotti suggests that the settlement at Tîrguşor Urs ranged over 7 ha though the density of building was low: nine surface-level buildings, one pit-structure and eleven storage or rubbish pits (Haşotti 1986c). Other sites cover large areas with similarly few buildings: two structures and a storage pit in a 50 × 50 m area excavated at Durankulak; three structures over 250 sq m at Medgidia-Satu Nou.

Absence of any, even relative, stratigraphic, chronological control among individual structures on Hamangia sites prevents secure conclusions about whether the sites were large, contemporaneously occupied, village camps or whether they represent longer sequences of much smaller groups using and reusing one place as part of a more mobile existence. If there is any chronological pattern to settlement, then it is a trend of increasing popularity of surface-level buildings matched by a decrease of pit-structures; thus the earlier phase of buildings at Tîrguşor Urs (Hamangia I) is dominated by pits while the later phase (Hamangia III) has a larger number of buildings constructed above ground (Haşotti 1986b; 1997: 27). However, it would unwise to see the two forms of buildings as mutually exclusive; many sites have both (e.g., Ceamurlia de Jos), though the lack of chronological control makes impossible any better understanding of the relationships between them.

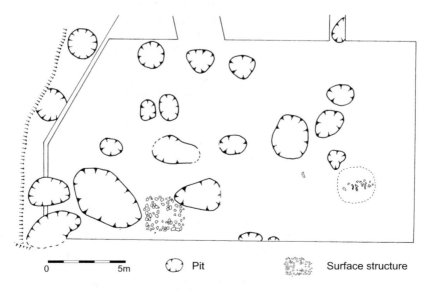

Figure 3.7 Plan of Hamangia site at Ceamurlia de Jos (after Berciu 1966).

HAMANGIA

At many sites, pits contain large assemblages of material but have no obvious, internal, architectural features such as walls. At Medgidia Cocoaşa, a pit 4 m in diameter contained animal bones (mostly of cattle), pottery, bone and stone tools, fragments of a hearth and figurines. Material was concentrated in two parts of the pit: bones to the south; the other objects to the north. Similar pits have been found at Baia-Goloviţa (Berciu 1966: 240, 242; Lăzurcă 1980: 9–10), Ceamurlia de Jos (Berciu 1966: 146–7) and Limanu (Galbenu 1970: 78). The excavators suggest that these pits had a ritual function though there is no obvious reason to interpret them as such. It is more likely that they were rubbish or storage pits; equally possible is some other, as yet, unrecognizable function that fits within temporary activities or short-term residences (e.g., linked to hunting, herding or other causes). Again, the imprecision of published excavation records precludes further deliberation.

Other material culture

In addition to the tools, pots, animal bones, ovens, hearths and, we shall see below, figurines, Hamangia pit-structures and surface-level buildings also contained ornaments and jewellery made of stone, clay, bone and shell. Bracelets and beads made from the marine mollusc, *Spondylus*, are not infrequent finds (e.g., at Ceamurlia de Jos and Medgidia-Satu Nou) nor are pendants made from boars' tusks (at Medgidia Cocoaşa) or marble (Ceamurlia de Jos). *Spondylus* bracelets and a pendant were also found at Agigea, a Hamangia phase III settlement, as were two copper bracelets (Slobozeanu 1959).[11] Marble was also used to make jewellery (e.g., at Tîrguşor Urs). Finds of large numbers of flint blades are not uncommon, witness the 600 that were found at Tîrguşor Urs, noted above. At many sites, such as Medgidia-Satu Nou, microliths dominate the flint-tool assemblages.

Settlement conclusions

The record of Hamangia settlement is not unusual for the Balkan Neolithic communities of the lower Danube region, though as we shall see in later chapters, it is different in important ways from the record to the south. Hamangia communities invested some effort into building places of residence and activities. In some places and especially in earlier phases, the amount of effort was limited to creating small, simple spaces, partly dug into the ground. Greater investment of time and materials is evident in other places, especially in later phases: larger, rectilinear, multi-roomed buildings built at ground level which suggest a greater commitment to particular places and which begin to suggest a firmer conception of a settled community. The density and arrangement of structures at any one site, however, does not suggest clear planning of a community over time or space. The absence of multi-strata settlement sites argues against long-term commitment to place. If people came together to live then they did so for short periods of time before moving to other places, perhaps to live with other people. Settlement has a fluidity about it that evokes mobility more than it does long-term residential permanence.

HAMANGIA

Burials

Though fewer in number than settlement sites, Hamangia burials have attracted the majority of research interest. Inhumation occurred in large cemeteries and of the few sites that have been excavated, two have been particularly intensely studied (Cernavoda and Durankulak) though only one has been satisfactorily published.[12]

Cernavoda

The Cernavoda cemetery was excavated as a rescue project from 1954 to 1961.[13] Over 400 burials were recovered, though many were disturbed; a large part of the cemetery had been destroyed by soil erosion. In almost all of the graves, bodies were positioned with their heads to the southeast and feet to the northwest. Most burials contained grave-goods and of these, stone tools, pottery vessels and animal bone were most common. Polished stone axes, adzes and chisels, many with no signs of having been used, were placed by the right hand or next to the head of the deceased. Fine-ware ceramics were common, though the pottery forms were different from those found on contemporary Hamangia settlements; funerary ceramics were more conservative, including older, more traditional shapes rarely found in pit-features or surface-level structures. Common forms were small cups (with rounded bodies and high, inward-sloping, small necks), small footed, open bowls and fuller-bodied bowls with wide waists and outward flaring rims. Well-made decorated fine-ware pots and poorly fired undecorated vessels were both deposited in the graves. Less frequent were inclusions of polished-stone pendants in the shape of discs, spheres and half-crescents and *Spondylus* bracelets and beads. A string of 21 *Dentalium* beads was found in one grave. Another burial contained a small anthropomorphic pendant made of marble and perforated with holes through the head and arms. Clay figurines, similar to those found on settlement sites were also deposited as grave-goods, though they were not frequent finds.[14]

Data on sexing and aging individuals from Cernavoda are available for the burials excavated during the 1956 season (Necrasov *et al.* 1959). Of the 48 individuals that could be aged, most were adults (over 80 per cent) and half of the adults were 30 years or older. Of the younger individuals, two were adolescents: one was 7–10 years old, and one was a year old. Of those for which sex could be determined, almost two-thirds (61 per cent) were male. The authors of the report interpret the age and sex distributions as a normal representation of natural mortality for a population. There is little information about the correlation of age and sex with grave-goods.

The Cernavoda necropolis also contained isolated deposits of individual human skulls, and more extraordinary, an assemblage of six human crania.[15] Two less easily understood pits contained human and animal bone, carefully arranged in different zones. Indeed, the majority of burials at Cernavoda contained animal bone, though in many cases, only the head of the animal was deposited. Bones, skulls and tusks from wild pig were most common; other animals include deer, oxen, and wild ass. Beaver was frequent; less so red or roe deer.

In some parts of the cemetery, later Hamangia burials cut into earlier ones. It is not clear, however, whether this informs on mortuary custom: did Hamangia conceptions of death, its ceremony and location focus exclusively on the events of burial? Was the event of inhumation the main component of mortuary ceremony with little or no importance

HAMANGIA

given to post-inhumation memory of the position or existence of the deceased? Is this the reason for the later cuttings of earlier burials? Alternatively, if, in the Hamangia conception of death, memories of deceased individuals lived on, then the cutting of earlier graves by later burials can be read another way; the cemetery had a long life, during which local memory faded and disturbances were unintentional. A third option is also possible; the cemetery was used by several communities none of which were permanent local residents. If this final possibility is most accurate, then Cernavoda would have been a common place for death but understood as appropriate for burial by several more mobile, Hamangia communities.

Durankulak

A fuller, more completely documented, record of Hamangia death is emerging from the Durankulak cemetery on the Black Sea Coast in northeastern Bulgaria (Avramova 1986, 1991; Dimov 1982; Dimov *et al.* 1984; Vajsov 1987; Todorova 1983, 2002a, 2002c, 2002e). The number of burials is almost twice than that for Cernavoda (750), and as at Cernavoda bodies were laid out in a common direction (N–S) though the arrangement of the body in the burial varied: placed flat on the back (in the majority of burials); crouched on the right-hand side; or crouched on the left-hand side. The cemetery contains the burials of men, women and children as well as bodiless burials (a.k.a. cenotaphs). Many (but not all) bodies were buried with one or more ceramic vessel (one burial contained eight); shapes include miniature pithoi, large storage jars, narrow-necked, round-bottomed or straight-sided cups, small closed bowls, carinated cups, lids, footed shallow bowls and large stands (Todorova 2002d: 81–116).

Many graves contain objects made of copper (arm-rings, beads and tooth-rings), malachite (beads), gold (finger-rings and beads), and *Spondylus* (beads, arm-rings, plaquettes). Beads were also made of *Dentalium* shell, lignite, chalcedony, bone, clay, and red deer teeth; some graves contained *Unio* shells, lumps of hematite or ochre. More frequent was the deposition of animal bones, especially the teeth, jaws and skulls of wild ass, wild pig, sheep, goat and cattle. In some burials small pots contained a specific assemblage of objects: a flint blade, a bone awl and a smoothening stone. Within the area of the cemetery, but unassociated with particular burials, were assemblages of animal bone (usually the skulls of wild ass and sheep but also cattle) and fragmented ceramic vessels which the excavators have argued are the remains of feasting complexes. Figurines made of clay and of *Spondylus* were placed in burials, though they are very infrequent inclusion, appearing in only 11 of the 750 Hamangia phase burials from the site.[16] Most of these graves contained a single figurine, though three burials[17] had two figurines each and one grave[18] had four (see further discussion below).

The disturbance of earlier Hamangia burials by later ones recorded at Cernavoda also occurred at Durankulak and similar conclusions can be drawn about the length of time that the cemetery was in use and about the depth of local knowledge possessed by different groups burying their dead in it. It is also the case at both Cernavoda and Durankulak that different areas within the cemetery were used either at different times or at the same time but by different groups. At Durankulak there are four spatially distinct areas of the cemetery, each of which corresponds to burials that have been dated to one of the Hamangia phases (Dimov 2002).[19] Thus, Hamangia I–II burials are located in the northeastern section of the excavated area,[20] Hamangia III graves are spread over the northwestern section, and Hamangia IV remains are found across the southern strip of the area. Without the precision that a substantial series of absolute dates could have provided, it is difficult to be certain that this pattern is best explained by successive uses of the cemetery and not by some other factors, perhaps related to status, or kin-group. If the spatial distribution does represent successive uses of the site for burial over a long period of time, then potentially important questions emerge. Was there a common understanding of where people had been buried in previous centuries, perhaps passed down over many generations? Was the location of the cemetery marked by long-perished grave markers? Does the cemetery mark the resting-places for individuals who lived nearby in communities for which we have so little architectural evidence (though note the Hamangia pit-feature excavated to the north of the cemetery)?

Burial conclusions

In addition to the bodies at Durankulak and Cernavoda, Hamangia burials have been found at Mangalia (Volschi and Irimia 1968) and Limanu (Volschi and Irimia 1968; Galbenu 1970). Both of these sites were very badly disturbed and, though published analyses are limited, the grave assemblages are similar to those found in better contexts at Cernavoda and Durankulak, particularly, the inclusion of the head and teeth of animals and of *Spondylus* bracelets and hundreds of *Dentalium* beads. An exception is the small marble bowl found at Limanu. For Hamangia communities overall, the ceremonies and places of death were significant foci for activities and material deposition. Though it is risky to draw inferences from the restricted data from Cernavoda and the other, either incompletely excavated or partially published cemeteries, the presence of a limited number of especially well-provisioned adult burials at Durankulak suggests some hierarchy of individual identities within the communities. The inclusion of both male and female burials in these particularly well-equipped burials argues against any sexually defined exclusion from positions of notoriety or power.

Economy

Hamangia communities were flexible hunter-herder-farmer-gatherers. At Techirghiol, for example, domesticates dominate the fauna (89.5 per cent) and of these cattle and sheep/goat are most frequent; pig and dog account for less than 3 per cent of individuals (Comşa *et al.* 1962; Necrasov and Haimovici 1962). The grinding-stone fixed into the building floor at Ceamurlia de Jos and the general increase in the frequency of grinding-stones at later, Hamangia III, sites supplement the Techirghiol faunal record to argue for the practice of traditional, settled, Neolithic farming.

It is difficult to get a full picture of Hamangia economy; the key sites were excavated before attention to sieving (let alone flotation) was acknowledged as mandatory. However, one gets the feeling that a lot of what Hamangia people did occurred away from the pit-structures and surface-level buildings. Indeed the record we have at present may be very badly biased in that it represents what may have been minority portions of communities' life: burial and short-term storage or activities based in temporary structures. At the very least, the small sizes of faunal assemblages from these sites suggest short-term usage; at most they make it difficult to generate general patterns of animal economies. Perhaps it is significant that finds of wild animal crania and long bones in burials are as numerous

HAMANGIA

and common as they are. Perhaps the traditional Neolithic understandings of the relationships among people, animals and places may need rethinking. The role of wild animals, the predominance of microliths among the flaked stone tools, and the mixed senses of transitory and settled existences arising from the Hamangia built environment suggest a very particular adaptation of Neolithic technologies, resources and ideologies. It was an adaptation in which the social and political importance of settlement space was limited and in which mobility and death were more important mechanisms for playing out the dynamics of individual and group identity and power relationships.

Hamangia community conclusions

As will become clearer in later chapters where other Balkan Neolithic cultures are discussed, Hamangia communities possess a marginal Neolithic identity. The people living the Hamangia way of life had adopted the critical elements of the generic Neolithic package; they grew plants (including cereals), they managed domesticated animals (including sheep and goat), they built social environments, and they made containers (and other objects) out of fired clay. However, Hamangia communities adapted the Neolithic way of life in their own particular fashion.[21] They avoided or rejected the long-term, permanent commitments to place that are so evident in the southern Balkans at this time, and indeed that had been a reality there for the preceding 1,000 years. The Hamangia exploitation of Neolithic economic technologies were similarly tempered; small-scale garden horticulture and grazing of small herds of domesticated herbivores were practices distinct from the larger-scale agriculture that took place elsewhere and which would eventually come to prominence in southern Romania and northern Bulgaria in the millennium after the Hamangia phenomenon. The particulars of burial, the inclusion of animal bone as a grave-good (and particularly, the high proportion of wild animal remains in burials) as well as the burial of disarticulated human skulls, all illustrate deep local roots within the north Balkan prehistory of the preceding millennia. The continuation of a microlithic industry among the Hamangia flaked tool assemblages adds yet another reference to the earlier times.

Running with these deeper links to the local past, however, were more provocative components leading forward to new fashions and protocols of living and dying. Use of exotic materials fashioned into body ornaments was a foretaste of the identity expression that came to permeate Balkan communities and which would continue, gathering strength until the middle of the fourth millennium BC. *Spondylus* and *Dentalium* and other less common materials such as copper and marble were Hamangia exotics of importance and expressive weight. Their presence in both the Hamangia domestic and funerary spheres is important and balances the embedded, traditional aspect of Hamangia with a less conservative, more forward-looking material enthusiasm.

Perhaps the essence of Hamangia is best reflected in the popularity of using boar's tusk as a material for making body ornament. On the one hand, boar's tusks referred to the traditional within the Hamangian character; the boar is a wild animal, very much a non-domesticate, possessing its own particular, probably dangerous, essence. Boars and their body parts, especially the parts that threatened injury during hunting, injected a dose of the untamed, the liminal, and the perilous into the identity of the person who wore a boar's tusk or who was buried with a boar's skull. On the other hand, the use of boar's tusk as an item of personal jewellery and the implicit emphasis on display during burial

59

ceremony look forward to the new ways of publicly displaying social relationships that were to remain fundamental to Neolithic communities across the regions for another 1,000 years.

About Hamangia communities, then, one senses that these people lived with relatively open-ended sets of protocols that defined the appropriate ways that things should happen, or that defined the special values that particular places held for ceremonies, for living and for expressing individual identities. This sense of looseness is underlined when one finds the same types of objects deposited equally in burial and domestic places. As expected, both mortuary and living contexts contain the mundane material of life and work: axes, pots, and bone and flint tools. Surprising, and indeed particular to Hamangia, is the deposition in both contexts not only of jewellery made from exotics such as *Spondylus* but also of figurines. This open looseness is a characteristic that sets Hamangia apart from other Neolithic communities in the Balkans; perhaps it is a symptom of a much less anchored existence, a life-style involving much movement across and through landscapes, perhaps determined in part by management of grazing animals such as cattle.

Does this understanding of Hamangia help us with a better understanding of the figurines found at Hamangia sites? One is tempted to try to fit the abstract, undetailed modelling and decoration of the figurines into the recognition that they are equally deposited in both settlements and burials. Does the lack of specificity in figurine appearance fit in the general looseness of rules over what should happen where, of the ephemeral temporality of settlements and use of cemeteries by different groups? Can the role of figurines in both burial and domestic contexts be understood in terms of that essence of Hamangia existence, the mixture of rootedness in the past with forward-looking behaviour? The general patterns reviewed above do not offer conclusive evidence. Perhaps a clearer understanding will come from the particularities of each figurine's archaeological context, its exact find-spot and associated finds.

Figurine contexts within Hamangia sites

As noted, Hamangia figurines are unusual in the context of the Balkan Neolithic as they are found both in domestic and funerary contexts. Indeed they are the exception to the Balkan rule that figurines are found only in settlement contexts.[22] What information can we draw from the specifics of figurine find-spots within Hamangia sites? Does a deep and full understanding of the spatial distributions of figurines within settlement and burial provide the information capable of satisfying our desire to understand Hamangia figurines and the reactions they cause?

Funerary contexts

Excavation of both major Hamangia cemeteries produced figurines. Grave 626 at Durankulak, for example, contained four figurines (fig. 3.8B). They were buried with a 20–25-year-old woman whose body had been placed on its left side with its legs drawn up and its head positioned to the north. In addition to the figurines, the burial contained an unusually large *Spondylus* bracelet, three strings of copper and malachite beads and three fragments of finger rings (Vajsov 1987, 1992a, 2002; Todorova *et al.* 2002: 62, 109). Preservation of the figurines was poor (they had been incompletely fired) and two survive only as fragments. Another only survives as head and feet, and the fourth is

HAMANGIA

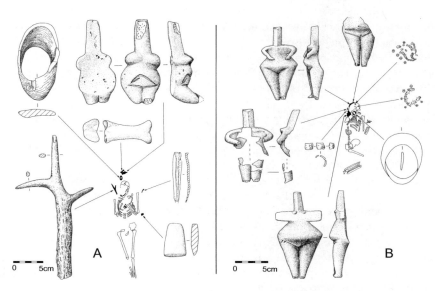

Figure 3.8 Hamangia phase graves from Durankulak: (A) 1036 and (B) 626 (after Todorova and Vajsov 1993).

nothing more than the torso and legs. As with other Hamangia figurines, the Durankulak Grave 626 figures are striking for the simplicity of their form and their lack of surface treatment. Necks are long, thin, triangular and without faces or heads. On the body of one figurine, two horizontal and curving incised lines form a pubic triangle and a short vertical slit suggests that this one is female. The other three have no sexually identifiable body parts, through two have small protuberances on their chests. Though these may be breasts, they may just as easily be men's as women's; indeed the potential breasts sit rather high on the chest and are as much part of the shoulders or neck as they are of the chest. Abdomens on each figurine bulge outwards, though to read these as signs of pregnancy would be to ignore their relative size in proportion to the width of the hips and the breadth of the figurine buttocks. Only two of the figurines have arms preserved; one has short, thick, square-ended arms that extend straight out to the sides. Arms on the other are thinner, bent at the elbows with hands resting on the top of the abdomen.

Other graves at Durankulak contain figurines. Similar in appearance to those found in Grave 626 is a figurine found in Grave 609; the burial also contains over 400 beads of malachite and *Spondylus*, *Dentalium* shell, a small pot, two fragments of a bone awl, a bone from a wild ass, a fragment of a ring and another tiny anthropomorphic figurine made of *Spondylus*.[23] Two similar, small *Spondylus* figurines were found in Grave 621; another one came from Grave 644. In Grave 1036 the body of a man was buried with a figurine placed above his head near a *Spondylus* bracelet and a cattle metapodial (Todorova and Vajsov 1993: 227–8; Vajsov 2002; Todorova *et al.* 2002: 80, 121) (fig. 3.8A). The almost completely destroyed traces of at least two other figurines were found on the man's chest where his hands had been positioned. Placed near his left shoulder was a flint blade; above his right shoulder was a deer-antler sceptre, though it just as easily could have been used as a digging-stick. Near the man's left elbow is a small ground-stone axe.

HAMANGIA

The many figurines from the Cernavoda cemetery include *The Thinker* and *The Seated Woman*, though neither of these comes from clear or undisturbed contexts. Berciu's publication of the cemetery provided few of the specific details of contexts and grave assemblages that would be expected in a modern project and we may be best served to rely of the full publication of Durankulak. What is clear about Cernavoda, however, is that figurines were found in a number of different graves (Berciu 1966: figs 45–55, 56: 1–3; 57: 2–7, 58).

What can we say about Hamangia figurines based on their inclusion in burials? Clearly, they were one of many objects deemed appropriate in Hamangia communities for inclusion with the body of the deceased. Were their meanings tied specifically to the mortuary ritual? They may have been, but in light of their recovery from settlement contexts, as we shall see below, it is unlikely that mortuary ceremony was their sole function. Vajsov has suggested that they were placed in the Durankulak cenotaph burials as replacements for a real body (Vajsov 1992a: 96); though this hardly makes sense in light of the inclusion of figurines in burials that also contained bodies. It is perhaps better to understand the placing of figurines in Hamangia burials as one of several material mechanisms employed to express part of the deceased's identity or to proclaim his or her membership within a particular stratum of a community. Perhaps they displayed individuals' attachments to a particular group of people and their differentiation from others. If this was the case then the location of figurines near the heads of the deceased makes sense: objects of identity expression usually concentrate around heads and hands. Identification of Hamangia figurines as a component of identity expression is further strengthened by the record of figurine deposition in a limited number of burials and in those burials that often contained disproportionately large numbers of grave-goods and especially those made of exotic materials. But other materials and objects (especially *Spondylus* and animal bone) also expressed identity. Was there something particular about figurines that made them work in ways that other objects did not? In identity expression did they speak to some particular element of personal character? The striking formal similarity among figurines suggests that if particular individuals' identities were the focus of figurine deposition, then it was an identity that several individuals shared: a group within a group. Most importantly, a detailed archaeological recording of Hamangia figurines within individual burials offers little information to help answer these questions.

Settlement contexts

In addition to the figurines from the Durankulak and Cernavoda cemeteries, Hamangia figurines are also recovered from settlement contexts. For example, four figurines were found in a building at Baia-Goloviţa (Berciu 1966: 276–8) (figs 3.9 and 3.10). The Baia-Goloviţa figurines were closely grouped, found with pottery and a stone axe in a substantially sized (6 × 5 m) surface-level structure. One of the figurines has a clearly defined pubic triangle; the other three have breasts, although only on one is the modelling of the breasts distinct enough for the viewer to be certain that this is also a female figure. Two of the figurines are standing. The one with a pubic triangle is modelled with legs slightly apart. Another stands with legs together. A third figurine sits with legs tucked underneath and the last one is depicted in a position somewhere between standing and sitting; slouching may be the best description. All four have extravagantly extended

HAMANGIA

necks; none has a face or head. The two standing figurines have hands modelled and placed on the abdomen. It is not clear whether the sitting and slouching figures have arms represented by stubby stumps or whether the arms are folded across the chest or, indeed, whether what we think are arms are actually breasts. There is no other surface decoration, and in general all of the figurines lack any distinguishing specificities in the way they were created.

Very few other figurines were found at Baia-Goloviţa (Berciu 1966: 232–79). One is a small and poorly preserved, seated figure, only 4 cm tall, with stubby little arms, a line incised around the neck (perhaps to depict a necklace) and other lines at the waist and across the hips forming a regular, horizontal zigzag. The only other anthropomorphic object was a fragment of a figurine leg found in another part of the site.

Excavation of the settlement at Tîrguşor Urs recovered many figurines, both complete and fragmentary (Haşotti 1986b). Most often they were found in pits that the excavator identified as domestic or residential. At Tîrguşor Urs and at Medgidia Cocoaşă, the inclusion of figurines in pits that have no architectural features is often interpreted as having a ritual function (Haşotti 1997: 23) though there is no reason that these are not merely storage or refuse pits. Another pit at Medgidia Cocoaşă also contained figurines, though the presence of a hearth, a large quantity of pottery, tools and animal bones led the excavators to interpret this as domestic and not ritual context. There are also half a dozen very fragmentary pieces of figurines from the pit-structures at Durankulak (Vajsov 1992a: fig. 21).

It is not easy to see how a knowledge of figurine locations in pits, pit-structures and surface-level buildings contributes to our understanding of the meaning of these figurines. Granted, investigation would benefit from more detailed excavation, tighter recording of features and deposits, and better attention to patterns and sequences of deposition within pits and buildings. It is not as clear, however, what the added detail would contribute to our ability to understand Hamangia figurine use or meaning. As with their location in burials, so also in domestic contexts; figurines were one of many different types of objects that ended up in the archaeological record of Hamangia sites. From these general assemblages of cultural and economic material it is impossible to tease out any special meaning or use that can be assigned to figurines. They were part of daily life or at least part of Hamangia life that is recorded in the built environments of these communities.

Conclusions of traditional approaches to Hamangia figurines

None of this examination of the archaeological context and the traditional typologies moves us any closer to a better understanding of Hamangia figurines. Most of the traditional research avoids or, worse, fails to recognize or acknowledge the reactions that people have when they see these objects and hold them in their hands. An in-depth knowledge of the typology of Hamangia figurines does not reveal information that helps us further understand our reactions to these objects. If there is an important distinction between standing and seated figurines, then what is it? What meaning might a sitting position contain? Is the seated individual in a subservient position, placed below and under a standing figure? Or do sitting, chairs and stools represent leisure, ease and dominance in the way that thrones and the modern western term 'chair' do? Indeed, the traditional division of Hamangia figurines into three separate types is itself misleading; examination of formal variation suggests that similarity rather than distinction

63

HAMANGIA

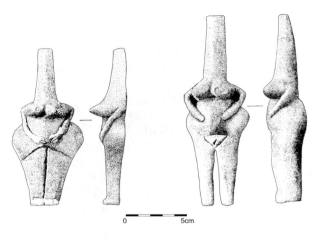

Figure 3.9 Hamangia figurines from Baia-Goloviţa (after Berciu 1966).

is the rule. The extravagant exceptions of *The Thinker* and *The Seated Woman* aside, Hamangia figurine appearance is tightly limited in shape or surface decoration. Furthermore, a full and precise knowledge of figurine find-spots provides information of no more help than do the traditional typological distinctions: figurines are one of several objects found in burial and settlement contexts. How can this help?

New questions

There are other important, potentially more fruitful questions to be asked of Hamangia figurines. What is the significance of the absence of representations of faces and heads on most Hamangia figurines? There is more at work here then merely the abstraction that accompanies the process of miniaturization. What special status does the head and face have that would make its exclusion of importance or meaning? How does the absence of a face affect an object's ability to perform in expressions of identity, if indeed figurines were part of a community expression of identity? Does the absence of faces suggest that other uses, beyond those connected with identity, were in play? Why the abnormally extended necks? Do they draw attention to the missing heads?

What is the significance of the similarity of body form among figurines? Why are they so recognizably similar to each other? Similarly, why was the amount of surface decoration so limited? When we look at Hamangia figurines, are we looking at one specific perception of the general understanding of the human body, or are we looking at a representation of a particular human body that has been reproduced, many times, in similar form? Why are Hamangia figurine bodies not covered with decoration and why is the body depicted in such a pneumatic, over-inflated fashion? What is the significance of the high degree of abstraction, the condensing-down of the elements of the human body from the living, human shape to the selection represented in the representation regime presented by Hamangia figurines?

Clearly, though the conditions of miniaturism and three-dimensionality help us understand how Hamangia figurines might have held a special place within the lives

HAMANGIA

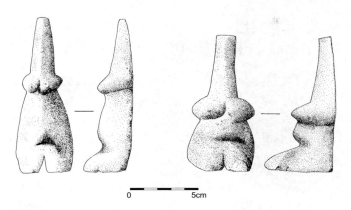

Figure 3.10 Hamangia figurines from Baia-Goloviţa (after Berciu 1966).

(and deaths) of these people, an understanding of miniaturism does not address all of these questions. In addition to miniaturism and its effects, two other conditions of figurines need to be examined. The first is anthropomorphism, the fact that these objects are human-shaped. As the human body contains an extraordinary potential for social, political and symbolic meaning, any representation, reproduction or manipulation of the body will engage and play out that potential. What happens then, when the body is made miniature? What happens, when the body-made-miniature is made in three dimensions? The other critical condition of figurines which needs to be examined is the exclusion of specific body parts from representation. True, the absence of heads, the overwhelming lack of surface treatment, and the decisions not to portray hands or feet are each a result of the abstraction that accompanies miniaturization. But what is the significance of the particular body parts that are depicted? What is it about the human head or breasts or hands that make them important foci for representational attention and, as importantly, for representational exclusion? To address these questions, the discussion in the following chapter focuses first on the significance of the human body as a subject/object of representation and then on different body regions and their significances within representation.

4

ANTHROPOMORPHISM

Dolls, portraits and body parts

In the late 1970s, a team of American and Yugoslav archaeologists collaborated on the excavation of the late Neolithic, Vinča Culture, settlement near the village of Selevac (Tringham and Krstić 1990). The excavation was remarkable in many ways and has had a major impact on our understanding of early farmers and herders in southeastern Europe. Neolithic Selevac was an aggregation of buildings in which people lived a life similar in many ways to the lives of countless people across central and eastern Europe from the seventh to the fourth millennium BC.

The excavation produced a large number of figurines (see Milojković's report for a full treatment of the material: Milojković 1990). Many were found in the remains of the village's timber-framed buildings. House 1, for example, contained twelve figurines. Five were individual finds recovered from the rubble of the structure; a group of seven were found together under the building's burnt clay floor (Tringham and Stevanović 1990: 86–93; Milojković 1990: 88–9). Two of the figurines are of particular interest (fig. 4.1). One is typical of objects dating to the transition from the Tordoş to Pločnik phases of the Vinča culture; radiocarbon samples from this phase at Selevac suggest a date of 4700 BC.

Of the two figurines, one is about 12.0 cm tall, the sort of size of a thing that would fit snugly in the hand. It is made of fired clay and has a face displaying clearly modelled eyes and nose though no mouth is represented. Arms are stumpy but positioned outstretched to the sides; there are no hands, nor any other features on the body below the neck. Two holes were made through each of the arms, and the figurine may have been suspended with a string or thong threaded through these holes. It is just as likely that the holes had some other purpose; perhaps something was suspended from the figurine or tied to it. The body of the figurine is cylindrical and straight-sided; it is the kind of thing that one could hold in one's hand with fingers wrapped around the cylindrical lower part while the arms and head would have been visible, on display even. The second figurine is different. It is much

Figure 4.1 Figurines from Selevac (Tringham and Dusan Krstić 1990).

ANTHROPOMORPHISM

smaller, *c.* 3.0 cm tall, and it is made of alabaster. In section it is flatter than the larger one, has breasts modelled on its chest, but no facial detail. Arms end in short, pointed protrusions at each side, and there is a visible indentation at the waist; below the hips there is little detail though the legs taper slightly towards the feet.

These two figurines were found together along with 70 snail shells and a lump of ochre pigment. The shells were perforated and originally formed a necklace, probably for the larger figurine. In other parts of the building there is evidence that people flaked and ground stone to make tools. How are we to understand these figurines? What can they tell us about the people who made and held them?

Introduction

As argued in Chapter 2, miniature objects, especially three-dimensional ones like figurines, are junctions at which a number of powerful and paradoxical conditions collide. In this sense any object that is made miniature has a particular potential to affect the viewer and to stimulate the viewer to act, to draw inferences, to bring the small thing into his or her personal space, to enter into alternative worlds. When the object made miniature is the human body, these potentials and consequences take on greater significances and meanings. The present chapter looks more closely at the significance of representing the human body in miniature. It asks two key questions. How does human representation work in other, non-ceramic media, in non-Neolithic contexts? For example, how does photography represent the human? Second, what can other media of anthropomorphism teach us that will help us understand Neolithic figurines?

Examination begins with modern dolls, looking at the how they help children understand and accept their positions in modern family life and how dolls function in police interviews of child abuse victims. I consider the politics of the Barbie Doll and how Barbie creates and promotes personal and group identities among young girls. Then I investigate the ways in which some twentieth-century artists have used three-dimensional anthropomorphs to provoke discussions about mortality, humanity and sexuality. Next I ask how photographic representations of the human body alter the ways in which we define individuals. We examine the photographic portraiture of the mid-nineteenth century (e.g., *cartes-de-visite*) and of the early part of the twentieth century (e.g., Stieglitz's serial portraits of Georgia O'Keeffe). I consider the consequences of photographers and painters, such as Manet, who cropped their images in order to segment and dissect bodies. Critical questions emerge. Why does portraiture focus on the head and the face? What is the significance of representing sexual body parts? Finally, I note the inherent paradox of an anthropomorphic miniature and ask how it and the other anthropomorphic manifestations discussed refine our understanding of the figurines from Selevac and from the Balkan Neolithic.

Dolls

As discussed in Chapter 3, miniaturism simplifies complexities and invokes other worlds, providing access to altered realities. When the thing made miniature is the human body, then the worlds that are opened up are especially vast and the things simplified are so particularly complex that they otherwise would avoid comprehension or manipulation (Hall and Ellis 1897; Carriker 1998: 29). When the human body is made into an image, an object even, then the body takes up a position in the domain of material relations.

67

It becomes the object of the spectator's look and touch. While the issues of spectation, the gaze and the caress arise in examination of the socio-politics of figurines in Chapters 6 and 8, the present discussion focuses on dolls as examples of the roles that the body-made-object plays in people's lives: positioning children in existing hierarchies of power; empowering child sex abuse victims; and as standard-bearers for girls' appearance and career aspirations. In all of these examples dolls work powerfully within the processes by which identities are created and manipulated.

Hierarchies of power

As miniature representations of the human body, dolls play powerful roles in children's unconscious understanding of their positions within power hierarchies. Hierarchies themselves are about scale; they are the physical spacing of relationships. Acconci suggests that dolls are one of the tools that children use to learn about their autonomy, that children use dolls to position themselves within our worlds (Acconci 1985). In this sense, the child sees himself as larger than the doll he holds. The doll is a thing (a person even) of the child's own kind: it is a human form with arms, legs, a head and other body parts; it is humanoid. The child understands that he is larger than the doll; also he understands the important inverse, that the doll is smaller than he is. At the same time, the child knows that he is smaller than something else, indeed someone else, of his own kind, an adult (a parent, guardian, or teacher). Furthermore, the child sees not only that the adult is larger than the child is but also that the adult is smaller than another anthropomorphic thing, God. As Acconci suggests, it is in these acts of scaled perception that the child places himself in the correct position in the larger scheme of things and in doing so learns the linearity of individual personality. Playing with dolls, in this sense, becomes an unconscious education in scaled perception, an indirect introduction to the hierarchies of power.

The hierarchical relationship that dolls propose is well illustrated in Gertrude Käsebier's photograph *A Christmas Scene* (1904). In this image, a child sits on a woman's lap, probably her mother's, and the child and her mother look down at a doll that lies on a seat next to them. The mother has her hand on the doll, seems to be adjusting the hem of its skirt, and appears to be speaking to the girl, perhaps talking about the doll, perhaps about the way that it is dressed. Hands on her own lap, at ease, the girl is watching what her mother is doing and listening to what she is being told. All three, doll, mother and child are clothed and coiffured similarly; all three are female. In this photograph, the position of female child in the hierarchy of relationships is clearly promoted. However *A Christmas Scene* is more than just a good illustration of Acconci's argument about the roles that dolls often play in children's auto-positioning within hierarchies; it represents an important moment in the modern representation of women and children.

Käsebier was a well-known photographer of the Pictorialist and then the Photo-Succession movements, both of which were major projects of late nineteenth- and early twentieth-century photography. She was particularly well known for her photographs of women in stereotypically domestic scenes. Her most noted images are of mothers with babies or children. Particularly good examples of this are *Manger* (1903), in which a woman cradles or, more probably, nurses a swaddled infant, and *Blessed Art Thou Among Women* (1899) (fig. 4.2), in which a woman and young girl stand in the doorway of a bedroom.

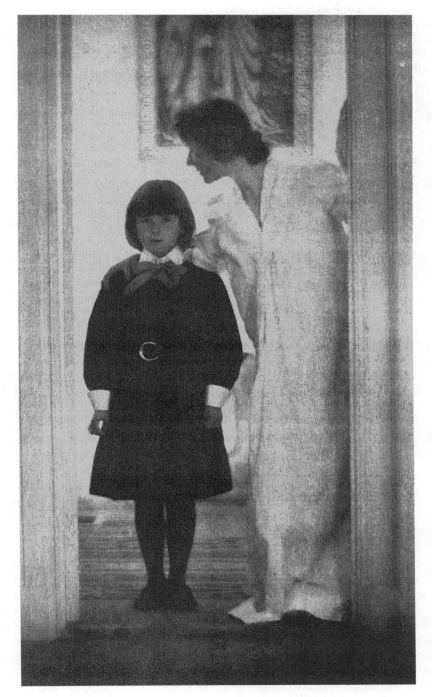

Figure 4.2 Gertrude Käsebier's *Blessed Art Thou Among Women* (1898). Library of Congress, Prints and Photographs Division, FSA/OWI Collection LC-USZC4-9109.

ANTHROPOMORPHISM

In this last image, the girl is fully dressed as if ready to go out to school or, perhaps, to some formal occasion. The child stands, almost to attention, with arms at her sides, feet together, looking straight ahead. The woman is dressed quite differently, not ready to leave the interior of the room or the house, wearing a loose dressing gown or house-coat. The mother's head is tilted down and towards the girl on whose shoulder, or at whose back, she places a maternal, nurturing hand. The inferences one draws are of a mother, having prepared her daughter for the world, sending her out from the domestic safety of the home.

Pictorialist photographers were especially interested in working with images of women's and children's bodies (Pultz 1995: 43). While some Pictorialists presented women as objects, often sexual ones (e.g., Clarence White and Alfred Stieglitz), Käsebier worked in a more traditional Victorian paradigm. She photographed women in interiors, in domestic spaces, where mothers and wives carried out procreative, nurturing, nuptial, maternal tasks, often in the company of children, and hardly ever with men (Pultz 1995: 43–6). Käsebier's images, like *A Christmas Scene*, and the photographic contexts within which these images were created, magnify the argument that Acconci makes about dolls as images of children being positioned with an accepted hierarchy. Photographs, or these photographs at least, and a child's engagement with a doll, project the orderings of relationships and the gendering of activities that were acceptable and appropriate within a particular part of a particular community at a particular phase of Western modernity.

Acconci's arguments about dolls are important for other reasons as well, because they ask us to revisit the discussion of miniaturism as an empowering process and because they bring those arguments into the realm of the anthropomorphic: the doll, as a minia-ture anthropomorph, empowers the child. Giving the child a doll that has body parts similar to those of the child, but that are smaller than the child's, provides a humanoid object that the boy or girl can dominate and control in the same way that a parent controls a son or daughter and, further, as the parent is controlled by a higher, divine, but still anthropomorphic being. Because of its acquiescence in play (i.e., it is inanimate), the doll forces the child to be assertive and to feel superior (Carriker 1998: 173). Furthermore, the child obtains, and then reaffirms, her sense of self and the personal viewpoint from which she perceives the world around her. In this way, dolls work within the development and understanding of the self and personal identity (Carter 1993a: 8). In the definition of an individual's personal world (which may be as much fantasy as reality), dolls work effortlessly because the image represented in the doll is made up of appropriate social conventions that dictate acceptable clothing or sexual representations (ibid.).[1]

Anatomical dolls and police interviews

While a condition of miniaturism in general is the ability to empower the viewer or handler, dolls empower in special ways. A good example is the use of anatomical dolls to gather evidence and to prosecute cases of suspected child abuse. Interviewing children who were suspected victims of abuse is a complex task. Problems of communication arise because children are reluctant to talk about abuse; reluctance comes from fear, embar-rassment, or the limits of children's vocabulary or their span of attention (Morgan 1995: 12). Language differences between child and investigator also hamper communication (ibid.: 40). Since the 1970s, law enforcement agencies have been using anatomical dolls

70

during interviews (ibid.: xiv) because they help remove the difficulty or embarrassment that children experience when describing abuse. The dolls offer an efficient bridge of communication linking child and detective, judge or prosecutor (ibid.: 2, 40). The dolls succeed because they create an environment in which the potentials for child trauma and emotional damage have been lowered (ibid.: xiv, 2).

The dolls used in interviews and court questioning are specially made (fig. 4.3). They are less toy-like than play-dolls, most obviously as they are more sexually explicit. Normal, off-the-shelf children's dolls are particularly unsuitable for legal work as they vary greatly in morphology and have inappropriately proportioned, or inadequately detailed, genitalia. Acceptable, purpose-made anatomical dolls are soft cloth figures that present a general replica of the human body, complete with sexual body parts such as a penis and testicles for male dolls, vaginal openings for female dolls, oral and anal openings, and pubic hair on adults. A set of dedicated interviewing dolls includes adult and child dolls and represents not only the abused child and the abuser but also the victim's siblings and other adults of the child's daily environment (e.g., grandparents).

The sizes of anatomical dolls are important; they are a size that is most comfortable for children to hold and manoeuvre. Dolls that are too large are difficult to handle and frustrate the children being interviewed; dolls that are too small make it difficult for the interviewer, judge or jury to see what the child is using the doll to demonstrate. Adult-dolls are larger than child-dolls, but not in proportion to reality. While a child-doll is usually 16 inches tall, the corresponding adult doll is only 4 inches, or 25 per cent, taller. These particular size differentials are part of the dolls' successes. The altered child–adult differentials between dolls and living humans empower the child victim; they make the child closer in size to the abuser and, thus, move them up the hierarchy of scale.

Though these dolls are sometimes referred to as anatomically complete or anatomically correct, they are not biologically accurate; not all body parts are represented. The dolls provide a basic map of the human body and, as such, are representations and not exact replicas or factual models (Morgan 1995: 3, 65). More importantly, where normal play-dolls have faces that bear precise expressions (smiling, frowning, laughing, crying) that represent particular emotions (happiness, displeasure, pleasure, fear, pain), anatomical dolls have faces intentionally left expressionless. The neutrality of the doll's facial expression allows the child to communicate a full range of emotions and ensures that the doll cannot be blamed for suggesting to the child a particular reaction or feeling, suggestions that could jeopardize court prosecutions (ibid.: 4). The expressionless face of the doll allows the child to demonstrate a variety of emotions depending on the child's experience and not on the toy designer's intention (ibid.: 8).

Figure 4.3 Anatomical doll use in court. From Morgan (1995), fig. 5.1, page 47. Reprinted by permission of Sage Publications.

ANTHROPOMORPHISM

Relevance of dolls in power hierarchies and anatomical dolls

Obviously it would be ridiculous to propose that Neolithic figurines are dolls used in sexual abuse interviews or that they dictate to children their place in status quo power hierarchies.[2] However, the conditions which make dolls work for these purposes and in these contexts are important. The fact that a child feels empowered enough to talk about and physically handle an individual (in miniature representation of course) who has harmed them is a significant product of the degree of empowerment that accompanies miniaturism. The fact that by handling a doll a child can understand and accept their place in the world is a product of the relations of scale and, in particular, the child's involvement in relationships of the essential, human-scale. Both uses of miniaturism empower as well as offer comfort and security. Significantly, they allow the child into another world. For the sexually abused child it is the world of the painful and needing-to-be-forgotten and, probably, the unconsciously blocked or actively displaced. For the child playing with any doll, it is the virtual world of a proposed social order in contemporary society (indeed Acconci suggests that it is an entry into the bourgeois hierarchy).

There is a further relevance particular to the anatomical dolls: the inclusion of certain body parts and the exclusion of others. The inclusion of genitals and anus is as expected. These body parts must appear in a standardized form; they are not open to negotiation or interpretation by child, interviewer, prosecutor, judge or jury. They are the firm ground of the interview; they are the evidence. They must be unequivocal parts of the investigation and the subsequent court proceedings. However, the absence of other body detail is suggestive. On the one hand, their absence is a factor of the legal exercise in which the dolls play a part and a product of law-enforcers' and prosecutors' efforts to prevent objections made in court by defence lawyers: for example that a particular part of a doll's appearance either led the child to think about sexual things that he or she would not have noticed otherwise or led a child to think of a particular person as the abuser (Morgan 1995: 6). Thus the faces of anatomical dolls are intentionally left expressionless. The expression and emotion must be supplied by the child. These elements are not fixed or agreed; in their description lies the maximum variability. It is up to the child to fill in these details. The abstraction of the facial expression forces the child to come up with the answers, to fill in the blanks, to supply the evidence.

Therefore, the body parts that are represented are fixed and not open to negotiation or alteration; the parts of the body (such as the face) that are left undefined invite consideration and imagination. This has direct bearing on the process of abstraction that is one of the critical conditions of miniaturism: what is left out determines the areas about which people must draw their inferences. Thus, the empty, undecorated or unmodelled areas of the Hamangia figurines discussed in Chapter 3 and the body parts not depicted are the areas of the figurines that provoke thought and contemplation. Paradoxically, in their absence, they are the elements that invite maximum attention and consideration. The static and fixed parts that are represented offer no room for such contemplation.

Dolls and identity

The roles that dolls play in child (and adult) affirmations of appropriate positions within hierarchies of relationships lead us to the use of anthropomorphic objects in the per-

ANTHROPOMORPHISM

ception, manipulation, expression and contemplation of identity. Dolls engage both child and adult developments in personal identity. While the microcosm of the doll simplifies extremely complex things, it also opens up a world of relationships so large as to be otherwise unmanageable. In addition to the contribution that dolls may make to positioning children in hierarchies of power, dolls also help fashion identities by providing reflections of the self, by providing an Other against whom identity is constructed, by supplying the companionship of a Same, and by creating test zones in which children practice caring and nurturing (as well, of course, as hating and harming) and other activities of real life but without the immediate consequences of flesh and blood. Obviously, the routine of doll play creates deeply ingrained perceptions of appropriate behaviour towards others which will, eventually, enter the real life of the child. The important point is that dolls provide a range of different components that a child uses to build up ideas of who she is, who others are and how she should behave towards others. Furthermore, objects such as dolls allow, encourage even, children to play out narratives of the self and the other. By manipulating and orchestrating ensembles of dolls a child practises and experiments in rudimentary social scenes (Carroll 1993: 27).[3]

Barbie Doll

For many women growing up in the twentieth-century western world, dolls encouraged appropriate behaviour and appearance: innocent, dependent, content, silent, mass-produced and compliant (Carter 1993a: 16). The epitome of this tradition is the Barbie Doll, a phenomenon of the toy world (on its success rested the success of the company Mattel) and a subject of considerable intellectual debate (fig. 4.4). Barbie was based on the Bild Lilli doll of post-war Germany whose appearance has been described as a three-dimensional pin-up, a hooker or, most evocatively, an actress between performances (Lord 1994: 8–9). Barbie was Lilli recast as a wholesome woman: the epitome of the middle-class All American girl. Over the years of her production Barbie was re-presented in a sensational series of outfits and occupations. She was fashion model, sportswoman, office secretary, doctor, singer, nurse, astronaut, *inter alia*. The frequent remodelling of Barbie was a successful marketing mechanism, stimulating mothers, fathers and daughters to purchase new sets of Barbie clothes and paraphernalia, as well as new Barbie Dolls themselves as they appeared with seasonal variations or annual developments in new and improved doll technology.

Defenders of Barbie praise her as a much-needed role model for girls. They point to the huge range of occupations and abilities that were projected as acceptable for women to pursue and possess. This is no small feat for a doll which appeared before the advent of popular feminism (the first Barbie went on the market in the early 1950s) and who has survived the post-feminist critique. Even the 1961 appearance of Ken, as a required male consort, did little to reduce Barbie's independence. From the start, Ken's position was problematic: he could never marry Barbie, and thus they can never have children (Ken has an impotent 'bulge' in the place of any reproductive equipment, anatomically correct or otherwise). Indeed, most often Ken is found dressed in Barbie's fashionable outfits (see Lord 1994 for extended discussion of these issues and a full bibliography). For many critics and commentators, Barbie represents a strong, modern woman, not tied down by marriage, domesticity or children, nor even restricted to the monotony of a single job for life: the perfect role model for the young women of the world.

Figure 4.4 Eli, Matilda and Eli's Barbie Doll.

On the other hand, there are many critics of Barbie who view her as harmful to young women's perceptions of reality. Some suggest that her body proposes an unattainable physical ideal which girls grow up wanting to emulate: Barbie is blemish-free, does not age, has a disproportionately narrow waist and the equivalent of a perfect, 38-inch bust. Indeed, one woman, Cindy Jackson, spent $55,000 on over 20 operations (face-lifts, breast implants, liposuction) so that she could become a living Barbie (Lord 1994: 244). Barbie's own body has not remained unaltered; the designers and engineers at Mattel have continued to invent new internal mechanisms that extend the doll's ability to bend and twist in increasingly complex ways and carry out new and different activities (e.g., the ability to tilt at the waist or the neck, to play tennis and volley-ball) (ibid.: 12). Other critics argue that in her multiple outfits and many vocations, Barbie represents someone with serious multiple-personality disorders. Indeed her personalities are invented; they are the things of fantasy. The most common criticism attacks Barbie as a stereotype, a prototype of bimboism, a woman-made-object: purchasable, undressable, controllable, disposable.

Engaging as these debates are, the relevance of Barbie does not depend on whether she is an empowering or a harmful influence on little girls. Barbie is relevant for my desire to better understand Neolithic figurines because she documents the emotive power

ANTHROPOMORPHISM

that a miniature anthropomorph can have in influencing our opinions. Even more important, Barbie provides an excellent example of an anthropomorph that was created in one context for one purpose (as a toy for girls), and which has been understood in many different, at times mutually exclusive, ways by many different groups of people. There is a wonderful disjunction between the intention of the doll's creation, its uses and its meanings to people.

Dolls in the art world

Because of the important positions that they occupy in our childhoods, dolls and other representations of the human body (life-size as well as miniature) possess implicit significances for us. Because dolls communicate social information and reproduce cultural roles, artists are particularly drawn to using them in their work (Carroll 1993: 28). Frequently, artists manipulate these deeper meanings by using dolls and other anthropomorphs to question our understandings of identity, of what it means to be human, and of what it means to be a man or a woman.

Artists use dolls to inspire spectator dialogue and viewer contemplation about the ways in which self and identity are constructed. They attempt this by projecting and manipulating human imagery to illuminate differentiation among individuals. Anthropomorphs become a physical means of defining the personal narratives that make up the individual self. Not only can dolls play the role of Another, through which an individual becomes conscious of his or her own self or person (Carter 1993a: 9), but dolls can also act as silent listeners (ibid.: 12). In a more fantastic sense that takes advantage of the powers inherent in dolls as miniatures, artists use dolls as metaphors for the universal concern that people have about personal identity (ibid.: 8). The doll-as-art becomes a medium through which both the exhibit's viewer and the artist can explore their own dimensions of identity (ibid.: 12).

Times when traditional values, roles and role models come under fire are particularly potent periods for artists to employ dolls and other anthropomorphs to engage and overthrow traditional ideals (Carroll 1993: 28). Many artists employ satire or irony by replacing the pretty, likeable childhood dolls with darker manifestations of the standard human form and reveal what is normally hidden. Hans Bellmer and his mannequin art, *Les Yeux de la Poupée* (1935) is one example of this (fig. 4.5). Bellmer created his dolls in 1930s Germany,[4] using metal, wood, and fibre ball-joints so that the dolls could be positioned in various poses of which the artist took a series of striking photographs (Pultz 1995: 76–7; Webb 1975: 366–70). The poses are startling and the photographs suggest violence and abuse, sadism and fetishism (Carter 1993b: 13). Bellmer's work had extraordinary powers to horrify, excite, illuminate and, at the same time, intrigue the viewer (Webb 1975: 366); his doll photographs blended the real with the imaginary in order to be provocative and to open peoples' eyes to new realities (ibid.: 370). Bellmer's dolls were not attractive and did not adhere to traditional conceptions of beauty; they do not inhabit the world of Barbie or of Käsebier's mother-and-child domestic world. Cindy Sherman is another artist who has used dolls as well as larger, life-size, plastic bodies to illustrate female bodies as objects that are repulsive and not desirable (Carter 1993a: 14). Thus, Sherman's *Untitled* (1992) portrays a female body that has been exploited and objectified. Usually erotic and sensual body parts (breasts, vaginas) are rearranged in order to fight against accepted visions of genitalia.

75

ANTHROPOMORPHISM

Bellmer and Sherman's questioning of the human body through their manipulations of anthropomorphs force the viewer to question stereotypical representations of women and sexuality. In installations and exhibitions that challenge standard perceptions of social groups, such as the identity of women in relation to the home or to gendered power relations, artists use dolls as biologically and psychologically significant symbols in order to provoke questions and uncertainties, to overturn accepted opinion and to propose alternative versions of the status quo (Carter 1993a: 23).

Artists have also used dolls to suggest ambiguity and to exploit that ambiguity to unsettle the viewer. Michele Oka Doner's *Doll* (1968) has a similar effect. *Doll*'s porcelain body is covered almost completely with impressed dots and spirals; they are potentially symbolic markings that defy decoding. Even if we cannot understand the surface decoration, we are challenged to decipher it (Carroll 1993: 28). In these cases and many others, artists have used dolls, mannequins and puppets to stimulate thought about important contemporary issues of humanity and sexuality. None has suggested answers or preferred philosophies; each has questioned stereotypes and the status quo by manipulating a single, inherently powerful, material form: the human body.

Figure 4.5 Hans Bellmer's *Les Yeux de la Poupée* (1935) © ADAGP, Paris and DACS, London 2004.

ANTHROPOMORPHISM

While the dolls that a child plays with and the dolls that artists manipulate in their work have very different contexts of use, intention and meaning, they share an important condition: as anthropomorphs they are inherently powerful vehicles for proposing and contesting identities on personal or community levels. Anthropomorphs such as Doner's *Doll* or Sherman's *Untitled* (1992) reveal a powerful feature of such objects: they are props whose drama is already built into them, scripts ready to be performed (Carroll 1993: 28). The body is a vehicle upon which ride all sorts of secondary intentions and meanings. It is perhaps the essential seductive form. As such it sucks in the viewer and allows stow-away symbols and decoration to sneak past otherwise impenetrable raised guards.

Portraits and mutable identities

Portraiture is the major medium of anthropomorphic representation (Clarke 1992a; Tagg 1988). Though previous research has suggested that Neolithic figurines functioned as portraits (Bailey 1994b), the preceding discussion and the closer look at the concept of portrait itself that follows here argue that such an equation is overly simplistic, if not in fact misleading. However, a critical look at portraiture as a social process does help us refine our understanding of anthropomorphic representation. Perhaps most importantly, thinking around portraits prompts us to see how images of individuals can be used to transform the ways in which spectators view and recognize identities and social positions.

Perhaps more than any other kind of photographic image, the portrait achieves meaning through the context in which it is seen (Clarke 1992b: 1). Portraits exist within complex and historical local iconographies and are created with reference to elaborate codes of pose and posture. These iconographies and codes are only readily understood within the communities in which the images have currency (Tagg 1988: 35). Portraits produce significances in which contending groups claim presence. They codify the person in relation to other frames of reference and to other hierarchies of significance (ibid.: 37). In these senses, a portrait is both a sign that describes an individual and a mechanism that inscribes social identity (ibid.: 37). Thus a portrait is only one form, though an extreme one, of one's relationship to others (Bourdieu 1999: 167).

Photographic portraiture

There is no surprise in the discovery that portraiture was one of the first explosions of photographic activity in the middle of the nineteenth century, nor in the fact that 90 per cent of all daguerreotypes taken were portraits, nor that in 1840s America 95 per cent of photographs taken were portraits (Tagg 1988: 43). The popularity of photographic portraiture was the consequence of combining photography (with its representational potential, low costs, and less time-consuming methods) with the long-present desire for personal images, a desire that had been satisfied, though inadequately, by growing industries of silhouette and profile engravings in the late eighteenth and early nineteenth centuries (ibid.: 39). As photography made portraiture accessible to more people and thus as more people possessed representations of their own and other people's bodies, the status that these people held and claimed to hold within society changed radically (Pultz 1995: 17).

ANTHROPOMORPHISM

Cartes-de-visite

The emergence of *cartes-de-visite* in the mid-nineteenth century is one example of the impact that portrait representation can have on people's perceptions of individual identities, their correct presentation, content and meaning. *Cartes-de-visite* are small photographs printed from negatives onto paper (and thus distinct from the other early portraits, the one-off daguerreotype). Inexpensive and quick to produce and thus easy to procure, *cartes-de-visite* radically broadened the range of people who could possess photographic images and who could have their own image reproduced photographically. Because they were cheap and widely available they became an efficient way of holding together families during a period when people were moving across America and Europe (Pultz 1995: 17): albums of *cartes-de-visite* portraits kept together long-departed and distant family members. *Cartes-de-visite* also linked generations of families through time, providing an easily readable record of the temporal depth of familial existence (ibid.: 18). Of course the use of visual representations to document family relationships, coherence and duration had a long, pre-*cartes-de-visite* history in other genres such as oil painting and sculpting. The important difference, of course, was that the use of these other media of portraiture had been limited to a thin stratum of society that could afford to commission oil portraits and marble or bronze busts. *Cartes-de-visite* made portraiture widely affordable and available across communities and in the process contributed to the reshaping of those communities. Indeed, low-cost photographic portraiture like *cartes-de-visite* was one of the key processes that helped define the new European bourgeoisie in the nineteenth century (ibid.: 17).

Like all anthropomorphic representation, *cartes-de-visite* were powerful because they provided an opportunity for people to acquire and advertise new or alternative personal identities: existences that could stand apart from their own physical presences and characteristics. They gave a wide range of people the symbolic power to use imagery to manipulate their own and other's identities (ibid.: 17). *Cartes-de-visite* albums created a virtual world where the pictures of family, friends or political figures could be presented on comparable terms and where the unwanted (e.g., the poor, the sick, the black sheep of the family) could be excluded (ibid.: 17). Collections of *cartes* into albums proposed photographically mediated hierarchies or equalities (ibid.: 18). In this way, *cartes-de-visite* made possible the mass production of images that could be manipulated to actively renegotiate and display relationships between individuals and among family groups. They were one of the important mechanisms with which the new bourgeoisie emerged out of a series of ever-changing social aggregations to form an entity of common, shared beliefs and practices (ibid.: 17).

Stieglitz/O'Keeffe portrait(s)

Cartes-de-visite were only possible because of photography, a technology that facilitated manipulations of the ways individuals were viewed and which provided extraordinary potential for radical transformations in the display and viewing of individual identities. Alfred Stieglitz's portrait study of Georgia O'Keeffe is another example of the potential that photographic representation has for reworking the dimensions of identity expression (Norman 1984; Pultz 1995: 67–8). One of the most influential American photographers at the beginning of the twentieth century, Alfred Stieglitz, took a series of over 300 photographs of his wife, the artist Georgia O'Keeffe, between 1917 and 1933. Fifty-one of these photographs have been published as *Georgia O'Keeffe: A Portrait* (Stieglitz 1978). The wording of the title so that the volume is in the singular (i.e., *A Portrait*) is significant; both Stieglitz and O'Keeffe were interested in exploring the role that visual representation could play in portraiture. Thus, no one photograph from the O'Keeffe series functioned, on its own, as an adequate or complete portrait; *A Portrait* only works as a portrait when all of the images are viewed together in series.

As one would expect, some of the images that make up *A Portrait* are traditional views such as the facial image (fig. 4.6: left). The majority of the images focus on particular parts of O'Keeffe's body. Some are limited to sexualized body parts: breasts and genitalia. Many more of the images however, are of O'Keeffe's hands (fig. 4.6: right): hands on their own, hands against the throat, hands on an aurochs skull. Stieglitz's focus on the hands was one way of drawing the spectator's attention to the parts of O'Keeffe's body that were responsible for her public identity as an artist: with these hands the art is produced. As O'Keeffe's public identity was grounded in her art, then her hands were the best part of her body to use to project that identity in a portrait. On the other hand, the images of the sexual body suggest another, not necessarily contradictory, identity or personality that was linked to O'Keeffe as a woman, of whom Stieglitz was the lover.

As Pultz has pointed out, the Stieglitz/O'Keeffe multiple-image portrait reflects interests that the photographer and his subject had in contemporary cinematographic techniques of representing unfolding narrative. In this sense, *A Portrait* suggests that our understanding of a person is built up over time and incorporates more than any one view, perspective or representation (Pultz 1995: 68). This conception of a multi-image representation of a single individual has radical implications for understanding any set of representations of the human body, but especially where there are multiple representations of potentially the same individual. It is for this reason that earlier work,

Figure 4.6 Two images from Alfred Stieglitz's serial portrait of Georgia O'Keeffe (1919 and 1918). The J. Paul Getty Museum, Los Angeles. © Estate of Georgia O'Keeffe.

ANTHROPOMORPHISM

including my own (Bailey 1994b) was overly naïve in arguing that any single figurine represented a particular Neolithic person; figurines may well be portraits, but only when a portrait is understood as a collection of different images of an individual.

Relevance of portraiture

The benefit of discussing *cartes-de-visite* photography and Stieglitz's study of O'Keeffe is not to suggest that Neolithic figurines functioned within early photo-albums or that they were multiple, serial representations of the same individuals. Rather, the importance is to recognize that changes in the technology and material media of representation can have profound consequences for how people projected their own or other people's identities. We are also forced to acknowledge the potential power that representational imagery of the body can have within deeper social and political changes such as the shifting of social boundaries within nineteenth-century Europe. A deeper discussion of the interplay between reality, politics and representation is the subject of Chapters 6 and 8.

The particular significance of the Stieglitz/O'Keeffe portrait is that it forces us to think more critically than we currently do about the range of possible components within the apparently, and misleadingly, simple concept of portrait or representation of an individual. We must rethink our conception of the link between a single representation of a body part or a single representation of an entire body on the one hand, and an individual being represented on the other. Many separate and differently fashioned and cropped bits of representation, such as O'Keeffe's hands or breasts, may very well refer to a single person. Attempts to identify individual people as portrayed in individual figurines become extremely complex, perhaps even pointless, exercises, the end of which may be of no value whatever: the importance may rest more securely in understanding the enabling (and restrictive) conditions of the medium and technology employed in making a representation. Furthermore, both the *cartes-de-visite* and the O'Keeffe portrait focus our attention on the potential of photography as a technique and on the impact of a new medium. The introduction of a new medium or technology of representation and the consequent alternation between different media and techniques have important consequences for the ways in which human imagery works within larger redefinitions of individual and social groups.

Body parts

In addition to revealing the complexities surrounding traditionally defined portraiture and suggesting the facility of multiple-image portraits, the Stieglitz/O'Keeffe images raise important questions about the representation of body parts in isolation from the body-as-a-whole. Dissecting the human body through representation is a significant act that has important repercussions. On the one hand, it removes a part from its natural context and then transfers it to an alternative place in which different restrictions and encouragements of conduct and of looking apply. Thus, cropping the body and focusing the viewer's attention on particular body parts isolate those parts and invite a scopophilic consumption that often would not be permitted in the more natural, complete contexts. It is no surprise, therefore that cropping is a fundamental tool of the pornographer; cutting up a body into visual bits and pieces invites aggressive acts of looking that are not acceptable in normal encounters (Mercer 1999: 440).

80

ANTHROPOMORPHISM

Segmenting the body has other important consequences. Linda Nochlin has shown how Edouard Manet selectively cropped many of his paintings, intentionally cutting off parts from bodies (Nochlin 1994). By doing so, an arm or leg is left truncated at the painting's edge. The fragment alludes to the rest of the body (often a female one) but also to other worlds that existed beyond the boundaries of the picture frame, worlds of sexualized bodies and body parts. Thus, the leering man in *Nana* (1877), the dancing girl in *The Beer Server* (1878–9), the trapezist in *A Bar at the Folies-Bergère* (1882). While cropping alludes to what is absent (and thus titillates the viewer) it also urges the viewer to draw inferences about what is missing, to create other worlds based on the suggestions made in the partial representations. Nochlin defines cropping as a way of playing with the normal borders of reality, as a tool for questioning and suggesting contemplation. Furthermore, removing a part from the body denaturalizes that body and thus lays it open to reconstructions (Pultz 1995: 162). The body can be built up from one piece into a reconstituted whole that is very different from the original being. Thus, many different whole bodies can be built from the same isolated part and no one reconstructed body need be the correct whole. Fragmentation of the body invites creation of the ungeneralizable, the particular and discrete, of series of differences more than of completenesses (Nochlin 1994: 56)

With the discussion of dissection and the titillating allusions that are proposed in Manet's cropping of his paintings, there are references to the discussion of the expressionless anatomical dolls as well as, in the more general sense, issues that arose from the definition of miniaturism. In those discussions, it was proposed that the thing that is depicted is less important than what is omitted; what is absent is the stimulus for the viewer to draw inferences.

Heads

One of the most frequently isolated parts of the body is the head. Identity cards, passports and drivers' licences represent our faces; museums are filled with portrait busts; coins, stamps and paper currency carry facial representation. The dominance of head and shoulders in representation occurs to such a degree that one assumes that this region of the body contains some essential truth of a person's being (Tagg 1988: 35). Why is this the case?

Physiognomy, phrenology and pathognomy

Part of the answer can be found in the implicit foundations of the now discredited pseudo-sciences of physiognomy, phrenology and pathognomy. Each of these approaches to the documentation of identity worked from the belief that a measurable relationship existed between people's visual appearance and their character, intelligence and morality.[5] Physiognomy is the study of static features of the human face and their relations to an individual's underlying character. Pathognomy is the correlation between different, changing, facial gestures with particular passions and emotions (Twain 2002: 71). Phrenology is based on the principal that the development of a person's mind could be externally documented by examination of the individual's head.

Physiognomy and phrenology had long and deep periods of popularity and appealed to the public's beliefs about an individual's appearance and character. Though the

81

basic tenets of physiognomy have pedigrees traceable to Classical sources (e.g., Plato and Aristotle), the significant popularization of the study occurred in the latter half of the eighteenth century and revolved around Johann Lavater's publication *Essays on Physiognomy* (1775–8). Physiognometric studies to identify and classify the unwell and unruly members of society were popular practices of the institutions of control that arose in nineteenth century Europe: the police, the prison system, asylums and hospitals, reform schools and homes for misdirected youth. These institutions emerged as part of a more general move towards photographic documentation of the abnormal components of communities both within western society and beyond (e.g., the early visual anthropology of 'primitive' tribes). Phrenology can also trace its roots to the end of the eighteenth century in the work of Franz Joseph Gall and in the first half of the nineteenth century in that of Johann Spurzheim (Spurzheim 1826).

None of these beliefs is accepted any longer. Among other things, physiognomy assumed, mistakenly, that the relationship between appearance and character was static; it also failed to recognize that character, morality and identity are social constructs and cannot be read from typologizing facial features. Much more damaging were the uses to which racists and eugenicists put the disciplines at the end of the nineteenth and in the early twentieth centuries to justify (and naturalize) their attempts to discriminate and exterminate (e.g., the Holocaust). Despite the death of these approaches, the scientific search continues for a key to unlock the secrets of individual characteristics and to allow their categorizations; the investigative role once played by the appearance and shape of the face and head has been overtaken by the genetic code. The current scientific study of character and identity differentiations among people has shifted inside the body and away from surface appearance and morphologies.

While scientific approaches to understanding character, identity and intelligence based on external appearance are no longer credited, their long-running and widespread popularity reveals the fascination with a person's outward appearance as an interpretive tool for recognizing character and identity. The widespread belief in the importance of individual appearance continues to dominate much modern daily life; the thriving cosmetic surgery industry is one example of the continuity of the underlying belief (Twain 2002). The desire to correlate external bodily appearance with less tangible components of individual identity may well rest deep within the human psyche.

Sexual body parts

If the head and face retain a fascination for personal representation and identity expression, similarly significant representational cropping and segmentation focuses on sexual body parts. The attention given in many Neolithic figurines to breasts and labia is at the core of their most widely followed interpretations: that figurines functioned within cults (or at least belief systems) of reproduction and fertility. As discussed in the opening chapter, these interpretations have little support. However, the weakness of fertility explanations does not affect the attention devoted to breasts and pubis on figurines. What is the significance of this attention? An answer may be found in examining why genitalia and breasts attract attention in other representational media and in other contexts.

One answer to this question is found in Kaja Silverman's discussion of the ways in which children learn to differentiate between particular parts of their bodies (Silverman 1999). Following the analytical psychology of Jacques Lacan, Silverman argues that a mother identifies specific areas of her child's body as being particularly erotic: parts which provide contact between the external and the internal somatic world (i.e., the anus, the penis, the mouth and the vagina). The mother pays particular attention and cares for these areas more than she does for other parts of the body. Because of the extraordinary attention that they receive, these areas become appropriate sites of pleasure and the child's libido is encouraged to focus on these locations. The mother's attentions inscribe these places as sexualized or erotogenic zones. The organization of the child's understanding of its body in terms of pleasure and body parts, several of which also have critical reproductive functions, is a process of erotic inscription. From a very early age, sexualized body parts have a deep-seated, perhaps unconscious, importance for people.

Again the importance for our project is not to assume that Neolithic figurines are prehistoric examples of erotogenic inscription nor that figurines can or even should be interpreted with psychoanalytical concepts, Lacanian or otherwise. There is scant support for either assumption. Rather the benefit is that we recognize that these areas of the body have attracted significant interpretive efforts from other perspectives in other disciplines. There is something important, perhaps inherently so, about sexual body parts which can be found in their frequent representation. Equally important, sexual characteristics, biological sex and gender are each important elements within the construction of personal identities and in the proposal of appropriate and inappropriate identities. Important issues of sexual politics, stereotyping and imposition of agreed realities revolve around these concepts and we will return to them in Chapter 6. There may also be value in considering sexual regions of the body as highly charged and potentially disruptive in character. Psychoanalysts propose that fear and desire dwell within sexuality, and that this combination produces a power and significance of its own that exist without need for justification. Sexual representation draws attention to differentiation of a particularly high status in structures of power and domination.

Much interpretive mileage has been made from the proposition that there is a higher proportion of female to male bodies among Neolithic figurines; reconstructions of a matriarchal society for the period are the most widely acknowledged. More critical examination of figurines has shown that the composition of figurine inventories is not so simply defined. While it is true that many clearly female representations are present (pubic triangles and breasts) and that exclusively male body parts (penises) are few, there are significant numbers of figurines which have neither male nor female parts represented (Bailey 1994a).

Anthropomorphic representation and the human scale

In Chapter 2, a series of paradoxes were proposed as a potential source of rhetorical power inherent in miniature three-dimensional objects. There is a further contradiction inherent in the making miniature of the human form: the paradox of miniature anthropomorphism. The paradox comes from the recognition that anthropomorphic figurines are the ultimate scaled-down abstractions. If the essential measure of scale is the human scale and if everything is judged in quantitative and qualitative reference to the human body, then the creation of scaled-down versions of the human body generates a critical problem: the human form is present at two different and conflicting sizes. The essential authority from which scale itself is determined is present at two different scales. Which version has priority? It is an irresolvable paradox and from its irresolution is released an energy of evocation for the spectator or handler.

Another dimension of the body and the human to be found within the miniature anthropomorph refers to another issue raised in Chapter 2: intimacy. As suggested there, a miniature is measured against the essential scale of the human body and any miniature representation can only be fully engaged when it is within the intimate zone of the holder, viewer or maker. Its existence is defined by its spatial and palpable relationship with the body. As a representation, a doll, a figurine or any other small anthropomorph collapses down onto the individual who is doing the holding and the looking. It is one-on-one in the most intimate sense possible.

Both the paradox of miniature anthropomorphism and the ultimate intimacy that is inherent in scaled-down representations of the human form further disturb our reactions to objects such as figurines or Barbie Dolls. Attempts to understand are unbalanced. Together with the paradoxes implicit in miniaturism that were proposed at the end of Chapter 2, the two paradoxes presented here, which are specific to reducing the human form, combine to further complicate the relationship between the figurine as a visual, palpable object and the person as spectator or handler.

Conclusions

A figurine is a body made object-ful; it is an object infused with the essence of the body. It is a conflation of the body (and all that it means) and the object (and all that it means). The power of the body is addressed in detail in Chapter 6. None of the discussion in the present chapter intends to suggest that Neolithic figurines are dolls, photographic portraits or works of art. Such equations are irrelevant; they seek the wrong information and they misunderstand meaning because they want to know what a figurine was. The preferred approach has been to ask how these more modern examples of anthropomorphic representation work and then to use the answers obtained to gain a fuller appreciation of Neolithic figurines as particularly powerful material culture. How do the modern examples succeed in doing what they do, whether that is empowering a child who has been sexually abused or becoming a focus for battles of the politically (in)correct as Barbie has become? What effects do they have on people and how do they stimulate those responses?

The relevance of the cases presented in this chapter is that, in each, representations of the human body engage people and their perceptions of themselves and others. They stimulate us to think. Dolls, portrait busts and mannequins engage us with our conceptions of identities and our senses of humanness, of who we are and of our relationships to others. In its essence, anthropomorphic representation questions viewers over viewers' existences. None of the representations offers a definitive answer about identity or humanness; however, each provokes us to think again about what it means to be human.

As stimulants for thought about ourselves and our relationships with others, figurines are best defined as philosophies. As philosophies, figurines have no exact meaning or function. Thus, it does not matter if particular figurines were used as toys by children, as referents or votives in ritual ceremonies or as portraits to remember distant or deceased family members. Each of these anecdotal equivalences is not an interpretation; each is merely a suggestion that fails to engage the real essences of figurines as active visual culture. It is most probable that any one figurine was understood, used if you wish, in different

ANTHROPOMORPHISM

ways by different people, or by the same person in different contexts and different places, or in the company of different people, or at different phases of different spectators' lives.

The fact that these philosophical stimulants were made in miniature is critical; miniaturism powers anthropomorphs in ways that are not available to the life-size or larger. Miniaturism reduces the massive scale of philosophical issues down to a manageable and manipulatable size. Miniaturism allows people to engage, display, discuss and handle issues of identity, status, inter-personal, inter-group differentiation in comfortable and unthreatening ways. Miniature anthropomorphism allows the abstraction of issues of human identity, individuality, difference and similarities from the highly complex, almost ethereal and inconceivable down to the simple, graspable and physical. However, just as it aids thought and enables philosophical contemplation about identity and humanity, miniaturism also complicates; it invests these engagements of issues of identity, status and philosophy with the mystery of the paradoxic and the unbalance of the uncanny.

Relevance to the Selevac figurines

How do these conclusions and the examples presented in this chapter refine and improve our understanding of the two Selevac figurines with which the discussion of anthropomorphism opened? One figurine is larger than the other though both are smaller than life-size. The larger figurine is a selective and partial human representation with reference neither to male- nor female-ness. The smaller one is more complete; it has legs. The smaller one has breasts that suggest female-ness though this is not secure: there is no pubic triangle and many men have chests that appear large either through a lack or an over-indulgence of exercise. The larger figurine has incised decoration on its face; the face of the smaller one is blank. In describing these figurines, there appears to be more that is missing than there is included. If this is all that we can say, then we have less of an interpretation than we started with. Let us ask a few more questions.

Who is represented?

Do the markings incised on the face of the larger figurine and the breasts modelled on the chest of the smaller one suggest analogies with particular beings? Was the ornamenting of the larger figurine an intention to represent a known, and thus named, individual? Was it to depict a particular god, goddess, spectre or fictional character, known and recognizable to a few or to many? Do the breasts on the smaller figurine make it a reference to women in general? Does it depict a particular female? Is a fixed relationship proposed between the asexual (larger) and the breasted (smaller) figurine? Is it better to see both figures as partial representations? Are they single, dislocated parts of some long-fragmented serial narration of a particular person's identity and status? Do they represent particular, separate but not mutually exclusive characteristics of one person's identity?

What are we to make of the size differential?

The excavators proposed that along with many shells, the smaller figurine was part of a necklace that hung around the neck of the larger one. Do the perforations in the arms of

ANTHROPOMORPHISM

the larger figurine tell us about another stage of suspension in which someone at Selevac wore the larger figurine which, in turn, wore the smaller figurine? Does this series of suspensions make a statement about or provoke contemplation over hierarchies of inter-relational power? Is it significant that the smallest anthropomorph occupying the lowest level of suspension has breasts? Is it significant that along with the figurines and the necklace shells was found a lump of ochre and that the ochre was probably used to decorate the body of the larger figurine, of the smaller, of the necklace wearer, or of all three? Does the series of size differentials multiply the figurines' significance? While the larger figurine invokes the paradox inherent in any individual miniature anthropomorph (i.e., that it is both miniature and potential essential scale), does the smaller figurine inject another level of the paradox: which of the three anthropomorphs has priority in establishing the essential scale?

What can we make of the absences?

What of the recognition that the two Selevac figurines are neither necessarily female nor male? In their absences, do the missing sexualized body parts provoke thoughts about male and female genitalia? Does their absence inspire a freedom of contemplation about sexual identity and sexual activity that would be constrained, predetermined or proscribed by the depiction and modelling of genitalia? On the other hand, does the absence of sexual referents remove any need for the spectator to think at all about issues of sexuality? Is it more avoidance than engagement? Are the figurines devoid of reference to sexualized activity or identity? Does the presence of breasts on the smaller figurine remove the element of sexuality from the viewers', the handlers', or indeed the wearer's contemplation? In its representation, is its sexual identity fixed and not open to debate?

What of the absence of most facial detail? In their absences, do the missing components of expression leave the viewers freer to imagine and provide their own feelings and emotions? What of the fact that legs are not represented on the larger figurine? What of the missing arms of the smaller and the missing feet and hands of both? Are these body parts left to the spectators' imagination as well? What of the recognition that neither of the figurines is a complete or precise representation of a living human body? Both are abstracted, cropped, distilled. Do all of these absences provide the real stimulus for thought, the true meaning of these representations?

Answers

Figurines are especially evocative, expressive objects. As such their uses, meanings and understandings will always remain a series of proposals and provocations. They will never escape into the apparent clarity and interpretive satisfaction found in statements of precise usage or of the representation of a particular man or woman.

Clearly the response to the questions raised above and the resolution of the initially contradictory readings of representation subjects, differentials in size and absences is not any single, exact answer. Each question and contradiction pushes us to accept that these objects had the powers to provoke the men, women and children who lived in the houses of Selevac to think about negotiable issues of identity, sexuality, status and the representation of the human. Indeed they lead us to conclude that far from being factual models or portraits, figurines are mutable, flexible philosophies of being human.

ANTHROPOMORPHISM

Towards the political

Out of these varieties of questions, conclusions and co-existent alternatives emerges one shared proposal: that the process of bodily representation is complex and our appreciation of it has a critical bearing on our interpretations of what figurines were and how they engaged the communities of southeastern Europe over a 3,000-year period. The representation of the body in visual culture and through visual events is central to society's construction not only of norms of sexual behaviour but of power relationships in general. Chapter 6 takes issue with the socio-politics of representations. Before we enter that discussion, Chapter 5 looks in detail at a second group of Neolithic figurines: those from the Cucuteni-Tripolye culture.

5

CUCUTENI/TRIPOLYE

In the summer of 1982, while widening and deepening a trench of his garden allotment near the village of Dumeşti (northeastern Romania), Ion Onofrei found several clay figurines. Researchers from the local museum widened the trench and recovered more figures, some complete pots and many sherds; all were characteristic of the A3 phase of the Cucuteni culture and date to the second half of the fifth millennium BC. Two years later Ruxandra Maxim-Alaiba carried out a larger excavation during which she uncovered the building which had originally contained the material that Mr Onofrei discovered (Maxim-Alaiba 1983–4, 1987). Of particular interest is a set of 12 figurines.

The figurines range from 14.0–20.0 cm tall, were shaped bent at the waist, and can be divided into two groups based on form and surface decoration (fig. 5.1). Six of the figurines are modelled with their legs apart and have very little decoration, though what is present is the same on each figure: one band of clay wrapped around the waist and another band running from the back over the shoulder and down diagonally across the chest and around the side of the body, forming a loop (fig. 5.1, left). Both the waist and the shoulder bands are decorated with groups of two, three or more parallel incised lines running diagonally across the bands. Each set of lines butts up against the neighbouring sets at a right angle; the impression is of a piece of fabric that has been twisted and folded over upon itself to make a narrow belt and shoulder strap. Each of these six, belted, figurines has small flattened pellets of clay in the place of breasts and all but one has a similar flattened pellet marking the navel. All six have a small penis pointing down between the slightly bowing, separated legs and all six have small impressions marking the knees. None have any detail of feet. Hands are also absent, though very short stumpy arms curve up from the shoulders. Expressionless heads with eyes and noses formed by pinching the clay sit on round necks. In summary, these six figurines have very little decoration and are all very similar to each other.

Clearly distinct from this first group are six other figurines which are highly decorated and all of which are very similar to each other (fig. 5.1, right). On one of these figurines, small flattened pellets of clay represent knees. On another, pellets mark the navel and knees and on two others, pellets mark breasts, navels and knees. On all six, legs are modelled tightly pressed together. Many fields of incised lines cover almost the entire surfaces of each of the figurines. Individual fields of parallel incisions butt up against neighbouring fields, sometimes at right angles, sometimes straight-on and separated only by a vertical line. In the centre of the figurines' fronts and backs the fields of incisions meet up in two vertical lines.

CUCUTENI/TRIPOLYE

Figure 5.1 Cucuteni figurines from Dumeşti; height *c.* 20 cm. Photograph by George Dumitriu (after Mantu *et al.* 1997).

Together, the fields of lines create a standard pattern across each figurine body. Though each field is slightly different from the others, there is very little overall variation. Exceptions occur on two figurines where a different pattern was incised on the chest: on one, a separate field with two tall U-shapes is marked off from the rest of the decoration by a wide V-shaped incision; on the other there are two chest motifs, an upper one, like the one just described, and a lower one that reaches down to the stomach and which consists of a single J-shaped incision.

As with the first set of six, mostly undecorated, belted figurines, the highly decorated ones are all very similar to each other in appearance and size. Though all 12 figurines were found together, differences in form and decoration provoke us to divide them into these two groups of six, and though each group is distinct from the other, there is tremendous similarity among the individual figurines of each set of six.

How are we to understand the Dumeşti figurines? What is the significance of the strict similarity between individual figurines within each group of six yet the substantial difference between the two groups? Does the presence of the penises on the undecorated figurines mean that one set represents males and the other six figurines females? If so, then why do the 'male' ones have the same size and shape of breasts as do the supposedly female ones? Why was so much attention directed at decorating the bodies of one set and not the other? Why are the bodies of the six decorated figurines completely covered? Why are the heads of each of all 12 figurines barely represented and the faces left plain and expressionless? What is the significance of the discovery of so many figurines together in one place? Are they a record of one particular activity or is their association merely an accident of deposition?

Ruxandra Maxim-Alaiba, who excavated Dumeşti, suggests that the six incised figurines are female, that the undecorated ones are male and that together, the 12 figurines represent a ritual dance, a ceremonial part of a domestic cult, which involved ancestor worship, and that each figurine represents a supernatural intermediary who acted between men [*sic*] and the gods (Maxim-Alaiba 1983–4: 105; 1987: 270). There are other anthropomorphic objects from Cucuteni/Tripolye contexts that have been associated with ritual dances. Hora-pots (i.e., hollow-topped vase-supports made from several anthropomorphic caryatid figurines: fig. 5.2) have been found at a number of sites: Frumuşica (Matasă 1946: 77, 123; illus. 27: 249); Larga Jijia; Traian-Dealul Fîntînilor; Dealul Bulgarului; Tîrpeşti;

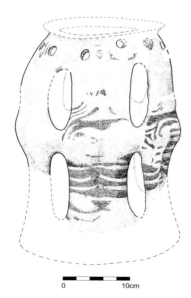

Figure 5.2 Hora-pot stand from Frumuşica (after Matasă 1946).

Drăguşeni; Luka Vrublevckaya; Grenovka (Marinescu-Bîlcu 1974c: 169–79); and three from Truşeşti (Petrescu-Dîmboviţa *et al*. 1999: 728). Hora-pots have been interpreted in terms of cult practices and magic dances.

One of the main authorities on Cucuteni figurines, Dan Monah, suggests that the building at Dumeşti, like structures at other contemporary sites, was a cult sanctuary (Monah 1997: 36–44). In the text that accompanies the superbly illustrated catalogue from the 1997 *Cucuteni* installation in Thessaloniki, Magda Mantu and Gheorge Dumitroaia describe the Dumeşti figurines as a cult complex and suggest that while the six incised examples are indeed female, the other six are not male but androgynous (Mantu and Dumitroaia 1997: 191).

There are many other assemblages of figurines from contemporary sites. From the PreCucuteni phase of the site of Poduri (i.e., the first half of the fifth millennium BC) comes a set of 15 figurines; again while some have intricate, body-covering decoration (though red paint in the place of incised lines) others are almost completely undecorated. A house from the site of Scânteia contains 75 figurines; a pit from the same site contains 24 (Mantu 1993a).[1]

The significance of sets of figurines has been addressed by Christina Marangou (1996) and John Chapman (2000a). In a lengthy and complex argument, Chapman suggested that concentrations of large numbers of figurines (particularly those found in houses destroyed by fire) are the remains of offerings that people had made to the soon-to-be destroyed (or in Chapman's terms 'dead') house (ibid.: 111). For Chapman an assemblage of figurines is a communal deposit. At work within them, and in other events of object deposition, are the principles which symbolize integrated community action that occurs at crucial moments in cycles of social practices (ibid.: 112).[2] Marangou suggests that associations and arrangements of anthropomorphic figurines, as have been found in a Cucuteni B context at Ghelăieşti (fig. 5.3) are the remains of events during which people purposefully assembled sets of miniature objects to represent preferred relationships among people, animals and the built environment of their community (Marangou 1996a:

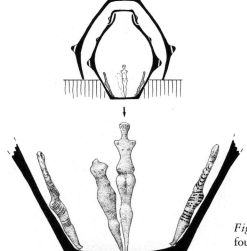

Figure 5.3 Four Cucuteni figurines as they were found at Ghelăieşti; figurine height *c*. 22 cm (after Monah 1997).

179). Thus, for Marangou, the groups of figurines and miniature objects (pots, furniture) reveal groups of somehow allied individuals, often women, in domestic settings.

But do these suggestions satisfy our search for the meaning of these objects? Though intriguing and positive as attempts to see objects working within complex community expressions of identity and local social history, are they any more than anecdotal suggestions for possible uses? Many thousands of figurines have been excavated from Cucuteni/Tripolye sites. How similar or different are they from the ones at Dumeşti or from the other assemblages of figurines? Can a closer look at these contemporary figurines refine our understanding of the Dumeşti assemblage?

Figurines from Cucuteni/Tripolye sites

Sites from the Cucuteni/Tripolye culture dating from 5000 to 3500 BC can be found across a broad area of northeastern Romania, Moldova and Ukraine, and have been categorized chronologically into the following phases: PreCucuteni/Tripolye A; Cucuteni A/Tripolye B1; Cucuteni A–B/Tripolye B2; and Cucuteni B/Tripolye C1 (Mantu 1998).

PreCucuteni/Tripolye A

Figurines from PreCucuteni/Tripolye A sites are decorated or undecorated, though many of the latter category have some limited surface treatment (e.g., one or two lines incised around the waist, at the tops of the thighs, and often marking the division between one leg and the other, or the modelling of small round breasts). These undecorated figurines have simple, squat bodies with very short stubby arms or with no arms at all (fig. 5.4). Faces are marked with impressions for eyes and slits for mouths.

Some of the decorated figurines have intricate, painted patterns of red lines tightly ordered in triangular or other rectilinear shapes. Individual fields of painted lines are tight against each other and give the appearance that they overlap and interweave as if they represent bands of cloth criss-crossing each other and wrapping around the body. By the end of the PreCucuteni phase (i.e., PreCucuteni III), organized patterns of incisions, like the decorated ones from Dumeşti (which date to the successive Cucuteni A/Tripolye B1 phase), start to appear and cover every part of the body. Spirals or sets of parallel incised lines are tightly grouped into interlocking and interwoven rectilinear fields. Particular decorative attention is focused on the buttocks where patterns range from spirals to hexagons to unrecognizable chaotic arrangements.

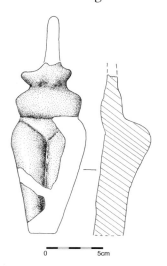

Figure 5.4 PreCucuteni figurine from Traian-Dealul Viei (after Marinescu-Bîlcu 1974a).

On some PreCucuteni/Tripolye A figurines decoration covers a much smaller proportion of the body: lines of shallow impressed dots or incisions running across the legs. On both decorated and undecorated figurines, heads were modelled very simply and faces were shaped by finger-pinching that formed two convex depressions for eyes and a vertical ridge for a nose. On these, eyes and mouth are occasionally marked by small, shallow impressions. There are also figurines without any facial detail but with elongated, tapered, undecorated neck-heads. A few have small round breasts formed by adding a pellet of clay to the body and then flattening it. A fragment of a figurine from Luka Vrublevckaya has the remains of an enormous penis that runs along the side of one thigh.[3] On a few others, at the base of abdomen, there is a small slit to represent the labia.

Many of the PreCucuteni/Tripolye A figurines were modelled in a sitting position: legs are straight and together, the body is bent at the waist and the torso and chest arch backwards. This body position is difficult to understand merely in terms of sitting, regardless of whether the figurines were sitting in miniature chairs (that sometimes accompanied them) or whether they were sitting on the ground. The angle of legs to torso throws back the chest, shoulders and neck to a degree that is not only unnatural, but also uncomfortable and disconcerting to look at. If these representations were intended to depict seated individuals, then they do not appear to be seated very comfortably. Was another position or purpose intended?

Common to many PreCucuteni/Tripolye A figurines is an extraordinary exaggeration in the size of the buttocks and thighs. On the undecorated examples, beyond the buttocks and thighs the body receives little attention; on the decorated ones, it is the buttocks that portray the greatest variation of the otherwise standard fields of incised decoration. Arms are seldom modelled; when they are depicted, they are tight to the body or reach to the head. On several figurines from Tîrpeşti and Traian-Dealul Fîntînilor, arms are modelled either so that elbows are on knees with hands placed on either side of the head (fig. 5.5), or they are wrapped around the chest, or they reach down to the abdomen (Marinescu-Bîlcu 1974a: fig. 73). There are also miniature pots which are scaled-down versions of regular vessels as well as uncommon shapes, and miniature chairs with square or rounded backs, and round tables (Marinescu-Bîlcu 1981: 43).

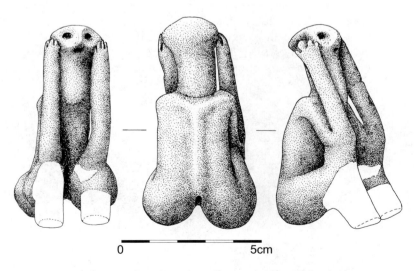

Figure 5.5 PreCucuteni figurine from Tîrpeşti (after Marinescu-Bîlcu 1974a).

Cucuteni A/Tripolye B1 figurines

Some of the Cucuteni A/Tripolye B1 figurines have the same uncomfortable posture as do the earlier ones (fig. 5.6). However, surfaces of many figurine bodies from the Cucuteni A/Tripolye B1 phase were intensively covered with regular fields of incised lines. Particular attention focused on placing irregular patterns on the buttocks, as before, but also on chests. Again, few figurines have any details applied to faces or heads. On some, a generic nose and empty depressions for eyes were formed by pinching the face. One or two examples have eyes marked by small, shallow impressions and mouths are depicted with a short horizontal incisions. In most cases, heads are undecorated, pointed, protrusions emerging from the shoulders but with little resemblance to the shape of a neck or a head.

While faces and heads carry little decoration, the rest of the bodies of the majority of Cucuteni A/Tripolye B1 figurines are covered with many dozens of vertical, horizontal or diagonal parallel incisions. Surfaces have sets of parallel incisions, most often running at the diagonal and most often meeting other sets in the centre of the front or the back of the body. Some of these lines are thin and tightly packed together; others are wider, deeper incisions spaced farther apart. The result is the same: body coverage is complete. As with the PreCucuteni/Tripolye A figurines, the patterning of individual fields of incisions is designed so that where they meet neighbouring fields the sets of parallel lines are at right angles to each other and give the impression of interweaving strands of fabric, of reeds or of other material (fig. 5.7).

On a few figurines the regularity of the fields of parallel incisions is broken, most often over the stomach, by the inclusion of interlocking spirals, curvilinear lines or short straight incisions. Such breaks in the otherwise regular patterning of body coverage are striking; they inject a more chaotic element into an otherwise highly ordered regime of surface decoration. However, even in these breaks from patterned coherence, there is a sense of order: spirals and rectilinear motifs are placed symmetrically opposed to each other. Curvilinear lines, dashes and short strokes that appear on one side of the torso are reproduced, flipped over, in the corresponding part on the other side of the stomach.

The attention given to covering the back and front of the torsos with decoration is equalled in the surface treatment of figurine legs. Again, parallel incised lines, either tightly packed or more widely spaced, leave no area uncovered. In many cases, lines are incised in strict, parallel order, running down from the hips to the ends of the legs (feet

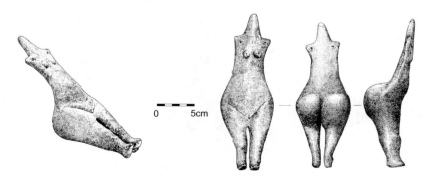

Figure 5.6 Cucuteni A figurine from Poduri (after Monah 1997).

CUCUTENI/TRIPOLYE

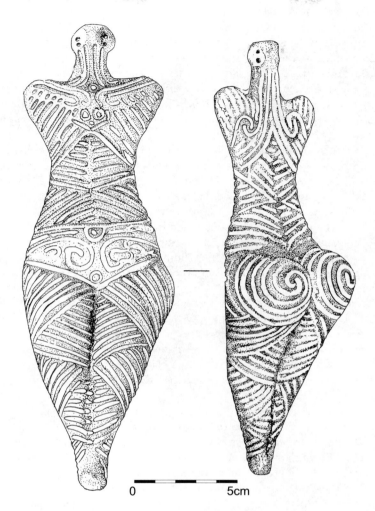

Figure 5.7 Cucuteni A figurine from Drăguşeni (after Monah 1997).

are seldom modelled); often each leg is covered by two fields of parallel incisions, one on the front, the other on the back with the two fields meeting on the outside of the leg. Lines run at a diagonal from the inside of the leg outwards or they are horizontal. Alternatively, on some figurines, the patterning is more haphazard; lines are incised with little attempt to maintain the parallel; indeed some lines cross others.

As in the previous phase, variation from the standardized sets of coherent parallel lines is found on two particular parts of the body: the chest and the buttocks. On some figurines, applications of clay add breasts or scarf-like wraps around the neck or chest. As before, breasts are small round pellets pressed into the chest, though not always in symmetrical positions and, at least in one example, with shallow impressions where nipples would have been located. On one example from Truşeşti, the application of a narrow band of clay, marked with parallel incisions, runs down from the shoulder, across

CUCUTENI/TRIPOLYE

one side of the chest, curves around the middle, and bears similarities with the incised designs positioned on the chests of other Cucuteni A/Tripolye B1 figurines (Petrescu-Dîmboviţa 1999). These incised designs wrap around one side of the chest. On a few figurines, running across the chest under the curving band of applied clay is an incised band of parallel horizontal lines which continues across the back of the figurine, though in diagonal parallel lines. Another Truşeşti figurine has a loop of applied clay running around the neck and down the front of the chest to the bottom of the stomach. Other figurine chests have curvilinear lines looping down from the shoulders, around low-relief breasts and finishing at the top of the abdomen. On yet other examples, short vertical lines descend from the base of the neck; in one case they form a zigzag that finishes at the tops of the breast which, again, are modelled in very low relief. Occasionally, the shoulders bear sets of three or four parallel lines running from front to rear. In many other cases, the chest carries no particular detail other than the mirrored or interwoven sets of parallel diagonal lines.

Like the chest, the buttocks stand out (literally) as a body part where variation in decoration is concentrated. If there is a common element to buttock treatment it is variation in pattern. On a few, the design of interlocking fields (perhaps representing interwoven pieces of material) is clear. On others each cheek is covered with two fields of parallel, vertical lines; the fields meet at a horizontal line running across the centre of the buttocks. Similar fields on other figurines do not have a horizontal separation and cover all of each buttock with vertical lines. On a few, short incised lines radiate out from the centre of each cheek. One of the figurines from Truşeşti has two semi-circles that touch in the middle of the buttocks and have their open sides pointing down to the leg or up to the torso. On yet others, a large incised spiral (or an interlocking set of spirals) covers each buttock; on another the spiral is to the side, on the hip, and the buttock bears several vertical lines.

There are also a large number of buttocks with surface treatment which does not fit into any readily recognizable, or repeated, pattern: overlapping sets of parallel incisions; overlapping non-parallel incisions; combinations of circles, spirals and rectilinear lines; sets of parallel right-angled lines; criss-crossed straight lines; large ovals with short lines within; and double loops of concentric semi-circles. Within this variety, some of the decorations were clearly planned and executed to a pre-set design; others appear to be nothing more (nor less) than unstructured attempts to fill the available space. The attention to the buttocks is of interest; buttocks are the most prominent of the very few body parts that are exaggerated by modelling on Cucuteni A / Tripolye B1 figurines. The absence of faces, the limited attention to breasts, and the absence of pubic triangles or labial slits makes the presence and variety of buttock decoration all the more noteworthy.

Body surfaces of Cucuteni A/Tripolye B1 figurines were also painted (Marinescu-Bîlcu 1981: fig. 188: 5): bands of red paint form horizontal, diagonal or semi-circular lines or spirals. Present in both the late PreCucuteni/Tripolye A and in Cucuteni A/Tripolye B1 phases, painted decoration is not common until the Cucuteni A–B/Tripolye B2 and Cucuteni B/Tripolye C1 phases. Indeed at Truşeşti, there were only two figurines with painting on them from the site's Cucuteni A/Tripolye B1 phase (Petrescu-Dîmboviţa et al. 1999: 727).

In striking opposition to the hyper-decorated incised and painted figurines are examples that have no surface decoration. Many undecorated figurines have featureless heads and faces, though some have small impressed dots for eyes and a thin slit for a

Figure 5.8 Cucuteni A3 figurine heads from Truşeşti (after Monah 1997).

mouth. A few have pellet breasts and at least two from Truşeşti have bulges where a penis would have been (Petrescu-Dîmboviţa et al. 1997: fig. 367). Body shapes are thin; occasionally an incised line circles the waist or an applied band of vertically incised clay wraps around the arms and waist. There are also small, face-shapes with simplest of detail (fig. 5.8).

Cucuteni A–B/Tripolye B2

While there are some decorative themes that continue from the Cucuteni A/Tripolye B1 phase, such as the use of incised decoration, the figurines from Cucuteni A–B/Tripolye B2 represent the body in different ways with greater attention to particular parts of the body, especially the head and face. While some figurine bodies are covered with parallel, interwoven or symmetrical sets of parallel incisions and spirals on buttocks, many others use incised lines that cover only parts of the body. Thus at Polivanov Jar II, incised lines are used both to cover large areas of the hips, legs and torsos as well as in more limited additions of smaller lines to the thighs. Where previous arrangements and positioning of incisions had suggested a generic, standard and complete body coverage, the new trends in decoration are more similar to what we might identify as clothing. Thus, long, narrow triangles filled with parallel horizontal lines cover the front of the legs between the waist and the knees (e.g., at Polivanov Jar II).[4] On other figurines from the same site, sets of very short parallel incisions run along other incisions and give the impression of a fringe attached to the edge of a garment.[5]

One of the most obvious changes is in body position, with the appearance of straight thin figurines with shoulders and hips of similar widths, and buttocks and thighs of less exaggerated width and prominence than in earlier phases. While some of these have dozens of parallel incisions over the torso and thighs, they are much less densely covered then were earlier figurines. As important a difference as the new elongated shape is the greater attention to modelling the head and face. Cucuteni A–B/Tripolye B2 heads are simple, flattened ovals of clay that sit upon short necks. Noses were modelled simply by pinching the clay. However, many heads have perforations where eyes should be and other perforations lower on the face, perhaps where the jaw line might have been if it were represented (but it is not). Some have three perforations running in a vertical line on each side of the face (e.g., at Soroki[6]); one from Karakušany[7] has thirteen perforations arranged in an arc running along the top of the head from one ear to the other. Perforations also appear at the shoulders and hips, usually one on each side of the body. Breasts are modelled, as before, by the application of small flattened pellets of clay.

On other elongated figurines, surface decoration is kept to a minimum: perforations for eyes and at the shoulders and hips; frequently, low-relief breasts; and single incisions around the waist. A few have a horizontal perforation through the front of the lower stomach or abdomen (Racovăţ[8]). Others have lines of small round impressions running from one shoulder to the waist: one example of this from Racovăţ also has a band of clay wrapped around the waist bearing four parallel rows of impressions.[9] On several figurines (e.g., from Polivanov Jar II,[10] Magala,[11] Karakušany[12]) there is a vertical incision, perhaps representing labia, within a pubic triangle. Others have the partially preserved base, or a thin vertical bulge, that represents a penis (Racovăţ,[13] Polivanov Jar II[14]). A more clearly depicted penis is made with the application of a tube of clay descending from a belt on a figurine from Šipency.[15] One example from Medvezha[16] has breasts as well as a penis bulge; also unusual is the face which has only one eye depicted (by perforation).

On some of the elongated figurines that have few or no incised decoration, the faint traces of painted lines suggest that much surface treatment has not survived. Where painted decoration is clear, as on several figurines at Vladimirovka,[17] widely spaced lines run horizontally across the chest, back and torso. Also depicted by painted decoration are parallel sets of diagonal lines running around the body (Krinički[18]), looping curves of lines across the chest and body (Krinički[19]), and sets of lines that meet in the centre of the front and back of the torso and which closely resemble the mirrored incisions of earlier phases (Krinički[20]).

While the heads of many of the Cucuteni A–B/Tripolye B2 figurines bear little detail other than perforation, a few are strikingly specific in expression and appearance. Two examples from Vladimirovka[21] have detailed faces with eyes, noses and mouths and flowing heads of hair; one has ears as well, the lobes of which are each perforated with two holes. From Krinički[22] another realistic head has eyes and mouth evoking a lively face as well as hair that is finely detailed with incisions (and a centre-parting).

Cucuteni B/Tripolye C1

The changes that distinguished the Cucuteni A–B/Tripolye B2 from the Cucuteni A/Tripolye B1 figurines continue in the material from Cucuteni B/Tripolye C1 sites: realistic faces (fig. 5.9), multiple perforations of heads, depictions of clothing. The practice

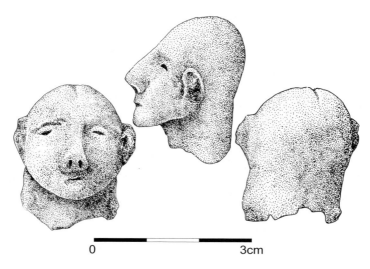

Figure 5.9 Tripolye C figurine from Kočeržincy (after Monah 1997).

of using incisions to cover the entire body has disappeared, though one or two incised lines encircle the waists of some figurines. Several examples from Suchostav[23] have four or five parallel horizontal lines running across the lower back just above the buttocks and three similar lines incised across the abdomen and above a pubic triangle that contains a vertical slit; a similar set of lines was found on a figurine from Košilovcy.[24] Many other figurines have similar vertical, labial, slits. As in the previous phase, a figurine from Košilovcy[25] has both breasts and a penis bulge and others[26] from the same site have similar bulges but no breasts. Other incised lines run down from the necks which are encircled by another line.[27] Many of the figurines have breasts, both as before, created with small, round flattened lumps of clay (a few[28] have tiny impressions where nipples should be) but also represented in new ways, with breasts more elongated, pointing out and hanging down from the chest.[29]

A few faces were modelled more realistically: eyes, nose, nostrils, ears and mouth are clearly depicted and evoke a specific appearance.[30] As in the previous phase faces are marked with perforations both in the positions where eyes should be and in other places: sometimes there are four perforations, other times six or eight (fig. 5.10). In a few cases[31] four large holes were surrounded by six or eight smaller perforations running around the edges of the head (fig. 5.11, left). Shoulders and hips also continue to be perforated, but again as with the heads, the numbers of perforations on figurines is greater than in the previous phase (e.g., four perforations on each side of the body on a figurine from Kočeržincy[32]). Some perforations are now made at the ends of stubby arms which are longer than previously and modelled to stick straight out or arch slightly upwards. One figurine from Košilovcy[33] even has fingers modelled at the end of its stumpy arms.

Lines made from series of small impressions and painting also decorate Cucuteni B/Tripolye C1 figurines. On several figurines from Suchostav[34] and Kunisovcy,[35] series of small impressions loop around the neck as if to represent a necklace. Less specific patterns cover the legs, buttocks and backs of a figurine from Čapaevka,[36] and fill in the area over the thighs of one from Košilovcy.[37] Painted decoration ranges from two criss-crossing lines across the chest and around the waist to many vertical lines descending from the waist,[38] to circles around eyes,[39] to looping lines around necks and down the front of chests,[40] to curving lines from shoulders to abdomen,[41] to solid painting of lower legs, and on to quite intricate short diagonals running down the front of the torso (fig. 5.11, right).[42]

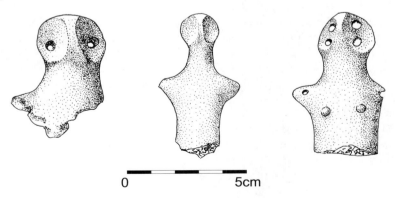

Figure 5.10 Cucuteni B figurines from Costeşti-Baia and Ghelăieşti (after Monah 1997).

CUCUTENI/TRIPOLYE

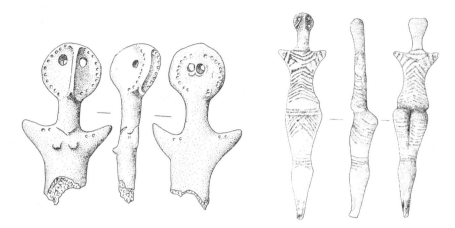

Figure 5.11 Figurines from Vîhvatinţi (left: Tripolye C) and Ghelăieşti (right: Cucuteni B) (after Monah 1997).

Even more specific and particular are two seated figurines from Košilovcy.[43] Other than the unconventional, downward-pointing breasts, only one had any decoration: four perforations through the face and two through the hips. Neither fits into any category yet discussed for Cucuteni/Tripolye. Together, the body positioning, the lack of surface treatment and the shape of the breasts create a figurine that is a long way from the tight and ordered repetition of body coverage that marked earlier phases. If in earlier phases there had been rules for the appropriate ways to decorate figurines, then those guidelines appear to have been relaxed. A more open system had replaced the tight strictures of the PreCucuteni/Tripolye A and the Cucuteni A/Tripolye B1 phases which controlled body form and dictated which body parts were represented and which were open to variation in decorative patterns.

Traditional approaches and explanations

For the Cucuteni/Tripolye region, figurine research benefits from several key works dedicated to figurines as well as chapters in excavation reports which describe and discuss figurine appearance, contexts and interpretation. The most comprehensive figurine-specific works are Dan Monah's *Plastica Antropomorfă a Culturii Cucuteni-Tripolie* (1997), Pogozheva's book *Antroporpfnaia Plastica Tripolia* (1983) and her article 'Die Statuetten der Tripolje-Kultur' published in *Beiträge zur Allgemeinen und Vergleichenden Archäologie*. Also, Silvia Marinescu-Bîlcu's volume on the PreCucuteni culture contains a chapter devoted to figurines (Marinescu-Bîlcu 1974a: 89–104). The excavation reports from Tîrpeşti (Marinescu-Bîlcu 1981), Truşeşti (Petrescu-Dîmboviţa 1999), and Drăguşeni (Marinescu-Bîlcu and Bolomey 2000) also contain particularly useful chapters on the figurines from these sites. There are many, many other articles and books on particular figurines or groups of figurines (e.g., Maxim-Alaiba 1987; Mantu 1993a, 1993b)[44] as well as several particularly useful attempts to transform the debate in original ways (e.g., Gheorghiu 1996, 1997, 2001; Chapman 2000a).

CUCUTENI/TRIPOLYE

As is common with the other regions examined in this book, considerable attention has focused on classifying Cucuteni/Tripolye figurines. Like many, Marinescu-Bîlcu focuses on the position of the body, for example, dividing PreCucuteni figurines into Type A (standing or semi-reclining statuettes) and Type B (sitting), identifying the latter as the 'classic' PreCucuteni type (Marinescu-Bîlcu 1974a: 89–95; 1981: 38), and then noting that A and B types each have sub-variants based on size, body parts presented and sexuality (e.g., A1–A4). Monah suggests a division of 'figurines' from 'statuettes'. The former, made with a coarse fabric, poorly fired, rarely decorated, have an ephemeral existence and were intentionally broken after ritual use. The latter, made with a finer fabric, were well-fired, are richly decorated, and had longer use-lives (Monah 1997: 220). Mircea Petrescu-Dîmboviţa uses the material from the excavations at Truşeşti to divide the figurines from the site into seated and flat figurines, though he notes that classification could be carried out based on body position (seated or standing), style (strongly stylized or realistic), sex (female, male or androgynous), and chronology (Cucuteni/Tripolye phasing) (Petrescu-Dîmboviţa *et al.* 1999: 727).

Considerable effort has also been invested in proposing referents for the various patterns of body decoration. Thus, Marinescu-Bîlcu sees the incisions as representation of tattoos, body ornaments, hairstyling, particular pieces of clothing, footwear or of other accessories such as waist- or shoulder-belts (Marinescu-Bîlcu 1981: 38; 2000a: 136; Dumitrescu 1979: 87–8). Others have suggested that incisions represent magic symbols (see Marinescu-Bîlcu 1981: 38).[45] Many investigators highlight the trends of decoration and form through the phases of Cucuteni/Tripolye. Monah notes that more realistic representations (with hair, jewellery, clothing) are made from the Cucuteni A–B/Tripolye B2 phase onwards, that incised decoration (popular in Cucuteni A/Tripolye B1) becomes less common over time, and that many figurines have a more 'svelte' form in later phases (Monah 1997: 220).

Furthermore, he suggests that, with Cucuteni B/Tripolye C1, realism increases, the elongated form becomes very popular, and the very small figurines which were made in earlier phases disappear (ibid.: 223). To explain the differences in shape and decoration, Marinescu-Bîlcu focuses on connections between different regional groups and resulting cultural influences (Marinescu-Bîlcu 1981: 38). Thus, the appearance of incised decoration on PreCucuteni figurines was the result of contacts with the Gumelniţa culture of southern Romania and northern Bulgaria (Marinescu-Bîlcu 1974a: 96; 1974b); similar contacts were also responsible for the introduction of perforations in later phases (Marinescu-Bîlcu 2000a: 133).[46]

In one of the most provocative attempts to broaden the debate, the Romanian art historian and theorist Dragoş Gheorghiu has argued that the incised patterning on many of the Cucuteni/Tripolye figurines represents funerary shrouding and that the figurines represent ancestors (Gheorghiu 1996, 1997, 2001). The absence of arms, the close modelling of the legs and the particular patterning of the incised (and painted) decoration all support Gheorghiu's suggestion.[47] On its own, the proposal that figurines represent the deceased is supported by little other than the assumption that figurines are direct representations of Neolithic reality. However, Gheorghiu's focus on the body and its significance in society is important. Gheorghiu contends that the body has particular power within communities and that at certain times it is necessary to hide or control this power. The covering of the body with fabric after death either protects and conserves the power within the ancestor's body or protects the rest of the community from the effects of that power. Gheorghiu also examines possible connections between the highly fragmented condition of most Cucuteni/Tripolye figurines, their scattered distribution across sites in structures and rubbish pits, and contemporary attitudes to the human body after death (Gheorghiu 2001: 79). Gheorghiu argues that figurines (as ceramic bodies) and corpses (as flesh and bone bodies) were both subject to dismemberment and decapitation; thus the physical treatments of figurines (breakage and discard) and bodies (dismemberment and discard) follow the same community perception of the body (Gheorghiu 2001: 79). The value in Gheorghiu's approach may not be in the direct connection of figurines to death but in the way that he approaches the figurines in dimensions of the human body and the potential power that the body has within societies.

In all of these approaches to Cucuteni/Tripolye figurines, the goal is either to understand the material in terms of diachronic trends in morphology and patterning or to find real-life Neolithic correlations to figurine body decoration (e.g., tattoos, clothing or shrouds) or to activities. Thus, Marinescu-Bîlcu has suggested that particular representations of arms give those figurines a ritual meaning (Marinescu-Bîlcu 1981: 40), and that figurines are representations of ritual dances (Marinescu-Bîlcu 1974c). Even Gheorghiu's refreshing arguments investigating the links between figurines and death, and Chapman and Marangou's suggestions, are limited to their assumptions that figurines are direct reflections of Neolithic reality.

Like Maxim-Alaiba's conclusions on the set of figurines from Dumeşti, as well as Gheorghiu's proposals for body-wrapping and Marinescu-Bîlcu's invocation of ceremonial dancing, most interpretations place the meaning of Cucuteni/Tripolye figurines in the contexts of rituals and ceremonies.[48] Petrescu-Dîmboviţa suggests that figurine-use had a magic-religious goal (Petrescu-Dîmboviţa *et al*. 1999: 726). Marinescu-Bîlcu has been most specific about this, arguing that the figurines 'foreshadow the divinity of the time', that the female ones represent the Great Goddess, the male ones the goddess's 'acolyte', and that the divinities in general relate to magic practices. While Marinescu-Bîlcu denies the presence of a pantheon (Marinescu-Bîlcu 2000a: 135–6), Gimbutas, as expected, takes the issue further. She describes a set of 32 PreCucuteni/Tripolye A figurines from a building at Sabatinovka II in terms of a tableau that suggests a mystery of death and regeneration (Gimbutas 1989a: 133). Because they have no arms and have snake-shaped heads, Gimbutas concludes that the Sabatinovka figurines were created in the image of the Snake Goddess (ibid.: 133), and the building in which the figurines were found is identified as a house-shrine dedicated to the Snake Goddess. Gimbutas sees the long bench (or table) built against the building's rear as an altar; on the altar are 16 figurines including one who holds a long, straight, thin cylinder of clay, which Gimbutas interprets as a baby snake. 'The baby snake is the bridge, an umbilical cord linking the subterranean womb with the living world. Initiation rites could have been practised in this shrine' (ibid.: 133).[49]

As with other regions covered in this book, previous research either restricts itself to the descriptive typology or loses itself in anecdotal reverie about ancestor worship and magic-cults of goddess veneration. Neither outcome is satisfactory, especially in terms of the issues that have been raised in the previous chapters. Unlike many sites in other southeast European regions, those of the Cucuteni/Tripolye culture have been well excavated and published. Perhaps an understanding of the cultural, social and archaeological contexts can broaden and refine an understanding of these figurines.

CUCUTENI/TRIPOLYE

Cucuteni/Tripolye archaeology

The archaeology of the Cucuteni/Tripolye phenomenon has a long history; recent conferences celebrated over a century of research (Petrescu-Dîmboviţa *et al.* 1987; Dumitroaia and Monah 1996), exhibitions have produced well-illustrated catalogues (Mantu *et al.* 1997) and there are good historiographies available (Zbenović 1996; Mantu 1998: 15–28). The publication of large-scale excavations of several sites provides good contextual information (e.g., Tîrpeşti, Truşeşti, Hăbăşeşti, Drăguşeni) (fig. 5.12).[50] Regional surveys document site location and distribution, and provide useful bibliographies (e.g., Monah and Cucoş 1985; Sorokin 1995); detailed studies review cultural evolution, chronology and interpretations (Marinescu-Bîlcu 1974a; Mantu 1998); synthetic analyses have attacked particular topics: Ellis's study of ceramic technology (Ellis 1984); Popovici's study of settlement (at least for one phase of the phenomenon) (Popovici 2000).

Geography and chronology

Cucuteni/Tripolye refers to a collection of sites that covers an area of eastern Romania, Moldavia and Moldova (the Cucuteni component) and to a culturally and chronologically corresponding sequence of sites to the east in the Ukraine (the Tripolye component). The phenomenon dates from 5000 BC to perhaps as late as 3000 BC.[51] The traditional subdivisions within the Cucuteni/Tripolye culture run from PreCucuteni/Tripolye A through Cucuteni B/Tripolye C and are based on chronology as much as on differences in ceramic technology, morphology and decoration.[52]

The built environment

Frequently, Cucuteni/Tripolye settlements were established in parts of the landscape where local geomorphology provided natural barriers to access: sites on high river terraces or at river canyon edges (Ellis 1984: 48–9; Markevic 1981: 70–2). Natural features were supplemented by man-made ditches and banks or, as at Cucuteni and Malnaş, by wooden and clay structures (Monah and Cucoş 1985: 45; Popovici 2000: 262; Florescu 1966: 27; László 1993; Florescu and Florescu 1999: 230–1). At Ariuşd there was a ditch flanked by banks; rows of wooden stakes created palisades on top of the inner ditch, outside of the outer ditch, and at the base of the ditch itself (Monah and Monah 1997: 58; Székély 1988). Other sets of ditches and banks and boundary markers made of stones have been found at Hăbăşeşti (Monah and Monah 1997: 57), Traian-Dealul Fîntînilor (ibid. 1997: 58) and the eponymous site of Cucuteni.

Sites ranged in size from less than 20 buildings in an area no larger than a hectare to several hundred structures spread over dozens of hectares (Popovici 2000: 261; Monah and Cucoş 1985: 43; Ellis 1984: 185, table 23). While some sites had temporary uses and narrow functions, such as salt extraction at Solca (N. Ursulescu 1977), Cacica (Popovici 2000: 261) and Lunca (Dumitroaia 1987a, 1994), most were settled village concentrations of buildings and activity areas.[53]

Buildings had rectangular floor-plans of 40 to 100 sq m, though some were substantially larger, reaching 350 sq m (Monah and Monah 1997: 60) and a few had more than one storey (e.g., at Racovăţ). Many structures contained hearths made from flat stones laid on the floor and benches made of wood and clay built along interior walls.[54] Grinding-stones, concentrations of debris and tools from particular activities, such as

CUCUTENI/TRIPOLYE

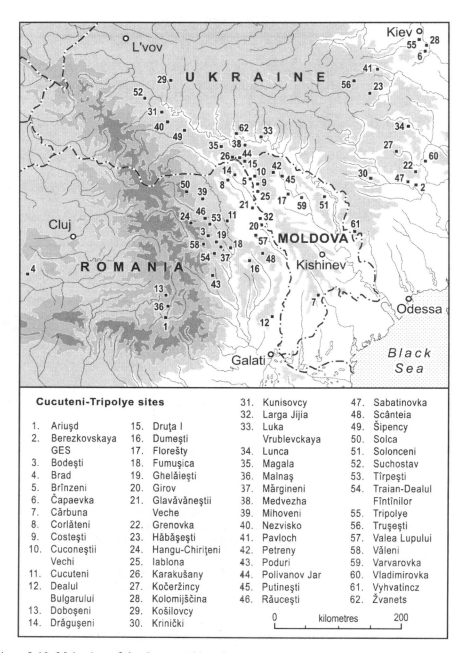

Figure 5.12 Main sites of the Cucuteni/Tripolye cultures mentioned in the text.

CUCUTENI/TRIPOLYE

stone-tool making and repair, and large numbers of ceramic vessels are common contents. Less frequently used for dwelling were circular structures dug into the ground (not unlike the pit-features of Hamangia sites to the south or at Makriyalos in Thessaly; see pp. 173–4); pit-features were common in earlier phases, especially in Bessarabia, where they were eventually replaced by surface-level structures (Monah and Monah 1997: 60). Some above-ground buildings have two or even three rooms: Building 12 at Tîrpeşti has three rooms, each of which has benches along its walls and one of which has an oven (Marinescu-Bîlcu 1981); Building 3 at Vladimirovka VIII has three rooms, each of which contained an oven (Markevic 1981; Monah 1992).

The spatial arrangement of buildings within the boundaries of individual sites was structured in relation to particular activities, such as pottery manufacture, or to less obvious social and political divisions (Popovici 2000: 264); in some cases there is no recognizable organizing principal.[55] At many sites, buildings were arranged in clusters: Traian-Dealul Fîntînilor (V. Dumitrescu 1963: 63; 1946); Drăguşeni (Marinescu-Bîlcu 1997: 170); Druţa I and Duruitoarea Nouă (Sorokin 1997: 13). At Brînzeni III, two, three or even four buildings were constructed close to each other in different parts of the site (Markevic 1981). A similar pattern is evident at Truşeşti (Petrescu-Dîmboviţa *et al*. 1999: fig. 423). At other sites, structures were arranged in parallel rows: Hangu-Chiriţeni (Popovici 2000: 261: 52–3, pl. 4); Balta lui Ciobanu (Popovici *et al*. 1992); Nezvisko; Vasilievka; Druţa I and Duruitoarea Nouă (Sorokin 1997: 13). At Cuconeştii Vechi I, there is a single row of structures (ibid.: 75), at Brînzeni III five buildings in the southern section of the site were built close to each other in a row (Markevic 1981), and at Truşeşti, six small buildings run along the southeastern edge of the site (Petrescu-Dîmboviţa *et al*. 1999: fig. 423).

The most common arrangement of Cucuteni/Tripolye structures was the placement of buildings in a circle at the centre of which was built an isolated structure. Thus, at Hăbăşeşti, two sequences of habitation are marked by two rings of 14 and 20 houses respectively. At the centre of each circle was one building that Dumitrescu assumed played a more important role in the community than did the others (V. Dumitrescu *et al*. 1954: 18, 201). In the Cucuteni A phase at Tîrpeşti, 17 buildings formed a circle around another structure, though the latter was not placed in a central position (Marinescu-Bîlcu 1981: 51). At Ioblona I, there are two circles of 29 and 30 buildings, and the buildings in each circle were arranged around a common yard; between the two circles were four other buildings. Around the periphery at Kolomijščina more than two dozen buildings form a large circle and share a common orientation with the shorter sides of their rectangular floor plans aligned with the circumference of the circle (Passek 1949); a larger building and several smaller ones sit at the centre of the circle. At Dobrovody, more buildings, more tightly concentrated, form a series of concentric rings within the site (Masson *et al*. 1982). At Putineşti III buildings were grouped in a semi-circle around open spaces, though it is unclear if all of these buildings were in use at the same time (Popovici 2000: 261). Other circles of buildings have been found at Corlăteni (Răşcani), Berezkovskaya GES (Sorokin 1993: 78), and Onoprievka (Tsvek 1996: 101).

Buildings in PreCucuteni sites were made from post and wattle-and-daub construction with larger pieces of timber placed on the ground to make a rectangular floor plan, sometimes with more than one room (Marinescu-Bîlcu 1974a). In the later Pre-Cucuteni phases, platforms made of logs, clay, sand, gravel and plant materials (sometimes fired) formed a platform upon which structures were erected (Ellis 1984: 20, after

CUCUTENI/TRIPOLYE

Marinescu-Bîlcu 1981). A good example of a PreCucuteni site is the settlement at Tîrpeşti (Marinescu-Bîlcu 1981: 24–49) which had two periods of use from this phase.

Tîrpeşti

Evidence for the earliest occupation of the site (end of PreCucuteni II) consists of three large pits located away from the main area of occupation, several pits within the settlement, a hearth and a small ditch. The ditch was over a metre deep, as wide at its surface, and enclosed an area of over 2000 sq m The large, extra-mural pits were created when people dug out clay to use for building; the pits were later filled in with sherds, bones, shells, ash, daub, fragments of figurines and a wide range of other broken and complete objects (Marinescu-Bîlcu 1981: 26–7). The record for the second phase of Tîrpeşti's PreCucuteni occupation (i.e., PreCucuteni III) is fuller (fig. 5.13, top). All of the buildings at the settlement were bounded by a larger ditch, almost 2.0 m deep, more than 3.0 m across, which enclosed an area of 4,600 sq m. The earlier ditch was filled in and was built over by PreCucuteni III structures (ibid.: 25). During the PreCucuteni III phase, Tîrpeşti consisted of ten rectangular buildings (large – 35–77 sq m, as well as small – 12–30 sq m) some of which had benches built along walls and one of which was constructed on a raised platform and had a particularly well-built oven (2.0 × 1.6 m). Other hearths, constructed on the ground and plastered with 2–3 cm of high-quality clay mixed with sand, were found both inside and between buildings. Associated with many buildings are shallow pits, most probably first dug to get clay before being used as rubbish dumps. Several buildings contained stone-grinding querns and some contained small copper objects (e.g., hooks, loops and bits of wire). Concentrations of material were not limited to buildings or pits: one area of 20 sq m contained a large concentration of pottery, almost three dozen figurines (most of which were fragmentary) and various miniature chairs and tables (ibid.: 26). All of the buildings were abandoned after being burnt, and two lie directly underneath a building from the later, Cucuteni A, phase of the site. Faunal remains suggest that during the PreCucuteni use of Tîrpeşti, domesticated cattle was the most common animal consumed, with domestic pig and sheep and goat less important; wild animals were very few but included red deer (Necrasov and Ştirbu 1981).

Many more buildings date to the Cucuteni A phases of Tîrpeşti. At a regional level, there are more sites distributed across a wider area and the sizes of individual settlements increased during this phase (Popovici 2000: 263; Ellis 1984: 184; Zaharia et al. 1970; Monah 1982; Păunescu et al. 1976; Coman 1980; Markevic 1973). Cucuteni A and A–B sites are increasingly large; phase B sites mark the culmination of the trend (Ellis 1984: 185). Sites are now found consistently located in naturally fortified positions (ibid.: 48).

During the Cucuteni A phase at Tîrpeşti, the earlier ditch was reused, widened and deepened, a second ditch was dug parallel to it, and a wooden fence was erected (Marinescu-Bîlcu 1981: 50). Buildings were distributed on both sides of the ditches and fence, though the majority was on the inside (fig. 5.13, bottom). Seventeen buildings date to this phase and most had hearths, though several hearths were in the open areas of the settlement. Ranging in size from 32 to 96 sq m (ibid.: 51), buildings were arranged in a circle around Dwelling 1 (9 × 5 m in size) with a fairly large open area at the centre of the settlement which Marinescu-Bîlcu interpreted as a place for meetings or ceremonies, or for keeping livestock (ibid.: 51).

CUCUTENI/TRIPOLYE

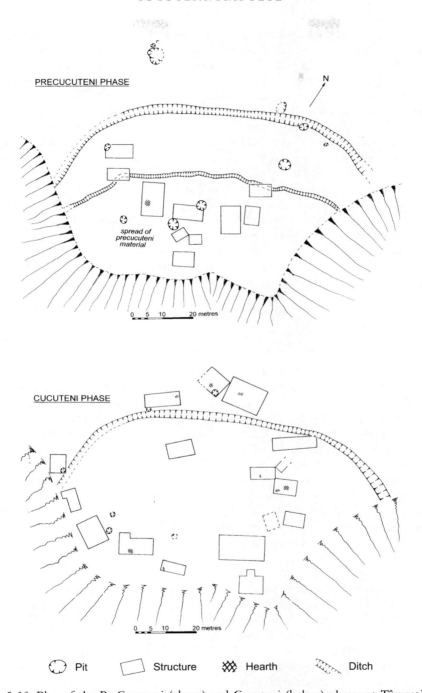

Figure 5.13 Plan of the PreCucuteni (above) and Cucuteni (below) phases at Tîrpeşti (after Marinescu-Bîlcu 1981).

CUCUTENI/TRIPOLYE

Individual buildings reveal evidence for structural repair and replacement: Dwelling 1 had several sequences of replastering and a hearth that had been repaired (ibid.: 73); Dwelling 5 had similar sequences of replasterings and repairs to its hearth. Outside of the ditch boundary, in Dwelling 9, there is evidence for the production of stone tools and inside the settlement a pile of partly worked diatomite raw material for tool-making was found to the west of Dwelling 21. The largest building (Dwelling 12) had thick wall plaster (8–15 cm thick), daub flooring (10–15 cm thick that had been recoated several times), at least three rooms, several ovens and grinding-stones, copper objects, figurines, miniature ceramic vessels and a sealing-stamp with a spiral pattern on it. Inside and outside of the building were large storage pots, some of which had ladles inside.[56] While there are copper objects, figurines, grinding-stones and ovens in other buildings, the combination of attention to the repair and maintenance of the building's internal appearance (the replastered walls and recoated floor), the location of storage jars and ladles and, especially, the sealing-stamp suggest that Dwelling 12 had a particular function or meaning within the Tîrpeşti community, perhaps one rooted in the storage and distribution of goods. The faunal record for the Cucuteni phase at Tîrpeşti provides much the same picture as for the PreCucuteni phase: domestic dominates over wild with cattle the most frequent animal consumed. All but one (Dwelling 17) of the Cucuteni A buildings were destroyed by burning.

Truşeşti

A larger Cucuteni A site has been excavated at Truşeşti (Petrescu-Dîmboviţa *et al*. 1999). The site covers 3 ha of a naturally isolated terrace spur to which the inhabitants of the site added a ditch on the eastern side. Almost 100 buildings and over 60 building annexes were uncovered and nearly 200 pits were located both within and outside of buildings. As at Tîrpeşti, the pits had originally been dug for clay and then filled with debris and rubbish. Some pits were used to store or prepare food or provisions; they contained large storage vessels as well as smaller pots, flint flakes and carbonized wood (ibid.: 720). Building size ranged from well over 60 sq m (the largest was 120 sq m and four others were 90 sq m) to less than 20 sq m: the majority were between 20 and 60 sq m and the remainder were evenly split between the large and the small (ibid.: 659–61, 741). Floors were made of wooden and clay platforms and floor-plans were rectangular. Buildings do not share a common orientation to each other and no easily recognizable pattern is evident in their arrangement, though in several places buildings may have been built in lines (Petrescu-Dîmboviţa 1963: 172–6).

Without a more refined understanding of the internal micro-chronology of building activity it is impossible to determine whether or not all structures that make up concentrations of buildings or lines of structures were contemporary (Popovici 200: 261). However, the excavators were able to identify three sub-phases of Cucuteni A activity at Truşeşti (Petrescu-Dîmboviţa *et al*. 1999: 670, figs 425–7). In the earliest phase[57] there were nine structures and more than a dozen pits spread across the site. In the centre of the site were four buildings, relatively close together, two of which contain remains of pottery-firing kilns. Further to the east (though not as close to each other as were the central buildings) are three more structures, and still farther to the east are two more buildings. Forty-one buildings date to the second phase of activity[58] during which a ditch was dug to bound the site to the east. Structures are strung along the length of the terrace

CUCUTENI/TRIPOLYE

with no shared orientation of floor-plans, though all buildings have a common rectilinear form. Along the southern terrace edge, at the eastern edge of the settlement, six small buildings were constructed in a row. At the western end of the village three structures contained ceramic kilns. In the third Cucuteni A phase[59] at Truşeşti, there are only 11 buildings with small clusters in the northeast and southeast of the settlement and more isolated structures in the southcentral and western portions.

At many Cucuteni/Tripolye sites, despite the recovery of floor-plans, ovens, benches and other architectural features, it is difficult to reconstruct particular activities in particular places. In a few cases, however, some suggestions can be made. Thus at Drăguşeni, several buildings contained large amounts of raw material and debris from the production of antler tools (Dwelling 16), flint tools (Dwelling 16 bis), and ground stone axes (Dwelling 14) (Marinescu-Bîlcu and Bolomey 2000: 183). However, for the majority of buildings and pits it is difficult, if not impossible, to propose with any certainty specific activities in particular places. On the one hand, the hundreds of pits at Truşeşti contain many thousands of artefacts. It is most likely that these pits were filled in with refuse and rubbish from activities that took place in and around the buildings. Despite the excavator's best efforts to reconstruct the sequences of pit-filling at Truşeşti, it is very difficult to determine if a pit was filled in a single event or in a series of perhaps widely separated events. If pit-fills are the results of gradual accumulations of rubbish from activities that took place within and among buildings, then it is difficult to reconstruct any particular activities. Furthermore, if buildings were periodically (frequently, even) cleared of debris which was then deposited in the pits, then the contents of the houses that excavators recovered may reveal very little *in situ* evidence for what people did, how often they did it or, even, exactly where they did it. In light of these difficulties, the excavators of Truşeşti suggested that several of the buildings at the site may have had special significance to their occupants. Thus, two of the buildings (nos 24 and 40) are proposed as 'community constructions'; others were assigned special cult functions due to the concentrations of figurines found within them (Petrescu-Dîmboviţa *et al.* 1999: 741). Similar arguments for the special status of structures at village centres have been made for Mărgineni where a small building in the middle of the village had an unusually constructed floor (made of a 5 cm layer of smoothed clay but without the beam platform that was common for other buildings at the site) and contained an oven, a copper axe, a sculpted anthropomorphic head made of clay and chaff (Monah and Monah 1997: 65).

Figurine distribution and concentrations

In the amount of detailed archaeological information provided for all of the individual pits and buildings, Truşeşti is an exception to most Cucuteni sites. From this information, it is clear that the distribution of figurines among different features is unequal. Not all pits and buildings contained figurines; of the 102 buildings listed in the final excavation report, 41 (40 per cent) contained figurines though most of those buildings (28) contained only one example. Two buildings (nos 16 and 87) had five figurines each; Building 2 had four. Only 19 of the 196 pits Truşeşti pits had figurines in them. Of these, only one (Pit 40) contained more than one figurine; it contained 14. In fact, most pits and buildings contained no figurines at all.

At one level then there is a clear pattern here. Indeed, ignoring the complexities of depositional practices and taphonomy, if one needed the security of statistical significance

109

CUCUTENI/TRIPOLYE

it would be possible to show that the figurine concentrations in these three buildings (nos 2, 16 and 87) and pit (no. 40) are statistically significant. But what do these concentrations really tell us? Do the buildings and the pits with extraordinarily high concentrations of figurines possess a special meaning or function? As noted above, it is common to read that the pits or the buildings with disproportionately high concentrations of figurines are the remains of sanctuaries for magical or religious activities. What other information do these features contain that might help us to understand the concentrations of figurines within them and, in turn, in what ways does such information help us towards a fuller meaning for Cucuteni/Tripolye figurines?

Pit 40 dates to the first phase of the Cucuteni A occupation at Truşeşti and is located on the southern-central edge of the site (Petrescu-Dîmboviţa et al. 1999: 202). When the pit was excavated, it had a top circumference, at modern ground level, that measured 2.20 × 2.0 m and when it was fully emptied, it was 3.4 m deep. The soil of the pit-fill was coffee brown with remains of carbon and traces of burning in the upper part and lenses of ash in the lower parts. The pit was distinct from others at Truşeşti in terms of the richness of its contents: a flat stone axe, a horn chisel, cups with incised, channelled or painted decoration, fragmentary high-necked vessels with rounded bodies, pot supports, incised bowls, fragments of binocul-pots,[60] broken ceramic scoops and ladles, fragments of bases from miniature footed pots, a fragment of a miniature cup, fragments of zoomorphic pot lugs, and six fragments of zoomorphic figurines.

Of the 14 figurines found in Pit 40, ten are decorated with incisions. Of these, six are fragments of hips and thighs, one is a fragment of one side of a chest-to-knee section, one is a fragment of a thigh, one is a fragment of a leg from the thigh down, and one is a fragment of the body from the waist upwards. Four of the figurines are undecorated: two are fragments of one side of the hip-to-foot section, one is a fragment from the chest-to-knee section of one side of a body, and one is a fragment from a torso. In addition to the figurines there were found isolated fragments of painted vessels whose decoration may be anthropomorphic, though not enough of the pot is preserved to be certain. Also found was a 10-cm-long ceramic object, roughly shaped as a tapering cylinder, with concavities at each end and which the excavators suggest is a phallus (Petrescu-Dîmboviţa et al. 1999: 202). In light of the heavily fragmented condition of the figurines and the other material it is difficult to read the contents of Pit 40 as anything other than rubbish fill.

The relatively high concentrations of figurines from Buildings 2, 16, and 87 cannot be explained away so easily. Building 16 is of average size (8 × 5.8 m) (Petrescu-Dîmboviţa et al. 1999: 49) and contains, in addition to numerous fragments of ceramics, very few other objects: two flint tools, a flat stone axe and three fragments interpreted as 'ornithomorphic protomes' (Petrescu-Dîmboviţa et al. 1999: fig. 384). Like the ornithomorphs, the five figurines are broken, though they were found in the same part of the building (i.e., the northeast corner). What does the concentration of figurines in this structure tell us? Was this a special building? Perhaps the key to the presence of figurines in these places is to be found in the ways in which people abandoned the structure. Clearly, it is important that the figurines (and most of the other objects in the house) are fragments. There is no evidence to connect the objects that were recovered from the building during excavation and the many different activities that must have occurred there during (and after) the structure's primary use-life. Is what we see anything other than the scattered, splintered and partial fragments of a portion of what people once did there?

CUCUTENI/TRIPOLYE

Building 87 is a bit smaller (5 × 6 m) than Building 16 but contained many more objects in addition to five figurine fragments (and a zoomorphic figurine); there is also an annex (no. 55) located 1.0 m to the northeast of the building which contained another figurine fragment as well as a lot of ceramic fragments and animal bone (Petrescu-Dîmboviţa 1999: 169–70). In the building, there are the remains of an oven, more animal bones, flint tools, scrapers, a ground stone chisel, a broken ground stone axe, a broken flint core, lots of sherds of incised, painted and undecorated ceramics, a fragment of a painted lid, one leg from a small table, a small cone and a miniature pot (Petrescu-Dîmboviţa 1999: 169–70).

Building 2 is larger (9 × 10 m) and, in addition to four anthropomorphic figurines, contained an oven, two simple grinders and a stone scraper, four fragmentary cups, two of which have incisions and two of which have channelled decoration, a vase support, a high-necked, round-bodied pot with incised decoration, a fragment of a similar vessel, an undecorated bowl, a painted zoomorphic head on a fragment of pottery, a ladle, one complete storage pot and fragments of another. All of the figurines are fragmentary: two are densely incised, one has a single incision at the hip and the other has a relief band around neck, shoulders and waist: three preserve nothing more than one section of a hip and thigh; the other lacks one leg below the knee and the other the legs from the hip down (Petrescu-Dîmboviţa 1999: 31, figs 356:10; 358: 5; 366: 4 and 8).

Rubbish or ritual?

What is the likelihood that these concentrations of figurines, both those in Pit 40 and in Buildings 2, 16 and 87 are merely results of random discard or, even, concentrated rubbish disposal? The fact that most of the figurines in pits (but also in buildings) are fragmentary suggests that this may be the case. Indeed Petrescu-Dîmboviţa suggests that most pits at Truşeşti were dug when people extracted clay for building structures and pots and then filled in with domestic rubbish (Petrescu-Dîmboviţa 1999: 219). Other pits (about 30 or so) were dug specifically as places to deposit rubbish. To be fair, Petrescu-Dîmboviţa argues that some pits were used first in ritual practices after which they were quickly in-filled and then built over by the platforms of later buildings. Pit 40 was an exception. It was dug for the extraction of yellow clay used in building and then the pit had a short-lived ritual use when cult objects were deposited in it, though after the acts of deposition it is likely that the pit was used to dispose of rubbish (ibid.: 219, 221–2).

If anything, one could argue that the buildings and pits with multiple figurines, especially in fragmentary form, are more likely to represent accumulations of discarded material and thus to refer to several (many, even) activities and several sets of objects. Trying to read any single activity from these deposits would be an error; attempting to impose a single, specific meaning to the building or pit, such as ritual or religious would be equally misleading.

A very different suggestion for the significance of rubbish disposal and the function of these and other similar pits from contemporary sites has been made by John Chapman (Chapman 2000a: 49–104; 2000b; 1996: 210–14). Chapman argues that pits like the ones at Truşeşti contain the remains of deliberate acts during which objects such as figurines, but also ceramics and bones, were intentionally broken and deposited as part of the 'nexus of social relations' (Chapman 2000a: 49); people intentionally broke and deposited objects (ritual and others) as a means of 'enchaining' social relations (ibid.: 104). These arguments are unconvincing, not because they may be incorrect, but because they assume a degree of attention to recovery (i.e., 100 per cent sieving) and to micro-stratigraphy and taphonomy which was never a part of excavation strategies at these sites. Without a rigorous understanding of the micro-depositional history of each pit, claims for structured deposition are baseless. Furthermore, to use the material from these sites in claims that most fragmentary objects were intentionally broken reveals a misunderstanding of depositional processes and the historical realities of excavation in southeastern Europe.[61]

Marinescu-Bîlcu's comments on the condition of the figurines from Drăguşeni are relevant here (Marinescu-Bîlcu 2000a: 132):[62] only two of the 150 (1.3 per cent) figurines from Marinescu-Bîlcu's Drăguşeni excavations were complete. Granted, it is possible that these figurines, the ones from Truşeşti and the ones that Chapman discusses, had a particularly short use-life after which (or even during which) they were broken and discarded. Thus, as Chapman suggests and as Talalay argued over ten years ago for Neolithic figurines in southern Greece (Talalay 1987, 1993), breakage may well have been an important part of figurine use (i.e., to mark the end of a ritual, ceremony or other use of the object). However, to assume intentional breakage and deposition for so many objects in so many different contexts throughout a site without any way of determining whether or not fragmentation was accidental or intentional is of little help and certainly cannot be used to conclude that all of these objects were ritually broken and deposited. It is much more likely that the contents of the majority of these pits represent nothing more (nor less)[63] than the discard of broken and finished objects and the detritus from activities, meals and house-cleaning.

Therefore, even when individual buildings and pits from the region's most detailed excavations are interrogated for information about figurine use or meaning, we gain little. Many possibilities emerge, such as Chapman's provocative ideas about fragmentation and deposition; however, none of them gets beyond the status of anecdote and indeed some of them deserve less courteous treatment.

Settlement conclusions and social significance

While it is not possible to determine any intention underlying the fragmentary state of objects such as figurines, it is possible to draw some preliminary conclusions about the communities that lived in these sites. The clearest record is for the delineation of settlement space from non-settlement space. By digging ditches and constructing banks and by the more widely followed tradition of placing villages on terrace edges or spurs, people exploited and manipulated the natural topography in order to delineate the place of the living. In this respect, then, there is a clear indication of the clustering of people, animals, activities, resources and products within a limited area.

Were these boundaries intended to keep (wild or grazing) animals out or to keep domestic herds in? Marinescu-Bîlcu suggests that the fence of the Cucuteni A/Tripolye B1 phase at Tîrpeşti was intended to protect the domestic herd from wild predators (Marinescu-Bîlcu 1981: 50). Were ditches and banks intended as defences against marauding enemies or did they provide a focus for gatherings of people and for the storage of produce and other resources? Perhaps both functions were at work and perhaps neither was the primary intention. Regardless of any originally intended functions, the unavoidable consequences were to reinforce divisions between parts of the landscape as well as

CUCUTENI/TRIPOLYE

to contribute to the distinction between groups of people, to reinforce the dynamics of group membership and of exclusion and inclusion.

If ditches and banks provided an ever-present, physical measure of being within or being without, of community belonging and of non-belonging, then the spatial arrangement of settlement interiors provides clues for other dimensions of social organization. Though varied across the region and through the phases, buildings were arranged in rows, in circles or, just as significantly, were not arranged to any set pattern, appearing scattered across settlement interiors. Dragomir Popovici has suggested that the individual clusters of buildings in separate parts of the same settlement represent individual multi-generational family groups (Popovici 2000: 261). Another type of interpretation would see the arrangements in rows and circles in terms of the different types of social relationships which may have developed among people within each community (Whitlelaw 1991, 1997; Bailey 1999a, 1999b). Thus, individual linear rows of buildings would have limited the number of immediate neighbours that any one household would have had while clusters or circles of buildings would have ensured that a single household would have had many different neighbours. Social consequences can be interpreted in terms of varying levels of co-operation within individual communities and between each household. Regardless of the differences in intra-site arrangement of structures, the majority of Cucuteni/Tripolye sites have substantial areas of open, unbuilt-upon space within the larger area that was bounded by ditches, banks and terrace edges.[64] As we shall see (pp. 168–75), the types of interpersonal relationships that can be read from the layout of Cucuteni/Tripolye sites are different from those that prevailed at contemporary sites in more distant regions, such as northern Greece. In any event, at Cucuteni/Tripolye sites there is a spatially supported (perhaps created) sense of residential coherence among the inhabitants of a site, living, working, sleeping and eating within the physically bounded settlement.

Beyond the spatial relationships among individual buildings within a site, there is little evidence for the spatial definition and organization of people, activities or resources at any finer resolution. True, it is clear that different buildings within any one site, and even different parts of a settlement, were the focus for particular activities: concentrations of pottery, stone or antler tool production in different buildings. However, there is little variation in the morphology of building floor-plans, especially in the earlier phases; most structures contained a single room. There are multi-roomed structures (e.g., Building 12 at Tîrpeşti), and there is variation in building size.[65] Furthermore, there are particular structures the position of which suggests that they may well have had a use or meaning within the community that was different from that associated with other buildings: for example, the buildings that sit within (sometimes at the centres of) the circles of structures, or the buildings that sit outside of the circles, and even, as at Tîrpeşti, buildings that were located outside of a site's boundary ditches. Thus while there is some variation among buildings and their arrangements within settlements, the impression is of communities living together without the highly structured restrictions on the precise placement of buildings within the space of the settlement.

If spatial patterns reveal little beyond a sense of community within a site, what can be concluded about the duration of residence? The replastering and repair of walls and ovens in some buildings at Truşeşti suggest that these buildings, at least, were in use over substantial periods of time. It is difficult to determine, however, whether the events of repair and redecoration occurred within a long-term, continuous period of residence or

113

whether they mark a series of reoccupations of a building (or of the site itself) after cycles of partial or complete site abandonment. What is clear is that the construction of successive buildings, one on top of the other, over significant periods of time, which is a hallmark of other parts of the Balkan Neolithic, was not a practice among Cucuteni/ Tripolye communities. Indeed, there is only one tell settlement, at Poduri, for the entire cultural sequence.[66]

At some sites there is evidence for the successive use of the same general location for occupation: thus the sequence of Cucuteni A buildings over PreCucuteni ones at Tîrpeşti. The three sequential phases of Cucuteni A occupation at Truşeşti also document the use of the same location for settlement over longer periods of time. Without more detailed micro-stratigraphic analysis and dating, however, it is difficult to know if all of the buildings (and pits) within a single cultural phase of a site were in use at the same time or whether different parts of a site went in and out of use throughout the larger phases of occupation at these sites.

Thus, the record of the built environment from Cucuteni/Tripolye sites suggests that the people who inhabited these places shared a common bond of living, working, eating and sleeping in a shared place that was delineated from the surrounding natural and social worlds. On another level within this sense of community cohesion, smaller groups of people lived and worked together and may well have associated more regularly with some groups (i.e., households) than with others. The degree of this lower-level community fragmentation may have been greater at settlements consisting of buildings that were scattered into small clusters or which were arranged in short single lines. At other sites, for example those where structures were arranged in a circle around an open communal space, the sense of division into separate household units, though still present, would have been much reduced. In the later phases of Cucuteni/Tripolye, when very large sites appear, particularly in the east, the significance of intra-village social and political organization would have increased as would have the potentially explosive dynamics of inter-household relationships, conflict and tension: private and public; sharing and hoarding; alliance, collaboration and isolation. Sites such as Majdanets'ke which covered over 250 ha and consisted of more than 1,000 buildings are of another dimension altogether (Ellis 1984: 187, table 23; Dudkin 1978; Šiškin 1973; Šmaglij *et al.* 1973a, 1973b, 1976, 1977, 1981; Artemenko 1979–1980).[67]

Mortuary record

While the evidence for Cucuteni/Tripolye settlement is strong, the record of mortuary activity is almost invisible (Mantu *et al.* 1994).[68] There are no Cucuteni cemeteries and the Tripolye ones which have been discovered are very late.[69] The majority of human bone has been found as isolated fragments, scattered across or at the edges of settlements.[70] In the northern part of the settlement at Drăguşeni, between three buildings and the site's periphery were found several unassociated pieces of human bone: a gnawed fragment of a femur from an adult male, a fragment of a mandible of an adult female, a fragment of a skull of an adult male, and a complete tibia of a 16–18-year-old female (Bolomey 2000: 153–5). The femur was found 4 or 5 metres from Building 14, the tibia was found in a waste pit at the edge of Dwelling 15, and the mandible and skull fragment were found half a metre from the same dwelling. Bolomey suggests that the bones come from at least three (and probably four) separate individuals (Bolomey 1983, 2000: 153–5).

CUCUTENI/TRIPOLYE

The discovery of skulls and parts of skulls is more frequent than the recovery of other body parts. Parts of skulls have been found at Cernatul de Sus (Chapman 2000a: 135; Székely 1965), Fumuşica (Mantu *et al.* 1994: 225), Girov (Chapman 2000a: 135; Bolomey 1983: 164; 2000: 156), Hăbăşeşti (Mantu *et al.* 1994: 225), Poduri (Chapman 2000a), and Scânteia (Mantu *et al.* 1994). At Tripolye two fragments of forehead were found; at Vreme'e skulls were flanked by a copper and a stone axe and three vessels; at Kolomijščina I a frontal bone was recovered (Movşa 1960: 59–76); and the skull of a 60-year-old woman was found at Traian-Dealul Fîntînilor (H. Dumitrescu 1954: 399–429; 1957: 97–116). At Luka Ustinskaia the skull of a 12–14-year-old girl was found in a pit along with *Unio pictorum* shells, animal bones, flint flakes and pottery sherds (Bolomey 2000: 156).

In the absence of excavators' discussions of taphonomy or post-depositional processes, it is particularly difficult to infer any significant patterns of behaviour from the apparent frequency of human skulls and skull fragments. Without discussions of the potentially disproportionate rates of preservation for crania versus other bones in the body, and with the knowledge that little or no systematic sieving was carried out at any of these sites, it is difficult to assess the propositions that skulls and skull deposition held special positions in Cucuteni/Tripolye attitudes to death and the appropriate treatment of corpses. Such absences in analysis and project design prevent any objective assessment of the more ambitious interpretations, such as Marinescu-Bîlcu and Bolomey's that the deposition of skulls represents family groups and refers to an ancestor cult (Bolomey 2000: 156), or Hortensia Dumitrescu's proposal that the partial bodies are the remains of human sacrifices (H. Dumitrescu 1957: 97–116).

While the majority of human bone recovered from excavation suggests haphazard discard of human remains, there are exceptions. Articulated bodies intentionally buried within the areas of settlement have been found at Costeşti (Mantu *et al.* 1994: 225), Cerniahovo (Bolomey 2000: 155), Kolomijščina I (Bolomey 2000: 155), Doboşeni (including the body of a child) (Mantu *et al.* 1994: 226), Vereme'e (Movşa 1960: 59–76), Nezvisko (60–65-year-old male) (Bolomey 2000: 156), Girov (including three children aged from 6 months to 12 years and a woman whose head bore traces of trepanation, all found in one building) (Chapman 2000a: 135; Mantu *et al.* 1994: 225), Mărgineni (Mantu *et al.* 1994: 225), Scerbanevski (a 25-year-old female) (Bolomey 2000: 156), Traian-Dealul Fîntînilor (a child less than 10 years old) (H. Dumitrescu 1954: 193–5), Soloceni II (an 18–19-year-old male) (Movşa 1960: 59–76), and Luka Vrublevckaya (a newborn in a pit near a hearth) (Bibikov 1953: 51–64).

At Scânteia, in addition to scattered bone fragments, a double inhumation was found between two houses (Mantu *et al.* 1994: 227–8). One body was badly disturbed, but less than a metre away was a second individual, in much better shape, lying on its back. Coarse-ware ceramic vessels had been placed near the head and the feet of the deceased and cattle and sheep and goat bones and a horse tooth were found nearby. A figurine was also found in the concentration of material near the head. Other double inhumations were found at Ozarintz and Doboşeni (Movşa 1960: 59–76). Incomplete but articulated skeletons have been found at Traian-Dealul Fîntînilor: an 8–9-year-old with no head found in a pit; the headless body of a 25-year-old male, in a pit, placed on top of almost 30 whole and fragmentary pots (H. Dumitrescu 1954: 399–429; 1957: 97–116; Bolomey 2000: 156; Mantu *et al.* 1994: 226).

CUCUTENI/TRIPOLYE

Mortuary summary and significance

What was happening with the dead in Cucuteni/Tripolye communities? Bolomey and Marinescu-Bîlcu suggest that the common practice was the abandonment of bodies to the 'good mercy of Mother Nature' (Bolomey 2000: 157). Passek (1949) and Movşa (1960) argued that some human bones possessed magic power and thus were scattered intentionally across the space of the settlement (Bolomey 2000: 158). The presence of possible cut marks on the badly gnawed femur fragment from Drăguşeni suggests at least excarnation, if not necessarily anthropophagy (ibid.: 158).

It is difficult to draw any conclusions from the Cucuteni/Tripolye mortuary record about individual or group relations in order to recreate social and political hierarchies among these communities, as is frequently possible in other regions. It is only possible to propose that in the vast majority of cases people did not think it appropriate or necessary to formally deposit corpses within the settlement area. The number of sites containing formally deposited bodies is very few and it appears that deposition of the dead within the limits of the settlement did not play the role in the expression of identity or of group intra-relationships that it did in many other regions of the Neolithic Balkans. If Cucuteni/Tripolye communities were not using burial to manipulate perceptions of identity and group politics, that is not to say that other ceremonies and objects were not involved in such activities.

Objects made of metal appear from the PreCucuteni/Tripolye A phase and evidence for processing and working copper comes from the Cucuteni B/Tripolye C1 settlement at Brînzeni: a lump of copper slag was found as was a large pot impregnated with copper (Monah and Monah 1997: 82). Common copper objects are bracelets, awls, needles and axes. A small gold pendant comes from a Cucuteni A–B/Tripolye B2 context at Traian and two gold discs come from a late Cucuteni A/Tripolye B1 phase at Brad (Ursachi 1991).

Significantly, as John Chapman has argued, copper (and other objects) were deposited in concentrations in pits and in pots placed in pits. At Brad, a pot contained two copper bracelets, a copper axe, and 274 copper beads as well as 15 paste beads, two made of marble and 190 perforated deer teeth (Ursachi 1991, 1992: Chapman 2000a: 248). At Ariuşd three bracelets and some copper beads were found in a pot with other beads and perforated deer teeth (V. Dumitrescu 1957; Chapman 2000a: 247). In the corner of a house at Hăbăşeşti were uncovered a copper disc, a fragment of copper sheet, two bracelets made of copper wire and copper beads as well as more than 20 deer canines, limestone beads and a fragment of a human skull (V. Dumitrescu 1957; Chapman 2000a: 249). In a building at Ghelăieşti a pot contained almost 500 pig and sheep and goat astragali (Cucoş 1973).[71] Perhaps most dramatic is the assemblage found in a pot at Cărbuna: two axes, five bracelets, two discs, eleven tubes, 14 pendants and 377 beads (all made of copper); over 100 perforated deer teeth, an animal tooth amulet, 143 shell beads, a stone amulet, two polished stone axes, 23 stone beads and 111 shell pendants (Sergheev 1961; Chapman 2000a: 250). These are the types and concentrations of objects that one expects (and finds) in contemporary graves in other parts of the Balkans, as discussed for Hamangia contexts (pp. 56–8). Perhaps Cucuteni/Tripolye communities used the events surrounding the deposition of these large assemblages to the same ends as other communities exploited the rituals of inhumation of the deceased.

Cucuteni/Tripolye conclusions

It is clear from the efforts that Cucuteni/Tripolye communities made to delineate the settled from the non-settled portions of the landscape that particular places had particular identities or significances to people. It is just as likely that the people who lived, slept and ate within the boundaries of the same village would have shared in the identity of that place and of each other. At some sites the evidence for this differentiation is clearer than at others; particular buildings are grouped together in clusters that were placed at a distance from other similar clusters. At other sites, there is a stronger sense of communality, at least as read from the layout of structures; buildings are arranged in inward-facing circles or in one or more linear rows. Critical to these social organizations, both within and between individual settlements, would have been the ways in which group and individual identities were expressed, maintained, contested and overturned.

The social relationships that existed among smaller groups of people within the larger village population distinguished these smaller associations one from the other; perhaps this occurred at the level of the household or at the very least at the level of activities that focused on individual buildings or clusters of buildings. However, there is no reason to believe that these relationships were fixed, static and unchanging; it is just as probable that participation (membership even) within different groups was temporary or chronic as it was permanent and stable. Most probably the apparently rigid social pattern that we try to read from building floor-plans or arrangements of structures was perforated by frequent, temporary and randomly located alternatives and contradictory relationships.

It was in the context of these alternatives (and the reality of these flexible and contestable relationships which threatened the status quo) that many Neolithic communities invested heavily in the ceremonies and paraphernalia of public rituals such as the formal disposal of the deceased or the demolishing (or burning) and then the rebuilding of houses in efforts to maintain preferred sets of social interrelationships. These reasons make conspicuous the Cucuteni/Tripolye absences of obvious formal mortuary rituals and of successive rebuildings of structures within a tightly controlled space (i.e., the growth of tell settlements).

In many contemporary communities in southeastern Europe, burial ceremony was one of the major foci for claims and counter-claims of identity, group membership, incorporation and exclusion. The absence of a frequently practised set of ceremonies revolving around the disposal of the deceased in Cucuteni/Tripolye settlements is unusual. It is possible, as John Chapman has argued, that the ceremonial burial and intentional breaking of particular objects in large concentrations was a Cucuteni/Tripolye alternative for making such claims (Chapman 1996, 2000a).

However, there is no need to assume that the event and consequence of death were unimportant to communities or to the on-going negotiations of group and interpersonal politics. If death was important within Cucuteni/Tripolye communities then its significance appears not to have adhered to the decomposing flesh and bones of the deceased; perhaps it is for this reason that in the majority of cases human bone was so casually discarded across settlement space in the same way as was other refuse such as animal bone and disused tools and broken ceramic containers. Another possibility is that the formal events of corpse deposition took place away from the space of the settlement, beyond the physical and social boundaries of the site. If this was the case, then further work off-site will eventually reveal the locations of these ceremonies, though it is highly suspicious that over a century of highly motivated fieldwork could have missed these off-site locations.

It is more likely that the former explanation for the absence of burial is the more accurate, that with death, the Cucuteni/Tripolye understanding of being, of personhood and of selfhood became detached from the physical container/vehicle of the body, if indeed identity had even been so tightly linked to individual corporeality. The relationship between identity and the body is important, because, as will be discussed in Chapter 6, perceptions of the body are vitally important components of community beliefs and philosophies of being. As will be elaborated in Chapter 6 as well as in Chapter 8, relationships between identity and conceptions of corporeality are fundamental parts within any people's understanding of who they are as a group as well as who they are as individuals within that group. An examination of the relationship between corporeality and identity is also important for our desire to better understand Cucuteni/Tripolye figurines.

Consequences for understanding figurines

One potentially fundamental consequence of this rendering of Cucuteni/Tripolye archaeology and, particularly, the absence of burial is that non-flesh manifestations and representations of the body would have occupied particularly critical positions within the village, household and individual understandings of one's place within a community. In Cucuteni/Tripolye contexts, figurines may well have been one of the main media through which were expressed appropriate appearances and relationships among individuals.[72] Is this one of the reasons why, in the early phases, such a strict adherence to stylistic principals is evident? Did figurines provide something tangible, visible and lasting that in other regions was supplied by burial ceremonies, burial grounds and the long-term declarations of ordered, residential permanence that were at the core of monumental tell settlements?

Design restriction

One of the most striking patterns among the Cucuteni/Tripolye figurines is the total body coverage and the regularity in patterning of incised decoration among the majority of figurines from the earlier phases. The regularity of repeated sets of incised lines is clear both across individual figurine bodies and between separate figurines. Even when the clarity and execution of the incisions breaks down (i.e., in the examples with more haphazard positioning of the lines) or when the density of parallel incisions is reduced (i.e., with the more widely spaced lines), the effect is the same: the ordered covering of the body. Marinescu-Bîlcu suggests that the production of these figurines was governed by rigorous canons of design, that unlike figurines from other regions, the surface treatment of the early Cucuteni/Tripolye figurines was limited by strict rules (Marinescu-Bîlcu 2000a: 131, 136).

On the one hand, a claim for a restrictive design canon that directed figurine production is unhelpful in its unsupported assumption that there was an intentional programme or industry of figurine production directed by masters and carried out in figurine workshops. It is much more likely that figurines were produced in a variety of ways and places

CUCUTENI/TRIPOLYE

and by a variety of people and even for a variety of purposes. What is significant is that many of the figurines were made in such a similar way, with particular attention to the amount of the body covered and to covering the body with a specific and shared means and pattern of decoration. Does the presence of such similarity suggest that there was a particular form and appearance of the body (wrapped at death or otherwise) that was deemed appropriate? Is this the way that the people living at Cucuteni/Tripolye sites thought about the human body? If so, whose bodies were they thinking about? Their own or others?

Another potential significance of the standard similarity of design is for the degree of diversity in body form and appearance that was expected or accepted as appropriate within Cucuteni/Tripolye communities. Do the tightness of design and the prevention of design alternatives reveal a restrictive desire to prohibit the display of alternative perceptions of the human body? If so, then what are the consequences for Cucuteni/Tripolye conceptions of individual identities? Was there a similarly restricted set of acceptable and appropriate ways of seeing oneself, of being seen and of individual physical appearances? There were, of course, other images of the human body portrayed in the same phases of the same sites, though these alternatives are in the minority. When we look at the early Cucuteni/Tripolye figurines, do we see one very specific perception of the human body and thus one of several strands of the ways that bodies and identities were perceived and presented?

What is the significance of the high proportion of figurine bodies that are covered by decoration? In terms of surface coverage, compared to the Cucuteni/Tripolye examples, the Hamangia figurines discussed in Chapter 3 are strikingly different; Hamangia figurines have very little, if any, attention to surface treatment. Following the discussion about the body in Chapter 4, are there particular open and flexible potentials for display, expression and the stimulus to think independently that accompany undecorated parts of the Hamangia bodies but which were not allowed in the Cucuteni/Tripolye material? Among the Cucuteni/Tripolye figurines, did clear, open parts of the body present some sort of threat to the preferred, approved, version of the way that the body should be seen and thought about? Did these figurines need to be completely covered by design to prevent alternative, free-wheeling, perceptions and treatments of the body to occur? Can we understand the relationship between the decorated to the undecorated in terms of distinctions between fixed and open expressions of being? Does the refusal to leave any undecorated space on the majority of early Cucuteni/Tripolye figurines bodies represent a desire to limit the ways in which people could think about their bodies and their identities within a predefined set of appropriate and controlled understandings of who they were and what were their relationships to others?

What is the significance of the changes, over time, which saw the standardized, repeated, body-covering incisions give way to a less structured and less complete coverage of the body in the later Cucuteni/Tripolye phases? Are we to read this as a shift in population, as traditional understandings of such changes have suggested, or did such a shift mark a fundamental change in the way, over many generations, that people thought about and understood the body and its role as a potent tool in identity creation and maintenance? This discussion raises important questions about the formal similarities and differences between individuals and the consequences for the construction and con-testation of identities. These questions and consequences form the core of the discussion to be held in Chapters 6 and 8.

CUCUTENI/TRIPOLYE

Body parts

Other questions emerge over the representational selection and exclusion of particular body parts on Cucuteni/Tripolye figurines. What is the significance of the placement of the unusual symbols and patterns on the buttocks and the chests of the restrictively incised early figurines? Why was it appropriate to break the otherwise standardized decoration in these places? Did buttocks and chests have some special significance within Cucuteni/Tripolye communities? Certainly the modelled exaggeration of the buttocks, hips and thighs on many of the earlier figurines was a fundamental part of their design.

What is the significance when this trend disappears, when the figurine body is no longer completely covered with decoration, when the regularity of treatment declines, when the hips and buttocks are less exaggerated, when the 'svelte' figurines appear in the later Cucuteni/Tripolye phases? Indeed, how are we to understand those very few figurines from the earlier phases which had little or no decoration? Again, can we understand these changes in terms of a looser, less restrictive concern for how individual people thought about their own bodies and in, perhaps, a wider range of ways in which they could portray their own and others' bodies?

Also of interest is the differential attention devoted to sexual body parts. While pubic triangles and labial incisions are more common in the later phases, the earlier figurines have little sexually specific decoration. Where small, round, flattened pellets of clay mark out breasts, it is not clear whether the intention was to represent female or male, child or adult breasts. Indeed on some figurines, such as those at Dumeşti, the typical Cucuteni/Tripolye breasts are found on figurines that also have clear representations of penises. The lack of specificity of breast representation using the flattened pellets is further complicated when pellets of the same size and shape were used to show the navel and knees on other figures.

Very different, however, is the modelling of downward pointing breasts on some of the latest figurines. For the earlier phases, at least, breasts and labia were not represented. Is their absence a factor of some untraceable restriction? Are they absent from the incised figurines because the incisions represent clothes or shrouds? What is the significance of the relative preference for representing breasts on the undecorated, early figurines? Perhaps, it is simply that breasts and labia were not deemed significant body parts to represent on the heavily covered figurines. Perhaps the presentation of one tightly controlled, appropriate body form and the correspondingly appropriate signifiers of identity did not include sexually specific ones.

Heads

If the buttocks and chests have a special status for patterning and decoration, how are we to understand the absence of heads and faces in the earlier periods and the dramatic attention to them in sites from the later periods? As discussed in Chapter 4, the head and the face are important contexts for presenting and reading identity in modern western societies. Can we read the Cucuteni/Tripolye shift in the status of head and face in terms of a shift in the parameters with which people perceived themselves as individuals similar to or distinct from others? Does the wider range of methods of treating the face in the later phases, the uses of varying numbers and locations of perforations, and the modelling of very realistic faces, suggest that the perception of identity had broadened to include a much greater variation of form and thus a greater range of different, perhaps personal, ways in which individual people thought about themselves and their relationships with others within their communities?

More questions

In all of this discussion, as with the discussion of the Hamangia figurines and as will be the case for the Thessalian material discussed in Chapter 7, we are left with more questions than answers. These questions engage several key debates, particularly about the ways in which visual culture, such as figurines, participates in individual and community representations of how things are or should be. Particularly relevant are debates over how visual representation succeeds in creating realities that people view and accept as truthful and appropriate. In Neolithic figurines, but also in a wider range of representational media with which we interact in our modern world, the significance and political potential of the body is married to the power of the visual. Part of the attraction of figurines both to modern researchers and collectors but also, I suggest, to Neolithic people, rests within this combination of corporeality and its representation in visual culture. The critical issue then revolves around the rhetoric of the visual and the ways in which people can manipulate visual representation to create regimes of truth and, in turn, can attempt to subvert, block or disrupt those regimes of truth that are accepted as the status quo. These issues are the basis of the final two theoretical chapters of this book (Chapters 6 and 8).

Back to Dumeşti

Many of the questions raised in this concluding section are engaged in the set of 12 figurines from Dumeşti with which this chapter started. Especially relevant is the presence of the highly decorated and the almost completely undecorated figurines, together not only in the same phase of Cucuteni/Tripolye or even the same site, but in the same assemblage. The important lesson from Dumeşti is that regardless of how we choose to understand differences in body form and surface treatment, we must understand that the variations in the representation of the human body shared common community contexts; they were seen together and in reference to each other. The issue of similarities and differences in the human form resurfaces with these figurines and needs further discussion. In the following chapter I turn to these issues, especially in terms of the ways that people propose identities.

6

VISUAL RHETORIC, TRUTH
AND THE BODY

In the late 1960s Colin Renfrew and Marija Gimbutas directed excavations at the Neolithic and Bronze Age settlement tell at Sitagroi near Drama in eastern Macedonia (Renfrew *et al.* 1986). Almost 250 figurines typical for the region were recovered from the site's Neolithic phases (Sitagroi I–III) (Gimbutas 1986a, 1986b). One fragment from Phase III (4600–3500 BC) is particularly evocative (fig. 6.1): a poorly preserved head only 5.2 cm from chin to forehead and 3.7 cm from one cheek to the other. Both sides of the face are damaged and the upper right portion of the forehead is missing; the neck is broken under the chin and the rest of the figurine is long lost.[1] The fragment was not found in any clear architectural structure or other special context (Renfrew 1986: 212). Gimbutas does not discuss the figurine in detail other than to suggest that it is probably a human (and not a divine) head (Gimbutas 1986b: 298). It is the black-painted decoration of the figurine face and head that is so striking. Eight parallel lines run from the bottom of the forehead, up and over the top of the head and straight down to the back of the neck (and perhaps further down the back – the fragmentation interrupts the lines), and probably represent hair. The eyes, made from the application of oval clay pellets and horizontal slits, bulge out from below eyebrows; above and below the slit of each eye is a painted line of triangles that represent exaggerated eyelashes. The mouth also bulges out though it has no painted details. Running from each side of the nose and mouth towards the side of the face and along the jaw-line are other painted lines. Two lines run down from the mouth over the chin and onto the neck. Other lines are on the neck, though the break of the neck from the body cuts them off just below the chin. Gimbutas comments on the protruding 'high cheek-bones', and that the figurine is a naturalistically rendered face of a woman (Gimbutas 1986a: 239). It is a highly decorated face, painted and modelled in order to create a particular appearance. Gimbutas recognizes eyelashes as female; in the cheek-bones and thick lips Gimbutas sees a shape that 'does not reflect a Mediterranean type', that is specific to another type of people, from another place, that even may be a mask (Gimbutas 1986a: 239). I am struck by the attention to painting the face, to marking the head, the eyes, the cheeks, the chin and the neck with decoration.

How are we to understand this figurine? Does it represent an important individual in the community? Is it female? Is it indeed, as Gimbutas suggests, the face of a specific non-local, woman? At any event, it appears a straightforward representation. Many, like Gimbutas would term it naturalistic. Certainly compared to the headless, inflated Hamangia figurines or the bizarrely incised Cucuteni/Tripolye examples, the Sitagroi figurine is easier to understand and visually simple to consume.

VISUAL RHETORIC, TRUTH AND THE BODY

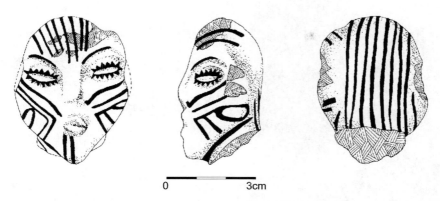

Figure 6.1 Figurine from Sitagroi (after Gimbutas 1986b).

How are we to understand this realistic and evocative figurine? How would it have been understood seven thousand years ago by the people living, eating and sleeping in the village of Sitagroi? Is this a representation of a particular individual whose hair was thus coiffured? Does it reflect a particular type of person, perhaps? Is it a statement of style of a particular kind of people, of a certain type of women from the Sitagroi region or does it refer to the appearance of a specific woman from another village in the valley or to the general appearance of a whole group of women from another community?

Why do we find this object evocative of these things in these ways? Why do we have these reactions? I find (and Gimbutas found) this object easier to understand then some of the other figurines from other regions. How does this object succeed in seducing us towards understanding? These are difficult questions and answers are not likely to be found in the specifics of the related archaeological record; rather they are to be found in discussions of relationships between truth and visual representation.

Representing the truth

In 1800, the French painter Jacques-Louis David (1748–1825) produced a heroic portrait of Napoleon Bonaparte: *Bonaparte, Premier Consul, Franchissant le Grand Saint-Bernard, 20 Mai 1800* (fig. 6.2). The painting captures Napoleon, in late autumn 1799, leading his troops over the St Bernard Pass in the Swiss Alps before they defeated the Austrians at Marengo. It is a superb portrait of the general (who would be crowned emperor in 1804) in charge of a dangerous and critical trek of the French army up and over the mountains before the winter made passage impossible. Looking towards the viewer almost nonchalantly, Napoleon appears in control while all around him is chaos. Pointing the way forward with one hand, he holds the reins of his horse with the other. The horse, terrified, rears on its hind legs, precariously near the edge of the icy rock underneath. A sharp wind blows a heavy yellow cape about Napoleon's shoulders, above the horse's head, and off to the left, in the direction of the marching army. The horse's mane and tail blow the same way. The ground is frosted stone, the sky looms above with angry dark clouds, and in the distance to the right, higher mountains are already covered in snow.

Figure 6.2 Jacques-Louis David's *Bonaparte, Premier Consul, Fraichissant le Grand Saint-Bernard, 20 mai 1800*. © Photo RMN – Arnaudet; J. Schormans.

In the distance to the left, more peaks lie in the path of the advance. In the middle ground, behind Napoleon, a cannon is wheeled to the left towards the pass; two or three soldiers are visible, though only from the chest up and without any individual detail. The painting is about Napoleon; with his horse he dominates the image just as Jacques-Louis David is suggesting that he dominates the danger of the pass and the ferocity of the conditions. Courage and heroism are required here and it is clear that Napoleon is the man for the job.

In the bottom left corner of the painting, three names appear hammered out of the rock. The clearest and most obvious is BONAPARTE; he has physically left his mark on the mountain as if in the epigraphy of legend. Below BONAPARTE, another name is

VISUAL RHETORIC, TRUTH AND THE BODY

cut into the stone: ANNIBAL. The mountain has its own legend and, as well as the recent addition of Bonaparte, there are others who had the courage and strength to succeed. ANNIBAL introduces Hannibal who triumphantly crossed the Alps in the third century BC on his way to outwitting the Roman Army. Just below and to the right of Hannibal, there is a third name, KAROLVS MAGNVS (i.e., Charlemagne) who led troops over the Alps in AD 774 to conquer the Lombards. Thus, not only is Napoleon a hero of his own time, a true and courageous leader, but he belongs in a select pantheon of extraordinary military men.

Bonaparte is not David's only painting of Bonaparte; he was an influential fashioner of an iconography of Napoleon as national leader and one of the artists that Napoleon chose to commemorate him and to help disseminate his new ideologies and politics (Johnson 1993: 174–5). Among David's other works is the massive (almost 10.0 m wide and more than 6.0 m high) *The Coronation of Napoleon and Josephine* (1805–7).[2] Indeed, David made part of his reputation in painting the *Bonaparte*. Beyond Napoleon's patronage, David holds a significant position in the history of western art (Brookner 1987; Johnson 1993). Acknowledged as a master of French painting, influenced by Poisson, he developed into a leading figure of Neoclassicism. His *Oath of the Horiatii* (1785) is a benchmark of the Neoclassical movement and served as a model for heroic portraiture through the first quarter of the nineteenth century. David's austere style dominated painting well into that century and he is seen as one of the forerunners of modern painting. An outstanding portrait painter and teacher, his students included Antoine Jean Gros and Jean-Auguste-Dominique Ingres.

Bonaparte projects an authoritative image of Napoleon as hero, a military man in perilous conditions providing exceptional leadership. The painting draws important analogies with well-established great men of European military history and provokes inspiration and awe. All of David's paintings of Napoleon were produced and appreciated in a period before the explosion in the production and distribution of visual imagery that accompanied the invention of photography in 1839.[3] The public that received the images created by David was a limited one, but it was the group that mattered, the landed, political and powerful, the viewers and connoisseurs of painting and of politics.[4]

Two questions of interest derive from David's *Bonaparte*. First, what is it about the painting that makes it work in doing its job, in presenting Napoleon as a heroic person within the late eighteenth- and early nineteenth-century structures of European, and especially French, power, politics and legend? Second, at a broader scale, how does one successfully create and maintain preferred versions of reality, such as the one that David proposed for the elevation of Napoleon, across different media and what is it about the visual media that make them such powerful vehicles of persuasion?

Regimes of truth

David's *Bonaparte* was created and praised within a historically specific set of conditions, in what Michel Foucault might have termed a regime of truth (Foucault 1977a, 1977b: 27–8): a system that produces, regulates, distributes and circulates statements that create and define truth and that allows or forces certain types of discourse to function as true. The regime of truth surrounding Napoleon encompassed a French military and political aristocracy and not a British nor necessarily pan-European one. Within its regime, the paraphernalia of battle, the symbols of national heroism and male power were tools

125

wielded to build and maintain individual positions of power and reputation. Equally important was the means by which this image of Napoleon was projected; oil portraiture was the medium of a particular stratum of society not only in France but also in England and other European countries. *Bonaparte* succeeds as personal and political propaganda within these regimes of truth; it, along with many other images, representations and artefacts, created the reputation of Napoleon as heroic leader.

Photography as truth

In 1839, less than half a century after David painted *Bonaparte*, the invention and rapid spread of photography revolutionized the graphic representation of people and ruptured existing regimes of visual truth (Tagg 1988). As discussed in Chapter 4, one of the earliest photographic productions was the *carte-de-visite*, a widely available, inexpensive means of photographic representation that extended portraiture well beyond the limits of the aristocratic or politically, militarily powerful. In addition to the low cost, speed and ease of production, photography was part of a new set of mechanisms and foundations of truth that emerged in the nineteenth century. As Tagg has argued in *The Burden of Representation* (1988), photographs became the most appropriate medium in which to create factual records; they provided a basis for a new kind of visual proof at a time when new types of knowledge were developing.

Almost immediately upon its introduction, the photographic image became authority. Cameras froze and recorded events and people objectively; they created tangible records that were not open to negotiation or query. The authority that photography possessed lent an unquestionable veracity to the records that photographs became. Photographs offered spectators an omniscience that allowed them to step inside the experience being pictured. Photography did not tell its audience about an event or a person: it showed them the event or person. Photographs delivered the experience and that experience was timeless (Sekula 1999: 189; Watney 1999).

Photography produced a new and potent reality because it possessed a new and superior evidential force and power of authentication. Authority derived from the camera as a mechanical instrument, from film, from laboratory processes (and their bases in optics and chemistry), and from the associated hard science and technology which were supported by objective laws and laboratory tests. The authority of the technical apparatus of the camera and the scientific-ness of the photographic processes seduced spectators when they looked at photographs. Existing and alternative forms of recording and representing could not compete for authoritative primacy. Photographs were straightforward, direct, seamless and clean. Furthermore, they offered the impression that they were transparent (Tagg 1988: 35), that what you saw is what you got, that the spectator can penetrate and expose any artifice that might colour the recorded truth and reality. There was an aura about photographic representation that possessed unquestionable, evidential force. Photography produced objective, tangible records of events, people and activities; they were the new facts.

In its social and political contexts, it is not surprising that photography became the dominant mode of representation immediately after its invention in 1839. John Tagg has written about the late eighteenth and the early nineteenth centuries as times when new regimes of truth and new regimes of the senses emerged. These new regimes were parts of larger changes in the organization of society that included the introduction of

VISUAL RHETORIC, TRUTH AND THE BODY

new authoritarian institutions which reorganized and classified people (Tagg 1988: 103–4). Especially important was a new professionalism that centred on the human body and which redefined individuals as objects (Foucault 1977b, 1980; Tagg 1988: 5). Hospitals, organized medical practices, asylums for the insane, prisons, houses of reform, law courts, police forces and large-scale programmes of public surveillance emerged as new mechanisms and institutions within new regimes of authority. Critically, these new organizations and classifications of people required legally binding, authoritative representations and records (Tagg 1988: 20). Photography met these requirements. One example of the way in which photography fed these new institutions was the popular, inexpensive *cartes-de-visites* which thrived (and helped to construct and maintain) the newly emerging institution of the middle-class family. Two other examples are relevant.

Social improvement of deviants

In 1871, Thomas Barnardo founded the Home for Destitute Lads to aid homeless boys in London. Barnardo took advantage of photography to create archives that recorded details of boys who entered the home and to document the improvements made in the boys' characters during their residence (Tagg 1988: 83–5; Pultz 1995: 27–8; Lloyd and Wagner 1974). Photographs were also used for comparison with police records and for tracing the parents and families of lost boys. In addition, Barnardo created a series of before-and-after photographs to illustrate the moral progress that particular boys achieved while they were in the care of the home. Sets of these photographs were used to advertise and raise money for Barnardo's: packs of 20 cards were sold for five shillings (Tagg 1988: 85). The before-and-after cards provided hard, objective proof of the success of the home in turning a dirty, dangerous, deviant youth into the clear, calm and courteous boy.

Abraham Lincoln's assassins

In July 1865, Alexander Gardner took a series of photographs documenting the hanging of George Atzerodt, David E. Herold, Lewis Payne and Mary Surratt, the four conspirators who, with John Wilkes Booth, had assassinated Abraham Lincoln four months earlier (fig. 6.3). Gardner also photographed these four after their capture by the police (fig. 6.4, showing Lewis Payne). Together the images are the photographic evidence of the preparation of the gallows at the Old Arsenal, Washington, DC, of the nooses placed around the assassins' necks, of the moment of hanging, and of the waiting coffins and dug grave-pits. Gardner's photographs created the documentary evidence that the criminals had been caught and punished, that justice had been served. Photographs with a similar purpose were published in Paris in 1871 showing the battered bodies of the Communards in their coffins; more recently the 2003 broadcast of videotape showing the capture of Saddam Hussein further illustrates how political regimes exploit the accepted authority of visual, especially photographic, imagery as documentation and proof.

The recognition that there are historically particular systems and media that propose what is appropriate and truthful in a particular context helps us understand how David's *Bonaparte* fit into a specific regime of truth in western Europe 200 years ago, how photographs served new institutions of authority within new regimes of truth half a century later, and how videotape continues this tradition today. However, we are not necessarily any closer to understanding what made *Bonaparte* succeed within its specific

Figure 6.3 Alexander Gardner's *Hanging at Washington Arsenal; Hooded Bodies of the Four Conspirators; Crowd Departing, Washington, D.C.* (1865). Library of Congress, Prints and Photographs Division, FSA/OWI Collection LC-DIG-cwpb-04230.

Figure 6.4 Alexander Gardner's *Lewis Payne, a Conspirator, in Sweater, Seated and Manacled* (1865). Library of Congress, Prints and Photographs Division, FSA/OWI Collection LC-B817-7777.

VISUAL RHETORIC, TRUTH AND THE BODY

regime of truth. Why this painting? Why in this style? Similarly, while the recognition that photographs of people were parts of transformations in how people saw and related to each other in the middle of the nineteenth century helps us to see how photography fit into new regimes of truth that developed at that time, it does not get us any closer to understanding why photographs succeeded in their role within that regime.

Relevance

The important note to take from the discussion of David's *Bonaparte* is that the painting has a political value within a specific regime of truth. It is not a statement of objective truth; rather it is one part (among many) of the construction of Napoleon's status and reputation. The point to take from the photographs of criminals and deviants and the videotape of a captured Iraqi leader is similar. These images also propose sets of truths within particular political systems. The individuals recorded in these pictures are dangerous and need to be documented and controlled. Indeed for many of them, the improved Barnardo's children, Lincoln's killers in chains and then hanged, and Saddam Hussein being examined by a US Army medic, photographic documentation provides evidence that society has solutions for these problems. As John Tagg reminds us, within these photographic portraits, there is a larger political process at work; photographs were one of several products of the disciplinary method of the time: the body made object, divided and studied, enclosed in a cellular structure (e.g., the record-card file-index), made docile and forced to yield up its truth, separated and individuated, subjected and made subject. When accumulated, such images amounted to a new representation of society (Tagg 1988: 76).

Regardless of their relationships to their own contexts of reality, regimes of truth and propaganda, all of these images impress us. More important, they succeeded in their nineteenth-, twentieth- and twenty-first-century tasks: to promote Napoleon as a hero positioned within a timeless legend, to persuade people to contribute to Barnardo's work because it succeeded in making the deviant decent, to persuade people to trust in the American and French governments' abilities to see justice done and criminals hunted down and punished, and to believe in the American-British invasion and occupation of Iraq.

Relevance to the Achilleion figurine

All of the examples discussed above force us to think about figurines as representations for a purpose and not only as representations of a person: *Bonaparte* is a representation of Napoleon for the elevation of Napoleon as legendary hero; a Barnardo's before-and-after card is a representation of a child for the manipulation of Victorian guilt in order to extract donations; the photograph of Lewis Payne in handcuffs is a representation of a criminal for the reassurance of the traumatized public; the video of Saddam Hussein is a representation of a deposed leader for reassuring a sceptical international audience of the existence of military and political control. Through these examples, we are forced to recognize that the conclusion that the figurine from Sitagroi is a representation of a woman is insufficient; we must try to understand what that representation was made for, in what regime of truth it took on meaning and succeed as a representation, if indeed it did succeed.

129

In addition, these examples make us realize that representational imagery is very often political, or at least exploited for political ends, whether or not there was any political intention. We need to ask why representational imagery is so successful in this type of highly charged use of imagery within large institutions such as governments as well as in smaller institutions such as families and households. How does visual imagery work to do its job? Important answers come below in a discussion of the power of the human body as a site of truth and in a discussion of identity. A recognition of the role that visual imagery plays in constructions of regimes of truth (and of individual reputations) forces us to question the veracity of the claims that various political and social institutions make when they rely heavily on visual representation. These examples make us realize that the woman from Sitagroi may not be so simple a representation after all.

In thinking about how these images work and succeed in representing *for* (as opposed to being simple representations *of*), we begin to examine the significance of particular media of representation; does oil on canvas do different things to the viewer with different degrees of success than do the camera, film and photographic process? What about clay that has been tempered, shaped and hardened by fire? If the emergence and rapid spread of photography as the common medium for imaging people is best understood in terms of social, economic and political events of the nineteenth century, then what can we say about the emergence and spread of ceramic pyrotechnology as the preferred medium of representing individuals in southeastern Europe in the seventh and sixth millennia BC? What were these ceramic representations for? Part of the answer is emerging in the chapters in this book that present specific sets of figurines and their contexts in different regions of the Balkan Neolithic. Another part of the answer will come closer to the end of the book in the concluding chapter. A third part is to be found in the present chapter, in an examination of the ways that visual imagery persuades the spectator.

Visual rhetoric

Wherein lies the power of the images of Napoleon, the Lincoln assassins, the Communards and Saddam Hussein? What is the rhetoric with which they persuaded the viewer? What advantages did their particular media have over textual or oral arguments? For many of these examples, the power and force of photography supplied the authority that derived from technology, science and the laws of physics and chemistry. As other, non-photographic, visual media also have significant force, we must address a wider issue: the rhetoric of the visual. How do visual images succeed? What are the processes, practices and institutions through which an image takes on meaning and has an effect? How does an image use depiction to persuade? How does an image attract and retain the attention of the viewer? How is the viewer engaged? Why did David's *Bonaparte* impress and please (Napoleon and his court at least)? Why are we convinced by videotape of Saddam Hussein being examined by a US Army doctor? What makes visual imagery successful? Understanding the rhetoric of the visual requires examination of the responses that spectators have to visual images. Regardless of the intention of the person creating the image, the meaning of visual culture rests with its reception by the viewer. Thus the question becomes, why do people react to visual imagery in the variety of ways that they do?

VISUAL RHETORIC, TRUTH AND THE BODY

Punctum, scopophilia and the sublime

One answer is found in Roland Barthes' concept of *punctum* (Barthes 1993).[5] Barthes argued that when a person looks at a photograph, he or she is struck by details in the picture and that these details remind the viewer of some part of his or her experience. More importantly, Barthes suggested that the appeal of the detail, or of the entire image, is irrational and cannot be clearly or easily explained by referring to the chemistry and optics of the photographic process. For Barthes, the picture evokes something uninvited and powerful. One's reaction is unexpected, and it is in this unpredictable reaction that part of the power of the image rests. Furthermore, the visual image provokes the viewer in an abrupt way, with an immediacy that sets the visual apart from the textual (Mirzoeff 1998). The reaction is a sudden personal attraction to particular aspects of an image that derives from whimsy, desire and memory (Mirzoeff 1999: 240). Most perplexing, the *punctum* is unknowable and thus the photograph is also unknowable (ibid.: 74). *Punctum* destabilizes. Almost by its own definition, it is impossible to put your finger on exactly what the *punctum* is or on precisely what constitutes our reactions to photographic images.

When John Tagg looks at an image he is 'flooded with a half-forgotten dream, bulking out its figures with forms of desire, opening its vistas to a physically sensed space and presence' (Tagg 1988: 199–200). Walter Benjamin described the reaction to an image as the bringing together of disparate things into a constellation like a flash of lightning; an image is a dialectic made stationary (related in Charney and Schwartz 1995: 284). Tagg argues that the power of images such as photographs rests in their ability to leave us feeling inadequate and incomplete yet with an appetite for more. They exert influence precisely because they are not real or complete. As representations, they are effective in deceiving in ways that the world of real actions and effects cannot match (Tagg 1988: 207). They are presentations of reality which deny the spectator the chance to physically move about in the represented place in order to test the value of its reference (Krauss 1999: 198).

While the reaction to visual imagery invokes the unexpected and the uninvited, and thus arouses curiosity, it also juggles pleasure and fear. Pleasure may come from many sources. Undoubtedly, for many French viewers looking at David's *Bonaparte* at the beginning of the nineteenth century (and undoubtedly today as well), pleasure derived from many factors (nationalist pride; hatred of the British or the Austrians; a hetero- and perhaps homo-eroticism riding on the backs of military prowess) as well as from other stimuli that, today, we can only guess at. For others, a modern auctioneer perhaps, or a collector, or a visitor to a museum, pleasure may accompany an appreciation of craftsmanship, from consideration of artistic, aesthetic quality, and without any concern for political contexts.

Pleasure may come as well from the satisfaction of curiosities aroused in the sudden provocation illuminated by Barthes' *punctum*; there can be pleasure in seeking out the unknown or the unsettling, and the optimism of finding out something (Rogoff 1998). Pleasure may be scopophilic, where looking becomes enjoyable because it objectifies and degrades what is being viewed or what is being represented. Scopophilia derives some of its pleasure from a not necessarily pleasurable sense: it is more than a satisfaction of superiority. The pleasure and security that miniaturism provides, as discussed in Chapter 2, derive, in some part at least, from this element of the scopophilic: the spectator is enlarged and made omnipotent. Scopophilia also engages the pleasure in causing (or at least recognizing) the misfortune of another. There are sexual undertones to the scopophilic (the concept is most thoroughly discussed in Freudian psychoanalysis) as well as relations of power and domination, and the discussion will turn to these issues below in relation to the gaze (pp. 143–5).

Paradoxically, pleasure can derive from pain. What is seen can threaten and scare, overpowering the viewer and injecting instability into the spectator's reaction. A British viewer of David's *Bonaparte* in 1800 may have felt anger, disgust, sadness or any mixture of these emotions. Responses to images of Lincoln's killers may have inspired fear, even if the conspirators are handcuffed: there are dangerous people out there. It is difficult to imagine that pictures of bodies hanging from the neck or of battered corpses in coffins do not provoke some feeling of revulsion, regardless of any relief or security that they might also provide. Images of Saddam Hussein's capture and medical examination provoked both relief (for US officials) and outrage (among human rights activists) and, undoubtedly, sadness (mixed with resolve perhaps) among supporters of his regime. One of the most powerful rhetorical stimuli is a combination of the pleasurable and the painful, the comforting and the dangerous, the calm and the tempestuous.

The sublime

In 1991, the British artist Marc Quinn exhibited a work entitled *Self*. *Self* is a portrait bust made at life-size, created from a mould made of the artist's head. In many places, the surface of the bust is rough where sections of the mould join. The eyes are closed, as is the mouth. The reference is to the tradition of portrait sculpture, particularly to death-masks. *Self* is striking to look at. There is something that is not quite right about it, something that unsettles the viewer. Part of this comes from the tradition of death-masks themselves: a mixture of the living and the dead, the surface of a face copied from death in advance of decomposition and decay. There is an added dimension of unease with *Self*; where one would expect the white of marble (or plaster) or the coppery-brown or patinized green of bronze, *Self* is deep red. The colour comes from the extraordinary conceit that Quinn employed. Instead of a traditional medium, Quinn made *Self* from four-and-a-half litres of his own blood, taken over a period of five months, mixed with anti-coagulants and antibiotics, poured into the mould and frozen. *Self* sits in a glass container on top of a refrigeration unit.

Quinn made two similar busts, one of which (*Shithead*) was moulded of excrement and another was made of coconut milk (which some wish to equate with semen). All three pieces are striking, arousing strong reactions from spectators, though *Self* and *Shithead* have made the greatest impression. Each piece plays with the viewers' expectations of what sculpture should be and especially about how sculpture should be created and which materials should be used. Marble, plaster and bronze are appropriate; congealed blood, excrement or semen is not. Quinn is working in between materials and conditions, between the artificial and the natural, literally between the blood and the stone. *Self* faces us with an instability between death (the death-mask tradition) and life (the blood). In earlier work Quinn counterpoised expectations of media and art-form by using bread to create traditionally shaped portraits of Marie Antoinette and Robespierre in bread; in more recent pieces (e.g. *Self Conscious*) he has used his own DNA. Quinn is not alone in creating work of this kind. Other artists have used body parts to create disturbing, yet provocative and stimulating work. Günther von Hagens takes human and animal corpses and replaces body fluids with silicone, epoxy and polyester polymers and exhibits them in extraordinarily evocative, and successful and popular, *Bodyworld* installations across Europe (von Hagens and Whalley 2002). All of these works arouse strong emotion, popular as well as academic press coverage and, often, police attention and intervention.

Regardless of what impact Quinn, von Hagens and others were intending to make, or what, if any, meaning they wished to attach to these pieces, their work has had tremendous coverage in the press and has attracted many thousands of people to see it in person. Why does this work create such a reaction? How are we to understand the power of these pieces? Why, like so much of the work created by the Young British Artists of the 1990s, did they arouse such emotions in the popular and academic press?[6] One answer is found in the sublime nature of *Self* and *Shithead*.

What is sublime?

In late eighteenth-century Britain, the sublime emerged as a trend in graphic and literary systems of representation.[7] Artists and writers pushed beyond the rational, regular and safe canons of traditional representation. Sublime representation engaged readers and viewers through provocation and astonishment. The sublime refers both to the reactions of awe and irresistible power that particular images and words generate and to the consequent strengthening and deepening of the spectator's or reader's mind as a result of the experience. It is the paradoxic mixture of incomprehension, pain, fear and pleasure.

A sublime visual event is one that cannot be completely comprehended or contained by the spectator. What is seen overpowers the mind (even if only for a nano-second) with incomprehension (Paley 1986: 2) and from this lack of understanding comes frustration and the recognition of human inabilities (Guyer 2000). In some examples, representations of the absolutely large or powerful (the mountain, the storm at sea) overpower the spectator's mind and its ability to conceive of what is represented: these things are too big for representation. In addition, in the subliminal image, the expected harmony of purposeful art is disrupted by frustration and incomprehension (Benjamin 1989: 202). Subliminal events are incomplete; they are distortions, fragments and selections (Burke 1759: 134, 142). Sublime events powerfully get in amongst your senses through the processes of apostrophe, ellipsis, hyperbole, misrepresentation, distortion and ugliness (Lawson 1758: 146). In these ways, a subliminal visual event causes unease for spectators because the viewers recognize that they are unable to fully understand what they are seeing, and they realize that their own sensibilities and imaginations are inadequate to handle and make sense of what they are seeing. Unease creates astonishment (Paley 1986: 2).

In defining and elevating the sublime, Edmund Burke drew the important distinction between a clear expression and a strong expression (Burke 1759: 142). While a clear expression simply describes something and aids in its understanding, it does not create an enthusiastic response, nor does it inspire or create awe or astonishment. On the other hand, a strong expression describes not what a thing is but how that thing feels; in doing so the strong expression moves the passions of the spectator. A clear image demonstrates; a strong, subliminal one grabs viewers and makes them feel (Benjamin 1989: 202). Quite simply the sublime image shocks.

A sublime visual event is complex, because the frustration of initial incomprehension gives way, or better yet, pushes and pulls against pleasure. Pleasure comes from the representation and engagement with something that would otherwise be painful or terrifying. Pleasure comes in recognizing, at a safe distance, the superior power of nature or technology over the human.[8] The distance created by representation provides the comfort that turns pain and danger into delight (Burke 1759: 131). Without such a distance between subject and object, the scopophilic pleasure collapses inwards onto itself, as the boundaries are erased and subject becomes object and object becomes subject. Juxtaposition of pleasurable attraction with unease, frustration, and incomprehension creates a vibration, an agitation, a transcendental feeling, a distraction (Benjamin 1989: 326–7, citing Kant section 27). In having these effects the sensations of the sublime raises self-consciousness and expands the mind outwards (Baillie 1747: 88).

Relevance of the sublime

In terms of the sublime, it is easier to understand reactions to Marc Quinn's *Self*, a piece of work that combines the fearful and dangerous with the pleasurable and the beautiful: the use of blood in place of a more traditional medium and the complex meanings and reactions to blood – it is dangerous, life-sustaining, reproductive. It is also easier to understand the attraction of the work of Quinn's contemporaries, such as Damien Hirst, who created *A Thousand Years*, a work which consists of a glass box containing rotting meat, consumed by flies who were then killed by an electric bug zapper, and *This Little Piggy Went to Market, This Little Piggy Went Home*, a bisected pig exhibited in formaldehyde, or Chris Ofili who used elephant dung in a piece called *Blind Popcorn* and Marcus Harvey who used hundreds of coloured, children's handprints (isn't that sweet) to create *Myra*, a faux-Impressionist portrait of the child-killer Myra Hyndley (isn't that disgusting). All of these pieces, and many others created by the YBAs, shock the senses: indeed most were shown together in 1997 in the provocative *Sensation* installation at the Royal Academy of Arts (Timms *et al.* 1999).

In terms of the sublime, it is also easier to understand the power of the photographs of the Barnardo's boys, the Lincoln conspirators, the dead Communards, the video of Saddam Hussein and even, perhaps, David's *Bonaparte*. Barnardo's deviant youths are dangerous, but they are somewhere else and the photographs prove that they are being taken care of and improved; there is also a scopophilic pleasure in looking down on them and if one bought a set of 20 before-and-after cards, then there also comes a warm, good feeling of having contributed to their moral correction. Lewis Payne and fellow conspirators are fearsome murderers, yet they are in chains, and then, hanged by the neck until dead; in looking at the photographs, there is the pleasure of knowing that they got what they deserved, the comfort in knowing that the authorities caught the arch-criminals, but also the evil of the crime (a presidential assassination), the danger in Payne's face, the grotesque display of their execution. Saddam Hussein for some, is evil personified, but on videotape he is docile and under control; there is pleasure for some in seeing him apprehended, but also an apprehension and disgust both about his treatment and about the justification for the war in Iraq. Each of these images contains dangerous and fearsome individuals or places, yet each image provides the viewer with safety and security created by the distance that the particular medium of representation inserts between spectator and person represented.

The subliminal mixture of pain and pleasure or of fear and security creates a paradox. How can something be both pleasurable and painful? How can an image make the spectator feel both secure and fearful? Why do millions of people enjoy watching

VISUAL RHETORIC, TRUTH AND THE BODY

accidents at motor-races? A paradox emerges; how can one image stimulate two mutually exclusive emotions? As argued in Chapter 2's discussion of miniaturism, paradoxes affect the way that people think and they lead to subtle dis-balancings of reason, to moments when guards are lowered and representations are accepted not for what they are for but for what they are of. These images don't describe; they make us feel. They are not logical.

Relevance to figurines

Saddam Hussein, Barnardo and Lewis Payne are a long way (and many thousands of years) distant from the Sitagroi figurines that started this chapter. There is, however, much about the Sitagroi example and in Neolithic figurines in general that engage the sublime. Figurines are human-formed, but they are not human. They are clay but they are understood as flesh. They are human bodies but most have missing limbs or heads. One figurine may have breasts and thus is female, but the same figurine also has a penis. In addition there are also the paradoxes introduced in the discussion of miniaturism: that what is smaller can be more powerful, and that there exist multiple scales, multiple worlds, and multiple temporalities. There are also the paradoxes of three-dimensionality: that no one can ever have a complete understanding of an object even though that form allows a 360-degree perspective. The figurines and the examples discussed in this chapter share the same ability to stimulate these types of responses. To be capable of creating these reactions is to be extraordinarily powerful in presenting preferred versions of reality, and in creating particular regimes of truth. In this sense all of these visual objects are unusually disposed to the political.

The politics of the visual, the body and identities

In the winter of 1936, Dorothea Lange took a photograph of a woman and several of her children sitting in a tent in Nipomo, California (fig. 6.5): *Destitute Pea-Pickers in California; a 32-Year-Old Mother of Seven Children. February 1936.* While it is a familiar picture (most of us have seen it before), it is no less striking now than it was in the decade when it was taken. Forehead creased in thought, the woman looks past the photographer into the distance, perhaps, towards some better future. One hand is up to her face, with fingers against her cheek, less for support than in contemplation. Her eyes are clear, sharp, angry, even. Three of her children frame her; one at each shoulder, the third on her lap. The two at the sides lean on their mother; both have backs turned to the camera. Are they asleep? Clearly they appear exhausted, at least unwilling to face Lange's camera. The mother's shirt is undone from feeding the baby who, with grubby face, sleeps on her lap. Clothing is coarse; one of the woman's sleeves ends in tatters. Within this scene, the mother appears calm and in control. There is a noble clarity in her face and a seriousness of expression that reassures the viewer: everything is going to be alright, the mother is in charge, protecting, nurturing, supporting, providing. There is dirt and depression on view in the image, but there is also cleanliness in the mother's face: hope. It is as beautiful, yet frightening, an image today as it was in 1936.

The photograph that Lange took of the mother and her children is one of six that are part of a group of pictures that she took of migrant farm labourers that winter. Lange later wrote that the mother had told her that she had been living on frozen vegetables collected from nearby fields and from birds that her seven children could

VISUAL RHETORIC, TRUTH AND THE BODY

Figure 6.5 Dorothea Lange's *Destitute Pea-Pickers in California; a 32-Year-Old Mother of Seven Children* (1936). Library of Congress, Prints and Photographs Division, FSA/OWI Collection LC-DIG-fsa-8b29516.

kill, that she had just sold the tyres from her car so that she could buy food (*Popular Photography*, Feb. 1960). The photograph told us as much. John Pultz notes how Lange composed the image, with the mother positioned above the level of the camera, in such a way that she is empowered and attracts sympathy (Pultz 1995: 93).

Regardless of the stimulus to a visual image, there is an immediacy of a spectator's reaction to the visual images such as Lange's *Destitute Pea Pickers* which sets it apart from textual representation (Mitchell 1994). The power of this reaction has important

VISUAL RHETORIC, TRUTH AND THE BODY

consequences for the successes that visual culture has in proclaiming, negotiating and contesting relationships among individuals, of assigning and displaying identities and establishing the dominant and subordinate groups' relationships. As we shall see, Lange's image was part of larger programme of government-orchestrated propaganda during the American Depression which aimed to propose a particular set of realities to the American people.

Spectacle, illusion and virtuality

Visual culture is a powerful means for proposing alternative realities, because it can exploit the processes of representation to replace the real with the fictional. In *The Society of the Spectacle*, Guy Debord suggests that people are dazzled by the spectacular and end up passively preferring the representation to the real thing (Debord 1967). Debord's spectacle is more than the mere collection of images; it is the way that images mediate between people (ibid.: 12). In the spectacle, appearances predominate; in fact, human, social life is nothing but appearances (ibid.: 14). Following Feuerbach, Debord argues that people give primacy to the sign as opposed to the thing signified, to the copy rather than the original, to the representation over the real, to the appearance and not the essence: illusion becomes sacred (ibid.: 11). In the society of the spectacle, people cannot directly perceive their world because it is only visible through particular visual mediations (ibid.: 17). Furthermore, the spectacle congeals all of those things which, in actual human activity, exist in a fluid state (ibid.: 26). Sets of images replace the real world and are superior to the real thing; they impose themselves as the appropriate perception of reality (ibid.: 26). The spectacle is the ideological form of pictorial power (Mitchell 1994: 327).

Similar to the spectacular is the simulacrum, a copy that has no original and thus no relation to reality (Baudrillard 1988). For Baudrillard, it is possible (and common) to create a model of a real thing that is, paradoxically, without any reality; it is hyper-real. Importantly he suggests that there are four phases of the image: one that reflects a basic reality; one that masks or perverts a basic reality; one that masks the absence of a basic reality; and one that bears no relation to any reality. In this final phase, the image is its own pure simulacrum. Debord's specular society and Baudillaud's simulacrum bring us into the world of the virtual where images or spaces that are not real appear to be so (Mirzoeff 1999: 91–5). For Nicholas Mirzoeff a virtual space is the one that comes into being when he is on the phone: it is a place that it is neither exactly where he is sitting nor is it where the other person on the phone is sitting. Rather, it is the space of the conversation, the virtual space; it is somewhere in between. Mirzoeff provides other examples of these virtual worlds, including the Neoclassical creation of the space of a virtual Classical antiquity, the stereoscopic images of the nineteenth century (and their magical creation of a three-dimensional image), the dioramas of the eighteenth and nineteenth centuries (in which illuminated translucent water-colours created three-dimensional effects), the television and the cinema (and the presentation of deaths, explosions and stunts), and most recently, computer-generated virtual worlds which cannot be known in any other form outside of the computer screen. In all of these, the actual reality of the world around us is transformed into poly-dimensional interior worlds of the spectator (ibid.: 92–3). By playing on the uneasy paradox that exists between the real and the representation, the virtual provokes imbalance and instability.

VISUAL RHETORIC, TRUTH AND THE BODY

Discussion of the virtual brings us to the ideologic where the actual conditions of relationships between individuals are replaced with imaginary ones. Ideologies do not correspond to reality; they constitute an illusion and only make allusions to reality (Althusser 1999: 317). Ideologies propose a world-view to be shared by people and in which things are taken for granted (Burgin 1999: 42). We enter the world of illusion, where proposals for reality jostle and contest, each offering a preferred regime of truth and values. Ideology disguises explicit power politics so that they appear to be part of the natural, eternal order of things (Nochlin 1991: 14).

Political currency of the image

How does the recognition that visual imagery can powerfully create other, virtual worlds, world-views and ideologies of preferred realities refine our political understandings of particular images, such as the figurine from Sitagroi or, even, of Lange's *Destitute Pea Pickers*? The answer lies in understanding not what the image is a *representation of* but what it was a *representation for*. Lange's image is perhaps the most famous of many pictures that she and other photographers took on assignment for the Resettlement Administration and, later, the Farm Security Administration (FSA). The FSA was a cultural programme within American President Franklin Roosevelt's New Deal reforms that were assembled during the American Depression of the 1930s. Within this context, the FSA was as much a political institution as a cultural one: it aimed to show that poverty was noble and aesthetic and that destitute people could appear as moral and dignified. The FSA was charged with employing cultural tools to create a unified nation (Lesy 2002). Although other media, such as writing for the press and the stage, played important roles in the FSA programme, it was documentary photography that had the greatest influence in projecting an image of an America which, though desperately poor, was noble and full of achievable ambitious hope and the belief that there was a brighter future ahead.

The FSA used photography and the power of its rhetoric to propose an image of society for public consumption. FSA-sponsored projects created hundreds of thousands of images. Though poor beyond the imagination of many Americans, the woman in Lange's *Destitute Pea Pickers* is represented as a strong, noble survivor. Through such orchestrated depictions of people in crisis, especially in the American South, the FSA commandeered human misery within the philanthropic reform of Roosevelt's government. The government used the FSA images as evidence of its good intentions (Lesy 2002: 11). As importantly, the file of FSA images became an official source of information about the rural poor to be used by non-government-associated writers: John Steinbeck visited the archive while writing *The Grapes of Wrath* (1938); the FSA sent 500 carefully selected images to Archibald MacLeish when he was composing his seminal *Land of the Free* (1938); by 1940, the FSA was placing 1,400 images a month in American newspapers and magazines (Lesy 2002: 318–20).

Not surprisingly, the FSA's photographic projects were tightly controlled. Under the direction of Roy Stryker, successful FSA photographers were asked to produce images that showed people who were in difficulty but who would be alright with a little help from the government (Tagg 1988: 169–70). Stryker gave his photographers shooting scripts to direct their work (Lesy 2002: 226), asking for pictures of men, women and children who appear as if they really believed in the United States; he wanted images of people who had a little bit of spirit about them; he wanted more contented older couples,

138

VISUAL RHETORIC, TRUTH AND THE BODY

Figure 6.6 Example of a negative that has been 'killed' by Roy Stryker of the Farm Security Administration. Library of Congress, Prints and Photographs Division, FSA/OWI Collection LC-USF33-031334-M4.

women sewing, men reading. Negatives of images that did not fit in with this doctrine were rendered unusable: of the more than 140,000 negatives produced almost half were never printed. Some negatives Stryker 'killed' by punching holes in them so that they could never be printed (fig. 6.6). Stryker's criteria for killing or not printing images extended beyond the control of image quality: politics and ideology were as important, if not more so (ibid.: 470). Stryker wanted images that showed determination that not even the Depression could kill, that showed endurance and dignified suffering (ibid.: 470). Some photographers' images were killed more often then others; some photographers, such as Walker Evans, were more infrequently printed than others (ibid.: 469). Walker Evans and Dorothea Lange (whom Stryker fired in 1939) took steps to preserve their work: Evans used two cameras, one shooting film for himself, the other for the FSA; Lange set up her own darkroom to process her negatives away from Stryker's hole-puncher (ibid.: 469).[9]

For the FSA and for the other examples noted in this chapter, photography emerges as an extremely potent instrument of ideology (Burgin 1999: 41). Photographs are not evidence of history; they are, themselves, historical. They are particularly powerful at the personal level where they engage the power relationships that revolve around the body (Pultz 1995: 10).

The body, identities and corporealities

In Chapter 4, we examined ways in which two- and three-dimensional representations of the human form work to create standards for appropriate behaviour and physical appearance. While that discussion focused on the manipulation of particular representations of the human body (the Barbie Dolls, the interview tools of the police), it avoided confronting the body as political phenomenon with its huge significance as a cultural, social and political object, indeed in its position as the most important site for the negotiations of power politics of the individual and the group. There is now a vast literature on the anthropology and archaeology of the body,[10] and the intention is not to regurgitate all of that here. There are three topics, however, which help us in our project: the constructed body, identity creation and the politics of the gaze.

The constructed body

The recent appearance of body literature in archaeology has disrupted traditional thinking about people and about images of people in the past; much of the recent work derives from the writing of Moira Gatens (1996), Judith Butler (1990, 1993), Elizabeth Grosz (1994, 1999a, 1999b) and other feminist authors. A critical conclusion that these authors share is that bodies are political, social and cultural objects par excellence; they are not natural, passive, or simply overlaid with cultural inscriptions. Bodies are neither reflections of static, individual and social relationships, nor are they metaphors for social and political structures. Indeed there is no single, stable, unified concept or definition of the body, nor can there be any single body image; the body is always precarious and always requires construction, maintenance and renewal (Grosz 1994).

Bodies are fluid things that have no original, essential definition or shape. At any one moment, different, contemporary communities and individuals have different ways of seeing, valuing and thinking about the corporeal. At many different moments, the same community or individual can have varying conceptions of the body. In this sense, bodies are specific rather than universal; their meanings lie in local understandings, truths, lies and fictions. There are specific historical contexts to each perception of the body. Corporeality is not an abstract category that can be defined and tied down; rather it refers to the ways in which bodies are materialized (Butler 1993).

As bodies are incomplete, indeterminate, fluid and amorphous, they require ordering and management. Body management derives from relations among individuals within (and from without) a community (Grosz 1999b: 382, 386). Bodies are constructed (Butler 1990; Grosz 1994). Bodies' meanings and functions are open to transformations through processes of contestation and re-signification (Grosz 1999a: 270); bodies are constantly altering (Riley 1999b: 223). For Butler, the body is part of deliberate acts, or performances that can deceive people, leaving them (and the performer) uncertain about what is real and what is not. In fact, performativity questions whether or not there is a distinction between a real body and one that is a non-real, or performed body or self. Bodies are performative and as such they are always in the process of becoming.

Furthermore, bodies are political and there exist body politics: power relations that surround the corporeal body and its representations, the inescapable relationship between embodiment, power and knowledge (Foucault 1980; Shildrick and Price 1999b: 18). The focal point for struggles over shares of power is the definition and shaping of the body (Bordo 1999). As political entities, bodies become the signifying practices within fields of hierarchy and of compulsory community organization and structure (Butler 1999b: 419).

Identity creation

Though not the only tool for creating and manipulating identity, the human body is one of the most powerful. The body's participation in acts, gestures, and performances constructs identity. The repetition of performances builds identities which become, unintentionally even, community-wide norms (Butler 1990). Concealed within such reiterations are the original, perhaps tenuous, proposals and claims. Repeated performance creates conventions and promotes acceptance of one alternative as a norm (Butler 1999a: 241). In this sense, there is no true or false, real or apparent, original or derived identity (Butler 1999b: 421). A person does not have a single identity, but is constituted from a host of identities. Identity is subject to change and is multiple. Identities are not facts; rather they are the result (intended or otherwise) of various acts and performances without which there would be no identity at all (ibid.: 420). The acts and performances of identity

VISUAL RHETORIC, TRUTH AND THE BODY

construction compel us to believe not only that a particular identity is appropriate and real, but even that an entity such as a corporeal 'identity' itself is a necessary and natural component of being human (ibid.).

Furthermore, bodies contain the power to resist, to contest and to refashion corporeal norms. Often, iterations of the bodily form or performance are disruptive and troubling. Categories and hierarchical oppositions emerge along boundaries between the normal and the abnormal (Price and Shildrick 1999). Radically altered body forms challenge norms in an aggressive manner. Performing in different ways and in inappropriate media transgresses expectations (Butler 1990); when repeated, such transgressions establish new norms.

In particular places and in particular times, distinct normative corporeal identities emerge. The normative body, itself constructed and maintained, constrains and prevents alternative presentations of the self. Sustained social performances create and maintain identities. Iterations of bodily form become instruments of cultural hegemony (Butler 1999b: 419). Acts repeated over long periods of time lay down the sediment of reality and produce a set of corporeal styles that congeals over time (Butler 1999a: 244 n. 5; 1999b: 420). Normative corporeal practices are acts through which the body is shaped, defined and impelled. Identity is in constant flux, creating a sense of self or selves from a range of possibilities (Mirzoeff 1999: 174) and the construction of identity requires repeated performances during which an already established set of meanings becomes mundane and legitimate (Butler 1999b: 420). So, identity does not exist on its own as a seamless, timeless quality; it is tenuously constituted in time and requires repeated presentation, representation. The failure to repeat (or, better yet, the repetition of a parody of one representation) threatens to expose the constructed-ness of identities (ibid.: 421).

A critical process within identity construction is the perception and expression of distinctiveness from others (Silverman 1999: 350). The definition one holds of one's own body is dependent on one having not only a discrete image of oneself but also of the orientation of one's own body in relation to others (Gatens 1996, 1999: 229; Schilder 1978). Individuals become aware of themselves when they recognize that they are different from others (Dyer 1999: 461). Divisions and statements of difference create the subject not in terms of what one has and is, but in terms of what one does not have and what one is not; difference creates identity by promoting a sense of lack in the individual (Silverman 1999: 250). Articulations of formal differences result in the creation of the subject where differences are played out over the shape and surface of the individual's body (Bhabha 1999: 371). Body surface is thus the critical signifier of difference (Bhabha 1986) and thus there is a surface politics of the body (Silverman 1999: 341) which we can expand to include a morphological politics of the body. Therefore, identity is the product of recognizing similarities (evoking cohesion) and by recognizing differences (evoking lack) from others through the media of the body's shape and surface schema. When a group of people construct their identities by recognizing differences from others, they participate in an exotropic activity; not only do they see other groups but also they recognize how they themselves are seen (Shohat and Stam 1998). This has important consequences: what Silverman refers to as self-alienation, where people know themselves through their external images (Silverman 1999: 344).

Difference is not about biological facts; it is about the ways that cultures mark bodies and recreate themselves (Gatens 1999: 230–1). Thus social practices create power relations between people. Social activities and performances present contexts for the

VISUAL RHETORIC, TRUTH AND THE BODY

expression and articulation of difference (ibid.: 232). Boundaries include and exclude; they regulate what is of reference and what is not (Butler 1999a: 241).

Also important is the recognition that within a group, the exotropic self-definition creates a standardized notion of the self in which individual differences are minimized in order to sustain overarching categories (Mirzoeff 1999: 170). Identity categories work better across the larger scale (the community, the household, the male, the female) than they do at a small scale (the particular individual), where the specific is blurred into the general. The visual repetition of a limited range of representations produces and reproduces particular definitions of the person and, at the same time, of the group (Mercer 1999: 437). In such economies of definition, articulations of image, reality, otherness and stereotypes appear (Doane 1999: 454). Just as the spectacular or simulacrum drains fluidity from the actual dynamics of social discourse, so with stereotypes come the fixity and imposed stability that is absent from the flux of actual relations and identities (Mercer 1999: 438).

In contexts of the stereotypic fixing of identity and the definition of self in terms of Other, dominant groups construct fixed identities in order to establish and maintain order, to apply reason and authority to communities in which identities flex, shift, morph and flow in ways that threaten and endanger emergent dominant groups. Importantly, bodies are part of the construction of social-community coherence, a process that suppresses differences (Butler 1990).

Sex is one, though only one, of many dimensions of corporeal difference. One does not simply have a 'sex' that statically describes what one is; rather sex is one of many different norms that qualify an individual within an historically specific, culturally coherent community (Butler 1999a: 236). Thus, the identification of a sexed body is not an unproblematic process; the sexed body is itself constructed by practices that engage the body as target and medium (Gatens 1999: 230). Importantly, sex is an idealized construct, it is yet another reiterative process through which norms emerge or are imposed. The process is ongoing and the construction is never quite complete because bodies do not comply precisely with the norms imposed (Butler 1999a: 235–6). Sex is a constructed dimension of difference along which one becomes culturally intelligible or coherent: many other dimensions of construction materialize through the body: volumetric dimension, colour, smell, texture.

Corporeal thinking

Out of these arguments, the body emerges as a good thing to think with, a good way to think about who one is and is not. Bodies are things that give themselves to the construction, reconstitution and, especially, contestation of the boundaries between individual and individual, between individual and group, and between group and group. Patterns of bodies (and body patterns) create appropriate mental images and instil moral qualities (Jackson 1983). Because boundaries inspire the recognition of difference, they are the norms that create and justify inequality within specific moral orders (Lock 1993: 138). Any investigation of the body and its representations engages our understanding of what it is that constitutes the human being, the human individual and human corporeality (Shildrick and Price 1999a: 10).

Therefore, visual representations of the body are never politically innocent nor are they inherently stable. Furthermore, if, as Butler argues, a large part of identity creation is performative then three questions arise: what are these performances, how can we see

142

VISUAL RHETORIC, TRUTH AND THE BODY

them in the Neolithic, and what is the relationship between performer and audience? While, the first two questions form the basis for discussion in Chapter 9, one answer to the third question derives from the concept of the gaze.

The gaze

In 1978, Mattel, the makers of the Barbie Doll, released *Fashion Photo Barbie* (Lord 1994). The doll came with four pre-printed photographs of Barbie in various poses, a cardboard portfolio for storing the pictures, a stand for Barbie to pose on and a camera that was connected to the stand by a wire. When the child turns the camera lens, Barbie changes her pose on the stand. While *Fashion Photo Barbie* can be read as another example of how Barbie gave girls examples of women taking on an ever-expanding range of occupations (in this case a fashion model), Lord has proposed an equally plausible, less sympathetic interpretation (Lord 1994: 103–4): *Fashion Photo Barbie* reflects a masculine understanding of the female experience, that the doll taught children a code of feminine erotic styling in which women are defined as a thing to-be-looked-at; indeed the product description invites the child to 'Be a fashion photographer'. For the child, the pre-printed photos supplied with *Fashion Photo Barbie* pre-define which poses and looks are appropriate and desirable for women. Most importantly, Lord argues that in this iteration of the Barbie Doll, the child (boy or girl) plays the role of the male gazing at the female and controlling feminine erotic style (ibid.: 104). Lord's criticism forces us to consider the political importance of the processes of looking at and being looked at, most influentially proposed by Laura Mulvey's arguments about the gaze (Mulvey 1975).

In a major contribution to feminist film criticism, Laura Mulvey argued that the visual pleasures of Hollywood films are based on voyeuristic and fetishistic forms of looking (Mulvey 1975; see also Stacey 1999). Mulvey argued that film viewers identify with male protagonists in movie narratives and that, in doing so, they objectify the female figure through the lens of the male gaze. The resulting visual pleasure is based on the objectification of the image, the fact that the spectators are looking at a private world (i.e., that they are voyeurs). The film audience identifies with the male protagonist's power to possess the female character that is displayed as a sexual object for his pleasure (Stacey 1999: 391).

As mentioned above in the discussion of scopophilia, visual rhetoric benefits from the pleasure that spectators derive from looking, especially when that pleasure comes from the recognition of superiority over the subject of observation. The politics of exploitation reside in this pleasure of looking and it is at the core of Mulvey's argument. Mulvey's gaze theory is an adaptation of Freud's thinking about how the gazer constitutes his or her identity by distinguishing himself or herself from that which is gazed at (Freud 1905; Mirzoeff 1999: 164) and of Lacan's work on the symbolic power of the gaze, which he related to desire and to the complex, often contradictory, motivating forces of the eye (Lacan 1977): power, evil, benevolence, envy and love (Adams 1993: 6). In terms of the gaze, looking becomes a process of controlling people, associating action with the spectator and passivity with the person looked at. The gaze establishes a relationship between two people, an unequal relationship, where before there had been none.

While Mulvey's application of Lacanian and Freudian thought to gendered power relationships on screen has been influential, her original argument has important flaws. Most importantly, Mulvey's conception of the gaze is restricted to a simple male/female

143

relationship. Clearly, the male figure can just as easily be the object of erotic attention as can the female. Robert Mapplethorpe played with this limitation in his erotically changed images of black men (Mapplethorpe 1986) where both spectator and the viewed were male. However, even Mapplethorpe's manipulation of the gaze remains within the masculine fantasy of a sexual other (Mercer 1999), and if anything, has replaced a subordinate female body with a subordinate male black one. Stacey has pushed the criticism further, by examining the pleasures and desires that female movie viewers experience (Stacey 1999). For the films that Stacey investigated, she concluded that looking-derived desire is driven not by sexual difference but by a fictional fulfilment of becoming an ideal female other. More important though, is Stacey's argument that the same films can be enjoyed from different, gendered positions and that there is no single male or female spectator's position (ibid.: 393). Most critically, Mulvey's gaze theory polarizes everything: masculine/feminine, voyeuristic/exhibitionistic, active/passive. The value of Mulvey's article, the original work by Freud and Lacan, and the criticisms of Mercer, Stacey and others is that they force us to recognize that the process of looking and, equally importantly, the mechanisms and apparatuses of looking, are politically powerful things. Thus, it is not essentially women, nor even men, who are the victims (or the perpetrators) of the gaze; what matters is that acts and artefacts of looking are powerful mechanisms through which dominant relationships are established and experienced.

Relevance of the gaze

Regardless of the limitations of Mulvey's original argument, thinking about the gaze forces us to realize that looking is a form of power and that power inequalities based on bodily forms and surface texture emerge through the act and apparatuses of looking. Along with other recognitions of the power of looking, such as Foucault and the panopticon (Foucault 1977b), the gaze makes us realize that spectatorship (the look, the gaze, the glance, the practice of observation, surveillance and visual pleasure) contains the potential for exploitation (Mitchell 1994: 16). Thus, any mechanism, process or performance that engages acts of looking and being seen is inextricably caught up with the power politics of inequality between those represented and those looking (and representing). Any apparatus that shapes, limits or expands the actions and relationships of looking is politically important and potentially exploitative.

There are immediate and important relevances to Neolithic figurines. First, if looking and the apparatus of looking at the human body are politically significant, then the creation, handling, destruction and discard of representations of the human body become particularly potent political behaviour. In representing the human body, a figurine is one side of the politically charged relationship between looking and being looked at. Furthermore, figurines provide opportunities to gaze in ways and for durations and foci that may not be possible or indeed appropriate or permitted in real life. At the other side of the relationship, the gaze illuminates the importance of being able to look, of having sight. The power of looking can be inverted by removing this ability. In addition to being an apparatus of the represented gaze, those figurines without representations of eyes, indeed those without heads, are further objectified in their inability to return the gaze. They are doubly disabled, doubly reduced to passivity and subordination. The gaze is also relevant because it links the creation of identities, the mechanisms of recognizing similarities and differences and the political relationships between the spectator and the object of looking. Also important is the way that the gaze makes us aware that we may be looked at and this awareness becomes a part of our identity. Lacan's idea is that the gaze is a two-way process: I see myself seeing myself (Mirzoeff 1999: 164, 236).

More generally, the clear question emerges, what was the place of figurines within strategies of spectatorship and of looking that would have had political connotations and consequences in Neolithic communities? Perhaps it is best to argue that figurines were one of many parts of sets of apparatuses that continually established, contested and replaced appropriate relationships between individuals and within groups. It is equally important to realize that the gaze is about fixing a relationship between the viewed and the viewer.

Furthermore, figurines are three-dimensional objects that implicate the politics of handling as well as of looking. We need to take the gaze to the third dimension, to examine the political permutations of the physical handling, moving, creation, decoration, transformation, breakage and discard of a representation of the body. If the gaze is a power relationship over the visual field, then the caress is a power relationship (and a much stronger one) over the tactile field. What are the consequences of this? What of the desire to physically control, touch, handle, possess other bodies, or to hold in one's hand a particular manifestation of humanness? What of the opportunity that figurines would have supplied to people, for whom, normally, in the real world, it might not have been appropriate (or possible perhaps) to touch, control, possess the human body, and for whom miniature bodies created a world in which such rules of appropriateness did not exist? Figurines-as-miniatures open up alternative worlds for the spectator and the handler. Figurines-as-objects of the gaze and the caress introduce apparatuses of political relationship and control. Figurines-as-bodies play with the dimensions of similarity and difference which construct identities. The layers and convolutions of social and political dynamics make figurines everything but simple representations of men or women of the Neolithic.

Conclusions

This chapter has suggested that visual images are especially powerful means of proposing realities, that those realities (and the means of their proposals) are political acts/constructs, and that when those acts/realities contain bodies, there is an added layer of political significance. Therefore when we look at figurines from a Neolithic, southeast European village, what are we looking at? If we follow Debord and Baudrillard, it is just as likely (more likely, even) that figurines do not reflect the actual Neolithic person as he or she was. We are forced to ask ourselves another important question: based on the politics of control inherent in the gaze, what are we doing when we look at bodies of the Neolithic represented by figurines? Are the politics of the gaze one component of the satisfaction and pleasure (perhaps unnoticed) that comes from undertaking a detailed visual examination of these 7,000-year-old bodily representations in a museum, in the excavation archive, in this book? Together these understandings of the potency of miniature representations push us to think about the politics of what is represented. How might figurines have worked within proposals for alternative realities in the Neolithic?

Clearly one possible alternate reality would have contained constructions of identities. If this is the case, then why did there exist a need to materially propose body-based identities? What was it that made the period 6500–3500 BC different from other periods of the Balkan prehistoric past? Perhaps, if as was suggested in the introductory chapter, the Neolithic was about the regularization of living, literally the domestication of the human, the animal, the temporal and the spatial, then there would have been no place for fluid and loose conceptions of identity. Just as in the Neolithic, landscape was tied down, bounded and contained, so the need would have arisen to solidify the dimensions of what it meant to be a person, to be linked to a particular part of that landscape. Fluidity, instability and flexibility would have threatened any emerging patterns of regularization. In tying down the human, particular sets of similarities and differences came to dominate increasingly standardized notions of individual-self and group identity.

Although there are differences of shape and decoration among figurines within any one cultural corpus (e.g., there are different types of Cucuteni/Tripolye or Hamangia figurines), the greatest differentiation is between different cultural corpuses (Cucuteni/Tripolye figurines are distinct from Hamangia figurines). There is tremendous similarity among figurines from one particular culture group.[11] One way to understand this similarity has been to rely on the satisfying simplicity of the culture-history approach where the identification of types is the goal. Based on the discussions in this chapter, another way is to recognize the politics of differentiation, similarity and stereotyping that runs through identity constructions. An important part of living in the Balkan Neolithic was based on new modalities of power, one of which was based on proposing particular body morphologies and surfaces.

Figurines were a potent means by which specific forms and characteristics were sedimented into the foundation of the Neolithic way of living and thinking. They created ways in which people were to see other people and in which they were to see and portray themselves. Perhaps we should argue at a more general level, as Butler does for the body, that the Neolithic witnessed a fundamental reformulation of the materiality of the body and of people's conception of articulations between being and body.

In this reformulation, the material body took up a pre-eminent and indissolvable position in the regulatory norms that emerged as the basis of identity in the seventh, sixth and fourth millennia BC. If bodies are not static but continually constructed, then the limited ranges of figurine form and decoration (especially given the exceptional morphological potential of clay) suggest that, in the Neolithic, there was a reduction in the mutability of the being, that there was a move towards tying down the body and to bounding the dimensions of being.

During this, new, developing corporeality-of-being, figurines stood as evidence of the number of acceptable and appropriate selves and of Others. They were normative restrictions of being, manifest through representations of the body. Through the reiteration of a material corporeality (via figurines), the Neolithic body becomes a major political norm governing dimensions of being, of being similar and of being different. Figurines are traces of the emergent regulation of identificatory practices. They are part of a process of materialization that created the boundaries of similarity and difference that we understand as personal identity. The Balkan Neolithic was a new corporealization of power relations; figurines were one part of that. Figurines are sites of struggles for value and power in the representation of reality. However, at these sites occurred not only the presentation and maintenance of the fundamental constituents of reality (such as identity), but also the subversion of those fundamentals. Chapter 8 takes up this theme.

7

THESSALY

In the summer of 1973, a team of American and Greek archaeologists were digging into the Early and Middle Neolithic (6500–5600 BC) settlement at Achilleion on the southeastern edge of the Thessalian Plain, near the modern town of Farsala in northcentral Greece. In one of the upper layers of the excavation, in an area lacking built features, and consisting of discarded Neolithic material, the team recovered an extraordinary figurine (fig. 7.1).[1] The figurine, or at least what remains of it (for it survived only from the neck upwards and part of the forehead is missing) consists of two independent pieces of fired clay, slipped with white paint. One piece represents a cylindrical neck. It is a thin, rounded column of clay, broken at the lower end, where the neck would have met the shoulders, and at the top end where the column tapers to a point. The other piece of the figurine is a representation of a human face. It is very schematically modelled and, seen from the front, is an oval or lozenge shape, widest at the level of the eyes, and almost pointed at the chin and forehead. Running horizontally across the middle of the face, two eyes, formed by two deep, thin incisions are separated by a pointed nose. Low on the face, near the chin, is a mouth, incised and impressed as a flat oval. While it is clear that the mouth is open, the eyes are more difficult to understand: are they closed, or are they open? No other features of the face or head are depicted: there are no ears and no hair. Indeed the face, though clearly human, bears no expression. Seen from the side, the eyes have a more sinister appearance; the look of a person squinting in anger, or even perhaps in incomprehension. I have described expressionless faces in earlier chapters and discussed the potential significances of omitting facial expression. But the face of this Achilleion figurine is something more, or more accurately perhaps, something less. It is life-less, though it does not appear to represent death. It is human, but is it anything more?

In addition to the unsettling appearance of the facial expression, other features give pause for thought. Running along the right jaw and under the left eye are visible the impressions of the fingerprints of the person who made the figurine: traces of the fingertips that pushed and pinched the clay into shape, fingers of a Neolithic hand that held the face while another hand held a stick or a pointed bit of bone or a flint flake and slit the eyes and formed the mouth. More remarkable is the way that the face fits snugly upon the cylindrical neck. The two separate parts were fashioned out of clay and the face was then stuck onto the neck: even now the result is a face that can be removed from the neck. Like others, including the excavators of Achilleion, I am struck by the similarity between this figurine and a person wearing a mask. Just as a mask shields a living, facial expression by covering it with the static set of features of a mask, so do the eyes and mouth of the Achilleion figurine present a face without living expression. This is an

147

Figure 7.1 Figurine from Achilleion. *Reprinted from Achilleion: A Neolithic Settlement in Thessaly, Greece* (Monumenta Archaeologica 14), edited by Marija Gimbutas, Shann Winn and Daniel Shimabuku (Los Angeles, CA: The Cotsen Institute of Archaeology at UCLA, 1989).

extraordinary little ensemble. What are the significances of a figurine with a removable face? Were there many different, interchangeable faces that could be fitted onto one neck? If so what does this mean, especially in terms of the importance of the face and the head as vehicles within expressions of personal identity?

There is one other figurine with a removable mask from Achilleion[2] (Gimbutas 1989b: 179) and there are another nine examples from the site which have representations of masks fixed to their faces.[3] All have eyes represented, though some eyes are no more than thin incisions made into the surface of the mask; others are slits cut into small pellets of clay that had been pressed onto the mask. Some masked figurines have eyes and noses represented but no mouths. On a number of them, the cylindrical necks continue above the mask to form the tops of figurine heads; on others the tops of the masks mark the tops of heads. The body of one masked figurine is preserved down to the waist and shows that while the face is expressionless, other corporeal details were represented: head, neck and shoulders are disproportionately large in comparison with the torso; the shoulders have incised lines running front to back and the one arm that is preserved is bent at the elbow with its hands placed on a swollen abdomen.[4]

THESSALY

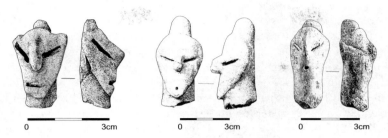

Figure 7.2 Figurines from Roidies (left) and Bei (centre and right) (after Gallis and Orphanidis 1996).

At Achilleion, mask-like faces are also modelled onto the surfaces of pots (ibid.: 201) and a masked face was found on the surface of a hollow vessel which itself was anthropomorphically formed.[5] In addition to these, there are masked figurines from many other sites in this region[6] (fig 7.2) some of which have additional detail on the head, such as ears.[7] On some of the masked heads, it is difficult to determine where the mask ends and where the human head begins and, indeed, it is even unclear whether or not it is a mask that is represented. There are contemporary cylinder-necked figurines which have the same expressionless eyes, mouths and noses as the masked versions, though often these have incised or modelled hair or head-dressings. Are these simply more elaborate masks that include wigs? Are they masks worn under the hair? Perhaps they are not masks at all, but only representations with an odd, expressionless face which appears to us similar to the one represented on masks?

Traditional studies of Thessalian figurines

In her report on the Achilleion excavations, Marija Gimbutas recognizes the likelihood that the figurine described above bears a representation of a mask, though she does not explore the potential meaning of the phenomenon beyond noting that it is ambiguous and thus can refer to two or three different divinities (Gimbutas 1989b: 179). Gimbutas' general approach to Thessalian figurines is perhaps the most widely known, though, as we shall see below, there are other, critically overlooked, local lines of attack that are more sophisticated and of greater value. In her general works (Gimbutas 1974a, 1980, 1989a, 1991), Gimbutas uses Thessalian figurines (as well as those from other regions) to propose a pantheon of Neolithic divinities. In the more detailed reports of her excavations in Thessaly (at Achilleion; Gimbutas 1989a, 1989b: 171–250) and in neighbouring regions at Anza (Gimbutas 1976) and at Sitagroi (Gimbutas 1986a), she follows a common approach: the classification of figurines, based on morphology and style, produces associations with particular divinities (Gimbutas 1989b: 171).

At Achilleion, six deities (and one human category) are said to be represented: Bird Goddess, Snake Goddess, Pregnant Goddess, Birth-giving Goddess, Frog Goddess, Male Gods and nurses (ibid.: 171). There is no analytical discussion, only the statement that 'the purpose of making figurines was not to create beautiful sculptures but to make goddesses, sacred animals, or participants in cult activities' (Gimbutas ibid.: 177). Implicit justification for interpretation takes the form of descriptive catalogue entries for each complete or fragmentary figurine (Gimbutas 1989c). Although Gimbutas presents contextual information for figurines from different phases of Achilleion (Gimbutas 1989b: 213–18) she subsumes analysis of any trends in form, decoration or find-context under discussions of 'cult types' (ibid.: 177). Figurines are found in religious or ceremonial places which have been defined, tautologically, as having religious or ceremonial purpose because they contain figurines (Gimbutas ibid.: 218–20). Patterns of variation among Achilleion figurines reflect variety in hierarchy within divine groups: smaller figurines of one particular cultic type represent assistants to one particular type of goddess (Gimbutas ibid.: 220). For Gimbutas, Achilleion figurines make two fundamental contributions to our understanding of the Neolithic: they show that goddesses ruled over human, animal and plant life; and they reveal a nearly complete 'assemblage of stereotypes of mythical images' (ibid.).

Beyond Gimbutas

Though Gimbutas' Achilleion work has had a wide influence on research in Thessaly and other regions, there are other important and often overlooked Greek works that move the discussion well beyond assumptions of divinities: the works of Georgios Hourmouziadis (1973), Evangelia Skafida (Skafida 1986), Laia Orphanidis (1998), and Kostas Gallis (Gallis and Orphanidis 1996). These publications share a common descriptive typology for Thessalian figurines, though for Hourmouziadis at least, there is the recognition that, on its own, classification on morphological grounds does not get us very far (Hourmouziadis 1973).

Description

Clay is the main material of figurine manufacture, though stone, especially marble, was also used, particularly towards the end of the Neolithic (Hourmouziadis 1973: 32–51, figs 4–5). Orphanidis has argued for the possible use of wood as a material of manufacture; she also suggests that the preference for construction material depended on the location of a particular site, the local soil and geomorphology, and the particular type of figurine intended: naturalistic or schematic figurines required the use of softer or harder materials respectively (Orphanidis 1998: 269). Clay figurines were made of the same materials as were used to make ceramic vessels. Frequently, separate lumps of clay were joined together to form a single figurine body, and thin layers of clay covered joins. The final object was smoothed, burnished and painted before firing (ibid.: 269–70). Sometimes, clay was fashioned around a core made of some perishable material which, after firing, produced a hollow figurine; in other examples, a pebble formed a core around which clay was applied.

All authors agree that there are two main types of Neolithic figurines (schematic and naturalistic/realistic[8]) and that each of these categories contains a series of loosely defined sub-types. Diachronically, many of the earlier figurines are more realistic than later ones and have well-defined body parts and diagnostic sexual features (Gallis and Orphanidis 1995; Kokkinidou and Nikolaidou 1997: 90). There are exceptions and one wonders about the actual homogeneity of any trends defined in these general terms. At Sesklo, for example, the earliest figurines were highly schematized with no diagnostic sexual

Figure 7.3 Figurines from Orenia (left) and Bezil (right) (after Gallis and Orphanidis 1996).

features (Perlès 2001: 257; Theocharis 1973: fig. 206, pl. 22; 1967: fig. 92) and body parts merge together with no distinct head, neck or breasts; arms are short stubs and buttocks are large (Wijnen 1981: 45–6). In the middle Neolithic, there was a move towards stylized representation and figurine decoration followed trends in contemporary pottery production. By the end of the Late Neolithic, a decline in quality of manufacture matched an increase in stylization, as trapezoid, oval and other plain shapes took the place of detailed facial rendering (Gallis and Orphanidis 1996: 155, 159). Also common is the descriptive importance given to whether a figurine is standing or sitting and whether or not the seated ones sit on a chair (or even 'throne'), sit on their knees or sit with their legs folded to the side or crossed. Female figurines outnumber male ones (the latter are represented by men sitting or standing and by phallus-shaped objects), though the assignment of sex to head fragments is problematic: elaborate headdress (fig. 7.3) need not be restricted to females (cf. Gallis and Orphanidis 1995: 158–9).

Interpretation

As Hourmouziadis suggests there is no single, secure view on the interpretation of Thessalian figurines.[9] Their meanings are dependent on their contexts of use and, as he suggests, these may well be diverse. Equally frustrating, contexts of use can vary from the original intention of a figurine maker (Hourmouziadis 1973: 199). Even Gimbutas admits the ubiquity of figurines within sites (Gimbutas 1989b: 213), and that attempts to use figurine find-spots as a key to unlock figurine function or interpretation are risky at best. To make the link between find-spot and function even more complicated, Skafida (n.d.) and Perlès (2001) have suggested that most figurines had a limited period of use after which they were broken and thrown away: thus information about find-spots has an even further reduced significance for determining use, and paradoxically moves us increasingly distant from any single, original, intended purpose or meaning if, indeed, there ever was one.

THESSALY

Thinking through figurines

While reference is often to Gimbutas, better work is available. Christina Marangou, for example, has published a major synthesis of figurines from Greece stretching from the Neolithic through the Early Bronze Age (Marangou 1992, 1996a, 1996b). Gallis and Orphanidis have detailed the realism in many figurines' appearances (Gallis and Orphanidis 1995) and Evangelia Skafida has written a useful dissertation and summary articles (Skafida 1986, 1992, n.d.; Skafida and Toufexis 1994). In addition to these works, four contributions are of particular value, each moving us towards a fuller understanding of the Thessalian material.

Talalay and the Peloponnese

The first of these other contributions is the research of Lauren Talalay who studied Neolithic figurines from southern Greece with special attention to material from Franchthi Cave (Talalay 1987, 1993). Though focused on a separate region, there is value to Talalay's approach and the direction that her interpretations take us. Talalay makes the important distinction between figurine use/function and figurine meaning: a particular figurine can be used as a votive but its meaning can refer to a range of things, from the way a community perceives the human body to their social attitudes to gender (Talalay 1993: 38). Importantly, figurines have a particular potential for manipulating ideologies within mechanisms of social control (ibid.: 38). Thus, some Middle Neolithic Peloponnesian figurines worked as identification or contractual props within inter-community agreements and alliances (ibid.: 46). More provocative is Talalay's discussion of the intentional cropping of figurines during their construction, and the consequent suggestion that figurine makers recognized two major divisions of the body: upper and lower; left and right (ibid.: 49). Regardless of the precise meanings of particular body divisions or zones, the significant contribution is the recognition that Neolithic men and women saw the body and its component parts as templates with which they structured and understood their worlds (ibid.: 50). Refreshingly, Talalay moves us away from the simple view that figurines are mere reflections of people; she makes us realize that they were specifically charged objects with which Neolithic individuals thought about their world and the position of the human body within it.

Kokkinidou and Nikolaïdou and body image

In an important paper on the ideological implications of body imagery in the Aegean Neolithic, Dimitra Kokkinidou and Marianna Nikolaidou took forward several of the points raised by Talalay (Kokkinidou and Nikolaidou 1997). Kokkinidou and Nikolaidou investigated how human representations can reveal Neolithic understandings of identities, how Neolithic people might have manipulated social roles and interactions, and how figurines functioned in constructions of gender and the interplay of power relations (ibid.: 88). They argue that body imagery was an organizing principal in the concepts, communications, symbols and social negotiations of Neolithic people (ibid.: 89) and they identify an iconography of sexuality that was embedded in Neolithic attempts to understand and interfere with fertility: attention to breasts, bellies, buttocks, and the schematization of pubis and phallus (ibid.: 93). Kokkinidou and Nikolaidou interpret the emphases on sexualized body parts as manifestations of Neolithic interests in the mysteries of human biology (ibid.: 93–4). While attention to breasts and pubis follows a long tradition in figurine interpretation (indeed it is at the core of the Mother Goddess approach), Kokkinidou and Nikolaidou push the connections in new directions. They suggest that figurine fertility-symbolism transgressed the boundaries of sexual division between men and women (ibid.: 94), and that figurines were material codes with which people represented and reshaped reality (ibid.: 103). Most importantly, like Talalay, Kokkinidou and Nikolaidou propose that the human body was an organizing metaphor that operated on collective and personal levels and with which Neolithic people created social bonds and ordered and understood their worlds (ibid.: 108). Emphasis on the body's image and its role in the Neolithic is exciting, though the article leaves us without a detailed discussion of how such an understanding might help us to better understand the particularities of a village or household community. Like so much good thinking on figurines, the stimulating discussion makes great progress at the level of generalization but stops short of working the provocative ideas through sets of data.

Orphanidis and repetition

Less widely circulated outside of Greece than the works of Gimbutas, Talalay or Kokkinidou and Nikolaidou is the important contribution that Laia Orphanidis made in her 1998 volume *Eisagoge Ste Neolithike Eidoloplastike: Notioanatolike Europe kai Anatolike Mesogeios {Introduction to Neolithic Figurine Art: Southeastern Europe and the Eastern Mediterranean}*. In addition to a survey of figurines from Greece and neighbouring regions, Orphanidis proposes an alternative approach through which analysis can move beyond sterile typological analysis (Orphanidis 1998: 285). She argues that people use symbols and other shared figurative formulations in order to mediate community agreement on critical concepts of being, especially in thought and in understanding one's position in a social group (ibid.: 283). Orphanidis suggests that an understanding of one's position in time and in space improves through repeated imitations of parts of one's surroundings. Orphanidis' imitations refer to figural representations, and their repetitions refer to the multiple creations of a similar form of figurine.

From these observations, Orphanidis develops a theory of repetition in which figurines find their new meaning as parts of the way that Neolithic people understand who they are and how they fit into their communities (ibid.: 254–62, 287). Thus, the control of many of the situations in which a person finds himself or herself lies beyond the reach of the individual's personal power; control rests in some other world. For Orphanidis, this other world is a magical or religious one and the consistent repetition of the body form provides the basis for a semiotics of peoples' shared acceptance of the belief in a divinity. Orphanidis identifies one such repetition of form in the figurines of women holding their breasts with their hands; the use of beaked noses on cylindrical necks is another (ibid.: 285). Orphanidis' theory of repetition is particularly relevant to the schematic figurines; they embody abstractive mental processes and facilitate human engagement with religious or social concepts (such as goddess or the qualities of a leader or healer) or with the ways that people understand a shared abstract social construction (such as a family or village) (ibid.: 287).

There are important consequences here for understanding the large number of figurines used and discarded at Neolithic sites, as well as the formal similarities of many figurines and the repetitions of particular forms over long periods of time and between separate villages. Significantly, just as the repetition of imitation from nature (i.e., repeated representations of the human form) is part of the human endeavour to understand, Orphanidis suggests that the variations between figurines (especially among the realistic ones) help to differentiate individuals from the rest of a social group. In all of these arguments, Orphanidis has pushed the discussion well beyond the limits of descriptive typology and she has done so in a way that resists the simple seductions of reconstructing pantheons of prehistoric deities or of uncovering ancestor portraits. Though the theory of repetition is not played out through the particularities of the Thessalian material, it is suggestive and provocative, moving us closer to an understanding of how these figurines worked and, critically, of what they were representations for.[10]

Hourmouziadis and synairesis

The fourth major work of influence and interpretive stimulation is Georgios Hourmouziadis' 1973 volume *Ne Anthropomorphe Idoloplastike tes Neolithikes Thessalias: Provlemata Kataskeues, Typologias kai Hermeneias, {Anthropomorphic Idoloplastic of Neolithic Thessaly: Construction, Typology and Interpretation}*. Hourmouziadis argued that analysts should not focus on morphology exclusively, but should examine the content of the figurine, the idea that the figurine maker tried to express in the clay (ibid.: 55–6). For Hourmouziadis, therefore, figurines are descriptions of ideas (Hourmouziadis 1973: 59). Particularly important is his discussion of the Neolithic tendency for unreal and distorted representation of anatomical details, a process that Hourmouziadis terms *synairesis*: an unnatural combination of perspective and of things not represented in nature (ibid.: 74). Thus, figurine body parts are not always represented in the correct positions, their sizes and relationships do not follow any natural reality: every figurine is not produced in harmony to a physical reality (ibid.: 74).

These manifestations of *synairesis* are not the result of carelessness or the lack of ability on the part of the modeller; rather, the distortions, altered perspectives and proportions are repeated and follow the principles of exaggeration and transformation (ibid.: 75). Transformation creates a recognizable form that is both easily repeated and easily recognized, and this is, I would add, a move towards simplification and abstraction as raised in the discussion of miniaturism in Chapter 2 above. Exaggeration is the selection and projection of particular anatomical detail (breasts, hips, hair) in order to produce a figurine of a particular character. Hourmouziadis suggests that we should approach figurines from two angles. First, we must look at figurines as constructions, objects that carry the personal views of the maker, though these views are also continuations of the views held by the community. On the other hand, we need to see figurines as instruments of particular social behaviour, as objects that worked within larger processes of social inscription. The presence in equal measures of these two perspectives inserts an unbridgeable gap between the intention of the maker and the purpose of the consumer and thus makes the task of interpretation a highly complex and nuanced one (ibid.: 199).

Conclusions of traditional approaches to Thessalian figurines

While the international understanding of Thessalian figurines has been dominated by Gimbutas' elevation of the divine and the goddess, a more exciting understanding comes from the work of Hourmouziadis, Orphanidis, Talalay and Kokkinidou and Nikolaidou. If we look again at the masked figurine from Achilleion, how do these latter works help us to better understand that object? All of those authors argued that we must consider figurines first in their relationship to other figurines (i.e., most clearly in Orphanidis' theory of repetition) and then in the context of the social and individual bodies of the people who made and experienced them. How does the masked Achilleion figurine fit into the larger corpus of material? To answer these questions, we need to take a broader look at the range of figurine form in the Thessalian Neolithic.

Simple representations

Like the masked example from Achilleion, many Thessalian figurines are made with long cylindrical necks that taper towards their tops. Many of these bear incised, horizontal (or slightly slanted) eyes and, frequently, exaggerated beaky noses (fig. 7.3 right). It is not always clear if this is the application of a face to an exaggeratedly long neck or if it is a head that is formed as one long cylinder. Some of these figurines have eyes made with pellets of clay pressed on the face and slit horizontally. Others have parallel zigzagging, incised lines on the sides and back of the head to represent hair. Some have hair modelled in a bun on top or back of the head.[11] There is also a series of schematic, triangular heads with prominent noses and with eyes formed from pellets of clay stuck on the face.[12] Are these representations of triangular masks, or are they something else altogether? More schematic are the triangular heads that lack even pellet or slit eyes or which have nothing more than small perforations where eyes might have been.[13] Simpler still are triangular heads made of white or grey marble.[14] Perhaps most basic of all the Thessalian figurines are the triangular or trapezoidal marble objects, the acroliths, that bear no resemblance to a head or face but which are found stuck into undecorated clay bodies in the place where one would expect to find a neck and head (fig. 7.4) (Theocharis 1973: fig. 30; Skafida 1986).[15] Other schematic marble heads are less like a person's head and neck and closer in form to the shape of a penis.[16]

A large number of figurines from the Thessalian Neolithic have similar lifeless or at least expressionless faces. Indeed a high proportion of figurines from the region lack specific details beyond a simplistic modelling of the head, often perched on an overly elongated neck; it is difficult to ignore similarities with the long-necked, and often faceless, Hamangia figurines, from regions further north (see Chapter 3). Although the chronological gap between the phenomena undermines arguments for cultural connection, are we looking at similar mechanisms of representation at work? If we were to revisit the faceless Hamangia figurines, would we now begin to see missing, detachable faces (masks even) and heads on top of their long thin necks?

Within the simplicity of form of the Thessalian figurines, however, different body parts receive unequal attention in modelling and decoration. On many of the cylindrical beaked forms, noses are modelled in a size out of all proportion to the rest of the figurine. Why has this been done? How do we understand such emphasis on the nose? Is there some special meaning that we are missing? Is there something important or distinctive about the sense of smell to which these examples refer? Are these representations of particular individuals who had particularly large noses? As we will see with other, more realistic Thessalian figurines, the decision to attend to particular body parts is not random; on the contrary particular body parts are elaborated in a common way on many figurines

THESSALY

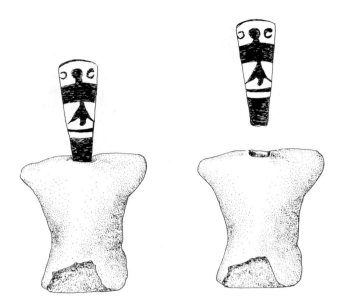

Figure 7.4 Acrolithic figurine from Rachmani (after Orphanidis 1998).

both from the same and from different sites. In addition to this emphasis on the face, similar processes of repetition and exaggeration of form are found on thighs, legs and stomachs. Though there are also dramatically realistic representations, the most noticeable pattern is the repetition of exaggerated, schematized form of a particular body part which appears in many separate examples; immediate reference is perhaps to something that extends well beyond the individual person.[17]

Realistic figurines

While many of the Neolithic figurines from Thessaly are schematic, a significant number are dramatically vital, full of facial and corporeal detail. In their realism there is an eerie disquiet not met when looking at the simpler, more schematic, figurines. One example, a fragment from Achilleion[18] (fig. 7.5), has a strangely unbalanced, disturbed face with an overly large, blob of a nose, modelled at an angle, twisted, and bent out of shape. Puffy eyes are shown as if swollen and sore. Thin lips are separated just enough so that one can almost see a breath being sucked in. We are far from the simplistic, almost mechanistic representations of the masks, the cylindrical neck and heads, the geometrical symmetry of the triangular heads, and the elongated trapezoidal stone of the acroliths.

This Achilleion head is slipped in white over which, around the bottom of the neck, is painted a red necklace or at least the top edge of a shirt or other garment, or even some sort of painted body decoration or tattoo. Though difficult to see in the photograph of the figurine, the top and sides of the head are covered, as if by a tight-fitting cap painted in red with small round, white dots on it.[19] This face is full of particular and individual expression; it speaks to the viewer in an emotional way. There is also a striking fragment of a face from Domokos (Gallis and Orphanidis 1996: 69; Gallis and Orphanidis 1995:

156

Figure 7.5 Figurine from Achilleion. *Reprinted from Achilleion: A Neolithic Settlement in Thessaly, Greece* (Monumenta Archaeologica 14), edited by Marija Gimbutas, Shann Winn and Daniel Shimabuku (Los Angeles, CA: The Cotsen Institute of Archaeology at UCLA, 1989).

156, 161, cat. no. 11, fig. 11); there, below fully modelled eyebrows, eyes are closed and, again, the impression of swelling emerges. Ears are modelled, as is a realistically sized nose with nostrils made from impressions. Mouth and lips are like those on the white-slipped figurine from Achilleion.

There are also figurines, though surprisingly few of them, of people in action. One from Early Neolithic Prodromos holds a pot on her head (Orphanidis 1998: 40); a pair of figures from early Neolithic Domeniko is modelled arm-in-arm (Gallis and Orphanidis 1996: 205; Gallis 1990: 19, figs 6–7; Demoule and Gallis 1991: 14; Gallis 1992: 118, fig. 22). A figurine from Late Neolithic Sesklo sits on a four-legged chair and is boldly painted in dark parallel rings that run around legs and body. The head is painted to represent hair, and the arms hold a baby (Orphanidis 1998: fig. 52). There are other examples of figurines holding babies at Agios Georgios I and Zappeio (Skafida and Toufexis 1994: 18).

Why aren't there more figurines shown engaged in activities? Is there some unrecognized significance of the immobility and stasis evoked by all of the schematic figurines and most of the more realistic ones? What is the significance of the almost complete absence of representations of active figurines? Perhaps part of an answer comes from the discussion in Chapters 2 and 4 about the potential that miniature objects such as figurines possess as media for thinking and doing in other worlds, that is, the proposal that in simplicity and a lack of expressive details (and also then in the absence of a particular activity) there rests the greatest potential for static and simple figurines to stimulate the independence of thought and to free the imagination of a person handling a figurine.

Heads, shoulders and backs

Figure 7.6 Figurine from Panagou (after Gallis and Orphanidis 1996).

Particular parts of the body receive more attention to detail than do others. Already discussed were the examples of schematic elaborations of eyes, noses, necks and heads. Beyond the simple modelling of the cylinder and masked heads and faces, special attention was focused on realistic modelling of hair on figurine heads (fig. 7.6). On some, clay was shaped into two or three long braids (dreadlocks even) that run down the length of long, cylindrical necks.[20] On others, the hair is parted down the middle and drawn up into a bun at the rear.[21] Thick, full heads of hair, modelled in straight vertical tresses, frame the face of a Middle Neolithic figurine from Sesklo, though the face bears a nose so exaggerated that it is longer than the hair (Orphanidis 1998: 43). On other figurines, the surface of the hair bears series of small impressions creating the appearance of a head of curly, shoulder-length locks.[22] On other heads, hair is represented in simpler ways by diagonal sets of parallel incisions. A figurine from Pyrassos has pellets of clay on the top and rear of its head and brings to mind the similarly sized and spaced painted pattern of white dots on the red cap of the realistic Achilleion figurine.[23] Though there is considerable variety in the ways that hair is represented in these Thessalian figurines, the common component is that hair is an appropriate element for detailed representation. What is the significance of this? Can we better understand Thessalian people of the Neolithic in terms of their hair and its styling, or is the attention to depicting hair an unimportant, decorative, background detail of these representations?

In addition to detailed modelling of hair on figurine heads, the shoulders and backs of Thessalian figurines also carry particular methods of surface decoration. Thus, small, clay pellets were stuck on to shoulders; a figurine from Paliambela[24] has parallel rows of four or five pellets running between the neck and shoulders and a figurine with similar shoulder treatment has been found at Mavrachades, Sofades.[25] Seven pellets, applied in a less carefully ordered fashion and, oddly, with eyelid-like slits incised into them, were placed on the shoulder of a figurine from Achilleion.[26] From Vassuli, there is a seated figurine with half a dozen pellets on each shoulder[27] and a seated figurine from Dragatsi has at least half a dozen on each upper arm.[28] On some figurines, instead of pellets, shoulders bear parallel rows of short parallel incisions running out from the neck.[29] Similar patterns of incised decoration were applied to the backs of figurines in single rows at Panagou,[30] in double rows at Zoodochos Pigi,[31] and in quadruple rows from Mezil.[32]

What is the significance of selecting these particular body parts (hair, shoulders, heads and faces) and subjecting them to similar treatment of shaping, application and incision? As with the attention to hair and heads, how are we to understand or read the parallel lines and the application of pellets of clay onto heads or shoulders? Can we ever pretend that we understand what these attentions to detail were attempting to portray or create? Perhaps not. What is possible, however, and what matters for our increasingly refined perception of the people who made, held and looked at these figurines, is for us to be able to recognize that people were creating, displaying and regularly looking at human figurines whose form and decoration established appropriate corporeal and facial appearances. Most probably unconsciously and unintentionally, the repeated, daily events of Neolithic people seeing and handling these figurines created and maintained standards of corporeal identity against which men, women and children subconsciously measured their own appearance and the appearances of others. Figurines engaged people in continual visual discussions of what it meant to be similar to and different from each other. In this sense, these figurines were one of many mechanisms through which communities interwove their shared (and contested) senses of how individuals were related to one another, indeed of who people were (and were not). Attention to head and the face would have worked well in these types of identity discourse, especially in light of the ways that heads and faces occupy positions of preference for more recent human understanding of who and what a person is (see discussion in Chapters 4 and 6). There is much here that fits in with Orphanidis' theory of repetition, though with the programmatic religious or ritual stimulus replaced in the more mundane, though perhaps more important, daily events of the social construction of reality.

Breasts, abdomen, pubes and penises

While figurine makers paid attention to heads, faces, shoulders and backs, they concentrated equally on modelling and incising sexualized body parts. While figurines in all southeast European Neolithic communities depicted sexualized body parts on figurines to some degree, the Thessalian examples are especially explicit in their attention to female breasts and to female and male genitalia. Many Thessalian figurines were modelled with clear representations of female breasts, and there is a particular, often repeated, manner of shaping figurine hands to rest on or under the breasts (fig. 7.7). In one variation, arms were shaped with elbows bent and hands placed in front of the breasts; often fingers cover the front of the breasts (though these hands often have only three fingers).[33] On other figurines, arms are modelled in the same way, but hands are placed under the breasts, touching or supporting them.[34] On yet other examples, hands are placed flat against the chest, below and away from the breasts.[35] What is the significance of the placements of hands to breasts? Indeed should we seek a single significance or several? Does any sort of physical connection between hands and breasts attract the viewer's attention to the breasts, or are we to understand each different positioning of the hands as having a different meaning or significance? Do hands placed under breasts support, project and draw attention to them? Do hands covering breasts serve to hide them? Similar questions emerge when we look at other representations of sexualized body parts.

THESSALY

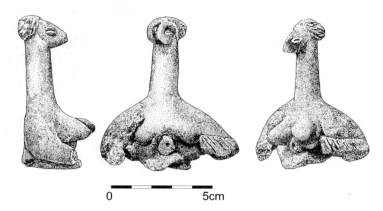

Figure 7.7 Figurine from Achilleion (after Gimbutas 1989c).

Abdomen and pubis

In addition to female breasts, attention in modelling and surface decoration is devoted to the abdomen and pubis. For the abdomen, as was the case with the breasts, the arms and hands play a part; hands are placed on the abdomen in various positions, above and below the navel.[36] Indeed the depiction of the navel itself is important in both its frequency on figurines but also, in some examples, in its modelling. While it is usually depicted by a simple impression, in a few examples it has been shown by the application of a flat, doughnut-like ring of clay around an impression. On many figurines, abdomens are depicted in extended, swollen or sagging forms. Exaggeration of this body region is important; indeed it is at the centre of widespread interpretations of these figurines as pregnant women or as representations of birth-giving or fertility divinities. However, there are rather unusual things happening here.

On many figurines that have breasts and navels, incised lines mark out an inverted triangular area covering the abdomen and the hips, with the triangle's tip marking the point where the tops of the thighs meet the crotch, and where there is usually a small vertical incision to suggest the closed outer labia of the vagina. There is nothing unusual in the depiction of pubic triangles and labia on Neolithic figurines from southeastern Europe: it is a common feature of figurines in these communities. What is unusual is the way that this pubic package is put together and, most especially, the relationship of the triangular area, the presence or absence of labia, and the shaping of the swollen, sagging (pregnant even) abdomen.

On many of the Thessalian figurines, the incised lines of the triangle mark out an area of a woman's body which, if the labial incision is present, work to exhibit this part of the body. If the triangle is present without labial incision, then the figurine represents the same area but in a different way: with some sort of covering or at least without explicit attention to labia. On many of the Thessalian figurines with the pubic region represented, the former arrangement is clear: labia are marked with a short slit and the incised triangle marks out the remainder of the pubic region. Though pubic hair is not depicted, it is difficult not to conclude that this representation refers to an uncovered, though simplified, female pubis.

THESSALY

A more perplexing combination is found in another series of Thessalian figurines. On these the same treatment has been applied to the pubic region: one incision marks the labia and others define the pubic triangle (fig. 7.8). There are, however, two odd things. First, the lines of the pubic triangle are not limited to the front of the figurine, but continue round the hips and across the buttocks: they appear to represent clothing or other forms of textile covering.[37] In some examples, the incised patterns are elaborated; usually they have many parallel lines running across and around the hips, buttocks and pubis. It is interesting that some of the figurines that have incised pubic triangles and labial incisions do not have breasts[38] and others have labia but neither pubic triangles nor breasts.[39]

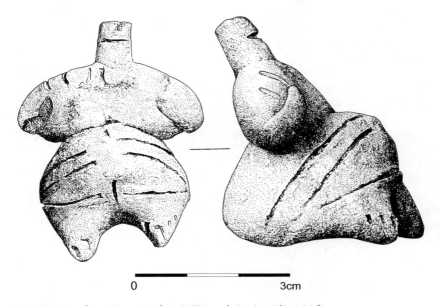

Figure 7.8 Figurine from Orenia (after Gallis and Orphanidis 1996).

None of these representations of a clothed/covered pubis would be perplexing if it were not for the fact that on some both labia and pubic triangles are represented together.[40] The labial slit cannot be both covered by clothing and visible at the same time. Or can it? There is a strange dynamic emerging when we look at these figurines, both the realistic ones and the more schematic ones, (especially, though not only, the masked ones); a series of contradictions emerges: between covering and uncovering, between hiding and displaying, between drawing the viewer's attention to particular parts of the body but then of confounding and confusing by failing to provide the full picture. The breasts are represented and presented to be seen, yet they can be covered and hidden as well; the labia are depicted yet are covered with clothing, the face is there but it is not, it is covered by a mask.

There is also something odd about the way that the incised pubic regions are set into the bodies of some of these figurines: the incised lines that mark out the pubic region cut back deeply into the body of the figurine (fig. 7.9).[41] This cutting of the incisions

THESSALY

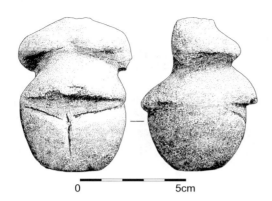

Figure 7.9 Figurine from Kyriaki (after Gallis and Orphanidis 1996).

into the body is less a factor of the technique used for incising the surface of the figurine and more a result of modelling the pubic region to appear as if a tight piece of clothing restricts and binds an otherwise swollen abdomen. Thus, above the top line of the triangle, the stomach bulges forward, out above the constriction. Here we have a representation of a piece of clothing that pulls in the swollen, flabby or pregnant, female body in a most unnatural manner. What makes this odder still is that the labial incision is also represented on these figurines, visible through whatever this constrictive piece of clothing might be.

The contradiction of labia visible through the clothing is only odd, of course, if the intention was to represent clothing. If the constricted areas represent not flesh held in by clothing, but of an area of the body bound with straps or thongs or some other sort of ligature, then the combination of incision, constriction, overhanging belly and the presence of the labia is more understandable, though also clearly more provocative for our understanding of this formulation of representing the female body. With these figurines, the attention is drawn to the labia and the abdomen but the target of that visual attraction is not limited to symbols of reproduction (i.e., vagina, pregnant abdomen) as is so frequently assumed. If these particular incisions represent constrictive straps, then perhaps the multiple incised lines covering the pubis, hips and buttocks, noted above on the other figurines of this type, represent not clothing, but similar straps as well or, at the very least, decoration of the body by paint or tattoo or other markings.

Penises

Female genitalia are not the only sexualized body parts elaborated and exaggerated on Thessalian figurines; a small but not insignificant number of figurines have penises depicted. Perhaps the most dramatic of these comes from a Late Neolithic phase at Larissa (fig. 7.10) (Orphanidis 1998: 53). The figurine represents a man sitting on a low stool with his legs forward, bent at the knees with feet flat on the floor in front of him, shoulder-width apart; his back is straight. The left arm is bent at the elbow with its hand on the left knee; the right arm, also bent at the elbow, reaches upwards and its hand is placed on the side of the face. There is little decoration on the face itself, which is tilted upwards. Around the base of the neck runs a series of short parallel incisions that represent a necklace or perhaps the edge of a shirt or other piece of clothing. Similar, though longer, parallel incisions run from the lower abdomen out along the shaft of what must have been an enormous penis, the diameter of which is not much less than that of one of the man's arms and the length of which was probably longer than the man's thigh. The penis sticks straight forward, with testicles modelled underneath.

Another figurine with similarly large penis comes from Early Neolithic Mataranga Karditsas (Orphanidis 1998: fig. 33; Gallis and Orphanidis 1996: 196; Gallis 1990:

THESSALY

Figure 7.10 Seated figurine from Larisa (after Orphanidis 1998).

18–19, fig. 5; Demoule and Gallis 1991: 12). In this version, the man sits on the ground with legs slightly bent at the knees in front of him; the right leg crosses under the knee of the left one. Both arms are bent: the right hand rests on the right knee and the left is placed against the head. The penis, not as large in proportion to the body as is the Larissa example, sticks straight forward, though its full size is impossible to estimate as it is broken along the shaft. There are other figurines with penises. From Vrasteri comes a fragment of a seated individual with hands placed towards his lap and penis and testicle modelled, though they are poorly preserved (Gallis and Orphanidis 1996: 177). Even less well preserved is another seated example from Sofades which has traces of a penis (ibid.: 176). From the same site comes another seated male figurine with a large, rounded penis, to the base of which were modelled the figurine's two hands (ibid.: 179). Another seated figurine comes from Otzaki and has one hand on a thigh and the fragmentary base of what must have been another large penis (ibid.: 178).[42]

Many of the figurines with disproportionately large penises share a common pose, often seated and sometimes with one hand to their heads and often one or both hands resting on their thigh, knee or the base of the penis. There are exceptions. A seated male figurine from Stergiana has a smaller penis and hands placed one above the other, flat against the chest and abdomen (ibid.: 182). There are also standing figurines with penises from Chara (ibid.: 192); and one from Sitochoro (ibid.: 194), though both of these are fragmentary and neither have extraordinarily large penises.

In the context of the potential binding of female bodies, the figurine with a penis from Sitochoro is of further interest as it has incised lines leading from the hips and crossing over the penis. Are there similar contradictions of dress/undress, covering/exposing and bondage at play here as there were with the some of the female figurines? Clearer similarities between treatment of the female and male genitalia are found in another male figurine, though it comes from an unknown, though clearly Neolithic, provenance (ibid.: 375). Patterns of incised lines cover hips and buttocks in a fashion similar to many of the female figurines that have labial incisions: most relevant is that the shaft of the penis, made from a piece of modelled clay, applied flat against the body, is pointed upwards towards the stomach and chest, and has been decorated with incised parallel, diagonal lines. Do the lines on the penis represent binding and is this penis thus strapped against the body? Are male genitalia bound in the same way as were those of women?

There are other figurines, though very few of them, that complicate even further the image that is emerging of sexualized bodies and attention to male or female sexual morphologies. Clearest are the examples from Sarliki (ibid.: 186; and see Gallis 1992: 156, fig. 28, drawing 16) and from Panagou. Both are seated figures and both have penises modelled lying along the join of the thighs. Neither penis is unusually large. The extraordinary thing is that on the chests of both figurines, the application of round lumps of clay clearly reveals female breasts on the otherwise male figures (fig. 7.11). While the figurine from Sarliki has its hands on its thighs, the one from Panagou has arms that are

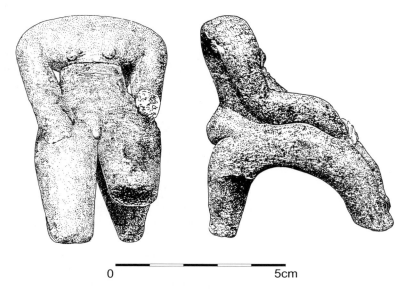

Figure 7.11 Seated figurine from Koutsouro (after Gallis and Orphanidis 1996).

bent at the elbow with hands to the breasts. How can we understand these composite figurines? Yet again, we are faced with irresolvable contradictions. Are these figurines male? Are they female? Are they something that lies beyond/between male and female? Are they even understandable at all within the dynamics of meaning that surround the other Thessalian figurines?

Part of an answer comes from Kokkinidou and Nikolaidou's illumination of the role that sexualized objects such as these figurines can play in defining sexual identities (Kokkinidou and Nikolaidou 1997). Especially relevant is their suggestion that some figurines might work to transgress normal biological distinctions of male and female. While this certainly is relevant to the figurines that have both male and female attributes, there must be something more here that speaks to the strange combinations of exposure and binding, of hyper-erect (or at least exaggerated) penises. What is going on?

Sex, sexuality and fertility

How are we to understand the explicitly, hyper-sexual figurines of bound women and of men with exaggerated penises, and indeed the possibility of men with bound penises as well? Regardless of how we choose to understand what is represented (and what is omitted) and whether or not we see incisions as simple representations of anatomical areas of the female bodies, or as clothing, or as body strapping and binding, we are drawn into complex thinking about these parts of the female body. Similarly, we cannot avoid wondering at the representations of exaggerated, enlarged, hyper-erect penises on other figurines.

On the one hand there is a clear desire to represent male and female genitalia in particular arrangements, perhaps, in states of bondage, which are unavoidable spectacles for the viewer of the figurine.[43] Just as important as any conscious desire of the people who modelled these figurines to display these corporeal combinations, perhaps more important is the presence of these overtly sexual bodies in the regular, daily visible regimes of Thessalian Neolithic lives. As noted above in the discussion of representations of heads, faces and hair on contemporary figurines (and as suggested by Orphanidis in her theory of repetition), the production and dissemination of repeated, standard modelling of the human form into a community's shared visual culture would have had important, probably unintentional, consequences for the ways in which people defined themselves in relationships to others. Similar consequences would have followed peoples' visual engagements with the hyper-sexualized figurines; these consequences would have affected peoples' definitions and understandings of their positions as men, women and, more critically, as sexual beings. But there is something else that sets aside the figurines with particularly elaborated pubes, labia and penises. Something that is less easy to deal with, something that unsettles, disturbs, or perhaps, even, arouses or angers the spectator (ourselves and the Greek collectors included) in ways that do not apply to the other examples in this and other chapters. What is this other sensation and how does it contribute to our wider understanding of these and other Neolithic figurines?

The common interpretation of the attention to sexual body parts in Thessalian figurines, indeed in sexualized figurines in all regions of southeastern Europe, is to refer to fertility and reproduction. Though widely invoked and popularly accepted, the connection of sexual body parts with fertility has only ever rested on tenuous assumptions. As discussed in Chapter 1, there are just as many ethnographic and historical examples that can be cited in which representations of sexualized body parts do not refer to fertility or reproduction, where body parts are engaged in much more complicated negotiations of identity and the contestation of interpersonal politics. In Chapter 8, the specific political potentials and consequences of representing sexuality will be explored in more detail. In the context of the present discussion of the particularities of the Thessalian material, what other meanings can be explored through the especially sexualized figurines?

Representations of sexual body parts may just as easily refer to more sensual dimensions of acts of conception, labour and birth: dimensions that are measured more in pain and pleasure than in reproductive units, assumed matriarchies or agricultural revolutions. Indeed, in the *petit mort* of the orgasm (male and female) there is not only access to the other worldly, the in-between, but there are also the physical and emotional foundations for realigning who one is and what one's relationship to others is, could be and should be. There is the potential mix of pain and pleasure that comes both from bondage (if we accept this reading of some of the Thessalian figurines), from such physical abuse (which these figurine appear to evoke) and, furthermore, from the distanced spectation of the abuse of others (which the act of looking at the figurine of a bound woman evokes). Issues raised in the discussion of the sublime in Chapter 6 resurface here. There is a dynamic tension between pain and pleasure in the bound bodies, especially the female; that tension, though it can be ultimately pleasing to some, more importantly, is unsettling and unnerving to most.

Perhaps a perspective that focuses on the emotional response, pain, pleasure and fear (which are all parts of the reality of bodies-in-the-world) and on the potential of these responses to access the other worldly, can reconnect figurines to birth, gestation and reproduction in a new and more productive way. Sexual engagements are physically, mentally, emotionally and sensually charged series of events. Similarly charged emotional atmospheres envelope pregnancy and birth: pain, danger, worry, threat to life (maternal and infant), blood, viscera, but also the rudiments of generating life, and the pleasure this can entail; engaging the dangerous and moving through and beyond it. Opposites, contradictions and challenges all are at work here.

Perhaps most importantly, and disregarding our own personal interpretative acceptance of an overly sexualized engagement within these figurines, and regardless of whether or not we retain an allegiance to a simpler, safer, more pleasant, fertility-based understanding of these objects, any perspective on these figurines illuminates their vital position as one of the fundamental means through which Neolithic people understood who they were. Not only was this relevant to their relationships with others, but it was fundamental to the gradual development of the standards and terms with which those relationships were regulated. If nothing else, these figurines, like those from Hamangia (Chapter 3) and from Cucuteni/Tripolye contexts (Chapter 5) fuel the proposition that Neolithic communities in southeastern Europe defined, negotiated and contested individual and group identities through a corporeal means. Definition, redefinition and, critically, the stimuli to think about one's relationship to others emerge equally from representations of sexual body parts, from physical binding of bodies and through the introduction of new members to community groups, whether that is through birth or through the recognition of similarities in facial or bodily appearance and decoration. Regardless of what we see in these sexualized figurines, they prompt us to think about human interrelationships between man and woman, men and women, woman and men, though not necessarily in that order nor limited to these heterosexual juxtapositions. The consequences for a broader understanding of Balkan Neolithic communities and the proposition that figurines were critical components of new sets of community and interpersonal relationships is taken up in full in Chapter 9.

How does the recognition of a hyper-sexuality help us develop our understanding of the masked figurine from Achilleion? Clearly there is some relevance in the concept of hiding or covering a highly charged part of the body: the context of unsettling contradictions. Furthermore, faces and pubes share equal decorative attention and, perhaps, shared equal Neolithic importance in presentations and negotiations of identity. To develop further our understanding we need to look at the broader archaeological, cultural and political contexts within which these figurines were made, seen, handled, broken and discarded.

Thessalian Neolithic contexts

The archaeology of Neolithic Thessaly has a long and distinguished history of research with major Greek and multinational excavations dating back to the beginning of the twentieth century; in many respects it is the best studied of the three regions considered in this book and thus we are better equipped here to push further with interpretive issues and socio-political reconstructions.[44] The Thessalian Neolithic refers to a collection of sites located in central northern Greece (fig. 7.12). Among these are some of the classic sites of the southeast European Neolithic, including Sesklo, Dimini and Achilleion. Other important contemporary sites, such as Makriyalos and Nea Nikomedia are not far away, to the north, in Greek Macedonia and the discussion here uses these sites, Makriyalos especially, as proxies for similar sites in Thessaly proper. Chronologically, the beginning of the Neolithic is earlier here than in regions to the north. The sequence runs from 6700/6500–3100 BC with major divisions for an Early Neolithic (67/6500–58/5600 BC),

166

THESSALY

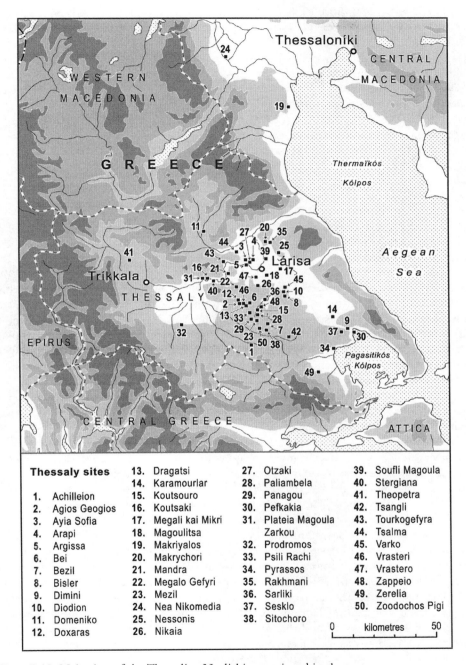

Figure 7.12 Main sites of the Thessalian Neolithic mentioned in the text.

THESSALY

a Middle Neolithic (5800/5600–5400/5300 BC), a Late Neolithic (5400/5300–4700/4500 BC) and a Final Neolithic (4700/4500–3300/3100 BC) (Andreou *et al.* 1996).[45]

Of all the southeast European regions, Thessaly possesses the clearest picture of diversity of settlement-site types for the Neolithic. Our understanding of Thessalian settlement tells, such as Sesklo and Dimini (long held up as homogeneous standards of Neolithic settlement), must now be tempered by the growing information about contemporary, extended, flat sites, such as Makriyalos, as well as the cave occupations, such as Theopetra. Across these different engagements with landscape and environment, there are variations in the forms and intensities in peoples' connections with the landscape and much can be inferred about local political relationships and social organization.[46]

Tell settlements

Thessaly was densely settled from an early period (Halstead 1999: 87; Perlès 1999) and tells developed particularly in those parts of the landscapes which had the most varied micro-environments; variation reduced economic risks resulting from over-reliance on individual resources (Halstead 1981a, 1990; Halstead and Jones 1989; Kotsakis 1999: 73). Tells are restricted areas of the landscape which were deemed appropriate for residence and on which there developed cycles of building and rebuilding of structures made of mud brick with stone foundations. The built environment within a tell's circumscribed horizontal ground-plan shared a common architectural order and regular form of structures (Kotsakis 1999: 68): with a few important exceptions, individual buildings in tells have very similar floor-plans, methods and materials of construction, and overall dimensions.

Independent, competing, social and productive units lived within the shared intra-mural space of a tell. At Sesklo for example, free-standing buildings often had open yards around them; building floor-plans reveal rectangular structures of good size (e.g., 8.5 × 5.5 m) with individual entrances and several rooms containing stone-built platforms, storage vessels, hearths and areas for grinding grain (ibid.: 70, 73; Andreou *et al.* 1996: 541). With these buildings, their maintenance and their diachronic replacement with formally identical structures, one can infer the processes through which people permanently marked their places of residence and activities in what was, at a regional scale, a crowded landscape (Halstead 1999b: 88).

The division and internal arrangement of tell village space was highly ordered; this is particularly clear at mid-fifth-millennium BC phases at Dimini. Six concentric perimeter walls enclosed four main domestic areas, each of which consisted of a larger building and a number of food preparation and storage areas (Andreou *et al.* 1996: 543; Hourmouziadis 1979). At the centre of the settlement a large, megaron-shaped building and courtyard occupied more than half of the total area of the village. Together, the perimeter walls, the separate domestic areas, and the larger central megaron building complex created a settlement area that was well demarcated and internally divided (Andreou *et al.* 1996: 543; Souvatzi in press a; Nanoglou 2001). While some argue for uniformity of activity, food preparation and storage among individual building complexes across the site (e.g., Andreou *et al.* 1996: 544), others suggest that there is a variability (between complexes and within individual buildings) which runs beneath any external uniformity and which may only exist at the broader level of the village itself (Souvatzi and Skafida 2003;

168

THESSALY

Souvatzi in press a, in press b). Concentrations of *Spondylus* rings, buttons and cylinder beads in different buildings suggest some spatial distinctions through the site (Andreou *et al.* 1996: 544; Halstead 1989a, 1993; Tsuneki 1987, 1989), though the distribution of waste from working the shell is found evenly distributed across the settlement (Halstead 1993; Andreou *et al.* 1996: 544, n. 46). Regardless of the particularities of activity and building diversity between individual units and the village as a whole, Dimini provides evidence for some form of institutionalized, community-level authority, perhaps linked specifically to the large megaron in its central courtyard (Halstead 1999b: 90).

At Sesklo there is ordering both within space of the settlement itself (though the arrangement of buildings is different from Dimini) and between the tell and the extra-mural non-tell areas. Individual buildings sit on their own, surrounded by open courtyards. Building interiors are divided into separate rooms, perhaps distinguished by different activities. The layout of the site interior, the relationship of building to building, is relatively uniform and appears to be centred on principles of orientation and symmetry (Souvatzi 2000). At the broader spatial scale, the distinctions seen at Dimini, between the interior of the walled village, are also present at Sesklo where walls separate the space that contains the buildings from the external non-tell area of the site, and contribute to what Kotsakis has termed a dual habitation pattern (Kotsakis 1995: 1999).

Regardless of any intra-mural distinctiveness of individual buildings, the architecture of Thessalian tells reveals an ordered variability that works at both building and village levels (Souvatzi 2000): between internal and external spaces (at Dimini the various peri-meter complexes and the central megaron and its large yard; the relations between a building's private internal and shared external space) and through the overall inter-building spatial organization (the concentric pattern at Dimini; the stand-alone one at Sesklo). The political inferences that can be drawn from these patterns range from arguments stressing the need for intra-community sharing and the establishment of binding inter-building and intra-village alliances to the opposite suggestions that indi-vidual buildings represent private places in which particular, constricted sets of people hoarded and hid their activities, produce and problems.

As well as a source of information about internal architectural and social relationships, tell settlements show the degree to which individual communities were locked into specific parts of particular landscapes. Tells speak to us as statements of permanent resi-dence; the repeated patterns of house and village reconstruction over many generations created places that had deep local histories (Bailey 1990; Chapman 1990; Nanoglou 2001). Repeated reconstructions of buildings in the same places and with the same floor-plans imply continuity in claims to settlement space (Milojčić 1960: 12; Theocharis 1973: 65; Kotsakis 1999: 69); efforts to establish and maintain residential continuity of individual households may well have clashed with equally motivated claims for group cohesion or communal reciprocity that worked at a village level (Kotsakis 1999: 74).

It is clear from the records of tells and, particularly, their constituent structures, that a particular social and political importance was attached to individual buildings (or houses) within a tell. Similar importance may have been attached to the social correlates of these buildings (i.e., households) represented by groups of people who co-operated in living, eating, nurturing, and caring for the young and the elderly as well as producing, con-suming and working together. Thus, any single tell village contained many individual, independent households. If this was the case, then the physical events of (re)building a house were important and powerful ways for individual household groups to construct and maintain distinct identities (Nanoglou 2001: 316; Bailey 1990; Chapman 1990). The house(hold) became one of the means by which people identified with certain people and distinguished themselves from others: tell houses were mechanisms for marking small group identities. Undoubtedly another dimension of identity expression existed at the broader level of a coherent village community: the larger group was tied together through inter-household bonds and alliances linked to co-residence in the tell village. Thus, two levels of identity functioned at the same time, in the same place, and engaged the same groups of people: at the village level, there was a general familiarity among people who see each other on an almost day-to-day basis; at the household level, there was a more intimate familiarity among people who eat and sleep together on a regular basis (Kotsakis pers. comm.).

The significance of the house as a social and political entity is reinforced by the production of miniature house models (Toufexis 1996; Toufexis and Skafida 1998).[47] Some models, particularly those from Middle Neolithic contexts, represent the exteriors of buildings; others, especially those from the Late Neolithic, show details of building interiors.[48] A good example of the latter trend is the model from Plateia Magoula Zarkou (Gallis 1985) which contained a set of eight anthropomorphic figurines (fig. 7.13). These have been interpreted as a nuclear family of two adult couples (the four larger figurines) and four children (ibid.: 22). Beyond the discussion in Chapter 5 of sets of figurines found together and regardless of the accuracy of Gallis' reconstruction, it is perhaps more important that these representations of people were attached to the representation of a building: people's identities were expressed in terms of their associations with a particular built place and, thus, with any other people who were linked to that place.

Also intriguing is the diachronic shift in house model form: from exterior representation in the Middle Neolithic to interior depiction (like the Plateia Magoula Zarkou example) in the Late Neolithic. Perhaps there was also a contemporary shift in the social and political importance of the house(hold) within tell village communities: from a more

Figure 7.13 House model with figurines from Plateia Magoula Zarkou; 17 × 15 cm (after Gallis 1985).

general perception of a generic building (without concern for the people associated with it) to a more specific concept of a particular building and the associated individuals and their specific characteristics, such as age and appearance. The definition and construction of a fundamental social unit had shifted from a physical, built structure to the persons who used that structure (Nanoglou 2001: 309). One could expand the significance of this shift to suggest that the earlier models of house exteriors were stable, static and fixed representations which were closed (literally) to any alternation of form or contents that a person handling them might wish to make. The later models of house interiors were very different; they were open and laid bare for alteration and manipulation particularly by the movement of figurines within them.

Permanence of tell residence

Despite the apparent monumentality of these tells (many were used over hundreds of years), there are unresolved disagreements over the degree and continuity of residential permanence. Some, such as Whittle (1996: 17–20) and van Andel *et al.* (1995), have argued that, for the Early Neolithic at least, communities were not fully sedentary, that mobility was as important as settled permanence and that the impressively sturdy buildings built with stone foundations and mud-brick walls need not represent continuous occupation or use throughout all of the seasons of the year, nor necessarily for more than one year in a row. Van Andel's work on patterns of river-flooding argued that some sites were used sporadically and only when episodes of flooding allowed. However, Halstead's most recent analysis of economic evidence from sites across the region suggests that Thessalian tells were occupied on a permanent basis throughout the year, though the number of people living in a settlement may well have varied in different seasons (Halstead 1999b, in press).

Critically, the attraction and concentration of people into a place of particular resources (spatial, building, social and otherwise) such as a tell village undoubtedly created political and economic instabilities: individual household units may have been too small to be economically or socially viable, and survival (especially in bad times) would have required individuals and groups to have relied on the assistance of neighbours (Halstead 1999b: 83). Social mechanisms through which alliances could be created between small groups (such as communal feasting, alliance-building, contact with other communities via exchange and mating networks) would have established and managed critically important support networks between normally separate and independent groups of people (either within or between villages): there emerged a system of mutual interdependence (ibid.: 89). Importantly, the success of these activities would have relied upon people understanding (or at least being cognizant of) the various particularities of personal and group identity at all levels: intra-household, intra-village, intra- and inter-regional.

There was of course variation within all of these social and architectural patterns: variation in house size perhaps reflects differences in social-group size and composition (e.g., extended households in larger buildings). Individual buildings with particular dimensions, floor-plan morphology, and the varying number of rooms or doorways may suggest particular variations in degrees of group cohesion or in the openness of different social units (Kotsakis 1981, 1999; Nanoglou 2001: 309). What remains constant through this variation, however, is that people were choosing to associate, for significant periods of time, with other people at an intimate, building-based level as well as at a looser, village level. While there was a spatial dimension to the expression and maintenance of allegiances within both levels of association, supplementary activities, involving other media (e.g., material, ceremonial, oral and performative), must have played equally important roles in structuring identities within and between Thessalian villages. All of this evidence defines tells as monuments, as ideological mechanisms that worked within various social and political narratives in the Neolithic (Kotsakis 1999: 74).

Importantly, there is nothing to suggest that the compositions of houses or villages were static or that there was not a constant tension against which considerable effort was required in order to maintain the coherence and distinctiveness of both the building-level and the village-level social units. Undoubtedly, strategies of house-building were one of the types of such maintenance activities. Other material such as highly decorated pottery and figurines must have contributed to these ongoing negotiations and contestations.

Flat sites and caves

A different set of social and political permutations is evident in non-tell engagements with the Thessalian landscape in the Neolithic. There is some evidence (though based on information from only one excavated site) for the use of caves for the same ranges of economic and productive activities as were present at tell sites. Thus, on the western edge of the Thessalian plain, there is a good record in the Theopetra Cave of occupation running from before the Early Neolithic (from as early as 9000 BC) (Kyparissi-Apostolika 1995, 1999; Andreou *et al.* 1996: 557). At Theopetra, all phases of the Neolithic are present though the depth of accumulation (1.5 m) is less than would be expected at contemporary tells (Kyparissi-Apostolika 1999: 144; and see Andreou *et al.* 1996: 557, n. 135). Most material comes from Middle and Late Neolithic phases; pottery is abundant and there are large storage jars, numerous mill-stones and a large range of charred plant remains, and domestic and wild fauna. A few figurines have been recovered, seven of which are anthropomorphic. *Spondylus* appears both as finished objects (beads and bracelets) and as a raw material. While there is also evidence for clay floors and perhaps hearths, the overall density of accumulation suggests a pattern of building (if indeed floors can be equated with houses; they may represent some other means of spatial organization) which was very unlike the substantial, mud-brick and stone walls of the buildings at tells such as Sesklo and Dimini.

Sesklo B

In addition to the role that caves played in the patterns of settlement in Neolithic Thessaly, there is an increasingly full record of non-tell settlement: sites that were not spatially restricted in the same way as were tells and which did not develop vertically though successive phases of residence. Thus, to the west of the Sesklo tell, there is a large area of Early and Middle Neolithic material and architectural remains (Kotsakis 1981, 1995; Andreou *et al.* 1996: 540–2). This part of the site, termed Sesklo B, is flat and has cultural deposits ranging in depth from a few centimetres to several metres. Unlike the Sesklo tell, the succession of activity areas and buildings at Sesklo B is discontinuous with material from different phases found in various parts of the site and a pattern of

THESSALY

habitation that is less intense (Kotsakis 1999: 69). While the majority of buildings belong to one period, the end of the Middle Neolithic (Kotsakis 1981), there are chronological gaps in the sequence. Furthermore, the buildings at Sesklo B are concentrated in tight clusters, have many common walls, and there is less open space between them, though there are significant empty areas between individual clusters. This is markedly different from the ordered and free-standing buildings of the Sesklo tell.

Where the tell at Sesklo can be defined in terms of continuity and residential permanence, Sesklo B is about spatial and temporal discontinuity. If tell-based lineage and descent worked through ideals of the house and the household, then the patterns of Sesklo B suggest a different focus: on the communal as opposed to the individual unit (Kotsakis 1999: 74). In contrast to the inferences that we take from the Sesklo tell (and from other tell settlements), the Sesklo B record implies a more dispersed and shifting pattern of habitation, less constrained and not subject to the regularization of architectural order on the tell (Andreou *et al*. 1996; Kotsakis 1995). Settlement on the flat, in an extended form, represents a radically different spatial organization with habitation drifting horizontally through time rather than building up in successive, horizontal, layers in the same place (Kotsakis 1999).

Makriyalos

With the exception of Sesklo B, much of the record for flat, extended settlements in the Thessalian Neolithic comes from survey.[49] A major exception is the recent rescue work at Makriyalos which is producing an exciting and detailed picture of what must also have been happening at contemporary flat sites in Thessaly (Besios and Pappa 1997, 1998a, 1998b, 1998c). The site of Makriyalos spreads over 50 ha of which 6 have been excavated (Pappa 1997a, 1997b; Pappa and Besios 1999: 108). There are two main phases of activity: Phase I dating to the beginning of the Late Neolithic (5300–4900 BC) and Phase II dating to the end of the Late Neolithic (4800–4500 BC). In Phase I, two ditches (up to 4.5 m deep and dug as a series of linked units which, in some places, appear to have been re-cut) enclose an area of 28 ha, which was sparsely populated with loose groups of pit-houses and small ovens and hearths which were located nearby in separate pits. In the fill of the inner ditch were traces of successive periods of site use: especially animal and human bone. A third ditch cuts across the middle of the enclosed area (Pappa and Besios 1999: 110–14). A much larger pit-feature contained a lot of ceramics and bone which were deposited over a short period of time (months rather than years), which probably represent large-scale feasting and the consumption of domestic animals, and which is distinct from the more casual patterns of daily consumption. The bones from this pit document year-round activity at Makriyalos during Phase I (Collins and Halstead 1999: 140).

Phase II reveals significant changes in the intra-site organization of space. The layout and concentrations of structures are dense: there are round pit-houses, but also oblong buildings with apsidal ends. In an early sub-phase, the round structures are large (5 m in diameter), have wattle-and-daub walls, distinct storage and rubbish pits, working areas, and external hearths and ovens, which are found on their own or in small concentrations that might represent communal cooking or working areas shared by a group of houses. In a later sub-phase the apsidal houses appear: they are large (up to 15 m long) and the internal space is divided by walls (Pappa and Besios 1999). In terms of plants

173

and animals exploited, the patterns from Makriyalos are no different from those recorded on contemporary tell sites (Collins and Halstead 1999: 139): domesticates dominate over wild animals with pig and sheep more common than cattle and goat (sheep were probably exploited for meat and cattle for milk) (Collins and Halstead 1999: 139–40).

Makriyalos is also significant in the patterns of mortuary deposition (and see broader discussion below). Bones from more than 50 individuals were recovered, mainly from the Phase I ditch. Most were adults, and of those that could be sexed (about half of all the bones recovered), the majority (24 of 33, or 73 per cent) were female (Triantaphyllou 1999: 130–2). While some bodies had been carefully placed in the inner, Phase I ditch, most bones were disarticulated and probably represent either secondary burials (after they had been buried or exposed elsewhere) or disturbances by subsequent ditch digging or deposition (ibid.: 129). Phase II human bone from the site is primarily disarticulated, represents less than a dozen individuals, and was recovered from settlement contexts and, less frequently, from a rubbish pit (ibid.: 131).

There are many important aspects to the Makriyalos excavations. In comparison with the settlement record from the tells, there are clear differences in duration of residence and in the inter-feature proximities of buildings and peoples' activities across the area of a settlement. To some degree the pattern of pit-houses at Makriyalos resembles the activities at Sesklo B, especially the dispersal of small collections of living features; there is also the similarity in the range of plants and animals consumed. On the other hand, there are important differences, not only in the materials used to create the built environment but also in the use of simple and small semi-subterranean features. There also appear to be important differences in the scales of consumption, in Phase I at least, where the evidence for ritualized feasting is very different from what is known from the economic records of tells. There are also important differences in the location and frequency of human remains, which will be discussed further below.

Boundaries

If there is a common element that connects these different forms of Neolithic Thessalian engagement with the landscape, it is the emphasis on bounding and separating space which comes from both tells and flat sites. The use of perimeter walls as well as internal building divisions at Sesklo and Dimini is unequivocal evidence for the exclusion of some people from others and, at the same time, for the incorporation of particular people either within individual houses and households, or within particular settlements, or both. It is clear that tell sites are about exclusion and incorporation, physical and social mechanisms manifest in monumental, architectural means (Bailey 2000: 156–60). It is also relevant that there is a wall that separates Sesklo A from Sesklo B and that within Sesklo B, individual, tight clusters of buildings were separated from other tight clusters by lots of empty space. Boundary walls have been found at other tells.[50] Other large dividers of space include ditches, like the one at Makriyalos, which run through sites or parts of them.[51]

To a large extent, flat extended sites, such as Makriyalos, do not divide space in the same ways as do tells: hence, the absence of significant internal building division (though the Makriyalos, Phase II, long, apsidal structures with internal walls are noted as possible exceptions) and the absence of monumental building materials. However, there is significant evidence for spatial (and thus potentially of social) division at the broader

THESSALY

scale at Makriyalos: the keys to this are the ditches. The Phase I boundary ditch may well have defined relations between the people doing things in the internal space of the site and whatever was happening on the outside (other people, animals, the wild).[52] Importantly the ditch may also have served as a depositional context within which different groups of people claimed and contested relationships among segments of society, kin-groups or other community units (Andreou *et al.* 1996: 573). The ditch may have been a communal (or at least communally visible) area that was accessible to everyone in the community and in which it was deemed appropriate to dispose of the deceased (Triantaphyllou 1999: 131). Did the deposition of the body or bones of an individual in the communal ditch represent the primacy of the group over the individual, as Triantaphylou suggests, or is this yet another example of multiple levels of identity expression working within and between individuals and the group? Furthermore, the inner of the two ditches in the Phase I double ditch consisted of a chain of large deep pits that had been continuously renewed, cleaned and joined to newly dug pits (Pappa and Besios 1999: 110–14). This ditch was not one original act but a series of linked units, a continuous process, maintained and adapted over time (Kotsakis pers. comm.). The acts of digging and renewing the pits may have been just as vital to expressing and maintaining site (re)occupation or residential continuity as were the building reconstructions on tells.

Are the differences between tells and extended sites merely factors of the duration of site use, the consequent degrees of residential permanence, and different attitudes to, desires and requirements for erecting boundaries which had the same political consequences but which differed in their intended duration? Regardless of the exact dynamics of their intended functions (and equally importantly, the reality of their unintended consequences), the important thing is that boundaries seem to be everywhere in the Thessalian Neolithic. Accompanying them, throughout the same landscapes, were vacillating social tensions between inclusion and exclusion, between being within and without, between us and them, same and other.

General conclusions about settlement

Being in Neolithic Thessaly, then, was about living through series of bounded spaces, about living in various (and potentially shifting) associations with other people, and about the spatial organization of these relationships. The distribution of individuals and groups across the landscape and the relationships between people suggests that contact, conflict, alliance, exclusion and incorporation were basic events of daily life. The participation of specific arrangements and repetitions of architectural form in claims and contests over membership within particular social groups can be related to contemporary patterns in the production and decoration of material culture. This is certainly one way of reading the particular patterns of ceramic decoration in the Thessalian Middle Neolithic where styles are particularly regionalized (Gallis 1996; Halstead 1989a). It may be more accurate to argue, at a less specific level, for a more general use of material culture and architecture within the constant negotiations of individual identities. For example, Halstead has suggested that the build-up of tells may not have been a community-wide thing to express the place of a village community. It may reflect, at a general level, the competition between individual households (Halstead 1999b: 88–9).

175

THESSALY

Burials

In light of the information about spatial organization and the increasingly clear (and increasingly dynamic and complex) social and political inferences that we can draw from them, it is surprising that the mortuary record for Neolithic Thessaly is so thin. In addition to the human bone remains at Makriyalos, there are only two formal cemeteries (at Plateia Magoula Zarkou and Soufli Magoula) and a scattering of isolated burials of infants and children at other sites.

At Soufli Magoula, at the edge of the settlement tell, in the lowest levels of the Early Neolithic levels, rescue excavations uncovered 15 Early Neolithic cremation burials, placed in closely spaced pits some of which cut into each other and some of which contain more than one cremation (Gallis 1982). Men, women and children are included and there is no clear pattern in grave-goods: some pots were fired when the body was incinerated, others were placed in the pits after the cremation; one cremation includes the skull of a goat. Also excavated were the remains of two circular ash pits (a metre in diameter and half a metre deep) in which the bodies had been burnt. These pits were not insignificant places used for a single cremation, but more substantial and repeatedly used pyres: indeed one was lined with mud brick (Cavanagh and Mee 1998: 8; Gallis 1982: 196–7). There was also an inhumation of an adult and a child at Soufli (Gallis 1982: 32, 46, 48–50; Cavanagh and Mee 1998: 6) and a similar burial, of a woman and two children from Nea Nikomedia, though this is farther to the north in Macedonia (Cavanagh and Mee 1998: 7). To the south of the Soufli settlement, though dating to the Late Neolithic use of the site, seven burials were made in urns placed in shallow pits and accompanied by one or two grave-goods.

Contemporary with the later Neolithic Soufli burials is the cremation cemetery at Plateia Magoula Zarkou (Gallis 1982). At least 70 cremations were found 300 m from the tell, though 20 of these had been disturbed. As the extent of the cemetery was not fully defined, the total number of cremations at the site must be higher still. The burnt bones were put in conical, one-handed beakers, amphorae or bowls and placed in pits. Other pots were included as grave-goods and, in one grave, a child's cremation was placed in a zoomorphic vessel (Cavanagh and Mee 1998: 11). Some pots contained the remains of different individuals and specific body parts (skulls and limbs) were selected for burial (Andreou *et al.* 1996: 556). The majority of the burials were of men and women; few children were included.

At other sites, there are isolated burials of individuals, often children or infants, inhumed within settlements. At Dimini, there are Late Neolithic burials of infants in houses (Hourmouziadis 1979; Halstead 1992a) including cremations of babies in pots and neo-natal infants (Kotsakis pers. comm.). There is an infant from Early Neolithic contexts at Sesklo (Cavanagh and Mee 1998: 7), another one at Argissa (ibid.: 7), and one from a Middle Neolithic phase at Agios Petros (ibid.: 6). At Rachmani an infant was buried in a pot (ibid.: 7) and at Prodromos, during two or three sequences of burial ceremony, 21 skulls, a leg and rib bones were deposited in a pit beneath the floor of a house (ibid.: 9). At Ayia Sophia, bones were placed in pits in abandoned houses, over which a thick covering of stamped, burnt clay sealed off the structures (ibid.: 10). Some grave-goods, such as the pots and bowls, are related to the consumption of food and thus, most probably, to the events surrounding death, its celebration and ceremonies, though cooking pots are rare. Occasionally flint blades are also found in burials. The overall impression, however, is that particular sets of objects were not buried with individuals, though of course, in the cremations, some objects may have perished during the burning ceremonies.

In the Thessalian Neolithic, it appears that rigid guidelines did not structure the treatment and disposal of a person's body after death. In some instances, as at Ayia Sophia, the building of a low mound of burnt, stamped clay over the abandoned houses which contained the burials may have had some significance linking the past and present uses of the settlement (Nanoglou 2001: 316), though closing-off the old space of the past and the dead may just as easily have functioned to sever links to that past. Cavanagh and Mee suggest that if death was a common occurrence and if child mortality was high, then the emotional impact would not have been significant enough to drive any more dynamic mortuary ritual (Cavanagh and Mee 1998: 6). More likely, the scarcity of cemeteries and burial in general may imply that within the contexts of the socio-political dynamism of settlement space, funerary ritual was not an important means of social integration (Souvatzi in press a).

Even in the cases where human remains are recovered, as in the ditch at Makriyalos, the bones are disarticulated and fragmented.[53] At the very least, the low incidence of formal burial and the destruction of bodies by incineration or exposure suggest a particular perception of the corporeal body and its potential for expressing identity and any trans-generational sequences or links. The very limited evidence from Plateia Magoula and Soufli for manipulating corpses in relation to the realms of the living suggests that generalizations about mortuary treatment would be dangerous. The destruction of the body by burning may be significant, especially as cremation is a Neolithic rarity throughout southeastern Europe. Perhaps the fully articulated, lifeless body (and obvious monuments to it) was not deemed an appropriate object to connect to the space and activities of daily life. In light of the common finds of isolated, disarticulated scraps of human bone across settlement sites (at least where rigorous recovery techniques are practised; i.e., wet or dry sieving), it appears that the corpse, as a material entity, had little or no value or positive meaning in the eyes of Neolithic Thessaly. Perhaps the most accurate conclusion is that the people just did not care about the corporeal remains of a person once they stopped breathing.

The particularities of the Thessalian attitude to death and the body are especially intriguing for the attention that was focused on death in other contemporary communities, for example the Hamangia cemeteries at Cernavoda and Durankulak (discussed in Chapter 3) but also in the communities in Bulgaria and Serbia, where Neolithic burial inserted the materials and rituals of death in highly visible fashions attached to settlement spaces (Bailey 2000: 116–23, 193–208). If, in the Balkan Neolithic, there was a new perception of the place of the body in social negotiations of identity and political positioning within and between these widely separated communities, then that perception did not include the use of the body after death in equal ways, to similar degrees, in different regions of southeastern Europe.

The contexts of figurines in Thessaly

While the settlement and mortuary records reveal the importance of the social group (at house or village level) and the unimportance of the body of the dead individual, they also provide valuable information for refining our understanding of figurines. Thus, in terms of the declarations of identities of people within small and large groups, there would have been a clear role for anthropomorphic objects such as figurines to have played. The establishment and daily display of standards of body appearance and shape (among the living at least) would have worked very well within communities through which conflicting claims for membership and inclusion were being aired at the close (intra-house), medium (inter-house), and more distant scales (inter-village). The information from the mortuary record is less clear, though the destruction and disassembling of dead bodies before final disposal may run parallel with the breakage and disposal of figurines.[54] Beyond fitting the non-specific 'use' of figurines into these general trends, what can we learn from the records of figurine provenance in these sites?

On the one hand, a large proportion of the published figurines comes from private collections (e.g., Gallis and Orphanidis 1996) and many others are from surface-survey projects. None of these have archaeological contexts beyond general ones that place them in a particular phase of the Neolithic or in a morphological category, such as schematic or naturalistic. However, for Thessaly, perhaps more so than for the other regions investigated in this book, we have detailed, published excavation reports with high-resolution information about figurine find-spots. The long history of multi-disciplinary work on Thessalian sites has created a solid base of contextual information.

There are spectacular figurine finds. Thus, the house model at Plateia Magoula Zarkou and the eight figurines it contained were carefully excavated from a deposit in front of an oven in a building from that site (Gallis 1985: plate 14a). Groups of figurines were also discovered in House T at Tsangli (Wace and Thompson 1912: 115–17, 123–4) and at Rachmani (ibid.: 39–41). At Achilleion as many as 14 figurines were found in a single assemblage and up to 20 were found in a single house (Gimbutas 1989a: 171–227). Indeed, as one would expect, the scientific attention devoted to identifying particular find-spots and associations of other artefacts was particularly heightened at Achilleion.

Paradoxically, the high level of contextual information for Thessalian figurines from work at sites such as Achilleion brings us no closer to a fuller understanding. Christine Perlès has noted three major problems that prevent us from benefiting from the documentation of figurine find-spots (Perlès 2001: 255–72). First, figurines are very numerous and are found in many different places within a single site. At Achilleion as at other sites, the rule is that figurines are found in houses, in pits and in the areas outside of structures: indeed, they are found everywhere. This is the problem of figurine ubiquity; if there are enough figurines spread over a site, any patterning in figurine location or association will be hard to isolate to any significant level of precision. Perlès suggests two other problems, both linked to depositional and post-depositional processes: very few figurines are found in their primary context of use; and the majority of figurines are found in an incomplete or broken state. Depositional history is the greatest obstacle, and depositional events are extraordinarily elusive, if indeed such things actually exist and can be recovered. If they do exist it is highly unlikely that there will be any consistency in any patterns of activity recovered. The related problem of breakage is equally dispiriting. While Talalay (1987, 1993) and Chapman (1996, 2000a) have both suggested potential activities that might contribute to deliberate breakage of figurines, their suggestions cannot apply to all fragments. More critically, while Talalay's argument comes into play when matched halves of figurines are recovered in different houses or villages, Chapman's suggestion contains no means for determining which figurines were intentionally broken and which were not (Bailey 2002). The situation is even less hopeful if one accepts Perlès' (2001:

263) attractive argument that many figurines were used for only a brief time, perhaps only as long as a particular ceremony, ritual (or even game) lasted and then discarded, maybe being broken before being thrown away. Even more depressing is Hourmouziadis' suggestion that figurine use varied from period to period and from individual to individual; thus we must recognize the probability that even after breakage (deliberate or other-wise), figurines were recycled and recirculated (Hourmouziadis 1973: 199). Perhaps the only primary depositions recorded through excavation are the spectacular ones, such as those in the house model at Plateia Magoula Zarkou, or the more frequent ones from Cucuteni/Tripolye sites (see Chapter 5). Perhaps all the rest are merely the detritus of life, kicked into the corners of the room, tossed out into the yard, thrown into rubbish pits.

Conclusions and return to the masked figurine

We are left in a difficult position. The region with the most detailed history of inter-disciplinary research on Neolithic sites, figurines, and the contextual links between the two, cannot provide answers to the questions most often asked about these figurines. What are we to do? Part of the solution lies in recognizing that the question is not what do these figurines represent, but rather what are figurines representations for. Furthermore, having considered the Thessalian material in detail, we are faced with an additional set of more specific questions that apply to this material. What is it about sexuality and why is it involved in figurine representations? Whether perceived in terms of reproduction or pleasure how does sexual representation affect the capabilities of figurines in their potentials as charged objects? Similar questions can be asked about the apparent binding of the female (and perhaps the male) body. And what about the ambiguity inherent in the figurines that have normally mutually exclusive, sexual body parts? A clear emphasis focuses on the display of sexual body parts (the penises and the breasts), body parts that are not usually displayed intentionally. While there is no need to assume that the people of Neolithic Thessaly shared our concerns for covering sexual body parts (particularly the breasts and penis) there is an unusual attention to promoting the breasts and female genitalia. Why?

If the suggestion is correct that some of the figurines represent bound genitalia, then how are we to understand this? Can we impose our own sensual (or moral) opinion on this practice, or are we fumbling with Neolithic conceptions of male dominance and physical control of women's bodies? Is this why the presence of the labial incision is an important element in these representations: to show which bodies are appropriate to bind? Or are we engaging the physical dynamics of sexual pleasure that accompanies dominance of an Other through bondage and especially through the bondage of sexual body parts and of specifically reproductive body parts? Does the potentially bound penis representation extend the category of dominance to include the male as well as the female? Why does it matter if these readings of these figurines are correct? What is the relevance? Beyond any voyeuristic pleasure (or revulsion) that might be derived by me or by you as reader of this book, or by the men who held many of these figurines in their private collections, what does it matter that so much attention appears to be devoted to the representation and manipulation of sexualized body parts? The use of (and consequences of producing and viewing) highly charged imagery, especially of the human body, is not limited to Neolithic figurines and a fuller discussion is provided in Chapter 8.

Perhaps the only interpretive conclusion that we can draw is that Thessalian Neolithic figurines made Neolithic people think about their bodies and about the bodies of others in especially sexual ways. The recognition that these figurines were stimuli (and continue to be stimuli) to think about the dynamics of identity, especially sexual identity cannot be ignored or hidden. That these bodies are cropped, fragmented, deformed, extended and exaggerated (Hourmouziadis' concept of *synairesis*) is equally important. That they are sexually ambiguous and apparently contradictory human forms were (and remain today) stimuli to think, rethink, question and challenge any existing, shared perceptions of how a person is defined by his or her body. Perhaps the meaning of the masked figurine from Achilleion rests in the answers to these questions: what is the appropriate appearance of a person; how does one attempt to hide (literally) a particular identity; how can a face be portrayed so as not to reveal the face? Contradiction and paradox, hiding and exposure are fundamental components of Thessalian figurines. Is it naked? Is it clothed? Is it bound? Is it male/female? The more we look, the closer we examine the figurines, the more we are unsure, the more we think about them and the more questions that arise. If anything we are moving away from any definite understanding or interpretation of these objects. Did the repetition of facial and genital form work within the creation and maintenance of politically potent standards of appearance? Were they parts of the accepted understandings of the exclusion and inclusion of individuals within social entities such as households or village? If so, were these standards accepted without objection or were there also attempts to disrupt the status quo? If such attempts to disrupt and subvert did occur, then how did people achieve this? Did attempts to disrupt the status quo unsettle the accepted standards and shared world-views that sub-consciously regulate and maintain what some parts of communities believed, implicitly perhaps, were appropriate behaviour, appearances and associations? The themes of contestation and subversion via visual media are explored in the next chapter and it should not be surprising that that chapter begins with another example from Thessaly.

8

SUBVERTING AND MANIPULATING REALITY

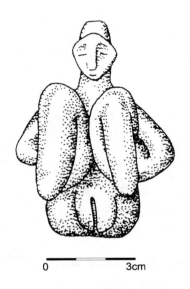

Figure 8.1 Figurine from Achilleion. Reprinted from Gimbutas *et al.* 1989.

During excavations that Marija Gimbutas directed in the early 1970s at the Neolithic village of Achilleion in northern Greece, a remarkable figurine was uncovered (fig. 8.1) (Gimbutas 1989c: cat. no. 32). It was found with other artefacts near a circular hearth in Phase IIa of the site and dates to *c.* 6200 BC. Like many Neolithic figurines it is made of clay and is small, about 5.0 cm tall and no more than 3.0 cm wide. It is only a fragment of the original representation; the head, hands, arms and legs below the knees have been lost. Even in its partial state, its appearance gives pause for thought. The most obvious feature of the body represented is its genitalia. The legs are pulled up and may have been held aloft by hands that are now missing; the vagina is clearly exposed, labia are modelled out of proportion to any anatomically correct size and are separated by a deep incision. The anus is also marked by an incision. There are other incisions on the figurine's back (two sets of three parallel lines) but these have less visual impact on the viewer. Though this figurine is extraordinary to look at there are two other examples from Achilleion which similarly display vagina and labia (one from an earlier and one from a later phase).

How are we to understand these representations of women spreading their legs and exposing their genitals to the viewer? Are they mere pornography? Should we be satisfied with the excavator's interpretation, that they are proof of a Neolithic Birth Giving Goddess (Gimbutas 1989b: 196–7)? We are faced with the very fundamental question, what are these representations for?

I discussed in Chapter 6 some of the ways that visual imagery persuades: the mechanisms and conceits with which it seduces and convinces the spectator. I offered a few examples of how such rhetorical power has been used to propose preferred realities, especially those that shore up large institutions: the government, the state, individual and group identities, the status quo in general. Equally important, and just as relevant to our investigation of figurines, is an examination of how people exploit visual culture and benefit from its rhetorical powers in order to disrupt, block and resist. In this chapter, we will examine a few examples of the ways in which the human form is used to subvert and resist established regimes of truth and accepted world views.

Subversion

In 1812, the British landscape painter J.M.W. Turner submitted to the Royal Academy a large canvas (5 × 8 feet) entitled *Snow Storm: Hannibal and His Army Crossing the Alps* (fig. 8.2). The painting depicts a moment in the nine-day crossing of the Swiss Alps by Hannibal and his army in 218 BC when leader and troops were moving through a high pass. Hannibal had been on a rampage, having laid siege to Saguntum in Spain, crossed the Pyrenees, and then defeated the Gauls in southern France. He was doing the unthinkable, outwitting the Roman army and taking his troops over the Alps and down into Italy. His goal was to destroy Rome. The manoeuvre is legendary, a classic, monumental, military success and an example of heroic leadership. Indeed, it was to this legend that David's *Bonaparte* had alluded 13 years earlier (see discussion in Chapter 6).

Turner's *Hannibal* is an evocative painting. Art-historically, it is an important work; it provides an early appearance of the Turnerian vortex (Paley 1986) and the arrangement of composition on the canvas introduces principles that organize many of the artist's later paintings (ibid.). The swirling clouds and snow, the feeling of instability thus created, the overall evocation of flux were all attacks against the then accepted, more balanced tradition of landscape painting (ibid.: 108; Kitson 1964: 73).[1]

Most importantly for our investigation of manipulation and subversion, *Hannibal* was a complex insult to Napoleon Bonaparte and to his reputation as a leader and military hero. England had been at war with Napoleon and France from 1793 until the signing

Figure 8.2 J.M.W. Turner's *Snow Storm: Hannibal and his Army Crossing the Alps* (1812). © The Tate Gallery, London.

SUBVERTING AND MANIPULATING REALITY

of the Treaty of Amiens in March 1802. In May 1803, Britain would once again declare war on France. In late summer 1802, Turner took advantage of the interim peace and travelled to Europe on a sketching tour, moving from Paris through France and spending considerable time in Switzerland, especially in the Alps (D. Brown 1999; Hill 1992).

Part of the recent successes of Napoleon's army had been their own heroic crossing of the Alps as they moved on to defeat the Austrians at Marengo in late autumn, 1799. Comparisons between Napoleon and Hannibal (as well as with Charlemagne) were clearly and visibly acknowledged. On his 1802 tour, and before leaving Paris for the Alps, Turner saw Jacques-Louis David's epic representation of Napoleon's 1799 crossing: the French leader on the back of a rearing horse, high in the mountains, arm outstretched, and one hand pointing the direction of advance to his troops. During his journey, Turner followed Napoleon's route and filled his sketchbooks with scenes of mountain passes, outrageously dangerous cliff-side paths and treacherous, narrow bridges (D. Brown 1999; Hill 1992). Turner also learned, without much convincing we may imagine, that in reality, Napoleon's part in the heroic crossing had amounted to little more than occupying a rearguard position, well below the pass, from which he arranged for the supply of his troops. In fact, Napoleon's journey up the mountain and through the pass had been on the back of a mule which had been led by a local peasant (D. Brown 1999: 18).

When Turner painted *Hannibal*, therefore, he constructed the picture to de-centre the heroes of Alpine crossings and to make them inconsequential. Thus, Hannibal is almost invisible in *Hannibal*, perhaps a minute figure on the back of an elephant in the mid-ground of the painting (ibid.: 18). In minimizing Hannibal in the representation of his heroic crossing, Turner attempted to deflate Napoleon and his reputation by puncturing the reputation of the referenced hero, to whom comparisons had been drawn in the creation of Napoleon's identity (ibid.: 19). The painting is a subtle but tremendously powerful put-down of Napoleon, the French hero of the moment, by one of Britain's foremost painters. Turner planted in the viewer's mind the stimulus to question the accepted opinion of a person's reputation. The put-down, the invitation to think in a subversive and derogatory way is subtle; the message is indirect, almost hidden, but it is there and it is all the more potent because of its subtlety.

Representation

The relevance of *Hannibal* is that, as argued in Chapter 6, representation is a complex process that is not straightforward and easily readable. Representation can be a versatile tool for subverting the status quo, for provoking and counteracting established perceptions and legends. In *Hannibal*, as in most representation, all is not necessarily as it appears. Representation can be provocateur and counter-agent; it can spread a story that attacks established reputations. Representation is able to do these things because of the ways in which reality is proposed through visual imagery, especially anthropomorphic imagery.

An important event therefore is the appropriation of the actual, the moment when the representation jettisons the real and enters a realm in which the symbolic and the fantastic are possible. It is in this event that meaning emerges (Silverman 1999: 350). I have argued throughout this book that the conditions that make up Neolithic figurines (such as miniaturism) constitute just such a movement into the fantastic and other worldly. In this chapter I argue that figurines also rupture the real, creating illusion through representation.

183

More complexity is introduced to our understanding of representation when we acknowledge the mutability of images and their meanings. The relationships that a visual image has with reality are not stable, but fluid. Images are not simple and straightforward; they are ambiguous, contradictory and multiform (Mirzoeff 1999: 257). Indeed this is one of the lessons of Turner's *Hannibal*: it can mean many things to many different people and it can even mean different things to the same person at different times.[2] So, the relevance of *Hannibal* for our examination of Neolithic figurines is that any representational link that we can establish between figurine object and a potential Neolithic person (or deity) is most likely to be deeply sedimented within local historical knowledges, politics and contradictions about reputation and status.

Blockage

In the summer of 1936, the photographer Walker Evans took a picture of a child's body lying on the coarse wooden floor boards of a cotton picker's home in rural Alabama (fig. 8.3). Laid out on its back the child is covered by a ragged and crumpled white cloth. One leg, visible only from the knee down sticks straight out from the cover towards the viewer. The other leg is bent at the knee with its foot bound in a scrappy bandage that leaves toes and ankle bare. The child's clenched left hand is visible along the body's side. The rest of the child's body and the face are covered. The photograph is disturbing. Is this child dead? My early twenty-first-century eyes find resemblances to bodies laid out after disasters, massacres and bombings. The rhetorical power of cropping the human body was discussed in Chapter 4 and Evans' incomplete body image forces my mind in particular directions. What does the rest of the body look like? What condition is it in? Is it battered? Is it bloodied? Are there other bandages? Are the child's eyes open? In death? These questions and unknowns edge me towards fear, worry and disgust. However, the image itself is stunningly beautiful, highly crafted (is it documentary or pictorial photography; news or art?): the grain of the wooden floorboards, the sharp contrast between the wood and the clean, rectilinear white of the bottom cloth, the shift to the crumpled covering. These are carefully registered components of the photograph. It is a beautiful image yet it is saturated with worry and fear for the fate of the child: it is sublime.

Figure 8.3 Walker Evans' *Squeakie Burroughs* (1936). Library of Congress, Prints and Photographs Division, FSA/OWI Collection LC-USF331-031294-M2.

The child under the sheet is Squeakie Burroughs (a.k.a. Othel Lee Burroughs), son of Floyd and Allie Mae Burroughs. The photograph captured Squeakie as he slept in the relative cool of the Burroughs' porch, with a sheet over him to keep the flies away. The Burroughs were one of three tenant families that Evans and the author William Agee lived with for four weeks in the summer of 1936 while they were gathering material for an

SUBVERTING AND MANIPULATING REALITY

article that *Fortune Magazine* had commissioned them to write about poor white agricultural workers in the American South. The finished article was rejected by *Fortune* though it was published eventually as a book, *Let Us Now Praise Famous Men* (Agee and Evans 1941). In the text of *Famous Men*, Agee evocatively described the existences that the three families scraped out from their surroundings; in the book's images, Evans illuminated the poverty of rural Depression America.

Famous Men is important because it uses its text, its images, and most particularly, the arrangement of text and image in an attack on the contemporary governmental and social system (Tagg 1988: 12–14, 168, 181–2; Mitchell 1994: 297–8; Pultz 1995: 89–93). Using what anthropologists would now term thick description and mixing stream-of-consciousness with hyper-detailed documentation, Agee's text criticized the human and political institutions that treated the farmers as little more than animals. In a powerful, yet indirect manner, the book criticized the system (i.e., the FSA as discussed in Chapter 6) that was funding and orchestrating large-scale documentary photography of American poor; in doing so, the book provided a powerful argument against governmental notions of progress and the ordering of the world.

As powerful as Agee's writing are the images taken by Evans. Like Agee, Evans refused to use his medium to construct illusions of nobility among the impoverished tenant farmers that the FSA wanted to promote. Evans photographed the Burroughs, Field and Tengle families as they were: dirty faces, grimy clothes, hang-dog expressions: drained and exhausted people. These images were not what Roy Stryker and the FSA or the editors of *Fortune Magazine* expected or wanted to see. In Agee and Evans' work there was no place for the determination and endurance in the face of hardship that Dorothy Lange evoked in her *Pea Pickers* (see fig. 6.5) and which ran through much of the FSA photography.

With *Famous Men*, Agee and Evans built difficulty into the representation of the rural American poor. They created what the cultural critic W.T.J. Mitchell has termed a blockage: an ethical strategy to impose a form onto the viewer (Mitchell 1994: 300). Agee and Evans' strategy was a resistance against the FSA's exploitation of the combined rhetoric of the photographic image and documentary description. In addition to the power of Agee's text and each of Evans' images, the critical component of *Famous Men* as blockage was the layout of the book. Instead of delivering easily consumed, standard photojournalism with simple, informative captions accompanying illustrative photographs, *Famous Men* presented the reader with unexpectedly disjoint and difficult sequences. The book begins with a series of images, including the one of Squeakie, but without any descriptive information or captions. Chapters, though they do resemble traditional book chapters of orderly, narrative prose, provoke more questions than they provide digestible description, explanation or apology. After the images follows an angry preface, a verse, a quote, two passages from a child's school geography textbook, a character list of persons and places of the book, the table of contents (presented as the 'Design of the Book'), a poem written to Evans by Agee and then the text itself. The combination of different and unusual elements and their sequence unbalances the reader, who struggles to know what to take from the volume. Agee and Evans ruptured readers' anticipated understandings of how one should look at (and understand) the rural poor, an anticipated understanding that was being generated and disseminated by the FSA.

As discussed in Chapter 6, Roy Stryker and the FSA commissioned photographers to create a particular sense of the crisis of the American south and west, to represent social

SUBVERTING AND MANIPULATING REALITY

disintegration and human misery within the terms of paternal philanthropy of President Roosevelt's reform strategy (Tagg 1988: 13–14). In *Famous Men*, Agee and Walker sabotaged the effectiveness of photography (and text) as traditionally used as the major apparatus of propaganda in the creation of malleable messages and narratives that supported political agendas (Mitchell 1994: 297–8). *Famous Men* showed (not told, but showed) that the rural poor had no chance. Evans took the images that appeared in *Famous Men* while on loan from his job at the FSA. As one might imagine, Evans and Stryker did not agree on many things and Evans left the agency in 1937, though it is unclear whether he quit, was fired by Stryker or was made redundant due to cut-backs that the agency experienced at the time (Lesy 2002: 228–9).

Relevance to figurines

Stryker and Evans' conflicting ethics of representation as well as Turner's attack on the Napoleon myth illustrate how manifestations of the human body are open to manipulation within large-scale party political ideologies, such as Roosevelt's New Deal reforms. Representations of the human body in more general terms are also open to manipulation within the less explicit political ideologies that surround individual and small group relationships and identities. If we accept that what-you-see-is-*not*-what-you-get, and that there is no one-to-one connection between represented reality and actual reality, then any attempt to read Neolithic identities from Neolithic figurines is precarious at best. More accurate, and more exciting I suggest, is an approach to figurines that views them as potent tools within the contemporary political struggles running through Neolithic households and villages. The ways that the human form is represented and the ways that those representations are used, displayed, disseminated, controlled and, as Stryker practised, killed become the critical actions and props of social engagement.

Distortions

While Stryker and Evans exploited the rhetoric of photographing specifically located people for their particular ethical projects, the Surrealist photographers of the 1920s and 1930s created images of the human body that posed ethical questions about the way that the human body in general was seen and represented. In 1933 the European photographer André Kertész took an extraordinary series of images (Ducrot 1977). In one of the least disorienting of these, *Distorsion no. 29*, Kertész has filled all but a third of the frame with a bizarre mutation of human body-parts (see discussion in Pultz 1995: 72–6). Two hands are joined by a stretch of a single arm, and a single stretch of legs joins two pairs of feet. The object of the image clearly is human but it is a humanity that has been fragmented and distorted: feet, hands, leg and arm but neither body nor face. The lower right quarter of the image is clearer: the naked upper torso of a woman's body, one arm extending towards the distortion and the other held across her body below her breasts; one side of a woman's face, eyes closed, face towards the distortion. Kertész made this and the other images in the series by photographing women reflected in large curved mirrors. Indeed, in *Distorsion no. 29*, the mechanism of distortion is clearly visible, the bottom of the mirror rests on the floor to the left of the woman; in the rest of the series the mirror is not apparent and the effect is even more disturbing. In all of the images, the effect of photographing the body reflected in the curved mirror is extraordinary. When I look at

SUBVERTING AND MANIPULATING REALITY

these images I can see body and body parts (i.e., I know that I am looking at a human body), but it is disturbingly difficult to recognize a specific body and body parts or to recognize where arm meets leg or torso leads to neck. I have to stop and work through each image, reassembling the body that I am trying to look at, trying to fit what I see into my personal idea of what a naked female body is and should look like.

Kertész was one of a group of Surrealist photographers and artists who challenged the principles of Realism in the 1920s and 1930s. By displacing and interrupting traditional and complacent perceptions, they aimed to disorganize and transfigure the normalcy of the everyday. In their constructions, they played with routine, ordinary objects such as tools and housewares. Paradoxically, by playing with things that people took for granted in their daily lives (mostly famously, Marcel Duchamp's lavatory urinal) the Surrealists released new visions from within the most mundane and standard products of peoples' lives. Surrealist representations were at once both strange and familiar. In his distortion series, Kertész played a double game, using the most everyday of objects (the body) while disorganizing the most everyday of representational institutions, the rhetoric of photographic technology.

Importantly, Kertész's distortions forced the spectator to think, to question and wonder about what he or she was looking at and, especially, to think about how the human body should be represented; indeed, what the human body meant and how it is defined. Kertész made body morphology ambiguous; what is usually seen as beautiful or sensuous becomes grotesque. The viewer cannot find any single, fixed, vantage-point in a Kertész distortion; the curved mirror has removed the traditional perspectival space that usually regulates relationships between model, photographer and spectator (Pultz 1995: 72). Looking at Kertész's distortions forces viewers to produce their own meanings within the process of looking at the human body; events of looking at the body become series of discoveries in which the spectator ricochets from what is secure in the observable world to the distorted representation of that reality, and then back again to the secure (Roberts 1998: 108–9; Kramer 1977). With his distortions and by destabilizing and detaching the body and body parts, Kertész confronted existing relationships between aesthetics and body politics (Roberts 1998: 99).

Relevance to figurines

How different are figurines to Kertész's distortions? Both present the human form in difficult and unusual manners. Also relevant is the more general Surrealist belief that the truth of things lies beneath any superficial moment of empirical verification, that objects are filled with motives and intentions not available on the surface (Roberts 1998: 100). At yet another level, Surrealists such as Kertész exploited the rhetorical power of photography as the medium of truth and turned the power of that rhetoric back against itself: photographs are truthful, they are the medium of evidence; yet what is represented is not anything of the real world. The result is bodies that do not look like bodies. The selection of fired clay as the dominant medium of Neolithic figurine manufacture raises and complicates the significance of clay (and of the body) among the world of Neolithic made-objects: did clay have one rhetorical significance as it was used to make pots; did it have another when it was used to make figurines? In using clay to make figurines, were they subtle inversions of medium-based significances that played themselves out in the everyday objects of ceramic pots and bowls? In their production, use, display and destruction, do figurines represent expropriations of a medium that held particular ideological significances? Is subversion to be found in the modelling of the human out of a material that is otherwise used for creating objects that were used to serve, mix, boil, simmer, contain, hoard and display?

Sexual disruption

If Kertész focused on distorting the human form with some reference to perceptions of the female body, many other artists have disrupted the accepted perception of human sexuality by drawing particular attention to the female form. In 1920, the German artist Hannah Höch created *Das schöne Mädchen* [The Beautiful Girl] (fig. 8.4). *Mädchen* is a collage (indeed Höch helped to develop the technique) in which several dozen images are pasted onto a light-coloured, solid background. As the title predicts, some of the images are feminine: the large wig of woman's hair in the centre-left; a seated girl in a bathing costume and beach/pool shoes, legs crossed, a hand holding a parasol; part of another woman's face; and a woman's hand (perhaps) that extends from behind the wig and holds a watch. However, most of the images in the collage are industrial: the largest is a metal crank, perhaps from a bicycle, with hexagonal nuts and round washers, sticking into the centre of the image; a studded, rubber car tyre; 20 or so BMW car badges distributed, overlapping each other, across the image's middle ground, which itself appears to be a poster with the word 'Motor' across its inverted lower half (though most of the word is covered by the wig). The watch, held by the hand, further refers to the mechanical as does an otherwise nondescript metal beam, upon which the bathing girl sits. Under the wig, where a human head should be, a lightbulb has been placed on the girl's shoulders. A male boxer emerges from the middle of the rubber tyre, punching his way towards the girl in the bathing costume. It is an extraordinary combination of images that seems to have no connection with the collage's title of feminine youth and beauty.

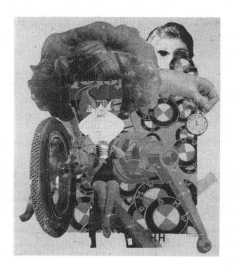

Figure 8.4 Hannah Höch's *Das schöne Mädchen* (1920). © DACS 2004.

Höch was a member of the Berlin Dada; the work of the Dada was troublesome and difficult on the eye. Dada engaged the problems of the day and, like its descendant/relative Surrealism, paid particular attention to the objects of everyday life (Ades 1986: 26). By juxtapositioning normally disparate created things, Dada artists disoriented and antagonized, creating apparently chaotic images that provoked the viewer to pull apart reality (ibid.: 12–13). In Höch's case the created things include both the represented objects (the car, the bicycle crank) as well as the means of representing them (the cutout and pasted photographs, posters and advertisements). Importantly, photomontage and collage were powerful media for attacking political ideologies: John Heartfield's creations, such as *Adolf the Superman* (1932), which suggested that Hitler spoke rubbish

SUBVERTING AND MANIPULATING REALITY

but swallowed funds; and *Hurrah, the Butter is Finished* (1935) which twisted a quote from a Goering speech (i.e., 'Iron makes a country strong, butter and lard only make people fat') by creating an image of a family sitting at the breakfast table chewing on metal (Ades 1986: 57).

As Linda Nochlin has argued, with *Mädchen*, Höch refuses the image of woman as a transcendent object of art and the male gaze, and denies the gaze, attacking the concepts of beauty, showing that the pretty girl of the title is literally a constructed thing (Nochlin 1991: 39–40). Not only is the concept of female beauty constructed (a sturdy metal beam supports the girl in the bathing suit) but the physical representation of visual beauty, here in the collage, is built out of ready-made materials, both the objects portrayed and their individual media within the collage (e.g., poster, advertisements). *Mädchen* attacks the mass-produced standards of beauty and the constructed nature of all representations of beauty. Like Kertész's distortions, Höch's collage disturbs viewers and disrupts their expectations of looking; it forces spectators to rethink how they see the human body and to recognize that concepts such as beauty, femininity (sexuality even) are constructed and not essential or straightforward. Collage was one way in which artists fractured the totalizing power of the gaze by allowing, forcing even, the recognition that bodies are deliberately created (Pultz 1995: 87). The pretty girl in Höch's title is clearly a product assembled from many others.

Many other contemporary women image-makers have focused their work on the problematics of gendered representation. Barbara Kruger and Mary Kelly refuse any straightforward mirroring of female subjects in representation (Pultz 1995: 150–3; Kelly 1998; Kruger 1999). They employ collage, photo-montage, self-indexical photography, combinations of texts, images and objects in order to call attention to the production of gender itself and its inscription in the unconscious as a social construction rather than a natural phenomenon (Nochlin 1991: 40). All of these artists use sexuality to disrupt and subvert. As discussed in relation to anthropomorphism in Chapter 4, Cindy Sherman also has played with common perceptions of sexuality and sexual body parts in order to challenge and overturn the way that people perceive identity and sexualized bodies. Jurgen Klanke has questioned conventional definitions of gender and sexuality in his *Physiognomien* (1972–3), a series of photographs which combine explicitly male traits such as a hairy chest with explicitly female body treatment such as facial makeup and a dress (Pultz 1995: 141). Because sexuality disrupts, it constantly worries and troubles anything supposedly as fixed as an identity (Mirzoeff 1999: 162; Mercer 1996: 119). Sexuality is the realm where fear and desire find their most intimate connection, where notions of otherness and the exotic/erotic are most often conflated. Sexuality often links the effects of differentiation to the structures of power and domination (Doane 1999: 451). In playing with sexuality by distorting, twisting, displacing and disorganizing a community's accepted understandings or perceptions of it, representations attack, subvert and resist contemporary perceptions of identity and political relations between people based on sexual or gendered difference.

Relevance to figurines

The overwhelming attention that figurine analysts direct to the representation of sexualized body parts and thus to reconstructions of social hierarchies within Neolithic villages has been misdirected. As noted in the introduction to this book and as elaborated in the discussion in this chapter, the relationships between representation and reality are more often than not a series of contortions. While it may not be easy (or even possible) to understand the precise political convolutions of subversion, blockage and resistance, it is clear that the least likely possibility is that what is represented in Neolithic figurine directly reflects what was happening in a Neolithic community.

Furthermore, the representation of sexual body parts can mean many, even simultaneously contradictory, things. The important lesson is that sexuality disrupts and that the representation of sexuality exploits the multifarious rhetorics of the visual in a struggle against what is appropriate and acceptable in a particular (pre)historical context. This is the argument that I put forward in two earlier articles on figurines from northeast Bulgaria (Bailey 1994a, 1996). In those articles, I argued that sexualized figurines would have worked well within villages where subordinate groups were muted and where the muted groups used particular media to 'voice' the reality of their private power. This private power thus was present in different material forms from those that dominant groups used to make louder statements about their more public power (i.e., through flash rituals surrounding male burials). Importantly, one of the examples I used in that argument was the female figurine from Achilleion (fig. 8.1) with legs spread and genitalia thrust into the viewer's face. In those articles, I suggested that sexuality disrupts and that the representation of sexuality was a fundamental mechanism of disruption. While it is clear to me, now, that my earlier arguments were rather inflexible reconstructions of what must have been more complex village dynamics, the main thrust of the argument remains valid: that the sexualized body is a powerful medium of resistance and subversion.

Affective ambiguities and the carnivalesque

There are subtler levels and contradictions within the political use of sexual representation in community politics. In the mid-1970s, social anthropologist David Gilmore was walking down a street in an Andalusian town in southern Spain during the annual carnival (Gilmore 1998). Gilmore watched as men, dressed up as women, walked along a street, grotesquely mimicking women's mannerisms, whining, pulling up their shawls to show off their padded breasts, lifting their skirts to reveal their bottoms and hairy legs, and shouting crude sexual obscenities: 'Stick it up my arse'; 'Touch my tits' (ibid.: 37–8). Gilmore's study of the Andalusian carnival and his book, *Carnival and Culture. Sex, Symbol and Status in Spain*, has become the authoritative, modern, text on the subject not only for southern Europe but for the phenomenon of carnival as a whole.[3] There is much to learn from carnival and in particular from Gilmore's analysis of it.

Carnival

With roots deep into Ancient Greek and Roman Dionysian and Saturnalian festivals, carnival is a socio-political institution best known from the pre-Lent celebrations of the European Middle Ages (Bakhtin 1968). In these communities, carnival played a central symbolic role, loudly proclaiming alternative world-views in which existing norms and values were inverted. During carnival, hierarchies were abolished, class distinctions dissolved, and power relations turned on their heads. Carnival decentralized and disrupted the official, hegemonic project of a community. Official and sacred boundaries were crossed; the most marginal of society was brought centre-stage (the pauper takes the role

SUBVERTING AND MANIPULATING REALITY

of the king; the Mayor the clothes of the wino), spectacles of participation erased boundaries between spectator and performer, and communities were brought together without regard for normal differences (Stam 1989: 85, 94). The powerful became grotesque; the vulgar became beautiful (Shohat and Stam 1998). Most often in carnival the status quo and power relations are overturned by a subordinate group, usually the poor or women and, in this, above all, carnival is an inversion of the world, a revolution in systems and order, a time for liberation, surrealism, intoxication, hysteria, impulsiveness, defilement and debauchery (Gilmore 1998: 10).

Bodies and sexualities

Paramount among the apparatus of such carnivalizations is the human body, especially in its most grotesque and unacceptable forms: the monster, the excessive, the obscene, the insane, the scandalous, the nonsensical, the distorted and disproportioned, the malleable and transformable, the unstable and mutated. In carnival, body form and bodily senses are exploited and corrupted: hunger, thirst, defecation, copulation take centre stage, literally. Carnival praises and promotes as positive all that society normally discards as gross, rude, of bad taste and inappropriate: farting, shitting, peeing, fucking, boozing, vomiting. Against static corporealities, carnival counterposes the uncontrolled body, the passing of one form into another, reflecting the never-completed character of being (Shohat and Stam 1998). Carnival is about corporal outrageousness, proposing abnormal concepts of the body, ones in which the body distorts to outlandish proportions, ones in which the body is laid open and unfinished (ibid.).

Within carnival, particular emphasis is placed on inversions of sexuality: the gay and lesbian, the bisexual and the transvestic. Indeed any release from socially imposed sexual roles is promoted: the display of genitalia, the illumination of the naked, the tart and the whore. In these ways, sexual suggestion is omnipresent, especially manifest in representations that annoy people and which irritate and stimulate (Gilmore 1998: 14). Transvestitism is particularly rampant. In Gilmore's Andalusian villages, transvestites present two images of women: a soft maternal one represented by middle-aged men dressed as women with faces made expressionless by a covering of white fabric or scarf (fig. 8.5); and a hideously destructive one, with younger men transformed by costume to have grossly misshapen bodies and faces bearing hideous, blood-stained and scarred masks (ibid.: 72). These are men that are women that are, in turn, male perceptions of women. Traditional boundaries are dissolved and no one is in his or her correct place. The resulting sexual ambiguity about who (or even what) is male or female leads to the merging of existing standards of gender identities (Stokes 1992: 122) and neutralizes what normally are extremely significant symbolic oppositions (Ivanov 1984). Above all else, the ambiguous, the double- or multi-faced is praised (Stam 1989: 94). The masks that Gilmore's transvestites wear obscure each man's particular identities as well as merging all of the wo/men into a faceless, anonymous mass (Gilmore 1998: 11).

The media through which the carnivalesque is delivered are diverse, but all deploy through spectacle or performance: pageants, festivals, speeches, songs, dances, banquets, feasts, oaths, foul language and slang. Together with participants (cross-dressers and others), material culture and the charged symbols and representations, carnival is an extraordinary form of artistic visualization, a peculiar sort of heuristic principle that allows the discovery of new and as yet unseen things (Shohat and Stam 1998). As

SUBVERTING AND MANIPULATING REALITY

Figure 8.5 Andalusian carnival participants. Photograph courtesy of David Gilmore.

spectacle, carnival is not only an entry into other worlds, somewhere beyond the actuality of everyday, but it is a glimpse, even, of the world(s) beyond the other worldly.

Revolution and reaffirmation

Significantly, carnival is much more complex than a simple attempt to overturn one existing power structure. Thus, carnival can work both in a vertical direction, against the authorities, and in a horizontal one, against peer-group deviance (Gilmore 1998: 16). Most paradoxically, as much as it subverts and inverts, carnival restores and maintains (ibid.: 4–6; see also Kertzer 1988: 144–50; Mintz 1997). While carnival-goers subvert the status quo, they also subvert their own altered statuses and sexual subversions; as Gilmore puts it they 'negate their own negations' and in doing so rehabilitate the traditional order (Gilmore 1998: 4). Through the rituals of carnival, the subjective, revolutionary world becomes reality. However, that reality, no matter how wild, violent or grotesque, never escapes its own terms of reference, the existing order against which it reacts. Bizarrely, the main effect is to reaffirm the status quo (ibid.: 31). While it provides an illusory sense of freedom, carnival, in fact, controls social tensions; it provides not a real release but nothing more than a simulacrum of freedom (Eco 1984). Most deflating is the realization that, when viewed through the bloodshot hangovers of the morning-after, a carnival appears as nothing more than an officially sanctioned and scheduled outlet for the expression of potential conflict, and as such remains an agent of social control (Gilmore 1998: 32; Brandes 1980: 90; 1988: 186; Le Roy Ladurie 1979; N. Davis 1973).

Philosophies

As Gilmore argues, carnival provides a screen upon which the key themes of sex, gender and status are projected, negotiated and understood through representations (Gilmore 1998: 3). It is a ludic, subversive but sane mechanism with which people can experience and negotiate the deep, troubling, emotional and philosophical conflicts and contradictions that demand some sort of psychological release. Carnival songs, symbols, performances and props break through normal barriers of reserve to convey and unwrap messages about sex and status and to make public and accessible what is usually secret. In his study of the Andalusian carnival *copla*, Gilmore shows how this song brings to the surface a diverse series of moral dialogues between singer and audience, between self and other, between concepts of high and low, between notions of good and evil, between categories of people: men and women, rich and poor, child and adult. The rhetoric of carnival reveals the ways that people perceive their own community and its traditions. Through the stories of the *copla*, the Andalusian villagers define 'themselves to themselves' (Gilmore 1998: 3; after Geertz 1983: 58).

Most important for our investigation of representation in the Balkan Neolithic is the recognition that carnival is two-sided, dualist, inconsistent, protean, contradictory and equivocal; carnival is dynamically ambivalent about the key issues in life such as sex and status (Gilmore 1998: 6). In this, Gilmore supports and expands Mikhail Bakhtin's original claim that above all carnival is essentially ambivalent, simultaneously praising and abusing, glorifying and humiliating (ibid.: 5; Bakhtin 1968: 416). Here then is the crux of carnival; in its ongoing dialectic and series of contradictions and juxtapositions, it produces what Gilmore calls the spice of life, the effervescent zest, the sparkle of juxtaposed antitheses, the open mingling of a community's internal contradictions (Gilmore 1998: 7). Carnival is a celebration of ambivalence and mixed feelings and a recognition of the fluidity of identity, status, sexuality and being in the world. It is the ultimate example of the dialectic nature of human relations. Carnival is the balance between alienation and identity; it is both about that which is the self and that which is not-the-self (ibid.: 207). The lesson is that all behaviour is always ambivalent, that all hierarchies are reversible (e.g., that men and women are on top and on the bottom, dominant and dominated, all at the same time); and, critically, that there can be no negation of the human imagination (ibid.: 123).

The ambivalence of carnival means that its rituals simultaneously challenge and support shared ideas, definitions and moralities. Carnival mixes otherwise incompatible symbols and affects, juxtaposing moral and ideological contracts and political (dis)order. In these senses, carnivals are philosophic: they engage people in thinking about who and what they are and about their relationships with others. In carnival, participants (and by-standers) experiment with criteria and standards of values, exploring their metaphorical and moral possibilities in order to make better sense of the logical inconsistencies of their worlds (ibid.: 121). People achieve new and powerful ways of interpreting the world and its possibilities (DaMatta 1991: 59). In Gilmore's Andalusian *copla*, the poets sing of shared concerns, of universal humanity; they merge the (always irresolvable) contradictions of life, juxtaposing the oppositions that face everyone, the problems of human contact, simultaneously highlighting and relieving the tensions that their songs produce (Gilmore 1998: 206). In Gilmore's words, carnival is a 'window briefly thrown open on the concealed machinery of life's complexities, a sudden *rendezvous* with the shocking unity of the sexes, a face-to-face encounter with the strange oneness of triumph and tragedy, and a sudden awareness of the disturbing linkage of dependency and autonomy' (ibid.: 207).

As philosophy, carnival functions out of time (Stam refers to carnival as 'time in parentheses': 1989: 94) and carnival functions out of space; it is life in a virtual world in which competing meanings become dialogue and get worked out, a place and a time which provide people with psychological relief (Gilmore 1998: 10), a revolutionary, other world that oppressed groups create in symbolic form (Scott 1976, 1985). Carnival allows people to destroy and transgress without fear of consequence or punishment (DaMatta 1991: 59).[4]

Relevance to figurines

Much of what Gilmore concludes about the Andalusian carnival and which Bakhtin and others have concluded about similar manifestations of the phenomenon bind together the critical themes and examples that run through the discussions of Neolithic figurines in the preceding chapters: the role of the body in definitions of identity, status, sexuality and hierarchy; the female body and the disruptive potential of sexuality; the body as spectacle of inversion; the sexual ambiguity and ambivalence of figurines that are neither male nor female; the hyper-sexualized figurines that seem to have both female attributes such as breasts as well as phallic-shaped necks or bodies; the use of the grotesque, over-inflated, cropped, fragmented and incomplete body; the importance not only of the head and the face, but significantly, the importance of faces left blank and expressionless and the significance of masquerade and the wearing of masks;[5] the rhetorical power that visual imagery has within political conflict, contestations and reaffirmation; the power to open up and allow access to other worlds that exist in some virtual place; and the power that both figurines and carnival possess to move people out of actual time and actual physical place. Both figurines and carnival are especially political, though not in the sense as is commonly understood (as simplistic one-dimensional attacks on the status quo or dominant group – e.g., Eagleton [1989] for carnival and Bailey [1994a, 1996] for figurines). Especially resonant are the contradictions and paradoxes at the core of the conditions that define both carnival and figurines. The power that drives carnival and figurines flows from irresolvable inner tensions created when the spectator experiences contradictory effects simultaneously.

However, none of these similarities supports (nor should we hope for or try to find such support for) an easy explanation which equates Neolithic figurines with carnival transvestites, an explanation that would close down both the argument and the vitality of figurines (and of carnival) as material culture (and of carnival as spectacle) and which would force us to generate reconstructions in which we see figurines as festival props in the hands of Neolithic carnival merry-makers, or even in which we see Neolithic people enacting carnivalesque ceremonies in miniature with a set of figurines.

SUBVERTING AND MANIPULATING REALITY

The connection is simultaneously more subtle and more obvious. At their most fundamental, both carnival and figurines are philosophic; they are mechanisms through which people play out positions (contradictory or otherwise) of identity, status, sexuality and belonging within their communities. Though planned and constructed, carnival, like figurines, has its greatest and widest impact in indirect ways, away from any conscious intentions of the individual who modelled the clay or the poet who sings the *copla*. Is there any difference in the scale (or content even) of the affects on the spectators provoked by a young Anadalusian man dressed as a hideous witch raising her/his skirt and the affects on the Neolithic woman, child or man holding the Achilleion figurine in her or his hand? If we need a more concrete interpretation, then the emphasis must rest on the local, (pre)historical context in particular inequalities of power and status. Both figurines and carnival carry with them implications and danger wherever there is a sharp stratification or inequality in which individuals find themselves pushed in one direction when they want to go in another, when rhetorics of persuasion are required. For Gilmore, such a situation pertains in the overcrowded towns in southern Europe (Gilmore 1998: 12); for Balkan prehistory, such a predicament can be found in the newly grounded alignments of people, in the consequences of the built environment and of the material things that gradually changed the ways people lived their lives after 6500 BC.

Chapter conclusion and relevances

Individual representations can act on their own or work within sets (or even iterations of the same image) of representations that attack shared perceptions of groups: Walker Evans, *Famous Men* and the impoverished; or Hannah Höch, *Das schöne Mädchen* and the feminine. Resistance and blockage can take on large party politics as well more general interpersonal and intra-group relationships. However, though it is possible to uncover a number of intriguing conditions of particular types of objects (the rhetoric of the photographic, the power of the sublime, the empowerment of the miniature), it is impossible to find explicit correlations between a medium or condition of representation and a particular target of attack. If the diverse material events of resistance have anything in common, it is that each exploits the power of internal contradiction and paradox to provoke the viewer. Beyond that, it is difficult to link any particular form or texture to any particular type of attack or system. There is no relevance for analogy here:[6] figurines are not surreal (though we may understand them better having looked at Kertész's distortions); they are not props in carnival (though we may benefit from recognizing the ambivalence of carnival representations). Without recourse to analogy we are turned back to particular (pre)historical contexts: to the rural poor of the American Depression; to the politics of the French–English wars and to the traditional perception of military hero and legend; and to the perception of women's bodies at the start of the twentieth century. One potential, shared characteristic of these resistances is that they attack the established and the commonly accepted. Another common element of engagement is the use of representations of the human body for the debate over individuals and the (in)balances of power, but also for the more general contemporary discussion of what it means to be human in a particular community: what does the thing called individual look and feel like; is it equivalent and representative in a corporeal person or is it something and somewhere else; is it a virtual entity only existing in a virtual place? In this sense then, an archaeology of Balkan figurines comes down to an investigation of the definitions and politics of being and of the relationships, definitions and politics that ran through the households, villages, gardens, fields and forests of the southeast European Neolithic.

Gilmore's work on carnival, however, shows that even iconoclastic assaults on the status quo turn in on themselves, that criticism only serves to reinforce the reality of what is being attacked. Even if one could establish secure connections between particular pre-historic subversive objects or specifically subversive media, there can be no certainty that subversion did anything other than stabilize existing structures of power and hegemony. Perhaps the only certain thing is that there were conflict and contestation, that everyday life was not secure but a constant flow of questionings and affirmations. Add to this the Surrealists' recognition of the depth and complexities of meanings contained in everyday objects and the result pushes us into even deeper levels of explanatory uncertainty. With what, than, are we left? What can we say about Neolithic figurines? One answer is that figurines, like all of the examples in this and the preceding chapters, are tools for thinking. They are philosophies. They make us think and they made Neolithic men, women and children think. Together, we think about what we are and about who we are. They make us think about how we relate to others and how we manipulate our bodies to express these relationships. They make us think through the body. They make our being manifest through the body. They make us ask questions.

9

CORPOREAL POLITICS OF
BEING IN THE NEOLITHIC

While discussion has investigated the ways in which figurines worked and on the particular conditions that made figurines successful as visual rhetoric, it has avoided answering the direct question, what do Neolithic figurines mean? One answer is the recognition that figurines were deeply sedimented within local (pre)historic knowledges, politics and negotiations over reputation and status. In this sense they worked within particular variations of physical, economic and social conditions. One of the most important of these local Neolithic conditions was the construction of architectural environments and the creation of bounded space. Exclusive mechanisms of marking off particular places for working, living, eating and sleeping were complemented by inclusive institutions such as households and villages.

Physically grounded in place for various durations (from the temporary to the monumental), Neolithic spatial arrangements were part of the variation in types of relationships that existed among individuals, small groups and larger congregations of people. As they had been for tens of millennia, Neolithic interpersonal relationships were the products of co-operation, competition, negotiation and (dis)agreements played out across the complete range of daily activities including both the mundane and the ceremonial. However, with the Neolithic, an intensified, significantly more permanent, articulation of particular people to particular places (i.e., sedentism) had fundamental consequences for community composition, particularly in the reduction of the flexibility of people's relationships to each other. One of the most important consequences of this adaptation of a permanent (or at least semi-permanent) architectural environment was a change to the character of relationships among people.

As significant as the consequences of the built environment in the Neolithic was the adaptation of ceramic pyrotechnology as a dominant medium for material culture. Beyond any functional advantages of making fired-clay vessels (e.g., for better, longer-term storage), the ability to use heat to transform a naturally malleable material such as clay into a fixed and durable object such as a pot marked a fundamental alteration to the types and numbers of objects with which people lived their lives, and to the capacities (functional, symbolic and sensual) that these objects possessed. If, as Vitelli has argued (see discussion in Chapter 1), the early developments of pottery-making in the Balkans were accompanied by conceptions of extraordinary and magical skills and knowledges, then the meanings of all ceramic objects, (pots and figurines included), may well have carried similar significances.

Together the development of the built environment and the dominance of a material world by ceramic objects had consequences that long outlived any novelties that their original uses in the region may have carried. Fundamental to the Neolithic was an arrangement of people, things and places, over durations and with particular boundaries, that was distinct from what had come before, in the late Upper Palaeolithic, as well as what was to came after, in the early Bronze Age. Similarly distinct were peoples' particular capacities, desires and needs to understand who they were as individuals and as members within households or village groups. To know oneself was to know one's relationship to others. While there was nothing specific to the Neolithic in the human need to understand social relationships, there were specific material and political conditions that made the Neolithic manifestations of human identities distinct. Specifically, new conceptualizations of society were created in new media, including the built environment and the formal deposition of the deceased; however, Neolithic perspectives on society found equally powerful manifestations in the repeated, daily, visual experience of people seeing representations of the human body in miniature, durable, three-dimensional form. Far from being defined in terms of a new economy (i.e., Childe's original shift from food-gathering to food-producing; Childe 1936), the Neolithic is better understood in terms of a particular appearance of the human body and in the articulations of corporeality, identity, community and individuality. The Balkan Neolithic was a particular corporeal politics of being and figurines were at the core of this politics.

The meanings of figurines

But what did these figurines mean? Were they used in the ceremonies of ancestor cults that involved votive figurines? Were they kept as portraits of relatives, friends and enemies? Were they children's playthings? Were they props set out on the altars of Mother Goddess priestesses? Were they mere doodlings in clay that accompanied the events of firing ceramic vessels? Personally, I am tempted to reconstruct Neolithic ceremonies and rituals in the terms that David Gilmore proposed for the affective ambiguities of the Andalusian carnivals (Chapter 8), or that Marc Quinn or Cindy Sherman's provoked about the human form (Chapter 6), or even in James Agee's and Walker Evans' attempts to overturn the New Deal documentary propaganda about Depression migrant labourers (Chapter 8).

The paradox of figurine meaning is that each of the proposed interpretations is at the same time both correct and incorrect. Neolithic figurines have at least two kinds of meanings. On the one hand they can be explained in terms of the particularities of their use or function, the reasons for which they were made. There is no reason to deny that any or all of the possible uses just listed or which have been listed elsewhere did not take place (Meskell 1998; Ucko 1968). Indeed figurines would have been very good at serving each of the proposed functions. This sense of figurine meaning consists of both a figurine's intended use as well as the uses to which it was actually put, recognizing of course that intended and actual use are often not the same thing.

On the other hand, there is a second meaning and it is this which may prove to be the more significant for understanding the social realities of living in the Neolithic Balkans. This second meaning works at a deeper level and has nothing to do with the intention of the person who modelled, decorated or fired a figurine. It does not have anything to do with the ceremony(s)/game(s)/prayer(s) in which that figurine was used. It does not even have anything to do with whether or not that figurine was found in a pit, a building, an oven, a burial or in the desk drawer of an antiquities' collector. This second meaning is the position of the figurine as an unintentional, but potent, manifestation of the body in Neolithic communities. In this sense, its importance is its frequent (perhaps continuous) circulation and visibility in people's daily lives. In this sense figurines are/were important because they are the habitual presentation of the human body in these communities. Regardless of the other superficial uses (as goddesses, as votives, as portraits, or as objects to be broken and deposited) figurines saturated communities with particular images/senses of being human. The ever-presence of these senses of being human was fundamental to the Neolithic understanding of being.

A corporeal politics of being

As is seen in existing figurine literature, it is possible to use differences in body morphology and surface treatment in order to build clear typologies within populations of Neolithic figurines from particular sites, cultures or regions. For example, some Cucuteni/Tripolye figurines are highly decorated and have no heads while others found at the same sites are undecorated and have full facial detail. Similarly, there are particular Thessalian figurines that are inescapably male and others that are just as clearly female. Indeed all figurine analysts focus on classifying figurines into types and sub-types.

However, examinations of these categories and sub-categories reveal that there is more similarity than there is variation across groups of figurines. This is especially clear within the early Cucuteni/Tripolye figurines where variation from the norm of body appearance was almost non-existent. A similar case can be made for the Hamangia figurines: even with variation in body position, the overwhelming impression is one of morphological, indeed corporeal, homogeneity. The high degree of corporeal similarity applies to almost all of the other groups and categories of figurines discussed in this book as well as those from the other major culture groups of the Balkan Neolithic (e.g., Vinča, Gumelniţa). Given the potential for formal variation that is inherent in clay when it is worked at this size, such similarity is particularly unusual. While there is almost no shape or variation on the human form that could not have been rendered in clay, figurine morphology varies little. There are exceptions to this internal similarity, for example the late Neolithic material from Cucuteni/Tripolye sites, though one is tempted to understand these in terms of the breakdown of long-accepted perceptions of the body and identity. On the whole, Balkan Neolithic figurines are striking in the absence of variation in specific, appropriate ways of modelling and decorating the body.

Traditional, culture-historical explanation reads the similarity of body form in terms of the expected homogeneity in the material culture of a common group of people. It is more likely that similarities in figurine body form represent sets of norms along with and against which people defined and positioned themselves. Definition and positioning need not have been conscious efforts. Rather, the presence of body representations, created for any range of primary functions (playthings, votives, portraiture) created a standard, corporeal, register that allowed people to visually judge differences and similarities between themselves and others. Importantly, then, the representation of a body through a figurine may have nothing to do with the rise of the individual (contra, Bailey 1994b); on the contrary, the presence of so many similarly formed and decorated figurine bodies suggests a shared conception of what a person was and should look like.

In her discussion of Thessalian Neolithic figurines (see Chapter 7), Laia Orphanidis emphasized the precise repetition of body form and decoration. In these repetitions and in the constraints on modelling and decoration are found the mechanisms of social conformity that are at work in modern body culture such as the Barbie Doll: created, purchased, given and played with as a toy but containing fundamental, highly political, yet unintended consequences for how young girls think about their bodies, the bodies of their mothers and the bodies of their friends. The inversion of these subconsciously created definitions of the female human body is at the core of the work by artists such as Cindy Sherman, who manipulate, rearrange and misrepresent the female form in order to force the viewer to think again about how they look at and understand women in modern society. While the stimulus of Cindy Sherman's work is intentional, the stimuli of the Barbie Doll and of the Neolithic figurine are less obvious (invisible and unintentional even) and are only found deep within the implicit of the everyday.

In the repeated, regular and habitual visibility of figurines in the Neolithic, it is possible to see a corporealization of the self and of the person. Critically (and para-doxically) through this ongoing, always present, process of body homogenization, the individual person, as defined as a corporeal being, was tied in to the greater social whole. It was a subtle, yet relentless, undetectable and, no doubt, unintentional process that led to the coherence of the group, that silently convinced people that, despite any range of actual differences among particular individuals, those individuals belonged together, linked by a common corporeality.

Furthermore, the Neolithic corporealization of the self and the person was a homog-enizing process through which diversity and differences were rejected and suppressed. Across these Neolithic landscapes, within village boundaries and between individual buildings, the corporealized individual (and its representation) became the core of social community. In this sense, it was the actual physical diversity among the living, breathing, flesh and blood individuals that were the greatest risks to community cohesion. The existence and long-term success of these forms of social aggregations (i.e., the 2,500-year survival of the Neolithic way of living) depended on the continuous, unintentional, suppression of the risks of social division and disintegration that diversity among living bodies posed. In itself, this was an incredible paradox: the individual body, through its repeated visual representation, was the essence of the communal. On the one hand there were public ceremonies linked to burials (at least for the Hamangia communities), possibly to rituals of deposition (as suggested by Chapman), and to events of house-building and destruction; these occasional ceremonies loudly proposed intra-group distinction and intra-community divisions. At the same time, however, figurines had saturated the visual world of these communities with particular images and arrange-ments of the human body; figurines were the quieter rhythm of social coherence. We can go further still and suggest that the homogenized representation of the body was the core of a subconscious politics of social homogenization that held together Balkan Neolithic communities.

In this sense, figurines were themselves interpretations and explanations: material interpretations of how it was to be, material explanations of how it was to be different and how it was to be the same. It is tempting, even, to suggest that Neolithic people preferred the virtual representation and definition of humans and humanity (seen in figurines) to the actual, dirty, fluid, flexing, Neolithic humanity (seen in their own bodies). This is close to Baudrillard's simulacrum (see Chapter 6): that figurines estab-lished a real thing (a clay human representation) that had no reality. This is also similar to Gatens' concept of an imaginary body: a body, constructed by a shared language and common institutional practices but which lacks any single fixed significance (Gatens 1996: 12; see Chapter 6). There were no living humans who looked like either the pneumatic Hamangia figurines or the many faceless examples from Thessaly or the Cucuteni/ Tripolye sites. In this sense the figurines were a hyper-reality. They were not a reflection of any basic, objective, reality; in fact they bore no relation to any one reality. They were their own pure simulacra.

The recognition that these Neolithic communities understood the human body to be the primary site of the individual and of the self opens up understandings for other communities, both those that shared these two and a half millennia and those that came before and after. There is no reason to assume that there were not other sites (in both the sense of settlements and of media) through which the individual and the self existed. Thus, in some communities the activities and materials of mortuary ceremonies engaged people's understanding of relationships and identities. All communities shared the socially organizing facility of the built environment. The rituals of architecture (and, to a more limited extent in the communities investigated in this book, of burial[1]) had particular effects on how people understood their relationships to others, whether those relationships were defined by prestige, status or hierarchy (as could be contested via burial ritual) or whether they were defined in terms of what activities one carried out where and with whom (as facilitated by the boundaries of houses and villages). The built environment (and the treatment of the deceased) were big and obvious ways in which social and political relationships were guided and fashioned; both treated the body in particular and highly visible ways either by decoration and deposition (or incineration) or by the choreography of movement into, across and out of a site. Figurines worked in much subtler and, thus, much more powerful ways, and made people think more deeply (without conscious recognition that they were thinking at all) and absorb the ways in which each person fitted into the larger social group. In this way, figurines did not actively prescribe systems of identities nor even did they represent preferred systems of identities; if anything, figurines were identity.

How did figurines work?

In the Balkan Neolithic, figurines were more successful than other media in engaging people's philosophies of identity and of being because of their particular physical conditions. Thus, as miniature objects, figurines imparted a sense of mastery, comprehension and well-being to the person looking at and handling them: the seductive illusion of comfort and security and the entry into alternative realities. As abstractions, figurines represented particular body parts and neglected others and, more importantly, forced viewers to draw inferences from what was represented and what was left out: the unbalancing provocation to inference. As compressions and distillations, figurines intensified what was represented. Figurines affected the ways that spectators thought, literally altering their perspectives on time and allowing them into other worlds. As visual, physical objects, figurines worked off the same hard-to-define power that makes the viewer of a photograph react in the ways that Benjamin, Barthes and Tagg noted: the flash of lightning, the *punctum*, and the half-forgotten dream. In many figurines there is also the disruption injected by the representation of sexuality.

More provocatively, figurines generated a series of contradictions and paradoxes within Neolithic spectators and it is from these paradoxes that they may have had their greatest effects. Figurines unbalanced viewers and put them on edge; as representations, they preferred the complex and convoluted to the straightforward and clear. They were the partial and unnatural combinations of elements that the philosophers of the sublime (in eighteenth-century Europe) recognized as being most powerful. Figurines provoked the spectator to think around an issue, such as identity and being, without offering a complete answer or solution to the enquiry. Miniaturism itself invoked a series of paradoxes: that the smaller object could be the more powerful; that there exist other worlds and other scales of being; that the spectator, though enlarged and empowered, can end up no closer to understanding what a small object might mean.

Contradictions and paradoxes also emerged in particular combinations of body parts on many figurines: the presence of female and male genitalia on the same figurines and the lack of sexual body definition on many others. As representations of the human form from which particular body parts were excluded, figurines drew on the apparently contradictory power that the most important areas of a figurine's surface may have been those without any decoration: figurines with little surface treatment were most open to thought and (Neolithic) interpretation. Similarly the cropping of figurine bodies (the frequent presentation of only the heads and shoulders) provoked thought about what was not represented, about what could not be seen and, thus, what must be imagined. There is also a deeper paradox that picks up again on Baudrillard's simulacrum: figurines were not what they were. They were recognizable objects (perhaps the most recognizable form, the human) that were reproduced in incompatible associations (clay, fired, miniature, incised, headless, faceless, broken).

Consequences

When spectators are confronted by these paradoxes, they are liberated in the sense that Bachelard noted in his *Poetics of Space* (1958: 154). It is a liberation of the senses most characteristic of the imagination. It is the potential to lose oneself in an alternative space, similar to the one that Michael Ashkin visits when he works on his table-top landscapes (see Chapter 2). It is the liberation of the narcotic. The recognition that Neolithic figurines worked in these ways and had the potential to stimulate thought, provoke inference and facilitate entry into other worlds, brings us closer to understanding their meaning. Figurines were philosophies in the politics of being in the Neolithic. Figurines do not mean any one thing, yet they meant everything; they were philosophies. They questioned the familiar and comfortable orientations and made people aware of their contact in the world. They altered the ways that people saw the world around them. They created a series of parallel realities that ran along the actual; in doing so they were part of people's (possibly subconscious) definition of the edges of their visible realities and of what made each person distinct (if they were distinct at all) from those other places, times and individuals. Figurines made people question who they were, where they were, what they were, and what their relationships to others were. In the Neolithic Balkans, figurines were at the core of a physicality of being that became visible in new conceptions of corporeality; the body became the key to understanding identities and relationships in the world. Therefore, if there is a meaning of figurines, if they had a function, then it is that they were philosophies of being human.

CORPOREAL POLITICS OF BEING IN THE NEOLITHIC

Relevance

The understanding that I am proposing for Neolithic figurines is similar, in spirit and form, to the arguments that run through the preceding chapters. Both figurines and arguments pose more questions than they provide answers. Both intend to provoke thought. Both conclude that there are no, simple, single solutions, either to the questions about what a figurine means or to the questions about what it meant to be human in the Neolithic. Both this book's arguments and Neolithic figurines agree that the point is not to answer these questions with definitive statements but to provide stimulation through questioning. Indeed, it perhaps does not matter what the answer is; it matters more that we are provoked to think about these issues. Both this book and figurines are stimuli to thought that leave the reader/spectator with as many (and perhaps more) questions than they had before reading/looking. Thus, the philosophy of both figurine and book is that by asking these questions and working through these issues we have a better understanding not only of the figurines and of the Neolithic people who made, used, and discarded them, but also a better understanding of the people who excavated, analysed and published them and, furthermore, of ourselves as people who are drawn to want to understand them.

What then of the applicability of such conclusions? What about the wider scale, across the Neolithic Balkans and beyond? How are we to use the proposals made above in attempts to better understand the material from other contexts, periods, and regions? Is it appropriate to speak of processes, uses, functions, or meanings that apply across southeast Europe as a whole? Is it possible to apply the discussion to other parts of the Balkans, for example, to the figurines of the Gumelnița or the Vinča cultures? Clearly there are some elements which are applicable. Perhaps useful is the approach to the material that moves beyond looking at simple function. Certainly the attention to the political nature of representation can be applied, as can discussions of the power of the body depicted and of the disruption caused by sexuality. However, what about the local, (pre)historical particularities of each culturally coherent tradition of figurines? Are specifics of region and site, period and phase important or is there some essential condition of figurines that allows a more generic engagement?

The question reduces to a consideration of the importance of context within the interpretation of figurines from Balkan Neolithic sites. In each of the examples examined for this book, I found no evidence from the details of excavation that facilitated a better understanding of what figurines mean. Obviously, there can be no question that a rigorous method of excavation for Neolithic sites in southeastern Europe requires absolute attention to contextual recording of stratigraphic units and must apply the full range of practices that this entails, such as sieving of all deposits and attention to deposition, post-depositional and taphonomic processes. Such an excavation methodology allows the recovery of the Neolithic record from which can be built the social, political and economic contexts for individual sites and phases of sites: it is in these contexts that discussions such as that of a corporeal politics of being must be anchored. However, the answers to the questions posed in this book are not to be found in even the most detailed data-base generated by the most dedicated excavation.

The solution that I have offered in this book is to work through the excavation-based data and then to look elsewhere, away from the Neolithic, for stimulation. Thus the attention to the modern uses of the body, the characteristics of miniaturism and the examination of the role of photography and portraiture. No analogies are proposed; no ethnographic links are constructed. The Neolithic is not modern Europe. The value is found in reading off different processes and engagements of meanings and significances from these other, non-Neolithic and non-archaeological places and then in thinking again in terms of the specifics of figurines.

Where does that leave us in terms of knowing what Neolithic people thought about these objects? If these people had any conscious idea of who they were (i.e., of their identities or senses of self and being) then these ideas were given life in the terms and forms that we find in figurines. If this was the case, then the people of the three regions discussed shared a common understanding of what it meant to be an individual within a Neolithic community. Similar material and symbolic media lay at the core of their understanding and acceptance of the nature of their relationships with others. Through the repeated, habitual display of the represented body, Neolithic people from all three regions recognized corporeal similarities and differences running along similar dimensions, though, of course, there were important variations among and within the three traditions.

In this sense, the Balkan Neolithic was about a particular corporeal politics of being, of identity and of relationships: figurines played a major role in the vitality of this politics. Obviously, there were other components that contributed to the politics of being in more active and intentional ways: houses, rooms, villages, graves and cemeteries. In the early Bronze Age that followed (from 3000 BC), the politics of identity and of the body slipped into other media and was played out with other sets of material and through other activities and rituals (e.g., burial and drinking). In these different social realities, objects such as figurines are not visible. Indeed, it is as if the body played a radically different role in more secluded, hidden places such as the large burial mounds that came to define the early Bronze Age ritual landscapes. Not unassociated with these changes was an equally dramatic disappearance of the permanent built environment as a part of the negotiation of relationships among people: basically long-term sedentism had no role. Furthermore, there was a move back to more mobile relationships with the landscape, similar to those that had been present before the Neolithic, in which buildings were less permanent and less visible and where there no longer existed the need to physically monumentalize the place of the living. The questions of who one was and how one related to others, the philosophical and political questions of being, had changed irrevocably.

NOTES

1 INTRODUCTION

1 For the purposes of this book, the Balkans are defined as the area bordered on the east by the Romanian, Bulgarian and Moldovan coasts of the Black Sea, to the south by Thessalian Greece, on the west by Serbia, southeastern Hungary and southwestern Romania and to the north by the Romanian Carpathians, northeastern Romania and Moldova.

2 Though there are figurines in the early Bronze Age Aegean and in the Middle Bronze Age Balkans, these are very different phenomena, discontinuous in time and meaning, distinct in form and decoration, and very much inferior in number.

3 For more detailed presentation of the Balkan Neolithic see *Balkan Prehistory: Exclusion, Incorporation and Identity* (Bailey 2000). For a more theoretically challenging perspective see *Fragmentation in Archaeology: People, Places and Broken Objects in the Prehistory of South Eastern Europe* (Chapman 2000a). For a general but excellent text that positions the Balkan scene within the rest of Europe see *Europe in the Neolithic: the Creation of New Worlds* (Whittle 1996).

4 For a recent critical review of the issue of sedentism in the Neolithic see Bailey *et al*. (2005).

5 It is becoming increasingly clear that many of these pit-huts were not habitations at all but places in which short-term activities took place and which were then filled in with Neolithic rubbish (Chapman 2000b).

6 The predominance of tells in this region may be more a reflection of research strategy than of actual Neolithic settlement activities.

7 The remarkable wooden bowl from Criş culture site of Grădinile in southern Romania (Nica 1983) is one example of part of this missing record.

8 This question gains weight when one realizes that the archaeological record for the period immediately before the Neolithic in the Balkans is almost empty and that the absence of sites is more a factor of research bias than it is of an empty landscape or an absence of people doing things, making, using and discarding material culture.

9 For a full discussion of these trends, see Bailey (2000: 116–23, 193–208).

10 Childe's economic definition of the Neolithic as the shift from food-collecting to food-producing has dominated since its publication (Childe 1936). It was assumed that the change in economy was the basis for changes in other realms of human behaviour and thought. The last 70 years of research has clarified Childe's original formulation. Variation in the degrees and adherence to different means of 'collecting' and 'producing' food mean that the economic change is just another one of many dramatic differences in how people lived their lives in the Neolithic.

11 See Bailey (1999a) on the particular requirements for the cultivation of spring-sown wheat at a tell in northern Bulgaria.

12 The key Gimbutas texts are *The Goddesses and Gods of Old Europe* (1974b), *The Language of the Goddess* (1989a), and *The Civilization of the Goddess* (1991). Key critiques are found in Meskell (1995); Fleming (1969); Ucko (1962, 1968); Haaland and Haaland (1995).

13 Tringham and Conkey have argued concisely that Mother Goddess interpretations of figurines

205

NOTES

(both Palaeolithic and Neolithic) reinforce modern sexist notions: the male–female sex and gender bi-polarity, the primary association of the female with reproduction and fertility, the conflation of anatomical sex with gender, the assumption that these images are unambiguously about femaleness or a limited nature (Tringham and Conkey 1998: 26). Meskell has criticized Mother Goddessism for the essentialism which allows it to ignore the large variety in figurine form and decoration (1995, 1998). More positive elements of the Gimbutas approach are less frequently noted. Haaland and Haaland argue that the questions that Gimbutas asked were of merit for their time, and are of note today, because they were an alternative to the sterile positivism of the 1970s and 1980s with its aim for absolute, quantifiable truths (Haaland and Haaland 1995: 120). They also argue that Gimbutas' objective has been misunderstood, that her goal was to project a picture of prehistoric society as a counterpoint to disagreeable tendencies in modern society, that she intended her reconstructions to stimulate us to think about modern concerns of sexism, violence and inequality (Haaland and Haaland 1995: 116–17). See also review by Talalay (1994) and comments by P. Davis (1993), Fagan (1992) and Lefkowitz (1992, 1993).

14 A crude example is Phelps' study of Neolithic figurines from Corinth which offers detailed description but avoids interpretation. As the authors states, the 'purpose of these figurines is anybody's guess' (Phelps 1987: 238).

15 Figurines with both male and female anatomical attributes and figurines with no sexually identifiable attributes are not uncommon (for examples of figurines with both male and female attributes see Marangou 1992: 362, fig. 15; Petkov 1934: fig. 244; Vajsov 1984: fig. 7, 20). The proportion of sexless to sexed figurines has been grossly underestimated, when it is acknowledged at all (Bailey 1994a). How do the sexless and multi-sexed figurines fit into existing definitions? Quite simply, they don't, and that is a major problem of current approaches: at best it assumes modern western categorizations of sex and gender; at worst it radically misrepresents human socio-sexual complexity.

16 Lesure (2002) identifies four schools of figurine analysis. The iconographic school asks what figurines were intended to represent, seeks conventional themes in body parts or coded attributes, examines positions of arms and body gestures, and assesses the divinity or immortality of the subjects. The functional school asks how figurines were used, characterizes the way that they fitted into social life, considers where they were used, who made and used them, and wants to know if they were sacred or profane. The social analytical school sees figurines as tools for understanding new dimensions of society, seeks to identify social tension and political struggle, or uses an understanding of the contemporary society to understand figurines. The symbolic school sees figurines as signifying more than they depict and seeks more abstract ideas in the subject matter.

17 Of course for publishing houses, the topic of figurines, and especially in connection with goddesses, is a good draw in the bookstores. See the review of *The Concept of the Goddess* for one example of how a major academic publisher traded on the word 'Goddess' to market what was otherwise a lightweight volume (Bailey 1997).

18 For excellent introductions to visual culture see Mirzoeff (1998, 1999) and Evans and Hall (1999a, 1999b).

19 For work on the Fur see Haaland (1984, 1990)

20 The Haalands had difficulty finding such cases. In the two other examples presented in their article (The Maconde of Tanzania [Saetersdal 1995] and the Fipa of Tanzania [Barndon 1992]) female imagery was linked to boys' initiation rites and male-dominated iron-smelting (Haaland and Haaland 1995: 117–18).

21 See Campbell (1982) on the presence of Mother Goddesses in communities that polarize male and female roles and on the inverse relationship between Mother Goddess worship and elevated female status. Also see Preston (1982) and Warner (1976) on the logic of the relationship of female objects of worship and female status.

NOTES

22 Richard Lesure has also raised this question (Lesure 2002).

23 On the inaccuracy of assuming that all Upper Palaeolithic figurines are female, see also Beck (2000) who suggests that although the majority of figurines (60 per cent) is female, some are androgynous and a few may be male. Similar cases for the diversity represented by Upper Palaeolithic figurines have been made by Rice (1981) and Rice and Paterson (1988). I have also raised this issue for the Neolithic (Bailey 1994a).

24 Indeed, both Meskell and Haaland and Haaland have argued that the Goddess interpretation has more to do with creating an idealized present that contrasts with today's impersonal and industrialized world. Meskell goes as far as to argue that the myth of matriarchy projected by Mother Goddessism is a tool that binds women in their places and that the only solution is to destroy the myth (Meskell 1998: 55). See also Biehl (1997).

25 Other types of figurines were used in other parts of Oaxaca society: complete figurines placed in women's burials; larger, hollow, sexless white-slipped 'baby-dolls' from house and midden contexts; male or sexless red-painted figurines (Marcus 1998: 29).

26 It is noteworthy that Formative Mesoamerican Oaxaca and the Sudanese Fur share similar socio-political contexts. At Formative Oaxaca, communities could not be managed in the same way as earlier, Archaic Period, food-collecting bands (they were too large) and yet they lacked the politically centralized social stratification that marked the following Classic period states. With Formative communities, rituals played critical integrative roles in establishing social obligations (Marcus 1998: 311). Among the Fur, society was organized in poorly developed, large-scale, corporate groups. Social solidarity was precarious, membership in a group did not ensure unity, and problems of trust were significant threats (Haaland and Haaland 1995: 115). In both cases rituals exploiting female imagery were mechanisms used to reduce the threats.

27 Undermined again are the traditional assumptions about the reflective simplicity of relationships between sexually attributable imagery and the social organization. In Formative Oaxaca, men had their own place to engage male ancestors: the men's house (Marcus 1998: 312).

28 If support is needed for this assumption, I refer to Steve Mithen's work on the prehistory of the mind and his conclusions that our brains' abilities have been unchanged since Anatomically Modern Humans arrived on the scene (Mithen 1996).

2 MINIATURISM AND DIMENSIONALITY

1 This scale is especially useful if one wants to concentrate on the interior of a building or look at certain aspects of how the construction is conceived (Jo Odgers pers. comm.).

2 For general information on *bonsai* see Stein (1990) and Koreshoff (1984). Of course, there are other traditions of dwarfed arboriculture such as the ancient Hindu Vaamantanu Vrikshaadi Vidya (literally: dwarfed body of tree and science) by which medicinal gardens were created from natural habitats.

3 Surrealist productions have similar effects on the viewer as do other philosophies of representation (e.g., Cubism, Minimalism).

4 Gaston Bachelard wrote eloquently on this in his *The Poetics of Space* (Bachelard 1958).

5 Gaston Bachelard makes a similar point suggesting that extreme images are virtual 'drugs' that 'procure the scenes of daydreams for us' (Bachelard 1958: 158).

6 Obviously, one could argue that there is no one, single, exclusive, reality, only constructions and representations of alternatives that are favoured by various political bodies. The distinction I am drawing is between the real world of physical, human-scale, existence and another place and time that are not found in that existence.

7 Disney employed the same reducing principle in other parts of Disneyland: the Matterhorn Mountain is built at 1/100th scale; Sleeping Beauty Castle is only 77 feet tall; the magic of

NOTES

forced perspective makes each appear taller than it actually is. The illusion of soaring height is founded on the reduction of stone building-block size; as one moves up the façade the blocks become smaller and smaller (Doss 1977: 181).

8 It is also not surprising, though important to note, that Disney took great care to separate the soothing world that existed inside Disneyland from the dirty and frantic world on the outside. Access to the park is tightly controlled and orchestrated. Visitors park their cars in special car-parks from which Disneyland cannot be seen. Transport from car-park and ticket booths to the park itself is only possible with Disney's monorail. Once you are inside, you cannot see the outside world: a large, banked berm surrounds the park and prevents any visual contact with the non-Disney reality.

9 Walt Disney's engagement with miniatures is interesting and further strengthens the links between small things, the empowerment of the viewer and the creation of security and comfort. Well before he created Disneyland, Walt Disney's doctors suggested that he take up a hobby when he complained of work-related stress. Disney became engrossed in miniatures and replicas, inspired first by the extraordinary Throne Room Miniatures that Disney saw at the 1939 Golden Gate International Exposition in San Francisco. Disney started making miniature replicas and models of buildings from his own childhood, particularly from his grandmother's Missouri cabin. Having seen model steam trains, he built a scaled-down train set in his backyard; this train was to provide the scale when Disney started to design Main Street (Jacobs 1995: 79–80).

10 The literature on Walt Disney and Disneyland is growing. Especially useful is Marling's book *Designing Disney's Theme Parks: the Architecture of Reassurance* (1997b) and the articles in it by Doss (1997), Tuan (1997) and Marling (1997a). Also see Zukin (1991). For Walt Disney see Schickel (1993).

11 All subjects played on both the smaller and the larger screens and the order of playing (i.e., whether on the smaller or the larger) was controlled to avoid biasing the results.

12 A 12–15 per cent improvement in their play.

13 Of course there is no reason to assume that any of these relationships between a person and an object are static; indeed they are not fixed. Pockets are emptied, jewellery discarded (wedding rings are a good example), clothes changed. Tattoos and other body ornamentation that have permanent consequences are a different matter.

14 It is interesting to note that, in the 1950s, the Hollywood studios turned to the power of the three-dimensional when the introduction of television threatened their hold on visual entertainment.

15 Two million people pay to visit Madame Tussaud's in London each year.

16 Another potential for the success of these mechanical attempts at three-dimensional replication is that they challenge our perceptual skills. They attempt to fool us, we know we are being fooled, but we derive pleasure from the attempt at deception.

17 While Disney brought to life these characters through their three-dimensionality and although he makes possible one-to-one engagements with visitors because of the characters' life-sizes, Disney was careful to prevent his visitors from being frightened by his creations. Thus all of the characters you meet while walking around Disneyland are just smaller than adult life-size: they will not threaten. There is other evidence that Disney guarded against fear in his manipulation of scale invoked when transforming the two-dimensional to the three-dimensional. A proposed ride based on Candy Mountain was scrapped because the Disney team felt that it would overwhelm and overpower people, especially children (Marling 1997a).

18 It is perhaps significant that the Ovcharovo miniatures from Building 7 are not the only examples of a set of objects, furniture, people and building. A house model with six people in it was found at Plateia Magoula Zarkou in northern Greece (Gallis 1985) and there are many other examples come from the Cucuteni/Tripolye sites in northeastern Romania, Moldova and Ukraine. These examples will be addressed in Chapters 5 and 7.

NOTES

3 HAMANGIA

1 Both come from disturbed contexts in the eastern part of the necropolis (Berciu *et al*. 1955).

2 Though this figurine, termed the *Thinker*, is known around the world (literally), it is, as we shall see, exceptional among Hamangia figurines. Romania sent it as its cultural signature to represent the country at the exhibition that accompanied the 1996 Olympic Games held in Atlanta. It also appeared on the Romanian 10,000 Lei note and graces the covers of several recent publications (Rudgley 1998; Hamilakis *et al*. 2001).

3 Marble figurines come from Cernavoda (three examples; Berciu 1966: 79, fig. 38: 3; Comşa 1976c: 23–7), Ceamurlia de Jos (Berciu 1966: 197, fig. 92: 6), and from Durankulak (Haşotti 1997: 43). Two other stone figurines, one which was of limestone, and one from Medgidia Cocoaşă (Comşa 1976c). One bone figurine each came from Cernavoda and from Ceamurlia de Jos (Berciu 1966: 188, fig. 95: 1). Numerous shell figurines were found at Durankulak.

4 Much of this scholarship is of course of little value or use beyond satisfying the narrow, descriptive goals of traditional culture-historical archaeologies of long-bankrupt nationalist ideologies.

5 For Hamangia in general see Berciu (1963), Haşotti (1982, 1984, 1986a, 1993, 1997). For specific sites see the following: Medgidia-Satu Nou (Haşotti 1980, 1987), Medgidia Cocoaşă (Haşotti 1986b), Tîrguşor Urs (Haşotti 1986c), Tîrgoşur-Sitorman (Haşotti and Wisoşenski 1985).

6 See Boyadzhiev (1995) for full discussion of the Bulgarian dates of relevance; see also Boyadzhiev (1992) and Dimov (1992a, 1992b).

7 One of the very few exceptions is Ceamurlia de Jos where there are three stratigraphic phases. There is the other concern that methods and research agendas in the older, but also the more recent work, have not focused on micro-stratigraphic sequences within individual Hamangia pit- or building-features.

8 Perhaps most tragic is the research programme of the recently publish Durankulak cemetery which contained over 700 graves but where only six burials were sampled for dating and of these only three provided dates which the excavators deemed to be reliable (Boyadzhiev 2002).

9 See Haşotti 1986b for a good example of such finds from the site of Tîrguşor Urs.

10 The published reports mention the recovery of ceramics and lithics but not any evidence for pit-structures or other buildings. The quantity of material was not insubstantial, however.

11 Haşotti has questioned the context of the copper bracelets, suggesting that they may well be later than the Hamangia phase of the site at Agigea (Haşotti 1997: 48).

12 The publication of Cernavoda is limited to the initial annual reports (Berciu 1961; Berciu *et al*. 1955, 1959, 1961; Berciu and Morintz 1957: 84–91; 1959: 99–105; Necrasov *et al*. 1959) and their subsequent reworking in regional syntheses (e.g., Haşotti 1997). Durankulak is a much more recent project with preliminary reports (Todorova 1983; Dimov *et al*. 1984; Vajsov 1987, 1992a) and a final publication recently available, though printed in limited numbers (Todorova 2002a, 2002e). Other cemeteries include Mangalia (Volschi and Irimia 1968) and Limanu (ibid.; Galbenu 1970). Haşotti lists other possible cemetery sites (Haşotti 1997: 32).

13 For Cernavoda excavations see Berciu (1961), Berciu *et al*. (1955, 1959, 1961), Berciu and Morintz (1957: 84–91; 1959: 99–105), and Necrasov and Cristescu (1965, 1978).

14 See Csalog (1976).

15 It is difficult to say more about these isolated skulls; the publications do not include clear plans, complete inventories or precise descriptions (see Morintz *et al*. 1955: 154). There are of course strong parallels with the deposition of human skulls and other body parts in the burials at Lepenski Vir in the Danube Gorges (see discussion and bibliography in Bailey 2000).

16 Hamangia graves from Durankulak that contained figurines were numbers 13, 88, 108, 601A,

NOTES

609, 609A, 621, 626, 642, 644 and 1036. All of these were dated to Hamangia III (Vajsov 2002).

17 Grave nos 88, 621 and 642 (Vajsov 2002).

18 Grave no. 626.

19 As the dating of the cemetery is disappointingly thin, the dating of individual graves relies on assignment of pottery form and decoration to established schemes of cultural sequences.

20 The distinction of individual phases within the Hamangia sequence was not always possible based on the ceramic correlates; thus Hamangia I and II are often, though not always, grouped together.

21 For a full discussion of the variation in degrees in uptake of the Neolithic in southeastern Europe see Zvelebil (1986), Halstead (1989b) and articles in Bailey *et al*. (2005).

22 There are claims that figurines were deposited in burials at Varna. These claims are mistaken. The objects claimed to be figurines have nothing in common with other anthropomorphic imagery from the Neolithic Balkans; they are small, circular, sheet-gold, appliqué disks which have one hole in their centres and one or two hole in their upper parts. The other mistakenly identified objects are more likely to be wrist-guards.

23 Todorova *et al*. 2002: 61, 109.

4 ANTHROPOMORPHISM: DOLLS, PORTRAITS AND BODY PARTS

1 See also ethnoarchaeological discussions of the socialization potentials of dolls, toys, and other miniature objects in Canyon and Arnold (1985), Guenple (1988), Briggs (1990) and Park (1998).

2 The second proposal is not entirely unlikely.

3 The same could be said for adolescents and adults, especially in light the popularity of role-playing and fantasy games.

4 Indeed he was persecuted by the Nazi Party in 1930s Germany from which he fled in 1938 (Webb 1975: 366).

5 See Twain (2002) for a good overview of the historiography of these trends.

5 CUCUTENI/TRIPOLYE

1 The Poduri set consists of 36 objects: 15 larger painted figurines, 6 smaller undecorated figurines and 13 miniature chairs (Mantu and Dumitroaia 1997: 179–81). Similar concentrations of numerous figurines and other 'cult equipment' (i.e., miniature or otherwise unexplainable objects) have been found at Truşeşti (Petrescu-Dimboviţa *et al*. 1999), Ghelăieşti (Cucoş 1970, 1971, 1973, 1993), Răuceşti (Dumitroaia 1987a) and Mărgineni.

2 Is it more likely that the discovery of multiple figurines together in burned houses is a factor of the preservation that the destruction of a building by burning provides and not a factor of any particular activities of deposition or offerings: the house-burning and collapse traps and preserves house contents which are not or cannot be retrieved after burning. While there may well be potential socio-political meaning for the burning of a building (see Stevanović 1997), it is critical that interpretation takes account of depositional and taphonomic processes. Indeed, it is just as likely (perhaps more so) that unusually rich assemblages of artefacts are the result of preservation and do not represent special acts of deposition.

3 Pogosheva 1985 (cat. no. 252).

4 Pogosheva 1985 (cat. nos 487–9).

5 Pogosheva 1985 (cat. nos 491, 494).

6 Pogosheva 1985 (cat. no. 684).

7 Pogosheva 1985 (cat. no. 617a).

NOTES

8 Pogosheva 1985 (cat. no. 547).
9 Pogosheva 1985 (cat. no. 541).
10 Pogosheva 1985 (cat. no. 499).
11 Pogosheva 1985 (cat. no. 534).
12 Pogosheva 1985 (cat. nos 610–11).
13 Pogosheva 1985 (cat. no. 546).
14 Pogosheva 1985 (cat. no. 511).
15 Pogosheva 1985 (cat. no. 604).
16 Pogosheva 1985 (cat. no. 606).
17 Pogosheva 1985 (cat. no. 549).
18 Pogosheva 1985 (cat. no. 655).
19 Pogosheva 1985 (cat. no. 652).
20 Pogosheva 1985 (cat. no. 653).
21 Pogosheva 1985 (cat. nos 569–70).
22 Pogosheva 1985 (cat. no. 665).
23 Pogosheva 1985 (cat. nos 790–1).
24 Pogosheva 1985 (cat. no. 808).
25 Pogosheva 1985 (cat. no. 919).
26 Pogosheva 1985 (cat. nos 920–2).
27 Pogosheva 1985 (cat. nos 788–9).
28 Pogosheva 1985 (cat. no. 746 from Kočeržincy).
29 Pogosheva 1985 (cat. no. 776 from Čapaevka and 906–7 from Kočeržincy).
30 Pogosheva 1985 (cat. no. 744 from Kočeržincy).
31 Pogosheva 1985 (cat. nos 801, 804 and 814 from Kočeržincy).The largest number of head perforations, 13, is found on a figurine from the Tripolye C2 site at Vyhvatincz (cat. no. 981).
32 Pogosheva 1985 (cat. no. 746).
33 Pogosheva 1985 (cat. no. 829).
34 Pogosheva 1985 (cat. nos 789–90).
35 Pogosheva 1985 (cat. nos 808, 812, 817, 825).
36 Pogosheva 1985 (cat. no. 782).
37 Pogosheva 1985 (cat. no. 800).
38 Pogosheva 1985 (cat. no. 755 from Stena).
39 Pogosheva 1985 (cat. no. 795 from Kočeržincy).
40 Pogosheva 1985 (cat. nos 798–800 from Kočeržincy).
41 Pogosheva 1985 (cat. nos 802, 804, 813 from Kočeržincy).
42 Pogosheva 1985 (cat. nos 830–1 from Kočeržincy).
43 Pogosheva 1985 (cat. nos 906–7).
44 Other important and early works include Marin (1948), H. Dumitrescu (1954), Makarevič (1954), Markevic (1981), Makarenko (1927), Cehac (1933), Kusurgaševa (1970), Movša (1969, 1973), and Popova (1980). See Pogosheva (1983, 1985) for a thorough account of previous work on Tripolye figurines.
45 One alternative of note suggests that the amount of decoration on a figurine is related to value, with the amount of time and effort expended on surface treatment an indicator of the level of value invested. Variations in surface coverage though time are then interpreted in terms of changes invested in production (Gheorghiu n.d.: 3).
46 See also Marinescu-Bîlcu's discussion of the relations between the Cucuteni and Hamangia cultures in terms of their figurines (Marinescu-Bîlcu 1964). Monah also traces the influences on Cucuteni/Tripolye figurines from other cultures (Monah 1991), and Sorokin suggests a Gumelniţa influence in the realistic figurines of Cucuteni A–B/Tripolye B2 (Sorokin 1994: 80).

NOTES

47 Gheorghiu also suggests, less convincingly, that the later Cucuteni/Tripolye figurines that have perforations in the faces, shoulders and hips, were wrapped as well with the perforations serving to secure the wraps. Similarly, he interprets as bindings the painted lines around the ankles and wrists of some Cucuteni B figurines (Gheorghiu n.d.).

48 See also Monah (1992).

49 For the excavation report on Sabatinovka II see Makarevič (1954).

50 For Tîrpeşti, see Marinescu-Bîlcu (1981); for Truşeşti see Petrescu-Dîmboviţa et al. (1999); for Hăbăşeşti see V. Dumitrescu et al. (1954); and for Drăguşeni see Marinescu-Bîlcu and Bolomey (2000).

51 The detailed dating of the subphases is as follows: PreCucuteni I–III/Tripolye A (5050–4600 BC); Cucuteni A/Tripolye B1 (4670–4050 BC); Cucuteni A-B/Tripolye B2 (4100–3600 BC); Cucuteni B/Tripolye C1 (4000–3500 BC); Tripolye C2 (3700–2700 BC (Chapman 2000a: 245)). There are many subtle alternatives and the interested reader should turn to Mantu (1998) and Chapman (2000) for more details.

52 Cucuteni 'C' refers to a type of pottery that is contemporary to Cucuteni A (as seen at Drăguşeni made with shell temper and fired to a low temperature in open pits). It is not a sequential phase of the Cucuteni/Tripolye phenomenon. Debate over the significance of Cucuteni C ceramics continues: see discussions by Marinescu-Bîlcu (1981: 82–4; 2000b: 104–110), Gâţă (2000), Passek (1949) and V. Dumitrescu (1963: 287–9).

53 Good evidence for pottery production has been found at many sites; see the detailed catalogue in Ellis (1984: 130–56).

54 For more detailed discussion of the methods of building construction see Marinescu-Bîlcu and Bolomey (2000: 25–30) and Passek (1949: chapter 1).

55 As with all regions in the Neolithic Balkans, little work has focused on understanding the micro-chronological relationships among structures within a site. Thus, the assumption usually made is that all structures were occupied at the same time and for the same lengths of time. At some sites, such as Truşeşti, attempts to breakdown the generic culture history have been made: there are three sub-phases of site use within the Cucuteni A phase of the site (Petrescu-Dîmboviţa et al. 1999: 666, 670–2).

56 Other buildings contained grinding-stones as well as copper objects (i.e., small tubular beads and pendants made from thin sheet-copper, small ringlets, thin bracelets of round wire and broad, thick bracelets and convex discs).

57 Cucuteni A2.

58 Cucuteni A3.

59 Cucuteni A4.

60 Binocul-pots are double-bodied, double-pedestalled, double-dished vessels.

61 See comments in Bailey (2002).

62 Christine Perlès has made a similar comment about the high rate of fragmentation among figurines from Neolithic Thessaly (Perlès 2001).

63 See Chapman 2000a for a recent discussion of rubbish in archaeology; on the archaeology of garbage see Rathje (1989), Rathje and McCarthy (1977), Rathje and Murphy (1992), Rathje et al. (1992) and Thompson and Rathje (1982).

64 The exceptions perhaps are the very large settlements with many concentric circles of buildings. At the late Tripolye site of Varvarovka VIII there are more than 200 structures arranged in circles, spread over 40 ha (Marchevici 1981; Ellis 1984: 185). On a large high plateau at the middle to late Tripolye site of Petreny there are almost 500 buildings of substantial size (8 × 5 m) arranged over 30 ha. Most of the structures are of a similar size, though there are almost ten that are larger and three dozen that are larger still. The Petreny buildings were arranged in ten concentric circles. At the centre of these circles was an area that contained two of the larger buildings; also on the outskirts of the settlement there was a row of larger buildings (15 × 6 m) (Marchevici 1981: 18, 74).

NOTES

65 Later, Cucuteni B/Tripolye C sites were larger and contained larger buildings: Kolomijščina I has buildings that are over 20 m long and which have several rooms (Passek 1949: 134–5; Monah and Monah 1997: 53). Ellis suggests that these are large enough to contain two or three families (Ellis 1984: 49).

66 Poduri is also of interest as it may have been surrounded by smaller, temporary satellite sites located up to 5 km away (Monah and Monah 1997: 56).

67 Other mega-sites have been found at Dobrovody (Šiškin 1973), Neblivka (ibid.), Glyboček (Štiglits 1971) and Talljanky (Šiškin 1973; Kruts and Ryžov 1983).

68 See also Bolomey (1983, 2000).

69 Thus there are 63 individuals buried at the Tripolye C site of Vyhvatincz in Moldavia (Ellis 1984: 172; Dergacev 1978).

70 Sites with bone found at the periphery of settlement include the following: Scânteia, Cucuteni, Hăbăşeşti, Frumuşica, Drăguşeni, Poduri, Ariuşd, Verem'e, Polivanov Jar, Kolodistoe, Kolomijščina I, Pavloch and Barnova.

71 The same building contained an assemblage of figurines (Cucoş 1973; Monah 1997: 42).

72 Of course this is not to suggest that, in other regions where formal burial or tell formation were present, figurines did not work in similar ways. Indeed figurines would have had similar significances in those communities as well. The point is that the particularities of mortuary and monumental settlement in Cucuteni/Tripolye communities would have elevated the role of objects and ceremonies that engaged perceptions of the body and identity to a higher level within the performative dramas of social reality and identity politics.

6 VISUAL RHETORIC, TRUTH AND THE BODY

1 However, Gimbutas does suggest that a fragment of figurine body (the abdomen, hips and upper thighs) may be part of the missing body (Gimbutas 1986a: fig. 9.38, cat. 165).

2 The principles that make miniaturism work (as discussed in Chapter 2) can work in the opposite direction as well: the gigantic stimulates submission, subservience and dependence (Stewart 1993: 70–103).

3 On the date and inventory of photography see Tagg (1988), Bolton (1989), Szarkowski (1989), Squiers (1990), Pultz (1995) and Rosenblum (1987).

4 *Bonaparte, Premier Consul, Franchissant le Grand Saint-Bernard, 20 Mai 1800* was painted for a very particular audience. It was commissioned by Charles IV of Spain to be hung in his *Salon des Grands Capitains* in Madrid's Royal Palace, where it would be one of many paintings of international military leaders (Johnson 1993: 179).

5 See also discussion of the *punctum* in Mirzoeff (1999:74–5, 240–4) and Tagg (1988).

6 For a thorough presentation and discussion of the Young British Artists see Timms *et al.* (1999).

7 Though reference was drawn to the Roman writings of Dionysus Longinus (or Pseudo-Longinus) on writing and speaking (*On the Sublime* [*Peri Hypsous*]), the key figures in the eighteenth century were Edmund Burke (with his *Philosophical Enquiry into the Origin of Our Ideas of the Sublime and Beautiful* [1756]) and Immanuel Kant (with his *Critique of Judgement* [1790]). See also Lyotard (1989, 1994) and Ashfield and de Bolla (1996).

8 For discussions of the technological sublime see McKinsey (1985) and Nye (1994).

9 The fact that the negatives of the unacceptable images were not destroyed completely but only hole-punched is of interest. By retaining the killed negatives of unprintable, unacceptable images, the FSA possessed not only examples of inappropriate work, but, more interestingly, proof of Stryker's power to control the image creators' output.

10 Lock (1993); Yates (1993); Knapp and Meskell (1997); Meskell (1996, 1999); Hamilakis *et al.* (2001); Sweeny and Hodder (2002).

11 In earlier publications (Bailey 1991, 1994b), I have underlined the great variation in figurine

NOTES

form and argued that the variation is evidence for individuation among figurines and among people. At one scale, that remains an accurate observation. At another scale, however, there are tremendous degrees of similarity within particular types of figurines within one culture group.

7 THESSALY

1 Gimbutas 1989c: 235–6, cat. no. 69.
2 Ibid. 1989c: 230, cat. no. 20.
3 Ibid.: cat. nos 17, 20, 21, 53, 61, 62, 69, 84, 126, 172.
4 Ibid.: cat. no. 17.
5 Ibid.: cat. no. 126.
6 For example at Bei (Gallis and Orphanidis 1996: 152), Koutsaki (ibid.: 111), Margarita (ibid.: 134), Soufli Magoula (three examples) (ibid.: 110, 153) and Mezil (four examples).
7 Mezil (Gallis and Orphanidis 1996: 115), Soufli Magoula (ibid.: 112); Bei (ibid.: 118), Doxaras (ibid.: 120), Petrino (ibid.: 122), Vrastero (ibid.: 142) and Psili Rachi.
8 Gimbutas chooses to call the latter 'articulate' (Gimbutas 1989b: 171).
9 Indeed the same general point was made forty years ago by Peter Ucko in his seminal work on figurines from Greece, the Near East and Egypt (Ucko 1962, 1968).
10 In another stimulating, though frustratingly abbreviated comment, Catherine Perlès suggests that figurines worked in the definition and integration of a complex, social dynamics (Perlès 2001: 262). Perlès contrasts the sparsely populated Peloponnesus in southern Greece with the more densely networked Thessalian landscapes in the north. In the Peloponnesus, inter-community relations were regulated through filiation and alliance; little use was made of objects such as figurines. In Thessaly, however, the opposite applied. A fuller, more densely occupied landscape led to more conflicts among people. To reduce the potential for conflict, people redefined individual status through ceremonies. These ceremonies integrated some segments of a community while alienating others; figurines were a part of these rituals, integration and alienation (ibid.: 262).
11 Examples come from Vrasteri (Gallis and Orphanidis 1996: 96, 99), Zappeio (ibid.: 98), Varko (ibid.: 137), Soufli Magoula (ibid.: 133), Platykambos (ibid.: 133) and Mezil (ibid.: 133).
12 Karditsa (ibid.: 157), Sofades (two examples) (ibid.: 158), Zappeio (ibid.: 159) and Neo Monastiri (ibid.: 160).
13 Arapi (ibid.: 162), Rachmani (ibid.: 162) and Argissa (ibid.: 163).
14 Tourkogefyra (ibid.: 164) and Nessonis (two examples) (ibid.: 165).
15 Rachmani, Karagioz (ibid.: 170–1), Tourkogefyra (ibid.: 172), Tsalma (two examples) (ibid.: 173) and Bisler (ibid.: 175).
16 Makrychori (ibid.: 167), Tourkogefyra (ibid.: 168) and Kalochori (ibid.: 169).
17 Indeed the recognition of widespread repetition of common bodily features goes a considerable way in understanding how Marija Gimbutas built her pantheons of divinities, such as the Beaked-Nose Bird Goddess. For Gimbutas the repetition of a selected anatomical detail identified the character of a particular god or goddess.
18 Gimbutas 1986b: cat. no. 177.
19 The strangeness evoked in the head's appearance was 'corrected' by the artist who drew the reconstruction for the Achilleion publication (Gimbutas et al. 1989: fig. 7.51). The nose was straightened, the face make more regular, the mouth made more lifeless.
20 See example from Paliambela (Orphanidis 1998: 37: epsilon).
21 Ibid.: 4.
22 See the example from Koutsouro which has a series of impressions that provides irregular modelling to the surface of the hair (Gallis and Orphanidis 1996: 12)
23 Orphanidis 1998: fig. 37, delta.

NOTES

24 Paliambela (Gallis and Orphanidis 1996: 211).

25 Ibid.: 341.

26 Gimbutas *et al*. 1989: fig. 7.37.1.

27 Gallis and Orphanidis 1996: 184.

28 Ibid.: 264.

29 See examples from Mezil (two examples) (ibid.: 286 and 328) and Achilleion (Gimbutas 1986b: cat. no. 132).

30 Gallis and Orphanidis 1996: 263.

31 Ibid.: 309.

32 Ibid.: 262.

33 See examples from Omorphochori (ibid.: 323), Magoulitsa (ibid.: 323), Nessonis (ibid.: 325), Psili Rachi (ibid.: 326), Panagou (ibid.: 329) and Prodromos (ibid.: 339).

34 See examples from Mezil (ibid.: 328) and Prodromos (ibid.: 338).

35 See examples from Bezil (ibid.: 334) and Diodion (ibid.: 348).

36 See example from Megali kai Mikri (ibid.: 340).

37 Indeed there are many figurines that have coherent incised patterns that consist of both a pubic triangle and hip and buttocks covering (ibid.: cat. nos 151, 153, 160, 165, 166, 168, 190, 221, 235, 236, 237, 238, 243, 244, 265, 304, 306, 311, 327, 328).

38 Ibid.: cat. nos 261, 265, 303 and 311.

39 Ibid.: cat. no. 303.

40 Ibid.: cat. nos 155, 222, 261, 311 and 327.

41 Ibid.: cat. nos 152, 153, 155, 161, 163, 164, 165, 166, 173, 200 and perhaps 178, 179, 193, 197. There is also a good example from Achilleion (Gimbutas 1989c: cat. nos 38, 112; 1991: 140, 142, fig. 218).

42 There is a fragment of another seated one from Megalo Gefyri (Gallis and Orphanidis 1996: 183).

43 It is especially relevant here to note that many of the figurines that I have included in this section of the chapter were donated to the Larissa Museum in 1992 by five male antiquities collectors (ibid.: 5). Are there not both modern and Neolithic significances to the sexuality of these figurines and to people's reactions to them?

44 See Andreou *et al*. (1996), Kotsakis (in press), Cullen (2001), Perlès (2001), Halstead (1999a), Papathanassopoulos (1996), Demoule and Perlès (1993). For historiographies see Kotsakis (in press).

45 Earlier, now discredited, schemes proposed an earliest, Aceramic phase (see Bloedow 1991 and discussion in Bailey (2000).

46 See discussion in Bailey (1999a, 1999b).

47 See examples at Crannon, Stephanovikion, Myrrini, Sesklo, Karamourlar (Theocharis 1973: 322, n. 72), Mavrachades 1, Sitochoro (Papathanassopolous 1996: cat. nos 262–3), Nikaia (Gallis 1992: 164), and Chaironeia (Theocharis 1973: 322, n. 72).

48 See examples from Kastro (Gallis 1992: 129) and Otzaki (Marangou 1992: 36)

49 See Galeni near Larissa (Toufexis 1997).

50 Arapi and Argissa (Andreou *et al*. 1996: 543, n. 36; Milojčić *et al*. 1962); Final Neolithic Pefkakia (Weisshaar 1989); Middle Neolithic Hatzimissiotiki (Grundmann 1937); Plateia Magoula Zarkou (Gallis 1982: 88–9); Paliambela (Kotsakis pers. comm.); and Mandra (Kotsakis pers. comm.).

51 See examples at Ayia Sofia (Milojčić 1976), Achilleion (Gimbutas *et al*. 1989), Otzaki and Mandra (Kotsakis pers. comm.).

52 See also the much broader discussion of the separation of domestic and wild by Hodder (Hodder 1990).

53 Indeed Sevi Triantaphyllou sub-titled her report on the material, 'A story from the fragments' (Triantaphyllou 1999).

NOTES

54 Indeed, Perlès has noted the possibility that the use-life of a Thessalian figurine may only have been short-term, with breakage and discard following shortly after relevant activities (Perlès 2001).

8 SUBVERTING AND MANIPULATING REALITY

1 See also Wilton 1980 on Turner and the sublime.
2 Thus, to the art student, at first it means a work of a noted artist, then it means a particular part of that artist's career and then later it might mean an example of a political act of visual culture. All of these meanings have the same value, each is just as accurate as the others. They only differ in the contexts of their consumption or dissemination: introductory art history class, upper-level class on British landscape painting, and graduate seminar on the politics of art.
3 The literature on carnival is vast. Other important texts include Lefebvre (1958), Eco (1984), Kertzer (1988), Le Roy Ladurie (1979), Bakhtin (1968), Stam (1989), and Shohat and Stam (1998).
4 Indeed, Bakhtin called carnival the construction of a second world (Bakhtin 1968: 11–12).
5 On masks see Pollock (1995).
6 One could draw up a large body of ethnographic cases in which people use(d) dolls, figurines, models and other anthropomorphic objects that are formally analogous to Neolithic figurines. The *nkisi* of the Congo are an excellent example of the direction that such research could take (Shelton 1995; MacGaffey 1993; see discussion in Mirzoeff 1999: 149–51). Links could be established and specific interpretations could be offered. My intention in the present book is to look elsewhere, specifically to the recent past and the present. Another project could take on the ethnographic record and may well expand and refine (perhaps reject even) the proposals that I am making here.

9 CORPOREAL POLITICS OF BEING IN THE NEOLITHIC

1 In other contemporary communities (e.g., Kodzhaderman-Gumelnița-Karanovo VI) in which figurines were present in similar numbers, formal disposal of the dead focused on extra-mural cemeteries. The same distinction can be found there between occasional, loud, public ceremonies proposing differentiations within communities and the quieter, continuous presence of body imagery that was at the core of social cohesion.

BIBLIOGRAPHY

Acconci, V. (1985) 'Playing with the word "doll"', in *The Doll Show: Artist's Dolls and Figurines*, pp. 3–7, no editor, Long Island: Hillwood Art Gallery.

Adams, L.S. (1993) *Art and Psychoanalysis*, New York: HarperCollins.

Ades, D. (1986) *Photomontage*, 2nd edn, London: Thames and Hudson.

Agee, J. and Evans, W. (1941; 1980 edition) *Let Us Now Praise Famous Men*, Boston: Houghton Mifflin.

Althusser, L. (1999) 'Ideology and ideological state apparatuses (notes towards an investigation)', in Evans and Hall, pp. 317–23.

Andreou, S. and Kotsakis, K. (1994) 'Prehistoric rural communities in perspective: the Langadas Survey Project', in P.N. Doukellis and L.G. Mendoni (eds) *Structures Rurales et Sociétés Antiques*, pp. 7–15, Paris: Les Belles Lettres.

Andreou, S., Fotiadis, M. and Kotsakis, K. (1996) 'Review of Aegean prehistory V: the Neolithic and Bronze Age of northern Greece', *American Journal of Archaeology* 100: 537–97.

Artemenko, I.I. (1979–80) 'Archaeological research in the Ukrainian SSR', *Soviet Anthropology and Archaeology* 18(3): 37–67.

Ashfield, A. and de Bolla, P. (eds) (1996) *The Sublime: a Reader in Eighteenth-century Aesthetic Theory*, Cambridge: Cambridge University Press.

Avramova, M. (1986) 'Nakite ot praistoricheskiya nekropol pri s. Durankulak, Tolbukhinski okrug', *Dobrudzha* 3: 76–84.

—— (1991) 'Gold and copper jewelry from the chalcolithic cemeteries near the village of Durankulak, Varna district', in J.-P. Mohen (ed.) *Découverte de Métal*, pp. 43–8, Paris: Picard.

Bachelard, G. (1958; 1994 edition) *The Poetics of Space* (trans. M. Jolas) Boston: Beacon Press.

Bailey, D. (1990) 'The living house: signifying continuity', in R. Samson (ed.) *The Social Archaeology of Houses*, pp. 19–48, Edinburgh: Edinburgh University Press.

—— (1991) 'The social reality of figurines', unpublished PhD dissertation, Cambridge University.

—— (1994a) 'Representing gender: homology or propaganda', *Journal of European Archaeology* 2(2): 193–202.

—— (1994b) 'Reading prehistoric figurines as individuals', *World Archaeology* 25(3): 321–31.

—— (1996) 'Interpreting figurines: the emergence of illusion and new ways of seeing', *Cambridge Archaeological Journal* 6(2): 291–5.

—— (1997) 'Review of "The Concept of the Goddess"', edited by S. Billington and M. Green (Routledge), *Antiquity* 71: 246–8.

—— (1999a) 'What is a tell? Settlement in fifth millennium BC Bulgaria', in J. Brück and M. Goodman (eds) *Making Places in the Prehistoric World*, pp. 94–111. London: UCL Press.

—— (1999b) 'Pit-huts and surface-level structures: the built environment in the Balkan Neolithic', *Documenta Praehistorica (Ljubljana)* 25: 15–30.

—— (2000) *Balkan Prehistory: Exclusion, Incorporation and Identity*, London: Routledge.

BIBLIOGRAPHY

—— (2002) 'Review of "Fragmentation in Archaeology: People, Places and Broken Objects in the Prehistory of South Eastern Europe" (Routledge)', by J.C. Chapman, *American Anthropologist* 103(4): 1181–2.

Bailey, D.W., Whittle, A. and Cummings, V. (eds) (2005) *(un)settling the Neolithic*, Oxford: Oxbow.

Baillie, J. (1747; 1996 edition) 'An essay on the sublime', in Ashfield and de Bolla (eds), pp. 87–100.

Bakhtin, M. (1968; 1984 edition) *Rabelais and His World*, Boston: MIT Press.

Barndon, R. (1992) 'Traditional iron working amond the Fipa', unpublished MA thesis, University of Bergen.

Barthes, R. (1993) *Camera Lucida*, London: Vintage.

Baudrillard, J. (1988) 'Simulacra and simulations', in M. Poster (ed.) *Jean Baudrillard: Selected Writinges*, pp. 166–84, Cambridge: Polity.

Beck, M. (2000) 'Female figurines in the European Upper Palaeolithic', in A.E. Rautman (ed.), *Reading the Body: Representations and Remains in the Archaeological Record*, pp. 202–14, Philadelphia, PA: University of Pennsylvania Press.

Benjamin, A. (ed.) (1989) *The Lyotard Reader*, Oxford: Blackwell.

Berciu, D. (1960) 'Deux chefs-d'oeuvre le "couple" de la civilisation de Hamangia', *Dacia* 4: 432–42.

—— (1961) *Contribuţii la Problemele Neoliticului din Românie, in Lumina Noilor Cercetari*, Bucureşti: Editura Academiei Republicii Populare Romine.

—— (1963) 'Neolitnata kultura Khamangia v Bulgariya', *Arkheologiya* 5(1): 5–7.

—— (1966) *Cultura Hamangia*, Bucureşti: Editura Academiei Republicii Populare Romine.

Berciu, D. and Morintz, S. (1957) 'Santierul arheologic Cernavoda', *Materiale şi Cercetări Arheologice* 3: 83–93.

—— (1959) 'Săpăturile de la Cernavoda', *Materiale şi Cercetări Arheologice* 5: 99–114.

Berciu, D., Morintz, S. and Diaconu, P. (1955) 'Şantierul arheologic Cernavoda', *Studii şi Cercetări de Istorie Veche* 6(1–2): 151–60.

Berciu, D., Morintz, S. and Roman, P. (1959) 'Săpăturile de la Cernavoda', *Materiale* 6: 95–105.

Berciu, D., Morintz, S., Ionescu, M. and Roman, P. (1961) 'Şantierul arheologic Cernavoda', *Materiale şi Cercetări Arkeologice* 7: 49–55.

Besios, M. and Pappa, M. (1995) '*Pydna*', Thessaloniki: Pieriki Anaptixiaki.

—— (1997) 'Neolithikos oikismos Makrigialou (1993)', *To Arkhaiologiko Ergo sti Makedonia kai Thraki* 7: 559–72.

—— (1998a) 'O Neolithikos oikismos ston Makrigialo Pierias', *Athens Annals of Archaeology* 23: 13–30.

—— (1998b) 'Neolithikos oikismos Makrigailou', *To Arkhaiologiko Ergo sti Makedonia kai Thraki* 8: 137–46.

—— (1998c) 'Neolithikos oikismos Makrigailou', *To Arkhaiologiko Ergo sti Makedonia kai Thraki* 9: 173–78.

Betz, M. (1998) 'Foreword', in *L.A. or Lilliput?* Long Beach, CA: Long Beach Museum of Art.

Bhabha, H.K. (1986) 'The other questions: difference, discrimination and the discourse of colonialism', in F. Baker, P. Hulme, M. Iversen and D. Loxley (eds) *Literature, Politics and Theory. Papers from the Essex Conference, 1976–84*, pp. 17–19, London: Metheun.

—— (1999) 'The other question: the stereotype and colonial discourse', in Evans and Hall (eds), pp. 370–8.

Bibikov, S.N. (1953) 'Luka-Vrublevetskaia na Dnestre na Dnestre', *Materialy I Issledovaniia po Arkheologii SSSR* 38: 1–408, Moscow: Itd-vo Akademii Nauk SSSR.

Biehl, P. (1996) 'Symbolic communication systems: symbols of anthropomorphic figurines of the Neolithic and Chalcolithic from southeastern Europe', *Journal of European Archaeology* 4: 153–76.

BIBLIOGRAPHY

—— (1997) 'Overcoming the "Mother-Goddess-Movement": a new approach to the study of human representations', *Latvijas Zinātņu Akadēmijas Vēstis* 51 (5–6): 59–67.

—— (2003) *Studien zum Symbolgut des Neolithikums und der Kupferzeit in Südosteuropa*, Bonn: Habelt.

Bloedow, E.F. (1991) 'The "Aceramic" Neolithic phase in Greece reconsidered', *Mediterranean Archaeology* 4: 2–35.

Bolomey, A. (1983) 'Noi descoperiri de oase umane într-o aşezare cucuteniană', *Cercetări Arheologice* 6: 159–72.

—— (2000) 'Man', in S. Marinescu-Bîlcu and A. Bolomey, pp. 153–8.

Bolton, R. (ed.) (1989) *The Contest of Meaning: Critical Histories of Photography*, Cambridge, MA: MIT Press.

Bordo, S. (1999) 'Feminism, Foucault and the politics of the body', in Price and Shildrick (eds), pp. 246–57.

Bourdieu, P. (1999) 'The social definition of photography', in Evans and Hall, pp. 162–80.

Boyadzhiev, Ya. (1992) 'Kulturata Hamangia', *Dobrudzha* 9: 10–19.

—— (2002) 'Die absolute Chronologie der neo- und äneolithischen Gräberfelder von Durankulak', in H. Todorova (ed.), *Teil 1 (Text)*, pp. 67–80.

Brandes, S.H. (1980) 'Giants and big-heads: an Andalusian metaphor', in S.B. Ortner and S.H. Brandes (eds) *Symbol as Sense*, pp. 77–92, New York: Academic Press.

—— (1988) *Power and Persuasion*, Philadelphia, PA: University of Pennsylvania Press.

Briggs, J.L. (1990) 'Play work as a tool in the socialization of an Inuit child', *Arctic Medical Research* 49(1): 34–8.

Brookner, A. (1987) *Jacques-Louis David*, London: Thames and Hudson.

Brown, C. (1997) 'Chinese scholars' rocks and the Land of Immortals: some insights from painting', in R.D. Mowdry (ed.) *Worlds within World. The Richard Rosenblum Collection of Chinese Scholars' Rocks*, pp. 57–83, Cambridge, MA: Harvard University Art Museums.

Brown, D.B. (1999) 'Turner's Grand Tour: the Alps and Switzerland in 1802', in Brown (ed.) *Turner et les Alpes'*, pp. 9–33, Martigny, Switz.: Fondation Pierre Gianadda.

Burgin, V. (1999) 'Art, common sense and photography', in Evans and Hall, pp. 41–50.

Burke, E. (1759; 1999 edition) *Philosophical Enquiry into the Origin of Our Ideas of the Sublime and Beautiful*, Harmondsworth: Penguin.

Butler, J. (1990) *Gender Trouble: Feminism and the Subversion of Identity*, London: Routledge.

—— (1993) *Bodies that Matter: On the Discursive Limits of 'Sex'*, London: Routledge.

—— (1999a) 'Bodies that matter', in Price and Shildrick (eds), pp. 235–45.

—— (1999b) 'Bodily inscriptions, performative subversions', in Price and Shildrick (eds), pp. 416–22.

Campbell, E. (1982) 'The virgin of Guadalupe and the female self-image: a Mexican case history', in J.J. Preston (ed.) *Mother Worship. Theme and Variation*, pp. 5–25, Charlotte, NC: University of North Carolina Press.

Canyon, D. and Arnold, C.D. (1985) 'Toys as indicators of socialization in the Thule culture', in M. Thompson, M.T. Garcia and F.J. Kerse (eds) *Status, Structure and Stratification: Current Archaeological Reconstructions*, pp. 347–53, Calgary: Archaeological Association of the University of Calgary.

Carriker, K. (1998) *Created in Our Image: The Miniature Body of the Doll as Subject and Object*, Bethlehem, PA: Lehigh University Press.

Carroll, N. (1993) 'Dolls in contemporary art', in C. Carter, pp. 27–32.

Carter, C. (1993a) 'Eye of the doll: art and personal identity', in C. Carter, pp. 7–25.

—— (ed.) (1993b) *Dolls in Contemporary Art: A Metaphor of Personal Identity*, Milwaukee, WI: Haggerty Museum of Art.

Cavanagh, W. and Mee, C. (1998) *A Private Place: Death in Prehistoric Greece*, Jonsered: Paul Åström.

BIBLIOGRAPHY

Cehac, H. (1933) 'Plastyka eneolitycznej kultury ceramiki malowanej w Polsce', *Światowit* 14: 164–252.

Černyš, E.K. (1973) 'Tripol'skoe poselenie Racovec', *Kratkie Soobščenija (Instituta Istorii Material'noj Kul'tury, Moscova)* 134: 48–58.

Chapman, J. (1990) 'Social inequality on Bulgarian tells and the Varna problem', in R. Samson (ed.) *The Social Archaeology of Houses*, pp. 49–92, Edinburgh: Edinburgh University Press.

——— (1996) 'Enchainment, commodification and gender in the Balkan Neolithic and Copper Age', *Journal of European Archaeology* 4: 203–42.

——— (2000a) *Fragmentation in Archaeology. People, Places and Broken Objects in the Prehistory of South Eastern Europe*, London: Routledge.

——— (2000b) 'Pit-digging and structured deposition in the Neolithic and Copper Age of Central and Eastern Europe', *Proceedings of the Prehistoric Society* 66: 61–88.

Charney, L. and Schwartz, V.R. (eds) (1995) *Cinema and the Invention of Modern Life*, Los Angeles, CA: University of California Press.

Childe, V.G. (1936) *Man Makes Himself*, London: Watts.

Clarke, G. (ed.) (1992a) *The Portrait in Photography*, London: Reaktion.

——— (1992b) 'Introduction', in Clarke, pp. 1–5.

Collins, P. and Halstead, P. (1999) 'Faunal remains and animal exploitation at Late Neolithic Makriyalos: preliminary results', in Halstead, pp. 139–41.

Coman, G. (1980) *Statornivie, Continuitate. Repertoriul Arheologic al Judeşului Vaslui*, Bucureşti: Editura Academiei Republicii Populare Romine.

Comşa, E. (1959) 'Săpături de la Dudeşti', *Materiale şi Cercetări Arheologice* 5: 91–7.

——— (1976c) 'Figurine din marmură din epoca neolitică de pe teritoriul Romăiei', *Pontica* 9: 23–8.

Comşa, E., Galbenu, D. and Aricescu, A. (1962) 'Săpături arheologice la Techirghiol', *Materiale şi Cercetări Arheologice* 8: 165–71.

Conkey, M. and Tringham, R. (1995) 'Archaeology and the Goddess: exploring the contours of feminist archaeology', in A. Stewart and D. Stanton (eds) *Feminisms in the Academy: Rethinking the Disciplines*, pp. 199–247, Ann Arbor, MI: University of Michigan Press.

Conroy, L.P. (1993) 'Female figurines of the Upper Palaeolithic and the emergence of gender', in H. du Cros and L. Smith (eds) *Women in Archaeology: a Feminist Critique*, pp. 153–60, Canberra: Australian National University.

Csalog, J. (1976) 'Die Idolen von Cernavoda und die sprechende Maske', *Archaeologiai Ertesítö* 103(2): 216–22.

Cucoş, S. (1970) 'Reprezentări antropomorfe în decorul pictat cucutenian de la Ghelăieşti (jud. Neamţ)', *Memoria Antiquitatis* 2: 101–14.

——— (1971) 'Reprezentări de încălţăminte în plastica cucuteniană de la Ghelăieşti, jud. Neamţ', *Memoria Antiquitatis* 3: 65–78.

——— (1973) 'Un complex ritual cuctenian descoperit la Ghelăieşti (jud. Neamţ)', *Studii şi Cercetări de Istorie Veche* 24(2): 207–17.

——— (1993) 'Complexele rituale cucuteniene de la Ghelăieşti (jud. Neamţ)', *Studii şi Cercetări de Istorie Veche şi Arheologie* 44(1): 59–80.

Cullen, T. (ed.) (2001) *Aegean Prehistory: a Review*, Boston, MA: Archaeological Institute of America.

DaMatta, R. (1991) *Carnivals, Rogues, and Heroes: An Interpretation of the Brazilian Dilemma* (trans. J. Drury), Notre Dame, IN: University of Notre Dame Press.

Darling, M. (1998) 'L.A. or Lilliput?', in *L.A. or Lilliput?*, pp. 1–9, Long Beach, CA: Long Beach Museum of Art.

Davis, N.Z. (1973) 'The rites of violence: religious riot in sixteenth-century France', *Past and Present* 59: 51–91.

Davis, P. (1993) 'The Goddess and the academy', *Academic Questions* 6: 49–66.

BIBLIOGRAPHY

Debord, G. (1967) *The Society of the Spectacle* (1995 trans. P. Nicholson-Smith), New York: Zone Books.

De Long, A.J. (1981) 'Phenomoenological space-time: toward an experiential relativity', *Science* August 7, 1981: 681–2.

—— (1983) 'Spatial scale, temporal experience and information processing: an empirical examination of experiential reality', *Man-Environment Systems* 13: 77–86.

—— (2000) *Experiential Space-Time Relativity: A Synopsis*. Pdf file made available by the author, June 2000.

Demoule, J.-P. and Gallis, K. (1991) 'L'un des plus anciens Néolithiques d'Europe', *Les Dossiers d'Archéologie* 159: 8–15.

Demoule, J.-P. and Perlès, C. (1993) 'The Greek Neolithic: a new review', *Journal of World Prehistory* 7(4): 355–416.

Dergacev, V.A. (1978) *Vykhvatinski Mogilnik*, Moscow.

Dimov, T. (1982) 'Zemlyanka ot neolitnoto selishte pri s. Durankulak, Tolbukhinski okrug', *Arkheologiya* 24(1): 33–48.

—— (1992a) 'Kulturata Hamangia v Dobrudja', *Dobrudzha* 9: 20–34.

—— (1992b) 'Kultura Hamangia v iujnoi Dobrudje', *Studia Praehistorica* 11–12: 122–30.

—— (2002) 'Entdeckung und Erforschung der prähistorischen Gräberfelder von Durankulak', in H. Todorova (ed.), *Teil 1 (Text)*, pp. 25–33.

Dimov, T., Boyadzhiev, Ya. and Todorova, H. (1984) 'Praistoricheski nekropol kraj s. Durankulak, Tolbukhinski okrug', *Dobrudzha* 1: 77–88.

Doane, M.A (1999) 'Dark continents: epistomologies of racial and sexual difference in psychoanalysis and the cinema', in Evans and Hall, pp. 448–59.

Doss, E. (1997) 'Making imagination safe in the 1950s: Disneyland's fantasy art and architecture', in Marling, pp. 179–89.

Ducrot, N. (ed.) (1977) *Distortions. André Kertész*, New York: Alfred Knopf.

Dudkin, V.P. (1978) 'Geofizicheskaja razvedka krupnykh tripol'skikh poselenij', *Ispol'zovanie Metodov Estestvennykh Nauk v Arkheologii*: 35–45.

Dumitrescu, H. (1954) 'Plastica', in V. Dumitrescu *et al.*, pp. 403–434.

—— (1957) 'Découverts concernant un rite funéraire magique dans la civilisation de la céramique peinte du type Cucuteni-Tripolie', *Dacia* 1: 97–116.

Dumitrescu, V. (1957) 'Le dépôt d'objets de parure de Hăbăşeşti et le problème des rapports entre les tribus de la civilisation de Cucuteni et les tribus des steppes pontiques', *Dacia* 1: 73–96.

—— (1963) 'Originea şi evoluţia culturii Cucuteni-Tripolie I–II', *Studii şi Cercetări de Istorie Veche* 14(1–2): 57–78, 285–308.

—— (1979) *Arta Cultura Cucuteni*, Bucureşti: Editura Meridiane.

Dumitrescu, V., Dumitrescu, H., Petrescu-Dîmboviţa, M. and Gostar, N. (1954) *Hăbăşeşti. Monografie Arheologică*, Bucureşti: Institutul de Arheologiă al Academiei RPR.

Dumitroaia, G. (1987a) 'La station archéologique de Lunca-Poieni Slatinii', M. Petrescu-Dîmboviţa (ed.) *La Civilisation de Cucuteni en Contexte Européen. Session Scientifique Dédiée au Centenaire des Premières Découvertes de Cucuteni*, pp. 253–8, Iaşi: Université Al. I. Cuza.

—— (1987b) 'Plastica antropomorfă cucuteniană de la Răuceşti-Munteni', *Memoria Antiquitatis* 15–17: 253–8.

—— (1994) Depunerile neo-eneolitice de la Lunca şi Oglinzi, jud. Neamţ, *Memoria Antiquitatis* 19: 7–82.

Dumitroaia, G. and Monah, D. (eds) (1996) *Cucuteni Aujourd'hui. 110 Ans depuis la Découverte en 1884 du Site Eponyme*, Piatra-Neamţ: Muzeul de Istorie Piatra Neamţ.

Dyer, R. (1999) 'White', in Evans and Hall, pp. 457–67.

Eagleton, T. (1989) 'Bakhtin, Schopenhauer, Kundera', in K. Hirschkop and D. Sheperd (eds) *Bakhtin and Culture Theory*, pp. 178–88, Manchester: University of Manchester Press.

BIBLIOGRAPHY

Eco, Umberto (1984) 'Frames of comic freedom', in T. Sebeok (ed.) *Carnival!*, pp. 1–10, New York: Mouton.

Ellis, L. (1984) *The Cucuteni-Tripolye Culture. A Study in Technology and the Origins of Complex Society*, Oxford: BAR.

Evans, J. and Hall, S. (1999a) 'What is visual culture?', in Evans and Hall, pp. 1–5.

—— (ed.) (1999b) *Visual Culture: The Reader*, London: Sage.

Fagan, B. (1992) 'A sexist view of prehistory', *Archaeology* 45: 49–66.

Ferenczi, S. (1955) 'Gulliver phantasies', in S. Ferenczi (ed.) *Final Contributions to the Problems and Methods of Psycho-analysis*, pp. 41–60, London: Hogarth Press.

Fleming, A. (1969) 'The myth of the Mother-Goddess', *World Archaeology* 1: 247–61.

Florescu, A.C. (1966) 'Observaţii asupra sistemului de fortificare al aşezărilor cucuteniene din Moldova', *Arheologia Moldovei* 4: 23–37.

Florescu, A. and Florescu, M. (1999) 'Şanţul de apărare', in M. Petrescu-Dîmboviţa, M. Florescu and A. Florescu (eds) *Truşeşti. Monografie Archeologică*, pp. 222–30, Bucureşti: Editura Academiei Romane.

Fontanills, L. (1997) 'Miniaturization', *Internet Bonsai Club* (http://www.internetbonsaiclub.org/index.php) Accessed November 2001.

Foucault, M. (1977a) 'The political function of the intellectual', *Radical Philosophy* 17: 13–14.

—— (1977b) *Discipline and Punish. Birth of the Prison* (trans. A. Sheridan) London: Allen Lane.

—— (1980) *Power/Knowledge*, Brighton: Harvester.

Freud, S. (1905; 2002 edition) *Three Essays on the Theory of Sexuality*, New York: Basic Books.

Galbenu, D. (1970) 'Aşezarea şi cimitirul de la Limanu', *Materiale* 9: 77–86.

Gallis, K.J. (1982) *Kafseis Nekron apo tin Neolithiki Epochi sti Thessalia*, Athens: Ekdosi Tameiou Archaeiologikon Poron kai Apallotrioseon.

—— (1985) 'A late Neolithic foundation offering from Thessaly', *Antiquity* 59: 20–24.

—— (1990) 'Prosphates Hereunes sti Neolithiki Thessalia', *Archaiologia* 34: 9–20.

—— (1992) *Atlas Proïstorikon Oikismon tis Anatolikis Thessalikis Pediadas*, Larisa: Etairia Istorikon Erevnon Thessalias.

—— (1996) 'The Neolithic world', in G.A. Papathanassopoulos, pp. 23–37.

Gallis, K. and Orphanidis, L. (1995) 'Twenty new faces from the Neolithic society of Thessaly', in J.C. Decourt, B. Helly and K. Gallis (eds) *La Thessalie, Colloque International d'Archéologie: 15 Années de Recherches (1975–1990)*, pp. 57–70, Athens: Tameion Archaeologikon Poron.

—— (1996) *Figurines of Neolithic Thessaly*, Athens: Academy of Athens.

Gâţă, G. (2000) 'A technological survey of the pottery', in Marinescu-Bîlcu and Bolomey, pp. 111–29.

Gatens, M. (1996) *The Imaginary Body: Ethics, Power and Corporeality*, London: Routledge.

—— (1999) 'Power, bodies and difference', in Price and Shildrick, pp. 227–34.

Geertz, C. (1983) *Local Knowledge*, New York: Basic Books.

Gheorghiu, D. (n.d.) 'Wrapping and unwrapping the ancestors: the rhetorics of anthropomorphic figurines in east European Chalcolithic', unpublished manuscript in the author's possession.

—— (1996) 'Pots and messages: the complex advertising of Eneolithic ceramics', in D.A. Meyer, P.C. Dawson and D.T. Hanna (eds) *Debating Complexity*, pp. 89–95, Calgary, Alberta: Chacmool.

—— (1997) ' Semenele stramosilor: rituri funerare şi transmitrea lor in societatea cucuteniana', *Acta Musei Napocensis* 34(1): 727–34.

—— (2001) 'The cult of ancestors in the east European Chalcolithic. A Holographic approach', in P.F. Biehl, F. Bertemes, and H. Meller (eds) *The Archaeology of Cult and Religion*, pp. 73–88, Budapest: Archaeolingua.

Gilmore, D. (1998) *Carnival and Culture: Sex, Symbol and Status*, New Haven, CT: Yale University Press.

BIBLIOGRAPHY

Gimbutas, M. (1974a) 'Achilleion, a Neolithic mound in Thessaly: preliminary report on 1973 and 1974 excavations', *Journal of Field Archaeology* 1: 277–302.

—— (1974b; 1982 edition) *The Goddesses and Gods of Old Europe, 6500–3500 BC, Myths and Cult Images*, Berkeley, CA: University of California Press.

—— (ed.) (1976) *Neolithic Macedonia as Reflected by Excavation at Anza, Southeast Yugoslavia*, Los Angeles, CA: Institute of Archaeology, UCLA.

—— (1980) 'The temples of Old Europe', *Archaeology* Nov/Dec: 21–34.

—— (1986a) 'Mythical imagery of Sitagroi society', in Renfrew *et al.*, pp. 225–89.

—— (1986b) 'Figurine catalogue', in Renfrew *et al.*, pp. 290–301.

—— (1989a) *The Language of the Goddess*, San Francisco: Harper Collins.

—— (1989b) 'Figurines and cult equipment: their role in the reconstruction of Neolithic religion', in Gimbutas *et al.*, pp. 171–227.

—— (1989c) 'Illustrated catalogue of figurines by phase', in Gimbutas *et al.*, pp. 228–50.

—— (1991) *The Civilization of the Goddess: the World of Old Europe*, San Francisco, CA: Harper Collins.

Gimbutas, M., Winn, S. and Shimabuku, D. (eds) (1989) *Achilleion. A Neolithic Settlement in Thessaly, Greece 6400–5600 BC* (Monumenta Archaeologica 14), Los Angeles, CA: Cotsen Institute of Archaeology, UCLA.

Grosz, E. (1994) *Volatile Bodies: Toward a Corporeal Feminism*, Bloomington, IN: University of Indiana Press.

—— (1999a) 'Psychoanalysis and the body', in Price and Shildrick, pp. 267–72.

—— (1999b) 'Bodies–cities', in Price and Shildrick, pp. 381–7.

Grundmann, K. (1937) 'Magula Hadzimissiotiki. Eine steinzeitliche Siedlung im Karla-See', *Athenische Mitteilungen* 62: 56–62.

Guenple, L.I. (1988) 'Teaching social relations to Inuit children', in T. Ingold, D. Riches and J. Woodburn (eds), *Hunters and Gatherers. Property, Power and Ideology*, pp. 131–49, Oxford: Berg.

Guyer, P. (2000) 'Introduction', in Kant, pp. xiii–lii.

Haaland, G. (1984) 'Fur', in R.W.V. Weeks (ed.) *Muslim Peoples. A World Ethnographic Survey*, pp. 264–9, New Haven, CT: Greenwood Press.

—— (1990) 'Øl og morsmelk. Symbol, moral og valg i Fur-Samfunnet', *Norsk Antropologisk Tidsskrift* 1: 3–16.

Haaland, G. and Haaland, R. (1995) 'Who speaks the Goddess's language? Imagination and method in archaeological research', *Norwegian Archaeological Review* 28(2): 105–21.

—— (1996) 'Levels of meaning in symbolic objects', *Cambridge Archaeological Journal* 6: 295–300.

Hall, E. (1966) *The Hidden Dimension*, New York: Doubleday.

Hall, G. and Ellis, A.C. (1897) *A Study of Dolls*, New York: E.L. Kellogg.

Halstead, P. (1981) 'From determinism to uncertainty: social storage and the rise of the Minoan Palace', in A. Sheridan and G. Bailey (eds) *Economic Archaeology*, pp. 187–213, Oxford: BAR.

—— (1989a) 'The economy has a normal surplus: economic stability and social change among early farming communities of Thessaly, Greece', in P. Halstead and J. O'Shea (eds) *Bad Year Economics: Cultural Responses to Risk and Uncertainty*, pp. 68–80, Cambridge: Cambridge University Press.

—— (1989b) 'Like rising damp? An ecological approach to the spread of farming in southeast and central Europe', in A. Milles, D. Williams and Gardner, N. (eds) *The Beginnings of Agriculture*, pp. 23–53, Oxford: BAR.

—— (1990) 'Waste not, want not: traditional responses to crop failure in Greece', *Rural History* 1: 147–64.

—— (1992) 'Dimini and the "DMP": faunal remains and animal exploitation in Late Neolithic Thessaly', *Annual of the British School of Athens* 87: 29–95.

—— (1993) '*Spondylus* shell ornaments from late Neolithic Dimini, Greece: specialised manufacture or unequal accumulation?' *Antiquity* 67: 603–9.

BIBLIOGRAPHY

—— (ed.) (1999a) *Neolithic Society in Greece*, Sheffield: Sheffield Academic Press.

—— (1999b) 'Neighbours from hell? The household in Neolithic Greece', in Halstead *et al.*, pp. 77–95.

—— (in press) 'Resettling the Neolithic: faunal evidence for seasons of consumption and residence at Neolithic sites in Greece', in D.W. Bailey, A. Whittle and V. Cummings (eds) *Sedentism in the Neolithic*, Los Angeles, CA: UCLA.

Halstead, P. and Jones, G. (1989) 'Agrarian ecology in the Greek islands: time, stress, scale and risk', *Journal of Hellenic Studies* 109: 41–55.

Hamilakis, Y., Pluciennik, M. and Tarlow, S. (eds) (2001) *Thinking Through the Body: Archaeologies of Corporeality*, London: Plenum.

Hamilton, N. (1996) 'The personal is political', *Cambridge Archaeological Journal* 6(2): 282–5.

Harţuche, N. (1976) 'Unele probleme ale postpaleoliticului în peşterile Dobrogei', *Pontica* 9: 13–22.

Haşotti, P. (1980) 'Aşezarea aparţinînd cultuurii Hamangia de la Medgidia-Satu Nou', *Pontica* 13: 199–214.

—— (1982) 'Aspecte privind începutul epohi neolitice în Dobrogea', *Pontica* 15: 33–46.

—— (1984) Noi date privind difuziunea comunitaţilor culturii Hamangia, *Pontica* 17: 25–36.

—— (1985) 'Noi descoperiri privind plastica Hamangia', *Pontica* 18: 25–34.

—— (1986a) 'Observaţii asupra plasticii culturii Hamangia', *Pontica* 19: 9–17.

—— (1986b) 'Observaţii asupra ceramicii dintr-un complex al culturii Hamangia de la Medgidia-Cocoaşă', *Studii şi Cercetări de Istorie Veche ši Arheologie* 37:119–31.

—— (1986c) 'Cercetările arheologice din aşezarea culturii Hamangia de la Tîrguşor – punctual Urs', *Materiale* 16: 26–33.

—— (1987) 'Sondajele din aşezarea culturii Hamangia de la Medgidia-Satu Nou', *Pontica* 20: 19–42.

—— (1993) 'Condideraţii privind originea, difusiunea şi cronologia culturii Hamangia', *Pontica* 26: 27–42.

—— (1997) *Epoca Neolitică în Dobrogea*, Constanţa: Muzeul de Istorie Naţională şi Arheologie.

Haşotti, P. and Wisoşenski, W. (1985) 'Descoperiri întîmplătoare în ašezarea neolitică de la Tîrgošur Sitorman', *Pontica* 18: 37–49.

Herbert, S. (1997) *Theodore Brown's Magic Pictures. The Art and Inventions of a Multi-media Pioneer*, London: The Projection Box.

Hill, D. (1992) *Turner in the Alps. The Journey through France and Switzerland in 1802*, London: George Philip.

Hodder, I. (1990) *The Domestication of Europe*, Oxford: Blackwell.

Hourmouziadis, G. (1973) *Ne Anthropomorphe Idoloplastike tes Neolithikes Thessalias: Provlemata Kataskeues, Typologias kai Hermeneias*, Athens: Ekdozeiz A. Karavia.

—— (1979) *To Neolithiko Dimini*, Volos: Society for Thessalian Studies.

Ivanov, V.V. (1984) 'The semiotic theory of carnival as the inversion of bipolar opposites', in T. Sebeok (ed.) *Carnival!*, pp. 11–37, New York: Mouton.

Jackson, M. (1983) 'Thinking through the body: an essay on understanding metaphor', *Sociological Analysis* 14: 127–49.

Jacobs, A.B. (1995) *Great Streets*, Cambridge, MA: MIT Press.

Johnson, D. (1993) *Jacques-Louis David. Art in Metamorphosis*, Princeton, NJ: Princeton University Press.

Jones, J. (1976) *The Wonders of the Stereoscope*, London: Jonathan Cape.

Kamps, T. (2000) 'Small world: dioramas in contemporary art', in Small World, pp. 6–11.

Kant, I. (1790; 2000 edition) *Critique of the Power of Judgment*. (edited by P. Guyer; trans. P. Guyer and E. Matthews), Cambridge: Cambridge University Press.

Kelly, M. (1998) *Imaging Desire*, Cambridge, MA: MIT Press.

Kertzer, D.I. (1988) *Ritual, Politics and Power*, New Haven, CT: Yale University Press.

BIBLIOGRAPHY

King, J.R. (1996) *Remaking the World: Modelling in Human Experience*, Chicago, IL: University of Illinois Press.

Kitson, M. (1964) *J.M.W. Turner*, London: Blandford Press.

Knapp, B. and Meskell, L. (1997) 'Bodies of evidence on Prehistoric Cyprus', *Cambridge Archaeological Journal* 7(2): 183–204.

Kokkinidou, D. and Nikolaidou, M. (1997) 'Body imagery in the Aegean Neolithic: ideological implications of anthropomorphic figurines', in J. Moore and E. Scott (eds) *Invisible People and Processes: Writing Gender and Childhood into European Archaeology*, pp. 88–112, Leicester: Leicester University Press.

Koreshoff, D.R. (1984) *Bonsai: Its Art, Science, History and Philosophy*, Portland, OR: Timber Press.

Kotsakis, K. (1981) 'Tria oikimata tou oikismou tou sesklou. Anaskafiki ereuna', *Anthropologika* 2: 87–108.

—— (1995) 'The use of habitational space in Neolithic Sesklo', in J.C. Decourt, B. Helly and K. Gallis (eds) *La Thessalie, Colloque International d'Archéologie: Quinze Années de Recherches (1975–1990), Bilans et Perspectives*, pp. 125–30, Athens: Tamio Arkhaiologikon Poron.

—— (1999) 'What tells can tell: social space and settlement in the Greek Neolithic', in Halstead, pp. 66–76.

—— (in press) 'Across the border: unstable dwellings and fluid landscapes in the earliest Neolithic of Greece', in Bailey *et al.*

Kramer, H. (1977) 'Introduction', in Ducrot, pp. 1–10.

Krauss, R. (1977) *Passages in Modern Sculpture*, London: Thames and Hudson.

—— (1999) 'Photography's discursive space', in Evans and Hall pp. 193–210.

Kruger, B. (1999) *Barbara Kruger*, Cambridge, MA: MIT Press.

Kruts, V.A. and Ryžov, S.N. (1983) 'Raboty Tal'janskogo otrjada', *Arkheologičeskie Otkrytija 1981 Goda*: 278.

Kusurgaseva, A.P. (1970) 'Antropomorphnaya plastika iz poselnija Novye Rusešty 1', *Kratkie Soobshcheniya Instituta Arkheologii AN USSR* 123: 69–77.

Kyparissi-Apostolika, N. (1995) 'Prehistoric inhabitation in Theopetra Cave, Thessaly', in J.C. Decourt, B. Helly and K. Gallis (eds) *La Thessalie, Colloque International d'Archéologie: Quinze Années de Recherches (1975–1990), Bilans et Perspectives*, pp. 103–8, Athens: Tamio Arkhaiologikon Poron.

—— (1999) 'The Neolithic use of Theopetra Cave in Thessaly', in Halstead, pp. 142–52.

Lacan, J. (1977) *The Four Fundamental Characteristics of Psychoanalysis*, New York: Norton.

Langdon, S. (1999) 'Figurines and social change: visualizing gender in Dark Age Greece', in N.L. Wicker and B. Arnold (eds) *From the Ground Up: Beyond Gender Theory in Archaeology*, pp. 23–9, Oxford: BAR.

László, A. (1993) 'Aşezări întărite ale culturi Cucuteni în sud estul Transilvaniei. Aşezarea fortificată de la Malnaş-Băi', *Arheologia Moldovei* 16: 33–50.

Lavater, J.C. (1775–8) *Essays on Physiognomy*, London: S.G. and J. Robinson.

Lawson, J. 1758. [1996] 'From lectures concerning oratory', in Ashfield and de Bolla, pp. 144–6.

Lăzurcă, E. (1980) 'Raport asupra noilor cercetări arheologice de la Baia (Hamangia), jud. Tulcea'. *Peuce* 8: 7–16.

Lefebvre, H. (1958) *Critique de la Vie Quotidienne*, Paris: Larche.

Lefkowitz, M. (1992) 'The new cults of the Goddess', *American Scholar* 62: 29.

—— (1993) 'The twilight of the Goddess: feminism, spiritualism, and a new craze', *The New Republic* 207: 123–45.

Le Roy Ladurie, E. (1979) *Carnival in Romans*, New York: George Braziller.

Lesure, R.G. (2002) 'The Goddess diffracted: thinking about the figurines of early villages', *Current Anthropology* 43(4): 587–610.

BIBLIOGRAPHY

Lesy, M. (2002) *Long Time Coming. A Photographic Portrait of America, 1935–1943*, London: W.W. Norton.

Lévi-Strauss, C. (1972) *The Savage Mind*, London: Weidenfeld and Nicholson.

Lloyd, V. and Wagner, G. (1974) *The Camera and Dr Barnardo*, Hertford: Barnardo School of Printing.

Lock, M. (1993) 'Cultivating the body: anthropology and epistemologies of bodily practice and knowledge', *Annual Review of Anthropology* 22: 133–55.

Lord, M.G. (1994) *Forever Barbie: the Unauthorized Biography of a Real Doll*, New York: William Morrow and Company.

Lungu, R. (1978) 'Cîteva figurine de la Dunărea de Jos şi unele probleme ale plasticii neolitice', *Studii şi Cercetări de Istoria Artei* 25: 203–9.

Lyotard, J.-F. (1989) 'The sublime and the avant-garde', in Benjamin, pp. 196–211.

—— (1994) *Lessons on the Analytic of the Sublime*, Stanford, CA: Stanford University Press.

McCoid, C.H. and McDermott, L. (1996) 'Towards decolonizing gender: female vision in the European Upper Palaeolithic', *American Anthropologist* 98(2): 319–26.

McDermott, L. (1996) 'Self-representation in Upper Palaeolithic female figurines', *Current Anthropology* 37(2): 227–75.

MacGaffey, W. (1993) *Astonishment and Power*, Washington, DC: National Museum of African Art.

McKinsey, E. (1985) *Niagara Falls: Icon of the American Sublime*, Cambridge: Cambridge University Press.

Makarenko, N. (1927) 'Sculpture de la civilisation Tripolienne', *Jahrbuch für Prähistorische und Ethnographische Kunst* 41(2): 119–30.

Makarevič, M.L. (1954) 'Statuetki tripol'skogo poselenija Sabatinovka II', *Kratkie Soobshcheniya Instituta Arkheologii AN USSR (Kiev)* 3: 7–16.

Mantu, C.-M. (1991) 'Vases anthropomorphes du site Cucuteni A3 de Scînteia', in V. Chirica and D. Monah (eds) *Le Paléolithique et le Néolithique de la Roumaine en Contexte Européenne*, pp. 328–34, Iaşi: Institut d'Archéologie.

—— (1993a) 'Anthropomorphic representations on the Precucuteni-Cucuteni cultures', *Anatolica* 19: 129–41.

—— (1993b) 'Plastica antropomorfă a aşezării Cucuteni A3 de la Scânteia (jud. Iaşi)', *Arheologia Moldovei* 16: 51–68.

—— (1998) *Cultura Cucuteni. Evoluţie, Cronologie, Legături*, Piatra-Neamţ: Muzeul de Istorie Piatra-Neamţ.

Mantu, C.-M. and Dumitroaia, G. (1997) 'Catalogue', in Mantu *et al.*, pp. 101–241.

Mantu, M., Botezatu, D. and Kromer, B. (1994) Une tombe double à inhumation de l'établissement de type Cucuteni de Scânteia (département de Iaşi, Roumanie), *Préhistoire Européenne* 6: 225–41.

Mantu, C.-M., Dumitroaia, G. and Tsaravopoulos, A. (eds) (1997) *Cucuteni: The Last Great Chalcolithic Civilization of Europe*, Thessaloniki: Athena Publishing.

Mapplethorpe, R. (1986) *Black Book*, New York: St. Martin's.

Marangou, C. (1992) *Eidolia. Figurines et Miniatures du Néolithique Récent et du Bronze Ancien en Grèce*, Oxford: BAR.

—— (1996a) 'Assembling, displaying and dissembling Neolithic and Eneolithic figurines and models', *Journal of European Archaeology* 4: 177–202.

—— (1996b) 'Figurines and models', in Papathanassopoulos, pp. 146–51.

Marcus, J. (1996) 'The importance of context in interpreting figurines', *Cambridge Archaeological Journal* 6(2): 285–91.

—— (1998) *Women's Ritual in Formative Oaxaca. Figurine Making, Divination, Death and the Ancesors*. Ann Arbor, MI: University of Michigan.

Marin, M. (1948) 'La plastica antropomorfa Cucteniana nella Dacia', *Revista di Scienze Preistoriche* 3: 17–57.

BIBLIOGRAPHY

Marinescu-Bîlcu, S. (1964) 'Reflets des rapports entre les civilisations de Hamangia et de Précucteni dans la plastique Précuctenienne de Tîrpeşti', *Dacia* 8: 307–12.

—— (1974a) *Cultura PreCucuteni pe Teritoriul României*, Bucureşti: Editura Academiei Republicii Socialiste România.

—— (1974b) 'La plastica in terracotta della cultura precucuteniana', *Revista di Scienze Preistoriche* 29(2): 399–436.

—— (1974c) '"Dansul ritual" în reprezentările plastice neo-eneolitice din Moldova', *Studii şi Cercetări de Istorie Veche ši Arheologie* 25(2): 167–79.

—— (1977a) 'Cîteva observaţii asupra sculpturii în lut a culturii Hamangia şi influenţa ei asupra plasticii culturii Precucuteni', *Peuce* 6: 13–17.

—— (1977b) 'Unele probleme ale plasticii antropomorfe neo-eneolitice din România şi relaţiile ei cu Mediterana orientală', *Pontica* 10: 37–46.

—— (1981) *Tîrpeşti. From Prehistory to History in Eastern Romania*, Oxford: BAR.

—— (1985) 'À propos de la statuette du type "Le Penseur" de l'Attique et le problème de ses éventuelles relations avec celle de Cernavoda', *Dacia* 29: 119–25.

—— (1986) 'O statuetă cicladică de 'Gânditor' şi eventualele sale legături cu piese similare din România', *Cultură şi Civilizaţie la Dunărea de Jos* 2: 83–90.

—— (2000a) 'Anthropomorphic representations', in Marinescu-Bîlcu and Bolomey, pp. 131–40.

—— (2000b) 'The pottery. Tradition and innovation', in Marinescu-Bîlcu and Bolomey, pp. 91–110.

Marinescu-Bîlcu, S. and Bolomey, A. (2000) *Drăguşeni. A Cucutenian Community*, Bucureşti: Editura Enciclopedică.

Mapplethorpe, R. (1986) *Black Book*, New York: St. Martin's.

Markevic, V. (1973) *Pamiatniki Epohi Neolita I Eneolita*. Arkeologicheskaia Karta Moldoavkoi SSSR 5(2). Chişină: Nauk.

Marchevici, I. (1981) *Pozdnetripolskie Plemena Severnoi Moldavii*, Chişinău.

Marling, K.A. (1997a) 'Imagineering the Disney theme parks', in Marling, pp. 29–178.

—— (1997b) *Designing Disney's Theme Parks: the Architecture of Reassurance*, New York: Flammarion.

Masson, V.M., Merpert, N. Ja., Munchaev, R.M. and Černyš, E.K. (1982) *Eneolit SSSR*, Moscow.

Matasă, C. (1946) *Frumuşica. Village Préhistorique à Céramique Peinte dans la Moldavie de Nord. Roumanie*, Bucureşti.

Maxim-Alaiba, R. (1983–4) 'Locuinţa nr. 1 din faza Cucuteni A3 de la Dumeşti (Vaslui)', *Acta Moldaviae Meridionalis* 5–6: 99–147.

—— (1987) 'Le complex de culte de la phase Cucuteni A3 de Dumešti, dep. Vaslui', in M. Petrescu-Dîmboviţa (ed.) *La Civilisation de Cucuteni en Contexte Européen. Session Scientifique Dédiée au Centenaire des Premières Découvertes de Cucuteni*, pp. 269–86, Iaşi: Université Al. I. Cuza.

Mercer, K. (1996) 'Decolonization and disappointment: reading Fanon's sexual politics', in A. Read (ed.) *The Fact of Blackness: Frantz Fanon and Visual Representation*, pp. 114–31, Seattle, WA: Bay Press.

—— (1999) 'Reading racial fetishism: the photographs of Robert Mapplethorpe', in Evans and Hall, pp. 435–47.

Meskell, L. (1995) 'Goddesses, Gimbutas and "New Age" archaeology', *Antiquity* 69: 74–86.

—— (1996) 'The somatisation of archaeology: institutions, discourses and corporeality', *Norwegian Archaeological Review* 29(1): 1–16.

—— (1998) 'Twin peaks. The archaeologies of Çatalhöyük', in L. Goodison and C. Morris (eds) *Ancient Goddesses. Myths and the Evidence*, pp. 46–62, Madison, WI: University of Wisconsin Press.

—— (1999) *Archaeologies of Social Life: Age, Sex, Class etcetera, in Ancient Egypt*, Oxford: Blackwell.

Millon, H.A. (1994) 'Models in Renaissance architecture', in H.A. Millon and V.M. Lampugnani

BIBLIOGRAPHY

(eds) *The Renaissance from Brunelleschi to Michelangelo: the Representation of Architecture*, pp. 19–74, London: Thames and Hudson.

Milojčić, V. (1960) *Hauptergebnisse der deutschen Ausgrabungen in Thessalien 1953–1958*, Bonn: Rudolf Habelt Verlag.

—— (1976) 'Die Grabung auf der Agia Sofia-Magula', in Milojčić *et al.*, pp. 4–14.

Milojčić, V., Boessneck, J. and Hopf, M. (1962) *Die deutschen Ausgrabungen auf der Argissa-Magula in Thessalien, I*, Bonn: Rudolf Habelt.

Milojčić, V., von den Driesch, A., Enderle, K., Milojčić-von Zumbusch, J. and Kilian, K. (1976) *Die Deutsche Ausgrabungen auf Magulen um Larisa in Thessalien, 1966*, Bonn: Beiträge zur Ur- und Frügeschichtliken Archälogic des Mittelmeer-Kulturraumes.

Milojković, J. (1990) 'The anthropomorphic and zoomorphic figurines', in Tringham and Krstić (eds), pp. 397–436.

Mintz, J.R. (1997) *Carnival Song and Society: Gossip, Sexuality and Creativity in Andalusia*, Oxford: Berg.

Mirzeoff, N. (1998) 'What is visual culture', in N. Mirzeoff (ed.) *Visual Culture Reader*, pp. 3–13, London: Routledge.

—— (1999) *An Introduction to Visual Culture*, London: Routledge.

Mitchell, W.J.T. (1994) *Picture Theory: Essays on Verbal and Visual Representation*, Chicago, IL: Chicago University Press.

Mithen, S. (1996) *The Prehistory of the Mind*, London: Thames and Hudson.

Model World (2002) *Model World*, Ridgefield, CT: Aldrich Museum of Contemporary Art.

Monah, D. (1982) Cîteva observații asupra causelor și efectelor exploziei demografice cucteniene, *Carpica* 14: 33–8.

—— (1991) 'Influence au traditions Vinča dans la plastique anthropomorphe de Cucuteni-Tripolie', *Banatica* 11: 297–302.

—— (1992) 'Grands thèmes religieux reflétés dans la plastique anthropomorphe Cucuteni-Tripolye', *Memoria Antiquitatis* 18: 189–98.

—— (1997) *Plastica Antropomorfă a Culturii Cucuteni–Tripolie*, Piatra Neamț: Muzeul de Istorie Piatra Neamț.

Monah, D. and Cucoş, S. (1985) *Aşezările Culturii Cucuteni din România*, Iaşi.

Monah, D. and Monah, F. (1997) 'The last great chalcolithic civilization of Old Europe', in Mantu *et al.*, pp 15–96.

Morgan, M. (1995) *How to Interview Sexual Abuse Victims. Including the Use of Anatomical Dolls*, London: Sage.

Morintz, S., Berciu, D. and Diaconu, P. (1955) 'Şantierul arheologic Cernavoda', *Studii și Cercetări de Istorie Veche şi Arheologie* 6(1–2): 151–63.

Morris, C. and Peatfield, A. (2002) 'Feeling through the body: gesture in Cretan Bronze Age religion', in I. Hamilakis *et al.*, pp. 105–20.

Movşa, T.G. (1960) 'K voprosu o Tripolskih pogrebeniah s obriadom Tripopoljenia', *Materialî I Issledovania po Arheologii Yuozapada SSSR I Rumînskoi Narodnoi Republiki* 34(1): 59–76.

—— (1969) 'Ob antropomorphnoj plastike tripol'skoj kul'tury', *Sovetskaja Archeologija* 2: 15–34

—— (1973) 'Novi dani pro antropomorphny realistyčnuju plastyku Trypillja', *Archeologija* 2: 123–34.

Mulvey, L. (1975) 'Visual pleasure and narrative cinema', *Screen* 16(3): 6–18.

Nanoglou, S. (2001) 'Social and monumental space in Neolithic Thessaly, Greece', *European Journal of Archaeology* 4(3): 303–22.

Necrasov, O. and Cristescu, M. (1965) 'Unele probleme ale populării territoruloi patriei noastre în neolitic în lumina noilor cercetări', *Omagui lui P. Constantinescu*, pp. 67–70. Iaşi: Institut d Archéologie.

Necrasov, O. and Haimovici, S. (1962) 'Studiul resturilor de fauna neolitica (cultura Hamangia)

BIBLIOGRAPHY

descoperite in corsul sapaturilor de la Techirghiol', *Materiale şi Cercetări Arheologice* 8: 175–85.

Necrasov, O. and Stirbu, M. (1981) 'The chalcolithic palaeofauna from the settlements of Tîrpeşti (Precucuteni and Cucuteni A1–A2 Cultures)', in S. Marinescu-Bîlcu, *Tîrpeşti. From Prehistory to History in Eastern Romania*, pp. 174–80. Oxford: BAR.

Necrasov, O., Cristescu, M., Haas, N., Maximilian, C., Nicolăescu-Plopşor, A. (1959) 'Observaţii preliminare asupra materialului osteologic uman descoperit în 1956 la Cernavoda', *Materiale şi Cercetări Archeologica* 5: 8–12.

Nica, M. (1983) 'Obiectele de lemn descoperite în aşezarea neolitică timpurie de la Grădinile (jud. Olt)', *Arhivele Olteniei* 2: 39–48.

Nochlin, L. (1994) *The Body in Pieces: the Fragment as a Metaphor of Modernity*, London: Thames and Hudson.

—— (1991) 'Women, art and power', in N. Bryson, M.A. Holly and K. Moxey (eds), *Visual Theory*, pp. 13–46, London: Icon.

Norman, D. (1984) *Beyond a Portrait: Photographs {by} Dorothy Norman, Alfred Stieglitz : an Exhibition, Alfred Stieglitz Center, Philadelphia Museum of Art*, Millerton, NY: Aperture.

Nye, D.E. (1994) *American Technological Sublime*, Cambridge, MA: MIT Press.

Orphanidis, L. (1998) *Eisagoge Ste Neolithike Eidoloplastike: Notioanatolike Europe kai Anatolike Mesogeios*, Athens: Athens Academy.

Paley, M.D. (1986) *The Apocalyptic Sublime*, New Haven, CT: Yale University Press.

Papathanassopoulos, G. (ed.) (1996) *Neolithic Culture in Greece*, Athens: Goulandris Foundation.

Pappa, M. (1997a) 'Neolithikos oikismos Makrigialou Pierias. Ta apotelesmata tis meletis', *To Arkhaiologiko Ergo sti Makedonia kai Thraki* 10A: 239–77.

—— (1997b) 'Neolithiki egatastasi ston choro tis Diethnous Ekthesis Thessalonikis', *To Arkhaiologiko Ergo sti Makedonia kai Thraki* 7: 303–17.

Pappa, M. and Besios, M. (1999) 'The Makriyalos Project: rescue excavations at the Neolithic site of Makriyalos, Pieria, Northern Greece', in Halstead (ed.), pp. 108–20.

Park, R.W. (1998) 'Size counts: the miniature archaeology of childhood in Inuit societies', *Antiquity* 72: 269–81.

Passek, T.S. (1949) *Periodizatsia Tripolskikh Poselenii* (Materialy i Issledovaniia po Arkheologii S.S.S.R. 10). Moscow.

Păunescu, A., Şadurschi, P. and Chirica, V. (1976) *Repertoriul Arheological Judeţului Botoşani*. Volum 1 şi 2, Bucureşti: Editura Academiei Republicii Populare Romine.

Pavlović, M. (1990) 'The aesthetics of Neolithic figurines', in D. Srejović and N. Tasić (eds) *Vinča and its World*, pp. 33–5, Belgrade: Serbian Academy of Sciences.

Perlès, C. (1999) 'The distribution of magoulas in Eastern Thessaly', in Halstead, pp. 42–56.

—— (2001) *The Early Neolithic in Greece*, Cambridge: Cambridge University Press.

Petkov, N. (1934) 'Materiali za prouchvane na predistoricheskata epokha v Balgariya', *Bulgarska Akademiya na Naukite. Zvestiya na Arkheologischeskiya Institu* 8: 429–34.

Petrescu-Dîmboviţa, M. (1963) 'Die wichtigsten Ergebnisse der archäologischen Ausgrabungen in der neolithischen Siedlung von Truşeşti (Moldauu), *Praehistorische Zeitschrift* 41: 173–86.

—— (1999) 'Plastica', in M. Petrescu-Dîmboviţa *et al*., pp. 496–533.

Petrescu-Dîmboviţa, M., Florescu, M. and Florescu, A. (eds) (1999) *Truşeşti. Monografie Arheologică*, Bucureşti: Editura Academiei Române.

Petrescu-Dîmboviţa, M., Ursulescu, N., Monah, D. and Chirica, V. (eds) (1987) *La Civilisation de Cucuteni en Contexte Européen*, Iaşi.

Phelps, W.W. (1987) 'Prehistoric figurines from Corinth', *Hesperia* 56(3): 233–53.

Podborský, V. (1983) *K Metodice a Moznostem Studia Plastiky Lidu s Moravskou Keramikou*, Brno: Breneske Universita.

—— (1985) *Těšetice-Kyjovice 2. Fidurááplastika Lidu s Moravskou Malovanou Keramikou*, Brno: Universita J.E. Purkyn.

BIBLIOGRAPHY

Pogozheva, A.P. (1983) *Antroporpfnaia Plastica Tripolia*, Novosibirsk.
—— (1985) 'Die Statuetten der Tripolje-Kultur', *Beiträge zur Allgemeinen und Vergleichenden Archäologie* 7: 95–242.
Pollock, D. (1995) 'Masks and the semiotics of identity', *Journal of the Royal Anthropological Institute* 1: 581–97.
Popova, T.A. (1980) 'Antropomorphnaja plastika tripol'skogo poselenija Polivanov Jar na Dnestre', *Archeologičeskij Shornik Gosudarstvennogo Ermitaža* 21: 7–19.
Popovic, D.N. (2000) *Cultura Cucteni Faza A. Repertoriul Aşezărilor (1)*, Piatra-Neamţ: Editura Constantin Matasă.
Popovici, D.N., Buzdugan, C. and Alexoaie, I. (1992) 'Aşezarea cucteniană de la Balta lui Ciobanu (com. Roma, jud. Botoşani)', *Sovetskaja Archeologija* 9: 12–29.
Preston, J.J. (1982) 'New perspectives on mother worship', in J.J. Preston (ed.) *Mother Worship. Theme and Variation*, pp. 325–45, Charlotte, NC: University of North Carolina Press.
Price, J. and Shildrick, M. (eds) (1999) *Feminist Theory and the Body: a Reader*, Edinburgh: Edinburgh University Press.
Pultz, J. (1995) *Photography and the Body*, London: Weidenfeld and Nicholson.
Rathje, W.L. (1989) 'The three faces of garbage – measurements, perceptions, behavior', *Journal of Resource Management and Technology* 17(2): 61–5.
Rathje, W.L. and McCarthy, M. (1977) 'Regularity and variability in contemporary garbage', in S. South (ed.) *Research Strategies in Historical Archaeology*, pp. 261–86, New York: Academic Press.
Rathje, W.L. and Murphy, C. (1992) *Rubbish! The Archaeology of Garbage*, New York: Harper Collins.
Rathje, W.L., Hughes, W.W., Wilson, D.C., Tank, M.K., Archer, G.H., Hunt, R.G. and Jones, T.W. (1992) 'The archaeology of contemporary landfills', *American Antiquity* 57(3): 437–47.
Renfrew, C. (1986) 'The excavated areas', in Renfrew *et al.*, pp. 175–224.
Renfrew, C., Gimbutas, M. and Elster, E. (eds) (1986) *Excavations at Sitagroi. A Prehistoric Village in Northeast Greece. Volume 1*, Los Angeles: Institute of Archaeology, UCLA.
Rice, P.C. (1981) 'Prehistoric Venuses: symbols of motherhood or womanhood?', *Journal of Anthropological Research* 37: 402–14.
Rice, P.C. and Patterson, A.L. (1988) 'Anthropomorphs in cave art: an empirical assessment', *American Anthropologist* 90: 664–74.
Riley, D. (1999) 'Bodies, identities, feminisms', in Price and Shildrick, pp. 220–26.
Roberts, J. (1998) *The Art of Interruption: Realism, Photography and the Everyday*, New York: St Martin's Press.
Rogoff, I. (1998) 'Studying visual culture', in Mirzoeff, pp. 14–26.
Rosenblum, N. (1997) *A World History of Photography* (3rd edition), New York: Abbeville Press.
Rosenblum, R. (1997) 'An artist collects', in R.D. Mowdry (ed.) *Worlds within Worlds. The Richard Rosenblum Collection of Chinese Scholars Rocks*, pp. 109–22, Cambridge, MA: Harvard University Art Museums.
—— (2001) *Art of the Natural World*, Boston: Museum of Fine Arts.
Rugoff, R. (1997) 'Homeopathic strategies', in R. Rugoff and S. Stewart, *At the Threshold of the Visible: Miniscule and Small-scale Art*, pp. 11–72, New York: Independent Curators Incorporated.
—— (2000) 'Bubble worlds', in Small World, pp. 12–16.
Saetersdal, T. (1995) 'Behind the mask. An ethnoarchaeological study of Maconde material culture', unpublished MA thesis, University of Bergen.
Schickel, R. (1993) *The Disney Version: The Life, Times, Art and Commerce of Walt Disney*, New York: Ivan R. Dee.
Schilder, P. (1978) *The Image and Appearance of the Human Body: Studies in the Constructive Energies of the Psyche*, New York: International Universities Press.

BIBLIOGRAPHY

Scott, J.C. (1976) *The Moral Economy of the Peasant*, New Haven, CT: Yale University Press.
—— (1985) *Weapons of the Weak*, New Haven, CT: Yale University Press.
Sekula, A. (1999) 'Reading an archive: photography between labor and capital', in Evans and Hall, pp. 181–92.
Sergheev, G.P. (1961) 'Ranetripolskii klad u s. Karbuna', *Sovetskaya Arkeologiya* 54(1): 135–51.
Shelton, A. (1995) 'The chameleon body: power, mutilation and sexuality', in A. Shelton (ed.) *Fetishism: Visualising Power and Desire*, London: South Bank Centre.
Shildrick, M. and Price, J. (1999a) 'Openings on the body: a critical introduction', in Price and Shildrick, pp. 1–10.
—— (1999b) 'Woman as body: introduction', in Price and Shildrick, pp. 17–20.
Shohat, E. and Stam, R. (1998) 'Narrativizing visual culture. Towards a polycentric aesthetics', in Mirzeoff, pp. 27–49. Routledge.
Silverman, K. (1999) 'The subject', in Evans and Hall, pp. 340–55.
Šiškin, K.V. (1973) 'Z praktyky dešyfruvannja aerofotoznimkiv u arkheolohičnykh tsiljakh', *Arkheolohija* 10: 32–41.
Skafida, E. (n.d.) 'Symbols from the Aegean world: the case of late Neolithic figurines and house models from Thessay, Hellas', unpublished MS.
—— (1986) 'Analisi formale e contestuale degli idoli Neolitici del sito di Dimini in Thessalia', unpublished thesis, Università di Pisa.
—— (1992) 'Neolithika anthropomorpha eidolia tou Diminiou', in *Praktika Diethnous Synedriou gia tin Archea Thessalia, Sti Mnimi tou Dimitri R. Theochari, Dimosieumata tou Archeologikou Deltiou* 48: 166–79.
Skafida, L. and Toufexis, G. (1994) 'Figurines de la fin de l'époque néolithique en Thessalie, (Grèce Centrale)', in P. Retomanu and M. Alexianou (eds) *Relations Traco-Illuro-Helléniques, Actes du XIV Symposium National de Thracologie, Baile Herculane, 14–19 Septembre 1992*, pp. 12–24, Bucureşti: Institute Roumain de Thracologie.
Skakun, N.N. (1982) 'Orudiyata na truda ot neolitnoto selishte pri s. Durankulak Tolbuhinshi okrug (tipologichno-trasoloigicheski analiz)', *Arkheologiya* 24(1): 49–53.
Slobozeanu, H. (1959) 'Consideraţii asupra aşezărilor antice din jurul lacurilor Techirghiol şi Agigea', *Materiale* 5: 735–52.
Šmaglij, N.M., Duckin, V.P. and Zin'kovskij, K.V. (1973a) 'Raskopki tripol'skogo poslenija', *Arkheologičeskie Otkrytija 1972 Goda*: 349–50.
—— (1973b) 'Pro kompleksne vyvčennja trypil's'kykh poselen', *Arkheolohija* 10: 23–31.
Šmaglij, N.M., Zin'kovskaja, N.B., and Zin'kovskij, K.V. (1976) 'Issledovanija tripol'skogo poselenija v s. Majdanetskom', *Arkheologičeskie Otkrytija 1975 Goda*: 406–7.
—— (1977) 'Raskopki na tripol'skom poselenii v Majdanetskom', *Arkheologičeskie Otkrytija 1976 Goda*: 391.
—— (1981) 'Razkopki v Majdanetskom', *Arkheologičeskie Otkrytija* 1980 Goda: 323.
Small World (2000) *Small World. Dioramas in Contemporary Art*, San Diego, CA: Museum of Contemporary Art.
Sontag, S. (1973) *On Photography*, New York: Farrar, Strauss and Giroux.
Sorokin, V. (1994) *Civilizaţiile Eneolitice din Moldova*, Chişinău.
—— (1997) Consideraţii referitoare la aşezările fazei Cucuteni A – Tripolie B_1 din Ucraina şi Republica Moldova, *Memoria Antiuitatis* 21: 9–19.
Souvatzi, S. (2000) 'The archaeology of the household: examples from the Greek Neolithic', unpublished dissertation, Cambridge University.
—— (in press a) 'Household dynamics and variability in the Neolithic of Greece: the case for a bottom-up approach', in D.W. Bailey, A. Whittle and V. Cummings (eds) *Sedentism in the Neolithic*, Los Angeles, CA: UCLA.
—— (in press b) 'The identification of Neolithic households: unfeasible or just disregarded?', in

BIBLIOGRAPHY

R.C. Westgate, J. Whitley and N.R.E. Fisher (eds) *Building Communities: House, Settlement and Society in the Aegean and Beyond*, Athens: British School at Athens Studies.

Souvatzi, S. and Skafida, E. (2003) 'Neolithic communities and symbolic meaning: perceptions and expressions of social and symbolic structures at Dimini, Thessaly', in L. Nikolova (ed.) *Early Symbolic Systems for Communication in Southeast Europe*, pp. 429–41, Oxford: BAR International Series 1139.

Spurzheim, J.C. (1826) *Phrenology, in Connection with the Study of Physiognomy*, London: Treuttel, Wurtz and Richter.

Squiers, C. (ed.) (1990) *The Critical Image: Essays on Contemporary Photography*, Seattle, WA: Bay Press.

Stacey, J. (1999) 'Desperately seeking difference', in Evans and Hall, pp. 390–401.

Stam, R. (1989) *Subversive Pleasures: Bakhtin, Cultural Criticism and Film*, Baltimore, MD: Johns Hopkins University Press.

Stein, R.A. (1990) *The World in Miniature: Container Gardens and Dwellings in Far Eastern Religious Thought*, Stanford, CA: Stanford University Press.

Stevanović, M. (1997) 'The age of clay: the social dynamics of house destruction', *Journal of Anthropological Archaeology* 16: 334–95.

Stewart, S. (1993) *On Longing: Narratives of the Miniature, the Gigantic, the Souvenir, the Collection*, Durham, NC: Duke University Press.

—— (1997) 'At the threshold of the visible', in R. Rugoff and S. Stewart, *At the Threshold of the Visible*, pp. 73–85, New York: Independent Curators Incorporated.

Stieglitz, A. (1978) *Georgia O'Keeffe: a Portrait*, New York: Metropolitan Museum of Art.

Štiglits, M.S. (1971) 'Razvedki tripol'skikh pamjatnikov v rajone Umani', *Arkheologičeskie Otkrytija 1970 Goda*: 236–7.

Stokes, M. (1992) *The Aradesk Debate: Music and Musicians in Modern Turkey*, Oxford: Clarendon Press.

Stuart, J. (1997) 'Where Chinese art stands: a history of display pedestals for rocks', in R.D. Mowdry (ed.) *Worlds within Worlds. The Richard Rosenblum Collection of Chinese Scholars Rocks*, pp. 85–107, Cambridge, MA: Harvard University Art Museums.

Sweeney, S. and Hodder, I. (eds) (2002) *The Body*, Cambridge: Cambridge University Press.

Szarkowski, J. (1989) *Photography Until Now*, New York: Museum of Modern Art.

Székély, Z. (1965) 'Contributions à l'étude de développement du Néolithique dans la Transylvanie sud-orientale', *Atti del Vi Congresso Internazionale delle Scienze Preistoriche e Protoistoriche* B (2): 270–5.

—— (1988) Raport asupra săpăturilor noi de la Ariuşd (jud. Covasna) 1968–1965, *Studi şi Comunicări (Sfânta Gheorghe)* 17–18: 101–14.

Tagg, J. (1988) *The Burden of Representation: Essays on Photographs and Histories*, Basingstoke: Macmillan.

Talalay, L.E. (1987) 'Rethinking the function of clay figurine legs from Neolithic Greece: an argument by analogy', *American Journal of Archaeology* 91: 161–9.

—— (1993) *Deities, Dolls and Devices. Neolithic Figurines from Franchthi Cave, Greece*, Bloomington, IN: University of Indiana Press.

—— (1994) 'A feminist boomerang: the great goddess of Greek prehistory', *History* 6: 165–83.

Theocharis, D.R. (1967) *I Augi tis Thessalikis Proistorias*, Volos.

—— (1973) *Neolithic Greece*, Athens: National Bank of Greece.

Thompson, B.E. and Rathje, W.L. (1982) 'The Milwaukee Garbage Project: archaeology of household solid wastes', in R.S. Dickens (ed.) *Archaeology of Urban America*, pp. 339–461, New York: Academic Press.

Timms, R., Bradley, A. and Hayward, V. (eds) (1999) *Young British Art / The Saatchi Decade*, London: Booth-Clibborn.

BIBLIOGRAPHY

Todorova, H. (1974) 'Kultzene und Hausmodell aus Ovčarovo, Bez. Targovište', *Thracia* 3: 39–46.

—— (1983) 'Ausgrabungen in Durankulak, Bezirk Tolbuchin (Bulgarien) in der periode 1975–1981', *Nachrichten aus Niedersachsen Urgeschichte* 52: 77–89.

—— (1986) *Kamenno-mednata Epokha v Bulgariya. Peto Khilyadoletie predi Novata Era*, Sofia: Nauka i Izkustvo.

—— (ed.) (1989) *Durankulak, Band I*, Sofia: Bulgarian Academy of Sciences.

—— (ed.) (2002a) *Durankulak, Band II. Die Prähistorischen Gräberfelder von Durankulak, Teil 1 (Text)*, Berlin and Sofia: Deutsches Archäologisches Institut.

—— (2002b) 'Chronologie, horizontale Stratigraphie und Befunde', in H. Todorova (ed.), *Teil 1 (Text)*, pp. 35–52.

—— (2002c) 'Die archäologische Geschlechtsbestimmung', in H. Todorova (ed.), *Teil 1 (Text)*, pp. 53–60.

—— (2002d) 'Die Sepulkralkeramik aus den Gräbern von Durankulak', in H. Todorova (ed.), *Teil 1 (Text)*, pp. 81–116.

—— (2002e) (ed.) *Durankulak, Band II. Die Prähistorischen Gräberfelder von Durankulak, Teil 2 (Katalog)*, Berlin and Sofia: Deutsches Archäologisches Institut.

Todorova, H. and Vajsov, I. (1993) *Novo-kamennata Epokha v Bulgariya*, Sofia: Nauka i Izkustvo.

Todorova, H., Dimov, T., Boyadzhiev, Y., Dimitrov, K. and Avramova, M. (2002) 'Katalog der prähistorischen Gräber von Durankulak', in H. Todorova (ed.), *Teil 2 (Katalog)*, pp. 31–125.

Todorova, H., Vasilev, V., Janusevic, Z., Kovacheva, M. and Valev, P. (1983) *Ovcharovo (Razkopki i Prouchvania 9)*, Sofia: BAN.

Toufexis, G. (1996) 'House models', in Papathanassopoulos, pp. 161–2.

—— (1997) 'Recent Neolithic research in the eastern Thessalian plain, Greece', unpublished paper presented at the International Symposium, 'The Aegean in the Neolithic, Chalcolithic and Early Bronze Age', Urla-Izmir.

Toufexis, G. and Skafida, E. (1998) 'Neolithic house models from Thessaly, Greece', in *Proceedings of the UISPP Meetings, Forli*, pp. 339–46, Forli: ABACO.

Triantaphyllou, S. (1999) 'Prehistoric Makriyalos: a story from the fragments', in Halstead, pp. 128–35.

Tringham, R.E. and Conkey, M. (1998) 'Rethinking figurines: a critical view from archaeology of Gimbutas, the 'Goddess' and popular culture', in L. Goodison and C. Morris (eds) *Ancient Goddesses. Myths and the Evidence*, pp. 22–45, Madison, WI: University of Wisconsin Press.

Tringham, R.E. and Krstić, D. (1990) *Selevac: A Prehistoric Village in Yugslavia* (Monumenta Archaeologica 15), Los Angeles: Cotsen Institute of Archaeology, UCLA.

Tringham, R.E. and Stevanović, M. (1990) 'Field research', in Tringham and Krstić, pp. 57–214.

Tsuneki, A. (1987) 'A reconsideration of Spondylus shell rings from Agia Sofia magoula, Greece', *Bulletin of the Ancient Orient Museum* 9: 1–15.

—— (1989) 'The manufacture of *spondylus* shell objects at Neolithic Dimini, Greece', *Orient* 25: 1–21.

Tsvek, E. (1996) 'Structure of the Eastern-Tripolye culture', in G. Dumitroaia, and D. Monah (eds) *Cucuteni Aujourd hui. 110 Ans depuis la Découverte en 1884 du Site Éponyme*, pp. 89–115, Piatra-Neamţ: Muzeul de Istorie Piatra-Neamţ.

Tuan, Y.-F. (1997) 'Disneyland: its place in world culture', in Marling, pp. 191–8.

Twain, R. (2002) 'Physiognomy, phrenology and the temporality of the body', *Body and Society* 8(1): 67–88.

Ucko, P. (1962) 'The interpretation of prehistoric anthropomorphic figurines', *Journal of the Royal Anthropological Institute* 92: 38–54.

—— (1968) *Anthropomorphic Figurines of Predynastic Egypt and Neolithic Crete, with Comparative Material from the Prehistoric Near East*, London: Andrew Szmidla.

—— (1996) 'Mother, are you there?', *Cambridge Archaeological Journal* 6: 300–4.

BIBLIOGRAPHY

Ursachi, V. (1991) 'Le dépôt d'objets de parure énéolithique de Brad, com. Negri, dép. De Bacău', in V. Chirica and D. Monah (eds), *Le Paléolithiue et le Néolithique de la Roumanie en Contexte Européen*, pp. 335–86, Iaşi: Biblioteca Archaeologica Iasseiensis.

—— (1992) 'Depozitul de obiecte de podoabă eneolitice de la Brad, com. Negri, jud. Bacău', *Carpica* 23(2): 51–104.

Ursulescu, N. (1977) 'Exploatarea sării din saramură în neoliticul timpuriu, în lumina descoperirilor de la Solca (jud. Suceava)', *Studii şi Cercetări de Istorie Veche şi Arheologie* 28(3): 3.

Vajsov, I. (1984) 'Antropomorphniya plastika iz praistoricheskogo poseleniya Kurilo-Kremenitsa Sophiskogo okruga', *Studia Praehistorica* 10: 103–41.

—— (1987) 'Pogrebeniya s idoli ot praistoricheskiya nekropol kraj s. Durankulak, Tolbukhinski okrug', *Dobrudzha* 4: 77–82.

—— (1990) 'La sculpture anthropomorphe du site néolithique d'Oussoé près du village d'Asparoukhovo, départment de Varna', *Studia Praehistorica* 10: 103–41.

—— (1992a) 'Anthropomorphe Plastik aus dem prähistorischen Gräberfeld bei Durankulak', *Studia Praehistorica* 11–12: 95–113.

—— (1992b) 'Antropomorphnata plastika na kulturata Hamandzhiya', *Dobrudzha* 9: 35–71.

—— (2002) 'Die Idole aus den Gräberfeldern aus Durankulak', in H. Todorova (ed.), *Teil 1 (Text)* pp. 257–66.

van Andel, T.H., Gallis, K. and Toufexis, G. (1995) 'Early Neolithic farming in a Thessalian river landscape', in J. Lewin, M.G. Macklin and J.C. Woodward (eds) *Mediterranean Quaternary River Environments*, pp. 131–43, Rotterdam: Balkema.

Vitelli, K.D. (1989) 'Were pots first made for foods? Some doubts from Franchthi?', *World Archaeology* 21: 17–29.

—— (1993) *Franchthi Neolithic Pottery. Volume 1. Classification and Ceramic Phases 1 and 2*, Bloomington, IN: University of Indiana Press.

—— (1995) 'Pots, potters, and the shaping of Greek Neolithic society', in W. Barnett and J. Hoopes (eds) *The Emergence of Pottery*, pp. 55–64, Washington, DC: Smithsonian Institute.

Voigt, M.M. (2000) 'Çatal Höyük in context: ritual at early Neolithic sites in central and eastern Turkey', in I. Kuijt (ed.) *Life in Neolithic Farming Communities: Social Organization, Identity and Differentiation*, pp. 253–93, New York: Plenum.

Volschi, W. and Irimia, M. (1968) 'Descoperiri arheologice la Mangalia şi Limanu, aparţinînd culturii Hamangia', *Pontica* 1: 45–87.

Von Hagens, G. and Whalley, A. (2002) *Bodyworlds. The Anatomical Exhibition of Real Human Bodies*, Heidelberg: Institut für Plastination.

Wace, A.J.B. and Thompson, M.S. (1912) *Prehistoric Thessaly*, Cambridge: Cambridge University Press.

Warner, M. (1976) *Alone of All Her Sex: The Myth and the Cult of the Virgin Mary*, New York: Alfred Knopf.

Watney, S. (1999) 'On the institutions of photography', in Evans and Hall, pp. 187–97.

Webb, P. (1975) *The Erotic Arts*, London: Secker and Warburg.

Weisshaar, H.J. (1989) *Die Deutschen Ausgrabungen auf der Pevkakia-Magula in Thessalien, I. Das späte Neolithikum und das Chalkolithikum*, Bonn: BAM.

Whitelaw, T. (1991) 'Variability in the social organisation of community space among foragers', in C. Gamble and W. Boismier (eds) *Ethnoarchaeological Approaches to Mobile Campsites: Hunter-Gatherer and Pastoralist Case Studies*, pp. 134–188, Ann Arbor, MI: International Monographs in Prehistory.

—— (1997) 'Order without architecture: functional, social and symbolic dimensions in hunter-gatherer settlement organization', in M. Parker Pearson and C. Richards (eds) *Architecture and Order: Approaches to Social Space*, pp. 217–43, London: Routledge.

Whittle, A. (1996) *Europe in the Neolithic: the Creation of New Worlds*, Cambridge: Cambridge University Press.

BIBLIOGRAPHY

Wijnen, M. (1981) 'The Early Neolithic I settlement at Sesklo: an early farming community in Thessaly, Greece', unpublished dissertation, Universitaire Pers Leiden.

Wilton, A. (1980) *Turner and the Sublime*, London: British Museum Press.

Yates, T. (1993) 'Frameworks for an archaeology of the body', in C. Tilley (ed.) *Interpretive Archaeology*, pp. 31–72, Oxford: Berg.

Zaharia, N., Petrescu-Dîmbovița, M. and Zaharia, E. (1970) Aşezări din Moldova de la Paleolithic pînă în Seculul al XVIII-lea, *Bucureşti: Editura Academiei Republicii Populare Romine.*

Zbenović, V.G. (1996) 'The Tripolye culture: centenary of research', *Journal of World Prehistory* 10: 199–241.

Zhao, Q. (1997) *Penjing: Worlds of Wonderment. A Journey Exploring an Ancient Chinese Art and its History, Cultural Background and Aesthetics* (trans. Albert), Athens, GA: Venus.

Zukin, S. (1991) *Landscapes of Power: from Detroit to Disney World*, Berkeley, CA: University of California Press.

Zvelebil, M. (ed.) (1986) *Hunters in Transition: Mesolithic Societies of Temperate Eurasia and their Transition to Farming.* Cambridge: Cambridge University Press.

INDEX

absence 64, 65, 71, 85–6; of body parts 71, 72, 81, 101
abstraction 22, 32–4, 48, 64, 72, 85, 154, 201
Achilleion 129–30, 147–9, 155, 156, 158, 166, 178, 180, 181, 195, 215n41, 215n51, figs 7.1, 7.5, 7.7, 7.12, 8.1
Agee, W. 184–6, 198
Agigea 55, fig. 3.6
Agios Georgios 157, fig. 7.12
Agios Petros 176
agriculture: consequences of 9; scales of 9, 59
ambiguities 187, 190–5; *see also* figurines, paradoxes
anatomical dolls 70–72, 81, fig. 4.3
ancestors 20–1, 90, 115, 198
animal: bone in burials 7; figurines 9, 110, 111; human relationships to 9, 112
anthropomorphism 25, 29, 65, 66–87
Arapi 214n13, 215n50, fig. 7.12
architectural models 28, 29, 207n1; *see also* house models
architecture *see* settlement
Argissa 176, 214n13, 215n50, fig. 7.12
Ariuşd 103, 213n70, fig. 5.12
Ashkin, M. 33–4, 202, fig. 2.5; *No. 43* (1996) 33, fig. 2.5
Atsipadhes Korakias 19
Ayia Sofia 176, 215n51, fig. 7.12

Bachelard, G. 202, 207n4, 207n5
Baia-Goloviţa 50, 53, 55, 62, 63, figs 3.6, 3.9–3.10
Bakhtin, M. 193, 216n4
Balchik fig. 3.6
Balta lui Ciobanu 105
Barbie-Doll 73–5, 84, 143, 200, fig. 4.4
Barnardo, T. 127, 129, 134

Barnovo 213n70
Barthes, R. 131; *see also punctum*
Baudrillard, J. 137, 145, 200
Beck, M. 205n3
Bei 214n6, 214n7, figs 7.2, 7.12
Berciu, D. 49, 50, 51
Berezkovskaya GES 105, fig. 5.12
Bellmer, H. 75, 76, 210n4, fig. 4.5; *Les Yeux de la Poupée* fig. 4.5
Benjamin, W. 131
Bezil 215n35, figs 7.3, 7.12
Biehl, P. 14, 22, fig 1.3
Bird Goddess 27, 149
birth 165
Birth Giving Goddess 149, 181
Bisler 214n15, fig. 7.12
Blessed Art Thou Among Women 68–70, fig. 4.2
Blind Popcorn 134
blockage 121, 184–6, 195
Bodeşti fig. 5.12
body 20, 39, 65, 66–87, 102, 118, 122–46, 152, 153, 177, 186–7, 191–5, 196, 197–204, 213n10; bound 161–2, 163, 164, 179, 198; constructed 139–40; cropped 80, 81, 152, 180, 186; defined 139–40; differences 75, 100, 141, 142, 144, 159; fragmented 81; and gesture 19; and identity 130, 139–42; morphology 19, 146; in the Neolithic 146; parts 47, 65, 71, 72, 79, 80–3, 101, 120–1, 150, 153, 154, 158–64, 179, 186, 188, 202; and performance 77, 140–1; and scale 28–9, 84; sexual 72, 75, 79, 81, 82–3, 120, 142, 144, 150, 153, 159–6, 179, 189, 191–5; similarities 64, 144, 199; surface 94, 97, 98, 118, 119, 121, 141, 146, 158, 159, 201; *see also* breasts, burial, faces, heads, intimacy, penis, pubis

INDEX

Bonaparte, Napoleon 123–6, 129, 182–3
  fig. 6.2; compared to Charlemagne 125;
  compared to Hannibal 125
*Bonaparte, Premier Consul, Fraichissant le Grand
  Saint-Bernard, 20 mai 1800* 123–6, 127,
  130, 131, 132, 213n4, fig. 6.2
bondage 161–2, 163, 164, 165, 179
bonsai 29–32, 207n2
books: miniature 29, fig 2.2
boundaries 191, 198; architectural 11, 103,
  105, 112, 113, 168, 174–5, 197, 201
Brad 116, fig. 5.12
breasts 61, 62, 63, 65, 82, 85, 88, 93, 95, 96,
  97, 98, 99, 100, 120, 135, 151, 152, 153,
  154, 159, 179, 186, 190, fig. 7.7
Brînzeni 105, 116, fig. 5.12
Bronze Age Crete 19
built environment *see* settlement
burial 7–8; cemetery 8, 11, 176, 201;
  cenotaph 8, 57, 62; cremation 176;
  Cucuteni/Tripolye 112–4; intra-village 7;
  grave-goods 8; Hamangia 56–8, links to
  settlement 7, 8; mortuary ritual 8, 11;
  social and political significance of 8, 58,
  116; Thessalian 174, 175, 176–7; *see also*
  human bone
Burke, E. 133; *see also* sublime
Butler, J. 140–1, 142
buttocks 93, 95, 96, 97, 99, 120, 152, 161,
  163

Cacica 103
camps 53
Căpaevka 99, fig. 5.12
Cărbuna fig. 5.12
car models 28, 9
carnival (and carnivalesque) 190–5, 196, 198,
  fig. 8.5
cartes-de-visite 78, 80, 126, 127
caves 54
Ceamurlia de Jos 53, 55, 209n7, figs 3.6–3.7
cemeteries *see* burial
cenotaphs *see* burial
ceramics 5–6, 130, 197; experimental phase
  5; hora-pots fig. 5.2; production 103
Cernatul de Sus 115
Cernavoda 45, 56–7, 62, 177, 209n12,
  209n13, figs 3.1–3.3, 3.6; *The Seated
  Woman* 45, 50, 64, 207n2; fig. 3.1; *The
  Thinker* 45–6, 50, 51, 64, 209n2; fig. 3.1
Cerniahovo 115

Chaironeia 215n47
Chapman, J. 91, 102, 111–112, 116, 117,
  178
Chara 163
Childe, V.G. 198, 205n10
A Christmas Scene 68, 70
collage 188–9
compression 30, 32, 201
Conkey, M. 23, 205n3
Conroy, L. 19
copla 193–4, 195
copper 7, 8, 55, 60, 108, 109, 116, 212n56
Corlăteni 105, fig. 5.12
The Coronation of Napoleon and Josephine
  (1805–07) 125
corporeality 118, 121, 139–41, 142–3, 146,
  177, 180, 195, 197–204; differences 48;
  similarities 48
Costeşti-Baia 115, figs 5.10, 5.12
Crannon 215n47
Criş Culture 205n7
cropping 80, 81, 152, 184, 202
Cuconeştii Vechi 105, fig. 5.12
Cucuteni 103, 213n70, fig. 5.12
Cucuteni Culture *see* Cucuteni/Tripolye
Cucuteni/Tripolye 88–121; built
  environment 103–14, 212n54, 212n64;
  burial 114–6, 117; Cucuteni A/Tripolye
  B1 94–6, 106, 108–9, figs 5.5–5.8;
  Cucuteni A-B/Tripolye B2 97–8;
  Cucuteni B/Tripolye C1 98–100, figs
  5.9–5.11; figurines 88–102, 109–112,
  118–21, 199, fig. 5.1; geography and
  chronology 92, 103, 212n51, 212n52;
  historiography 103; PreCucuteni/Tripolye
  A 51, 91, 92–3, 106, figs 5.4–5.5;
cult scene 27, 90

Dada 188; *see also* Höch, H.
David, Jacques-Louis 123–6, fig. 6.2;
  *Bonaparte, Premier Consul, Fraichissant le
  Grand Saint-Bernard, 20 mai 1800* 123–5,
  127, 130, 131, 132, 213n4, fig. 6.2; *The
  Coronation of Napoleon and Josephine*
  (1805–07) 125; *Oath of the Horiatii* (1785)
  125
Dealul Bulgarului 90–1, fig. 5.12
death *see* burial
Debord, G. 137, 145
Delong, A. 36, 37–8, fig. 2.6
Dentalium 56, 57, 58, 59, 61

INDEX

Destitute Pea-Pickers in California; a 32-Year Old Mother of Seven Children (1936) 135–7, 185, fig. 6.5

diarying 10

differences 48

Dimini 166, 168–9, 172, 174, 176, fig. 7.12

Diodion 215n35, fig. 7.12

dioramas 40, 137

Disney, W. 35, 207n7, 208n9

Disneyland 35–6, 40–1, 208n8, 208n17; *Snow White's Dangerous Adventure* 40–1; *see also* Disney, W.

distortions 186–8

Doboşeni 115, fig. 5.12

Dobrovody 105

dolls 67–77, 210n1; and art 75–7; Barbie Doll 73–5, fig. 4.4; and empowerment 70–2; hierarchies of power and 68–70, 72; and identity 72–5; police interviews with 70–2, fig. 4.3; sex 40

Domeniko 157, fig. 7.12

domestication: consequences of 9; of the human 146; of plants and animals 8

Domokos 156

Doner, M. Oka 76, 77

Doxaras 214n7, fig. 7.12

Dragatsi 158, fig. 7.12

Drăguşeni 91, 100, 103, 105, 109, 112, 114, 116, 212n50, 213n70, figs 5.7, 5.12

Druţa 105, fig. 5.12

Dudeşti Culture 51

Dumeşti 88–91, 120, 121, figs 5.1, 5.12

Dumitroaia, G. 91

Durankulak 51, 53, 57–8, 60–1, 63, 177, 209n8, 209n12, figs 3.6, 3.8

Duruitoarea Nouă 105

Ellis, L. 103

Evans, W. 139, 184–6, 195, 198, fig. 8.3; *Squeakie Burroughs* (1936) 184, fig. 8.3

faces 79, 81, 92, 93, 94, 97, 98, 99, 120, 122, 135, 147–9, 155, 156, 159, 191, 194; absence of representation 64, 71, 86, 88, 96

Farm Security Administration (FSA) 138–9, 185

fertility 51, 160, 164–6

figurines: acrolithic 155, fig. 7.4; anecdotal explanation of 12, 84, 92; breakage and fragmentation 20, 111–2, 151, 152, 178, 212n62; Bronze Age 19; criticism of current interpretations 12, 199; definitions of 15; depositional contexts of 60–3, 109–12; differences 88–90; empirical approach to 13, 14, 15; Cucuteni/Tripolye Cultures 88–121; Hamangia Culture 45–51, figs 3.1–3.5; historiography of research 12–24, 49–51, 100–102, 149–55; 210n4; intentional deposition of 23; Iron Age Greek 18; male 18, 162; materials 50, 150, 155, 187; meaning 197, 198–9; paradoxes of 42, 49, 161, 164, 166, 180, 194, 200, 201; as philosophies 84–5, 86, 195, 196, 200, 202; proposed functions 12; rhetoric of 12–13; sexless 19, 207n23; sexualities of 164–6, 206n15; similarities 90, 118–9, 146; Thessalian 147–66, 177–80; Upper Palaeolithic 16, 20; votives 20, 198

flora *see* Neolithic, Balkan, economy

Floresty fig. 5.12

Franchthi Cave 152

Frog Goddess 149

Fumuşica 90, 115, 213n70, figs 5.2, 5.12

Fur (Sudan) 16; *Bora Fatta* 16

furniture: miniature 26–7, 93, 157

Galeni 215n49

Gallis, K 150, 152, 170

Gardner, A. 127; *Hanging at Washington Arsenal: Hooded Bodies of the Four Conspirators; Crowd Departing, Washington, D.C.* (1865) fig. 6.3; *Lewis Payne, a Conspirator, in Sweater, Seated and Manacled* (1865) fig. 6.4

Gatens, M. 140–1, 200

gaze 132, 143–4, 145, 189

genitalia 75, 82, 159, 179, 181, 191, 202; *see also* breasts, labia, penis, pubis, sexuality

Ghelăieşti 91, 116, figs 5.3, 5.10–5.12

Gheorghiu, D. 101–2, 211n45, 212n47

Gilmore, D. 190–5, 198

Gimbutas, Marija 12, 16, 27, 51, 102, 122, 149–50, 151, 154, 181, 208n13, 214n17

Girov 115, fig. 5.12

Glavăvăneştii Veche fig. 5.12

Glybočok 213n67

gold 7, 8, 9

Gradeshnitsa-Krivodol Culture: figurines from 14, 22, fig. 1.3

Grădinile: wooden bowl from 6n7

238

INDEX

Grădiştea-Coslogeni 50, fig. 3.6
grave-goods *see* burial
Grenovka 91, fig. 5.12
Grosz, E. 140
Gumelniţa Culture 199, 203
Gura Dobrogei 53, fig. 3.6

Haaland, G. and R. 16, 18, 205n13, 206n20, 207n24
Hăbăşeşti 103, 105, 115, 212n50, 213n70, fig. 5.12
Hagens, G. von 132–3
hair 98, 101, 123, 151, 154, 155, 158–9, 214n22, figs 7.3, 7.6
Hall, E. 39
Halstead, P. 171
Hamangia Culture: 45–65, fig. 3.6; burials 56–8, 60–1, 62; economy 58–9; figurines of 13, 45–51, 60–4, 72, 119, 199, 201; fig. 1.2; material culture 55, 56; settlement 53–5, 62–3
Hanging at Washington Arsenal: Hooded Bodies of the Four Conspirators; Crowd Departing, Washington, D.C. (1865) fig. 6.3
Hangu-Chiriţeni 105, fig. 5.12
Harvey, M. 134; *Myra* 134
Haşotti, P. 49
Hatzimissiotiki 215n50
heads 81–2, 92–3, 96, 97, 98, 120–1, 147–9, 155, 176, 188, 202; absence of 65, 151; significance 64
Heartfield, J. 188–9
Hirşova fig. 3.6
Hirst, D. 134; *A Thousand Years* 134; *This Little Piggy Went to Market, This Little Piggy Went Home* 134
Höch, H. 188–90, 195; *Das schöne Mädchen* (1920) 188–90, 195, fig. 8.4
Hodder, I. 215n52
Hourmouziadis, G. 150, 151, 154, 179, 180
households 5, 11, 114, 118, 169, 170, 186, 198; activities 9; identities 7, 142
house models 6, 170–1, 178, 215n47
houses 5, 11, 170
human: body as essential scale 28; definitions of being 16, 75, 76, 118, 142, 153, 196, 199–201
human bone 7, 177; crania 56, 114, 115, 116, 209n15; *see also* burial
human form: differences 75; representation of 15, 19, 22, 24; *see also* body

Hussein, S.: representations of 127, 129, 130, 132, 134

Iablona 105, fig. 5.12
identities 10, 70, 77, 78, 81, 84, 85, 120, 146, 152, 159, 164, 166, 170, 180, 186, 189, 191, 195, 201; and the body 130, 139–42; construction 73, 75, 119, 140–2; 145; and dolls 72–5, 77; expression of 11, 59, 62, 64, 116; household 7; individual 7, 16, 119, 146, 175; village 7, 113, 175
ideologies 138, 139
illusion 137
imagery: political currency of 138–9; sexual and gendered 16, 18, 19; uses of 16; *see also* representation
inferences 32
intimacy 38–9, 84
Iron Age Greece 18

jewellery 7, 39, 55, 59, 99, 101, 169, 172

Kalochori 214n16
Karakušany 97, 98, fig. 5.12
Karamourlar 215n47, fig. 7.12
Karditsa 214n12
Käsebier, G. 68, 70, fig. 4.2; *Blessed Art Thou Among Women* (1899) 68–70, fig. 4.2; *A Christmas* Scene (1904) 68, 70; *Manger* (1903) 68
Kelly, M. 189
Kertész, A. 186–8, 195
Klanke, J. 189
Kočeržincy 99, figs 5.9, 5.12
Kodzhaderman-Gumelniţa-Karanovo VI Culture 216n1
Kokkinidou, D. 152–3, 154, 164
Kolodistoe 213n70
Kolomijščina 105, 115, 213n70, fig. 5.12
Košilovcy 100, fig. 5.12
Koutsaki 214n6, fig. 7.12
Koutsouro 214n22, figs 7.11, 7.12
Krinički 98, fig. 5.12
Kruger, B. 189
Kunisovcy 99, fig. 5.12
Kyriaki fig. 7.9

labia 48, 82, 93, 96, 98, 99, 120, 160–2, 163, 165, 179, 181, figs 7.8, 7.9, 8.1
Lacan, J. 82–3, 145
La Izvor 54, fig. 3.6

239

INDEX

landscapes: miniature 33
Langdon, S. 18
Lange, D. 135–7, 138, 139, 185, fig. 6.5;
 *Destitute Pea-Pickers in California; a
 32-Year Old Mother of Seven Children* (1936)
 135–7, fig. 6.5
Larga Jijia 90, fig. 5.12
Larisa 162, fig. 7.10
Lesure, R. 15, 208n16
Let Us Now Praise Famous Men 185–6, 195
*Lewis Payne, a Conspirator, in Sweater, Seated
 and Manacled* (1865) fig. 6.4
Limanu 55, 58, 209n12, fig. 3.6
Lincoln, A.: assassins 127–9, 132, 134, figs
 6.3, 6.4
looking *see* gaze, spectation
Luka Ustinskaia 115
Luka Vrublevckaya 91, 93, 115, fig. 5.12
Lunca 103, fig. 5.12

McDermott, L. 16, fig. 1.4
MacLeish, A. 138
Magala 98 fig. 5.12
Magoulitsa 215n33, fig. 7.12
Majdanets'ke 114
Makriyalos 166, 173–5, fig. 7.12
Makrychori 214n16, fig. 7.12
Malnaş 103, fig. 5.12
Mandra 215n50, 215n51, fig. 7.12
Manet, E. 81; *A Bar at the Folies-Bergère*
 (1882) 81; *The Beer Server* (1878–9) 81;
 Nana (1877) 81;
Mangalia 209n12, fig. 3.6
Manger (1903) 68
Mantu, M. 91
Mapplethorpe, R. 144
Marangou, C. 27, 91–2, 102, 152
Marcus, J. 20–22, fig. 1.5
Margarita 214n6
Mărgineni 109, 115, fig. 5.12
Marinescu-Bîlcu, S. 50, 100, 101, 102, 106,
 112, 118, 211n46
masks 23, 122, 147–9, 156, 194
Mataranga Karditsas 162
material culture 5–6, 197; expressive 6–7, 10
materiality 188; of the Neolithic 5
Mavrachades 215n47, 158
Maxim-Alaiba, R. 90
Medgidia Cocoaşa 55, 63, 209n5, fig. 3.6
Medgidia-Satu Nou 50, 53, 54, 55, 209n5,
 fig. 3.6

Medvezha 98, fig. 5.12
Megali kai Mikri 215n36, fig. 7.12
Megalo Gefyri 215n42, fig. 7.12
Meskell, L. 205n13, 206n24
metals *see* copper, gold
Mezil 159, 214n6, 214n7, 214n11, 215n34,
 fig. 7.12
Mihoveni fig. 5.12
miniaturisation 23, 24, 26–44, 64, 81, 154,
 201, 202, 210n1; effects of 33–6, 68,
 74–5, 85, 213n2; and empowerment 33,
 35, 70–2, 131, 195; versus models 29–30,
 32; narcotic effect 207n5; paradoxes of 33,
 83, 84, 86, 135, 195
Mirzoeff, N. 137
Mitchell, W.T.J. 185
model trains 28
models 71; versus miniatures 29, 32
Monah, D. 91, 100, 101
Morris, C. 19
mortuary ritual *see* burial
Mother Goddess 12, 16, 19, 198, 206n17,
 206n21, 207n24; relationship to feminist
 archaeology 12, 205–6n13
Mulvey, L. 143, 144
Myra 134
Myrrini 215n47

nano-art 29
Nea Nikomedia 176, fig. 7.12
Neblivka 213n67
Neolithic, Balkan: built environment 4–5;
 ceramics 5; defined 3–11; economy 8–10;
 engagement with landscape 4–5, 10;
 materiality of 5; pit features 4, 205n5;
 socio-politics 10–11
Neo Monastiri 214n12
Nessonis 214n14, 215n33, fig. 7.12
Nezvisko 105, 115, fig. 5.12
Nikaia 215n47, fig. 7.12
Nikolaidou, M. 152–3, 154, 164
Nochlin, L. 81, 189

Oath of the Horiatii (1785) 125
Oaxaca 20–22, 24, 206n25, 207n26, fig. 1.5
Ofili, C. 134; *Blind Popcorn* 134
O'Keeffe, G. 78–80, fig. 4.6
Omorphochori 215n33
Opovo 13, 23
Orenia figs 7.3, 7.8
orgasm 165

240

INDEX

Orphanidis, L. 150, 152, 153–4, 155, 159, 199

other worlds 19–20, 34–6, 38, 201

Otzaki 163, 215n51, fig. 7.12

Ovcharovo 26–8, 43, 208n18

Ozarintz 115

Paliambela 158, 214n20, 215n50, fig. 7.12

Panagou 159, 163, 215n33, fig. 7.12

pathognomy 81–2

Pavloch 213n70, fig. 5.12

Pavlović, M. 22

peak sanctuaries 19–20, 22

Peatfield, A. 19

Pefkakia 215n50, fig. 7.12

penis 48, 83, 88, 90, 93, 98, 99, 120, 135, 151, 152, 155, 159, 162–4, 165, 179, figs 5.1, 7.10, 7.11

penjing 29–32

Perlès, C. 151, 178–9, 214n10, 216n54

Petreny fig. 5.12

Petrescu-Dîmboviţa, M. 101, 102

Petrino 214n6

phallus *see* penis

Phelps, W. 206n14

photography 70, 77–80, 138–9, 143, 201; and authority 126–7, 130, 187, 195; daguerretypes 77; of dolls 75; origins of 213n3; Pictorialist 68, 70; Photo-Succession 68; as truth 126–9; *see also cartes-de-visite*

phrenology 81–2

physiognomy 81–2

pits 4, 23, 53, 55, 56, 63, 105, 111, 112, 173, 205n5

plants *see* Neolithic, Balkan, economy

Plateia Magoula Zarkou 170, 176, 177, 178, 179, 208n18, 215n50, figs 7.12, 7.13

Platykambos 214n11

Poduri 91, 114, 115, 210n1, 213n66, 213n70, figs 5.6, 5.12

Pogozheva, A. 100

Polivanov Jar 97, 98, 213n70, fig. 5.12

Popovici, D. 113

pornography 80

portraits 77–80, 126, 129

pots: hora 90, 91; miniature 27, 57, 93, 108, 110, 111

potters 5

pottery *see* ceramics

power relationships 86; and children 68, 72, 73

PreCucuteni Culture *see* Cucuteni/Tripolye

pregnancy: representation of 16, 61, 160, 162, 165, fig. 1.4

Pregnant Goddess 149

Prodromos 157, 176, 215n33, 215n34, fig. 7.12

Psili Rachi 214n7, 215n33, fig. 7.12

pubis 62, 96, 98, 99, 120, 152, 159–62, 165, figs 7.8, 7.9

Pultz, J. 136

punctum 131–2, 201, 213n5

Putineşti 105, fig. 5.12

Pyrassos 158, fig. 7.12

Quinn, M. 132, 133, 134, 198; *Self* (1991) 132, 133, 134; *Self Conscious* 132; *Shithead* 132, 133

Rachmani 176, 178, 214n13, 214n15, figs 7.4, 7.12

Racovăt 97, 98, 103

Răuceşti fig. 5.12

regimes of truth 121, 125–9, 130

Renfrew, C. 122

repetition 48; of body form 64, 100, 140–1, 142, 153–4, 155, 159, 198, 199–200, 214n17

representation 19, 22, 23, 65, 121, 130, 138, 154, 179, 183–4, 186, 187, 193; abstract 32; authority of 126; serial 80; of women 16–22, 68, 70, 75, 76, 88–91; *see also* absence, Barbie Doll, regimes of truth, simulacrum, spectacle

residence 10

rhetoric of the visual 121, 122–46, 190, 194, 197

ritual 90, 102, 111–2; dances 90, 91; scenes 20–2, 27, 55, 63

Roidies fig. 7.2

rubbish 111–2

Sabatinovka 102, 212n49, fig. 5.12

Sarliki 163

scale 28–9, 68, 83–4, 86; choice of 33, 40, 85, 71; paradox of multiple 42

Scânteia 91, 115, 213n70, fig. 5.12

Scerbanevski 115

scholars' rocks 29–32

INDEX

Das schöne Mädchen (1920) 188–90, 195, fig. 8.4

scopophilia 131–2, 134

The Seated Woman 45, 50, 64, 209n2; fig. 3.1

Selevac 66–7, 85–6

Self (1991) 132, 133, 134

Self Conscious 132

Sesklo 150, 157, 166, 168, 169, 172–3, 174, 176, 215n47, fig. 7.12

sets: of figurines 88–91, 178; of objects 208n18

settlement: cave 172–4; Cucuteni/Tripolye 103–14; flat sites 172–4; Hamangia 53–5; Neolithic 4–5; permanence of 4, 171–2; social and political significance of 5, 55, 112–4, 117, 169, 175, 197; tells 4, 5, 168–72, 205n6, 213n72; Thessalian 4, 168–75

sexuality 152, 179, 189, 195; definitions of 15; disruption 188–90; inversions 191; representations of 15, 61, 66, 75, 76, 82–3, 85, 120, 142, 153, 159–66, 181–2, 188–9, 191–5, 201

shell *see Spondylus gaederopus*; *Dentalium*; *Unio pictorum*

Sherman, C. 75, 76, 77, 189, 198, 200 *Untitled* (1992)

ship models 28, 29

Shithead 132, 133

Silverman, K. 82–3

similarities 48, 51

simulacrum 137, 200, 201, 202

Sipency 98, fig. 5.12

Sitagroi 122–3, fig. 6.1; figurines from 122–3, 130, 135, fig. 6.1

Sitochoro 163, 215n47, fig. 7.12

size: paradox of 42

size reduction *see* scale

Skafida 150, 151, 152

skulls *see* human bone

Snake Goddess 102, 149

Snow Storm: Hannibal and his Army Crossing the Alps (1812) 182–4, fig. 8.2

Snow White's Dangerous Adventure 40–1

Sofades 163, 214n12

Solca 103, fig. 5.12

Solonceni 115, fig. 5.12

Soroki 97

Soufli Magoula 176, 177, 214n6, 214n7, 214n11, fig. 7.12

spectacle 137–8

spectation 165; politics of 16, 143–4; *see also* gaze

spectator(s) 34, 38, 49, 76, 84, 126, 133, 134, 137, 143, 159, 161, 164, 187, 189, 195, 201; and miniaturism 33

Spondylus gaederopus 7, 8, 55, 56, 57, 58, 59, 60, 61, 62, 169, 172

Squeakie Burroughs (1936) 194, fig. 8.3

status: expression of 8, 10

Steinback, J. 138

Stephanovikion 215n47

stereoscopic 40, 137

stereotypes 19, 76, 142

Stergiana 163, fig. 7.12

Stieglitz, A. 78–80, 70, fig. 4.6; *Georgia O'Keefe: A Portrait* 78–80, fig. 4.6

Stryker, R. 138–9, 185, fig. 6.6

sublime 131–5, 165, 195, 202, 213n7, 213n8; paradox of 134–5

subversion 121, 182–3, 188–9

Suchostav 99, fig. 5.12

Surrealism 186–8, 195, 196, 207n4

synairesis 154, 180

tactility 37, 38, 145

Tagg, J. 40, 126, 129, 131; suturing 40

Talalay, L. 152, 154, 178, 205–6n13

Talljanky 213n67

Techirghiol 53, fig. 3.6

tells *see* settlement

Theopetra 172, fig. 7.12

Thessalian Neolithic 147–180, fig. 7.12; burial 174, 175, 176–7; figurines 147–66, 177–80, 201; historiography of 166, 168, 215n44; settlement 168–75

thighs 93, 97, 99

The Thinker 45–6, 50, 51, 64, 209n2; fig. 3.1

This Little Piggy Went to Market, This Little Piggy Went Home 134

A Thousand Years 134

three-dimensionality 22, 24, 36–8, 145; in miniature 34; paradox of 39–41, 135

time 194; compression of 36

Tîrguşor Sitorman 50, 209n5, fig. 3.6

Tîrguşor Urs 50, 53, 54, 63, 209n5, 209n9, fig. 3.6

Tîrpeşti 91, 93, 100, 103, 105, 106–8, 113, 114, 212n50; figs 5.5, 5.12, 5.13

Todorova, H. 26–7

Tourkogefyra 214n14, 214n15, 214n16, fig. 7.12

INDEX

Traian-Dealul Fîntînilor 90, 93, 103, 105, 115, fig. 5.12
Traian-Dealul Viei fig. 5.4
transvestites 191
Triantaphyllou, S. 215n53
Tringham, R. 23, 206n13
Tripolye fig. 5.12
Tripolye Culture *see* Cucuteni/Tripolye
Truşeşti 91, 96, 100, 101, 103, 105, 108–9, 113, 114, 212n50, 212n55, figs 5.8, 5.12
truth: regimes of 121, 125–9, 130; representation of 123–9
Tsalma 214n15, fig. 7.12
Tsangli 178, fig. 7.12
Turner, J.M.W. 182–4, 186, fig. 8.2; *Snow Storm: Hannibal and his Army Crossing the Alps* (1812) fig. 8.2

Ucko, P. 214n9
uncanny: paradox of 42
Unio pictorum 57, 115
Upper Palaeolithic 19, 207n23

vagina 83, 160, 181
Vajsov, I. 13, 49, fig. 1.2
Valea Lupului fig. 5.12
Văleni fig. 5.12
Varko 214n11, fig. 7.12
Varvarovka fig. 5.12
Vasilievka 105

Vassuli 158
Verem'e 115, 213n70
Vîhvatinţi fig. 5.11
villages 4, 11, 53, 118, 170, 186, 198; membership in 7
Vinča Culture 22, 51, 66–7, 199, 203
virtuality 137–8
visual: culture 206n18; politics of 130, 135–9; rhetoric 121, 122–46, 190, 194, 197
Vitelli, K. 5
Vladimirovka 98, 105, fig. 5.12
Vrasteri 163, 214n11, fig. 7.12
Vrastero 214n7, fig. 7.12
Vyhvatincz 213n69, fig. 5.12

women: representations of 16–22, 68, 70, 75, 76, 88–91, 122, 129, 143, 159–61, 164, 179, 181, 188–90; *see also* Barbie Doll, Sherman, C.
White, C. 70

Les Yeux de la Poupée fig. 4.5
Young British Artists 133, 134, 213n6

Zapotec State 21
Zappeio 157, 214n11, 214n12, fig. 7.12
Zerelia fig. 7.12
Zoodochos Pigi 159, fig. 7.12
zoomorphs *see* animal
Žvanets fig. 5.12